WMSCI 2019

I0036706

The 23rd World Multi-Conference on Systemics, Cybernetics and Informatics

July 6 - 9, 2019 – Orlando, Florida, USA

PROCEEDINGS

Volume III

Edited by:

Nagib Callaos
Elina Gaile-Sarkane
Bruce Peoples
Belkis Sánchez
Michael Savoie

Organized by
International Institute of Informatics and Systemics
Member of the International Federation for Systems Research (IFSR)

IIS

COPYRIGHT

The papers of this book comprise the proceedings of the conference mentioned on the title and the cover page. They reflect the authors' opinions and, with the purpose of timely disseminations, are published as presented and without change. Their inclusion in these proceedings does no necessarily constitute endorsement by the editors.

ISBN: 978-1-950492-07-7 (Collection)   ISBN: 978-1-950492-10-7 (Volume III)

PROGRAM COMMITTEE

Chairs: Michael Savoie (USA)
C. Dale Zinn (USA)

Adamopoulou, Evgenia	National Technical University of Athens	Greece
Alam, Delwar	Daffodil International University	Bangladesh
Alanís Urquieta, José D.	Technological University of Puebla	Mexico
Alhayyan, Khalid N.	Institute of Public Administration	Saudi Arabia
Altamirano, Patricio	Institute of Advanced National Studies (IAEN in Spanish)	Ecuador
Andersen, J. C.	The University of Tampa	USA
Ascacivar Placencia, Yanelli Karen	Mecoacc	Peru
Batos, Vedran	University of Dubrovnik	Croatia
Bermúdez Juárez, Blanca	Meritorious Autonomous University of Puebla	Mexico
Bernikova, Olga	St. Petersburg State University	Russian Federation
Bönke, Dietmar	Reutlingen University	Germany
Bubnov, Alexey	Institute of Physics of the Czech Academy of Sciences	Czech Republic
Cárdenas, José	University of Guayaquil	Ecuador
Carreño Escobedo, Jorge Raúl	Universidad Nacional Mayor de San Marcos	Peru
Castro, John W.	University of Atacama	Chile
Chen, Jingchao	University Donghua	China
Chiang, Po-Yun	The Ministry of National Defense	Taiwan
Chou, Te-Shun	East Carolina University	USA
Chukwu, Ozoemena Joseph	Riga Technical University	Latvia
Ciemleja, Guna	Riga Technical University	Latvia
Cilliers, Liezel	University of Fort Hare	South Africa
Dantas de Rezende, Julio F.	Federal University of Rio Grande do Norte	USA
Dasilva, Julian	Barry University	USA
Doherr, Detlev	University of Applied Sciences Offenburg	Germany
Dyck, Sergius	Fraunhofer Institute of Optronics, System Technologies and Image Exploitation	Germany

Edwards, Matthew E.	Alabama A&M University	USA
Eremina, Yuliya	Riga Technical University	Latvia
Fagade, Tesleem	University of Bristol	UK
Farah, Tanjila	North South University	Bangladesh
Florescu, Gabriela	National Institute for Research and Development in Informatics	Romania
Fries, Terrence P.	Indiana University of Pennsylvania	USA
Gaile-Sarkane, Elina	Riga Technical University	Latvia
Gourisetti, Sri Nikhil Gupta	Pacific Northwest National Laboratory	USA
Gvatua, Salome	Riga Technical University	Latvia
Haba, Cristian-Gyözö	"Gheorghe Asachi" Technical University of Iasi	Romania
Haferkorn, Daniel	Fraunhofer Institute of Optronics, System Technologies and Image Exploitation	Germany
Hanacek, Petr	Brno University of Technology	Czech Republic
Hassan, Md. Maruf	Daffodil International University	Bangladesh
Hendel, Russell J.	Towson University	USA
Hilkevics, Sergejs	Ventspils University of Applied Sciences	Latvia
Ho, Sophia Shi-Huei	University of Taipei	Taiwan
Hsiao, Jung	SMS Infocomm Corporation	USA
Hu, Wen-Chen	University of North Dakota	USA
Ismail, Zainab Z.	University of Baghdad	Iraq
Jakubik, Maria	Haaga-Helia University of Applied Sciences	Finland
Jaros, Jiri	Brno University of Technology	Czech Republic
Jenq, John	Montclair State University	USA
Jenq, Priscilla	Carnegie Mellon University	USA
Jiménez, Ricardo	Barry University	USA
Kabwende, Benjamin Ngongo	Riga Technical University	Latvia
Khan, Salam	Alabama A&M University	USA
Kocmanova, Alena	Brno University of Technology	Czech Republic
Lamr, Marián	Technical University of Liberec	Czech Republic
Lapina, Inga	Riga Technical University	Latvia
Leclerc-Sherling, Christine	ASTRACS	USA
Lo, Yen-Fen	Shih Chien University	Taiwan
Lo, Yen-Hsi	Shih Chien University	Taiwan
Lu, Shen	University of South Florida	USA
Makarov, Alexander	Institute for Microelectronics- TU Wien	Austria
Matin, Mohammad Abdul	North South University	Bangladesh
Mechan Méndez, Víctor	Universidad Nacional Mayor de San Marcos	Peru

Mendoza Rojas, Hubert James	Universidad Nacional Mayor de San Marcos	Peru
Meyer, Heiko	Gefasoft AG	Germany
Miyazaki, Jun	Komazawa University	Japan
Mohammed, Ali J.	Ministry of Construction and Housing	Iraq
Moraes, Altino José M. de	Brazilian Ministry of Planning- Budget and Management	Brazil
Mylrea, Michael	Pacific Northwest National Laboratory	USA
Naito, Katsuhiro	Aichi Institute of Technology	Japan
Nemecek, Petr	Newton College	Czech Republic
Oganisjana, Karine	Riga Technical University	Latvia
Oliveira, Álvaro	UFRN	Brazil
Omer, Ako K.	Koya Univeristy	Iraq
Orantes-Jiménez, Sandra D.	Instituto Politécnico Nacional	Mexico
Ozolins, Modris	Riga Technical University	Latvia
Pando Álvarez, Rosa	Universidad Nacional Mayor de San Marcos	Peru
Pastirčáková, Kateřina	Jan Perner Transport Faculty- University of Pardubice	Czech Republic
Pavlakova Docekalova, Marie	Brno University of Technology	Czech Republic
Peng, Michael Yao-Ping	Hsuan Chuang University	Taiwan
Pickard, John	East Carolina University	USA
Placencia Medina, Maritza	Universidad Nacional Mayor de San Marcos	Peru
Quintana Salinas, Margot Rosario	Facultad de Medicina- Universidad Nacional Mayor de San Marcos	Peru
Redkin, Oleg	St. Petersburg State University	Russian Federation
Rodríguez, Nancy	Autonomous University of Madrid	Spain
Sánchez Flores, Guillermo	Technological University of Puebla	Mexico
Sander, Jennifer	Fraunhofer Institute of Optronics, System Technologies and Image Exploitation	Germany
Santos, Irani	SEMPLA-Prefeitura de Natal	Brazil
Scappini, Reinaldo	National Technological University	Argentina
Schaetter, Alfred	Pforzheim University	Germany
Segall, Richard S.	Arkansas State University	USA
Selberherr, Siegfried	Technische Universität Wien	Austria
Shah, Syed Zubair A.	Jamia Millia Islamia	India
Shiraishi, Yoshiaki	Kobe University	Japan
Silva-Valencia, Javier	Universidad Peruana Cayetano Heredia	Peru
Simberova, Iveta	Brno University of Technology	Czech Republic

Singh, Harwinder	Guru Nanak Dev Engineering College	India
Skrbek, Jan	Technical University of Liberec	Czech Republic
Sohn, Han Suk	New Mexico State University	USA
Souza, Mônica L.	Intellectos	Brazil
Sturgill, Ronda	The University of Tampa	USA
Šulc, Jaromír	Jan Perner Transport Faculty- University of Pardubice	Czech Republic
Sulema, Yevgeniya	National Technical University of Ukraine	Ukraine
Sun, Baolin	Wuhan University	China
Sverdlov, Viktor	Institute for Microelectronics- TU Wien	Austria
Szygenda, Stephen A.	Suuthern Methodist University	USA
Tanaka, Katsuyuki	Aichi Institute of Technology	Japan
Tartari, Simone	Intellectos	Brazil
Terzidis, Orestis	Karlsruhe Institut of Technology	Germany
Tintin, Romel	Institute of Advanced National Studies (IAEN in Spanish)	Ecuador
Tsubaki, Michiko	University of Electro-Communications	Japan
Velázquez-Araque, Luis	University of Guayaquil	Ecuador
Vrána, Stanislav	Czech Technical University in Prague	Czech Republic
Windbacher, Thomas	Technische Universität Wien	Austria
Yang, Zining	ACERTAS	USA
Yoshida, Naofumi	Komzawa University	Japan
Zaman, Moniruz	Daffodil International University	Bangladesh
Zaretsky, Esther	Givat Washington Academic College of Education	Israel

ADDITIONAL REVIEWERS

Abariga, Samuel	Division of Epidemiology and Biostatistics	USA
Abbas, Ghulam	Ghulam Ishaq Khan Institute	Pakistan
Abd Jelil, Radhia	Higher Institute of Fashion Professions of Monastir	Tunisia
Abdel Hafez, Hoda	Suez Canal University	Egypt
Abdul, Hamed	University of Management and Technology	Pakistan
Abe, Jair Minoro	Paulista University	Brazil
Aboalsamh, Hatim	King Saud University	Saudi Arabia
Abreu, António	Higher Education Polytechnic Institution of Engineering	Portugal
Abrukov, Victor	Chuvash State University	Russian Federation
Abu Omar, Mohammad	Al-Quds Open University	Palestine
Abuhejleh, Ahmad	University of Wisconsin-River Falls	USA
Acharya, Sushil	Robert Morris University	USA
Agarwal, Arun	Siksha `O` Anusandhan Deemed to be University	India
Agrebi, Maroi	University of Polytechnique Hauts-de-France	France
Agulhari, Cristiano Marcos	State University of Campinas	Brazil
Ahmed, Shamsuddin	Islamic University of Medinah	Saudi Arabia
Aiordachioaie, Dorel	Tokyo Institute of Technology	Japan
Akdeniz, Rafet	Namik Kemal University	Turkey
Aksamija, Zlatan	University of Illinois at Urbana-Champaign	USA
Aksoy, Mehmet S.	King Saud University	Saudi Arabia
Alafaireet, Patricia	University of Missouri	USA
Alexik, Mikulas	University of Zilina	Slovakia
Al-Hamouz, Sadeq	The World Islamic Sciences and Education University	Jordan
Al-Hamzah, Khawlah Hussein Ali	Basrah University	Iraq
Ali, Kamal	Jackson State University	USA

Aliguliyev, Ramiz	Institute of Information Technology, Azerbaijan National Academy of Sciences	Azerbaijan
Alkhatib, Ghazi	King Fahd University of Petroleum and Minerals	Saudi Arabia
Als, Adrian	University of the West Indies	Barbados
Alsmadi, Izzat	Yarmouk University	Jordan
Amornyotin, Somchai	Mahidol University	Thailand
Analide, Cesar	University of Minho	Portugal
Andina, Diego	Universidad Politécnica de Madrid	Spain
Andrade Ramos, Ana Luisa	University of Aveiro	Portugal
Arato, Peter	Budapest University of Technology and Economics	Hungary
Arinyo, Robert Joan	Polytechnic University of Catalonia	Spain
Ariton, Viorel	Danubius University	Romania
Aruga, Masahiro	Tokai University	Japan
Asadi, Saeid	University of Queensland	Australia
Asemi, Asefeh	Corvinus University of Budapest	Hungary
Asproni, Giovanni	European Bioinformatics Institute	UK
Aveledo, Marianella	Simon Bolivar University	Venezuela
Aydogan, Hasan	Selcuk University, Technology Faculty, Campus Selcuklu Konya	Turkey
Aziz, Soulhi	National School of Mineral Industry	Morocco
Bagheri, S.	Eindhoven University of Technology	Netherlands
Bagnoli, Franco	University of Florence	Italy
Bai, Zhengyao	Yunnan University	China
Bakar, Ab Rahim	University Putra Malaysia	Malaysia
Baker, John	Johns Hopkins University	USA
Bakmaz, Bojan	University of Belgrade	Serbia
Balas, Valentina	Aurel Vlaicu University of Arad	Romania
Balicki, Jerzy	Warsaw University of Technology	Poland
Banerji, Sanjay	Amrita Vishwa Vidyapeetham University	India
Bang, Jørgen	University of Aarhus	Denmark
Barb, Adrian	Penn State University	USA
Barba, Leiner	Popular University of Cesar	Colombia
Barsoum, Nader	Curtin University of Technology	Malaysia
Bäßler, Ralph	BAM Federal Institute for Materials	Germany
Batos, Vedran	University of Dubrovnik	Croatia
Baudin, Veronique	Laboratory for Analysis and Architecture of Systems	France
Becejski Vujaklija, Dragana	University of Belgrade	Serbia

Belahcen, Anouar	Aalto University School of Science and Technology	Finland
Bernabé, Gregorio	University of Murcia	Spain
Bernardi, Ansgar	German Research Center for Artificial Intelligence	Germany
Bernardino, Jorge	Institute of Engineering of Coimbra	Portugal
Bernick, Philip	Hathority, LLC	USA
Bettaz, Mohamed	Philadelphia University	Jordan
Bidarra, José	Aberta University	Portugal
Biernat, Krzysztof	Automotove Industry Institute	Poland
Bigan, Cristin	Ecological University of Bucharest	Romania
Bilbao, Javier	University of the Basque Country	Spain
Bist, Ankur Singh	Krishna Institute of Engineering and Technology, Ghaziabad	India
Blaha, Martin	University of Defence	Czech Republic
Boenke, Dietmar	Reutlingen University	Germany
Bojcetic, Nenad	University of Zagreb	Croatia
Bolboaca, Sorana Daniela	Iuliu Hatieganu University of Medicine and Pharmacy Cluj-Napoca	Romania
Borangiu, Theodor	Polytechnic University of Bucharest	Romania
Bordignon, Alex Laier	Pontifical Catholic University	Brazil
Botti-Salitsky, Rose	University of Massachusetts Dartmouth	USA
Bubnov, Alexey	Academy of Sciences of the Czech Republic	Czech Republic
Bucchiarone, Antonio	Institute of Information Science and Technologies	Italy
Buchalcevova, Alena	University of Economics, Prague	Czech Republic
Caldararu, Florin	Ecological University of Bucharest	Romania
Caldeira, Filipe	Polytechnic Institute of Viseu	Portugal
Camargo, Maria Emilia	University of Caxias do Sul	Brazil
Canbolat, Huseyin	Yildirim Beyazit University	Turkey
Cardoso, Eduardo	Monterrey Institute of Technology and Higher Education	Mexico
Carmo, Elisangela Gisele Do	Paulista State University	Brazil
Carmona, Samuel	Development and Medical Innovation Center	Spain
Carretero, Jesús	University Carlos III of Madrid	Spain
Challa, Radhakumari	Sri Sathya Sai Institute of Higher Learning	India
Chang, Chin-Chih	Chung Hua University	Taiwan
Chang, Weng-Long	National Kaohsiung University of Applied Sciences	Taiwan
Chang, Ya-Hui	National Taiwan Ocean University	Taiwan

Chaudhari, Narendra	Indian Institute of Technology Indore	India
Chen, Jingchao	DongHua University	China
Chen, Jyi-Ta	Southern Taiwan University	Taiwan
Chen, Lisa Y.	I-Shou University	Taiwan
Chen, Yil	Huafan University	Taiwan
Chen, Zhe	Northeastern University	China
Cherinka, R.	The MITRE Corporation	USA
Chiou, Richard	Drexel University	USA
Chorikavil Thomas, Jose	Central Plantation Crops Research Institute	India
Chou, Tsung-Yu	National Chin-Yi University of Technology	Taiwan
Chou, Tung-Hsiang	National Kaohsiung University of Science and Technology	Taiwan
Chuvakin, Anton	Gartner for Technical Professionals	USA
Cialdea, Donatella	University of Molise	Italy
Cirella, Jonathan	RTI International	USA
Comite, Ubaldo	University of Calabria	Italy
Corcuera, Pedro	University of Cantabria	Spain
Cortés Zaborras, Carmen	University of Malaga	Spain
Cunha, Idaulo J.	Intellectos	Brazil
D`Ulizia, Arianna	National Research Council	Italy
Da Rugna, Jerome	University Jean Monnet of Saint-Etienne	France
Dalla Vecchia, Alessandro	Federal University of Rio Grande do Sul	Brazil
Danjour, Miler Franco	Federal Institute of Education, Science and Technology of Rio Grande do Sul	Brazil
Dash, Sujata	North Orissa University	India
De Aquino, Andre L. L.	Federal University of Alagoas	Brazil
De la Puente, Fernando	University of Las Palmas de Gran Canaria	Spain
Deakins, Eric	University of Waikato	New Zealand
Desilva, Mauris	3D PARS (US) and 3D PARS Limited (UK)	USA
Dhamdhere, Vidya	G. H. Raisoni College of Engineering and Management	India
Dhingra, Arvind	Guru Nanak Dev Engineering College	India
Dizdaroglu, Bekir	Karadeniz Technical University	Turkey
Do Nascimento Morais, António J.	Open University	Portugal
Doherr, Detlev	University of Applied Sciences Offenburg	Germany
Doma, Salah	Alexandria University	Egypt
Donko, Dzenana	University of Sarajevo	Bosnia and Herzegovina
Druzovec, Marjan	University of Maribor	Slovenia

Duchen, Gonzalo	National Polytechnic Institute	Mexico
Dugarte Peña, Germán Lenin	Charles III University of Madrid	Spain
Dursun, Sukru	Selcuk University	Turkey
Dvornik, Josko	University of Split	Croatia
Ebadati, Omid Mahdi	Kharazmi University	Iran
El Oualkadi, Ahmed	Abdelmalek Essaadi University	Morocco
Elçi, Atilla	Aksaray University (Emeritus)	Turkey
Elías Hardy, Lidia Lauren	Higher Institute of Technologies and Applied Sciences	Cuba
El-Kashlan, Ahmed	Academy for Science and Technology	Egypt
Elmahboub, Widad M.	Hampton University	USA
Encabo, Eduardo	University of Murcia	Spain
Englmeier, Kurt	University of Applied Sciences Schmalkalden	Germany
Ercan, M. Fikret	Singapore Polytechnic	Singapore
Erins, Ingars	Riga Technical University	Latvia
Falkowski-Gilski, Przemyslaw	Gdansk University of Technology	Poland
Farhaoui, Yousef	Moulay Ismail University	Morocco
Farias, Patricia	Federal University of Pernambuco	Brazil
Félez, Jesús	Technical University of Madrid	Spain
Feng, Tao	Aramco Service Company	USA
Feraco, Antonio	Nanyang Technological University	Singapore
Fernandes, Márcia	Federal University of Uberlândia	Brazil
Fernandes, Paula Odete	Polytechnic Institute of Bragança	Portugal
Ferreira, Andrea	Federal University of Paraíba	Brazil
Figueroa de La Cruz, Mario M.	National Technological University	Argentina
Finkbine, Ronald	Indiana University Southeast	USA
Fiorini, Rodolfo A.	Polytechnic University of Milan	Italy
Fisser, Erwin	Soa Aids Nederland	Netherlands
Flammia, Madelyn	University of Central Florida	USA
Floyd, Raymond	Innovative Insights, Inc.	USA
Foglia, Pierfrancesco	University of Pisa	Italy
Fox, Richard	Northern Kentucky University	USA
Frejlichowski, Dariusz	West Pomeranian University of Technology	Poland
Fujdiak, Radek	Brno University of Technology	Czech Republic
Furst, Jacob D.	DePaul University	USA
Furukawa, Susumu	University of Yamanashi	Japan
Gandhewar, Nisarg	SB Jain Institute of Technology, Managment & Research	India

Garai, Gautam	Saha Institute of Nuclear Physics	India
García, Alberto Eloy	University of Cantabria	Spain
Garcia Bedoya, Olmer	State University of Campinas	Brazil
García Marco, Francisco J.	University of Zaragoza	Spain
García-Aracil, Adela	Polytechnic University of Valencia	Spain
García-Ramírez, José Miguel	University of Granada	Spain
Gedviliene, Genute	Vytautas Magnus University	Lithuania
Genser, Robert	Institute for Handling Devices and Robotics	Austria
George, Alan	Montana State University	USA
Ghayoumi, Mehdi	Kent State University	USA
Ghosh, Uttam	Vanderbilt University	USA
Giampapa, Joseph	Carnegie Mellon University	USA
Gini, Giuseppina	Polytechnic of Milan	Italy
Gnatyuk, Volodymyr	V.E. Lashkaryov Institute of Semiconductor Physics of the National Academy of Sciences of Ukraine	Ukraine
Gnudi, Adriana	University of Bergamo	Italy
Gobron, Stephane	Iwate University	Japan
Gouyon, David	University of Lorraine	France
Grouverman, Valentina	Research Triangle Institute	USA
Guedes de Souza, Sergio	Federal University of Rio de Janeiro	Brazil
Gueorguieva, Natacha	City University of New York	USA
Gui, M. W.	National Taipei University of Technology	Taiwan
Gulbahar, Yasemin	Ankara University	Turkey
Györödi, Cornelia	University of Oradea	Romania
Haddad, Hisham	Kennesaw State University	USA
Hajduk, Zbigniew	Rzeszow University of Technology	Poland
Ham, Chan	Kennesaw State University	USA
Hamie, Ali	University of Brighton	UK
Hanakawa, Noriko	Hannan University	Japan
Haruvy, Nava	Netanya Academic College	Israel
Hashimoto, Shigehiro	Kogakuin University	Japan
Hieber, Hartmann	International Consulting Bureaux	Germany
Hilkevics, Sergejs	Ventspils University of Applied Sciences	Latvia
Hishiyama, Reiko	Waseda University	Japan
Holmqvist, Mona	Kristianstad University College	Sweden
Hong, Sungbum	Jackson State University	USA
Hong, Tzung-Pei	National University of Kaohsiung	Taiwan
Hsu, Ching-Hsien	Chung Hua University	Taiwan

Huget, Marc-Philippe	University of Liverpool	UK
Hunek, Wojciech P.	Opole University of Technology	Poland
Ilunga, Masengo	University of South Africa	South Africa
Imbalzano, Giovanni	MPI	Italy
Inci, Ahmet Can	Bryant University	USA
Inkinen, Tommi	University of Helsinki	Finland
Intakosum, Sarun	King Mongkut's Institute of Technology Ladkrabang	Thailand
Ionescu, Adela	University of Craiova	Romania
Ishikawa, Hiroshi	Niigata University of International and Information Studies	Japan
Ivasic-Kos, Marina	University of Rijeka	Croatia
Izydorczyk, Jacek	Silesian University of Technology	Poland
Jacobson, Jon A.	University of Michigan	USA
Jakóbczak, Dariusz	Politechnika Koszalinska	Poland
Jalal, Laassiri	Ibn Tofail University	Morocco
Janota, Aleš	University of Žilina	Slovakia
Jaoua, Ali	University of Qatar	Qatar
Jara Guerrero, Salvador	University of Michoacan	Mexico
Jaramillo-Núñez, Alberto	National Institute of Astrophysics, Optics and Electronics	Mexico
Jastrzebska, Agnieszka	Warsaw University of Technology	Poland
Jenq, John	Montclair State University	USA
Joshi, Dheeraj	National Institute of Technology Kurukshetra	India
Julião, Rui Pedro	New University of Lisbon	Portugal
Kabassi, Katerina	Technological Education Institute of the Ionian Islands	Greece
Kachanova, Tamara L.	Saint-Petersburg State Electrotechnical University "LETI"	Russian Federation
Kalganova, Tatiana	Brunel University	UK
Kaneko, Itaru	Tokyo Polytechnic University	Japan
Kaneko, Yoshihiro	Gifu Univiersity	Japan
Kaur, Kiran	University of Malaya	Malaysia
Kawaguchi, Masashi	National Institute of Technology, Suzuka College	Japan
Kawarazaki, Noriyuki	Kanagawa Institute of Technology	Japan
Kemmerich, Thomas	University College Gjøvik	Norway
Kenk, Mourad A.	Computer Science Department, Faculty of Science, South Valley University	Egypt
Keswani, Bright	Gyan Vihar University	India

Khademi, Aria	Pennsylvania State University	USA
Khalifa, Abdul Jabbar	Al-Nahrain University	Iraq
Khudayarov, Bakhtiyar	Tashkent Institute of Irrigation and Agricultural Mechanization Engineers	Uzbekistan
Kim, Eung Sang	Korea Electrotechnology Research Institute	South Korea
Kim, Hyunju	Wheaton College	USA
Kinser, Jason	George Mason University	USA
Kiriazov, Petko	Bulgarian Academy of Sciences	Bulgaria
Knipp, Tammy	Florida Atlantic University	USA
Kohir, Vinayadatt V.	Indian Institute of Technology	India
Kopparapu, Sunil Kumar	Tata Consultancy Services Limited	India
Korsakiene, Renata	Vilnius Gediminas Technical University	Lithuania
Koul, Saroj	Acadia University	Canada
Kouroupetroglou, Georgios	University of Athens	Greece
Kozlovskis, Konstantins	Riga Technical University	Latvia
Kozma, Tamas	University of Debrecen	Hungary
Kreisler, Alain	University Paris 06	France
Kroumov, Valeri	Okayama University of Science	Japan
Krovvidy, Srinivas	Fannie Mae	USA
Kucuksille, Ecir	Suleyman Demirel University	Turkey
Kumar, Prashant	Shivaji University	India
Kumar, Shashi Kumar	Bangalore University	India
Kumar Pandey, Sumit	Jharkhand Rai University	India
Kurtulus, Kemal	Istanbul University	Turkey
Kushida, Takayuki	Tokyo University of Technology	Japan
Lai, Yeu-Pong	Chung Cheng Institute of Technology	Taiwan
Lakhoua, Mohamed Najeh	University of Carthage	Tunisia
Lasmanis, Aivars	University of Latvia	Latvia
Latawiec, Krzysztof J.	Opole University of Technology	Poland
Law, Rob	Hong Kong Polytechnic University	Hong Kong
Ledesma Orozco, Sergio E.	Guanajuato University	Mexico
Lee, Chang Won	Hanyang University	South Korea
Lee, DoHoon	Pusan National University	South Korea
Lee, Jong Kun	Changwon National University	South Korea
Lee, Kyung Oh	Sun Moon University	South Korea
Lee, Yih-Jiun	Chien Kuo Technology University	Taiwan
Lee, Yusin	National Cheng Kung University	Taiwan
Li, Weigang	University of Brasilia	Brazil
Lim, Hwee-San	Science University of Malaysia	Malaysia

Lin, Hong	University of Houston Downtown	USA
Lin, Shu-Chiung	Tatung University	Taiwan
Lipikorn, Rajalida	Chulalongkorn University	Thailand
Lipinski, Piotr	Technical University of Lodz	Poland
Loffredo, Donald	University of Houston-Victoria	USA
Lopes da Silva, Paulo A.	Military Engineering Institute	Brazil
López de Lacalle, Luis Norberto	University of the Basque Country	Spain
López Román, Leobardo	University of Sonora	Mexico
Lorenzo, Carla	National University of San Juan	Argentina
Lyridis, Dimitrios	National Technical University of Athens	Greece
Lyudmila, Mihaylova	Lancaster University	UK
Magnani, Lorenzo	University of Pavia	Italy
Mainguenaud, Michel	Institut National des Sciences Appliquées	France
Malollari, Ilirjan	University of Tirana	Albania
Mandal, Pratap Chandra	Indian Institute of Management, Shillong	India
Mao, Xiao-Bing	Wuhan University of Technology	China
Marappan, Raja	SASTRA University	India
Marcelino, Roderval	Federal University of Santa Catarina	Brazil
Marinova, Rossitza	Concordia University of Edmonton	Canada
Marlowe, Thomas J.	Seton Hall University	USA
Marra, Cirley Barbosa	Universidade Federal do Sul da Bahia	Brazil
Martínez Rebollar, Alicia	Polytechnic University of Valencia	Spain
Marx Gómez, Jorge	University Oldenburg	Germany
Masum, Salahuddin Mohammad	Daffodil International University	Bangladesh
Mateen, Ahmed	University of Agriculture Faisalabad	Pakistan
Matsuda, Michiko	Japanese Standards Association	Japan
Maymir-Ducharme, Fred A.	IBM US Federal	USA
McConnell, Rodney	University of Idaho	USA
McMahon, Ellen	National-Louis University, College of Management and Business, Retired	USA
Memon, Imran	Zhejiang University	China
Mendes Gomes, Luis	University of the Azores	Portugal
Merten, Pascaline	Free University of Brussels	Belgium
Metrolho, Jose	Polytechnic Institute of Castelo Branco	Portugal
Mihai, Dan	University of Craiova	Romania
Milcic, Diana	University of Zagreb Faculty of Graphic Arts	Croatia
Mishra, Deepak	Indian Institute of Space Science and Technology	India

Misurec, Jiri	Brno Univerzity of Technology	Czech Republic
Moin, Lubna	Pakistan Naval Engineering College	Pakistan
Monti, Marina	National Research Council	Italy
Morgan, Theresa	Wudang Research Association	USA
Morshed, Ahmed Hisham	Ain Shams University	Egypt
Mozar, Stefan	Electrical Testing Services Pty Ltd.	Australia
Mróz-Gorgoń, Barbara	Wroclaw University of Economics	Poland
Muñoz García, Ana Celina	Los Andes University	Venezuela
Mylonas, Phivos	Ionian University	Greece
Nag, Abhijit	The University of Memphis	USA
Nagaiah, Narasimha	University of Central Florida	USA
Nagarkar, Mahesh	SCSM College of Engineering	India
Nagy, Endre L.	Society of Instrument and Control Engineers	Japan
Navas Delgado, Ismael	University of Malaga	Spain
Nayyar, Anand	KCL Institute of Management and Technology	India
Neaga, Elena Irina	University of Wales Trinity st David	UK
Nemec, Juraj	Matej Bel University	Slovakia
Neumüller, Moritz	Vienna University of Economics and Business	Austria
Newsome, Mark	Hewlett-Packard Company	USA
Niculescu, Virginia	Babes-Bolyai University	Romania
Nievola, Julio Cesar	Pontifical Catholic University of Paraná	Brazil
Nikolarea, Ekaterini	University of the Aegean	Greece
Novikov, Oleg	Tomko	Russian Federation
Nugroho, Heru	Telkom University	Indonesia
Núñez, Jose Luis	Technical University of Madrid	Spain
Objelean, Nicolae	State University of Moldova	Moldova, Republic of
Occelli, Sylvie	Economic Social Research Institute of Piemonte	Italy
Odella, Francesca	University of Trento	Italy
Odetayo, Michael	Coventry University	UK
Odhiambo, Marcel O.	Vaal University of Technology	South Africa
Olson, Patrick C.	National University	USA
Ong, Sim-Heng	National University of Singapore	Singapore
Ortiz Sosa, Lourdes Maritza	Andres Bello Catholic University	Venezuela
O'Sullivan, Jill	Farmingdale State College	USA
Oszust, Mariusz	Rzeszow University of Technology	Poland
Ow, Hock	University Malaya	Malaysia

Paiva, Teresa	Guarda Polytechnic Institute	Portugal
Pal, Tandra	National Institute of Technology, Durgapur	India
Park, Se Hyun	Chung-Ang University	South Korea
Parrilla Roure, Luís	University of Granada	Spain
Patel, H	University of Bridgeport	USA
Patel, Kuntalkumar P.	S. V. Institute of Computer Studies	India
Paul, Stephane	Thales Research	France
Pereira, Elisabeth T.	University of Aveiro	Portugal
Pereira, Rafael	Federal University of Santa Maria	Brazil
Periyasamy, Pitchapillai	Sree Saraswathi Thyagaraja College	India
Perjési-Hámori, Ildikó	University of Pécs	Hungary
Petrillo, Antonella	University of Naples Parthenope	Italy
Phakamach, Phongsak	North Eastern University	Thailand
Pickl, Stefan	Bundeswehr University Munich	Germany
Pieterse, Vreda	University of Pretoria	South Africa
Pilvere, Irina	Latvia University of Agriculture	Latvia
Pingitore, Alessandro	Council National Research, Clinical Physiology Institute	Italy
Plakitsi, Katerina	University of Ioannina	Greece
Poh, Elsa	Eastern Michigan University	USA
Polenakovikj, Radmil	Ss. Cyril and Methodius University Business Start-up Centre	Macedonia
Poniszewska-Maranda, Aneta	Lodz University of Technology	Poland
Poobrasert, Onintra	National Electronics and Computer Technology Center	Thailand
Poveda, Geovanny	Technical University of Madrid	Spain
Prasad, P. M. K.	GVP College of Engineering for Women, Visakhapatnam	India
Prykarpatsky, Anatoliy K.	Ivan Franko State Pedagogical University	Ukraine
Pshehotskaya, Ekaterina	InfoWatch	Russian Federation
Qabazard, Adel M.	Kuwait Institute for Scientific Research	Kuwait
Quadro, Martín	National University of Córdoba	Argentina
Quan-Haase, Anabel	University of Western Ontario	Canada
Quist-Aphetsi, Kester	Ghana Telecom University College	Ghana
Rachev, Boris	Technical University of Varna	Bulgaria
Rahmes, Mark	Harris Corporation	USA
Rahouma, Kamel	Technical College in Riyadh	Egypt
Rashid, Kasim	Amman University	Canada

Reichwald, Julian	Cooperative State University Baden-Wurttemberg Mannheim	Germany
Reis, Arsénio	University of Trás-os-Montes e Alto Douro	Portugal
Reis, Rosa	Porto Superior Institute of Engineering	Portugal
Renes-Arellano, Paula	University of Cantabria	Spain
Reuter, Matthias	Clausthal University of Technology	Germany
Reyes-Méndez, Jorge J.	University of Toronto	Canada
Riihentaus, Juhani	Docent (retired), University of Eastern Finland	Finland
Ripon, Shamim	East West University	Bangladesh
Rivza, Peteris	Latvia University of Agriculture	Latvia
Rizki, Mateen	Wright State University	USA
Rizzo, Rosalba	University of Messina	Italy
Rodi, Anthony	California University of Pennsylvania	USA
Rodrigues, Nelson	Polytechnic Institute of Bragança	Portugal
Rodríguez Florido, Miguel Ángel	University of Las Palmas de Gran Canaria	Spain
Rodríguez-Piñero, Piedad Tolmos	Rey Juan Carlos University	Spain
Rojas, Arturo	National University of Engineering	Peru
Rolland, Colette	University of Paris 1 Pantheon-Sorbonne	France
Romansky, Radi	Technical University of Sofia	Bulgaria
Romero, Luis Felipe	University of Sonora	Mexico
Romli, Fairuz	Universiti Putra Malaysia	Malaysia
Ros, Frederic	Orleans University	France
Rößling, Guido	Darmstadt University of Technology	Germany
Rot, Artur	Wroclaw University of Economics	Poland
Rout, Deepak	National Institute of Technology Goa	India
Roveda, Loris	University of Applied Sciences and Arts of Southern Switzerland	Switzerland
Rowe, Neil	Naval Postgraduate School	USA
Ruiz Rey, Francisco J.	University of Malaga	Spain
Ruiz Zamarreño, Carlos	Public University of Navarra	Spain
Rutkowski, Jerzy	Silesian University of Technology	Poland
Ščeulovs, Deniss	Riga Technical University	Latvia
Sadri, Houman	University of Central Florida	USA
Salazar, Antonio	Simon Bolivar University	Venezuela
Saleh, Magda M.	Alexandria University	Egypt
Salim, Siham	National Research Center	Egypt
Samcovic, Andreja	University of Belgrade	Serbia

Sanna, Andrea	Polytechnic University of Turin	Italy
Santagati, Cettina	University of Catania	Italy
Santos, Jorge	Polytechnic Institute of Porto	Portugal
Sarma, Himangshu	University of Bremen	Germany
Sasakura, Mariko	Okayama University	Japan
Sastry G, Hanumat	University of Petroleum and Energy Studies	India
Selberherr, Siegfried	Technische Universität Wien	Austria
Selim, Haysam	University of Nevada Las Vegas	USA
Seme, David	University of Picardie Jules Verne	France
Sencu, Razvan	University of Manchester	UK
Serôdio, Carlos M. J.	University of Trás-os-Montes and Alto Douro	Portugal
Shang, Yilun	Tongji University	China
Shanker, Udai	Indian Institute of Technology Roorkee	India
Shieh, Chin-Shiuh	National Kaohsiung University of Applied Sciences	Taiwan
Shieh, Hsin-Jang	National Dong Hwa University	Taiwan
Shin, Jungpil	University of Aizu	Japan
Shing, Chen-Chi	Radford University	USA
Shiraishi, Masatake	Ibaraki University	Japan
Shojafar, Mohammad	University Sapienza of Rome	Italy
Siddique, Zahed	University of Oklahoma	USA
Silva, Geraldo	Estadual Paulista University	Brazil
Simion, Gabriela	University Politehnica of Bucharest	Romania
Singh, Vijander	Netaji Subhas University of Technology (Formerly NSIT)	India
Siriopoulos, Costas	Zayed University	United Arab Emirates
Sllame, Azeddien M.	University of Tripoli	Libya
Sokolov, Sergey	Keldysh Institute for Applied Mathematics	Russian Federation
Sornkaew, Thanakorn	Ramkhamheang University	Thailand
Sotirov, Sotir	University "Prof. Dr Asen Zlatarov"	Bulgaria
Sousa, António	Institute of Biomedical Engineering	Portugal
Spalek, Seweryn	Silesian University of Technology	Poland
Srotyr, Martin	Czech Technical University in Prague	Czech Republic
Stasytyte, Viktorija	Vilnius Gediminas Technical University	Lithuania
Steinbacher, Hans-Peter	University of Applied Science Kufstein	Austria
Štork, Milan	University of West Bohemia	Czech Republic
Stosic, Lazar	Institute of Management and Knowledge, External Associate Coordinator for Serbia, Skopje, Macedonia	Serbia
Straub, Jeremy	North Dakota State University	USA

Strugar, Ivan	University of Zagreb	Croatia
Suárez-Garaboa, Sonia Mª	University of A Coruña	Spain
Subba Reddy, N. V.	Manipal Institute of Technology	India
Subban, Ravi	Department of Computer Science, School of Engineering and Technology, Pondicherry University	India
Subramoniam, Suresh	College of Engineering	India
Sundaram, Aruna	A.M Jain College	India
Sureerattanan, Nidapan	Independent	Thailand
Sutherland, Trudy	Vaal University of Technology	South Africa
Suviniitty, Jaana	Aalto University School of Technology	Finland
Swart, William	East Carolina University	USA
Szabó, Csaba	Technical University of Kosice	Slovakia
Tadepalli, Gopal	Anna University	India
Tadisetty, Srinivasulu	Kakatiya University	India
Tam, Wing K.	Zodicom Technology Pty Limited	Australia
Tansel, Abdullah Uz	City University of New York	USA
Tao, C. W.	National Ilan University	Taiwan
Taraghi, Zohreh	Mazandaran University of Medical Scienses	Iran
Taylor, Stephen	Sussex University	UK
Teixeira Pinto, Leonel	Federal University of Santa Catarina	Brazil
Tenreiro Machado, J. A.	Institute of Engineering of Porto	Portugal
Thapliyal, Mathura	Hemvati Nandan Bahuguna Garhwal University	India
Thompson, Laura	Keiser University	USA
Thurasamy, Ramayah	Science University of Malaysia	Malaysia
Tiwari, Rahul	Medi-Caps University, Indore M.P.	India
Tomar, Ravi	University of Petroleum	India
Trifas, Monica	Jacksonville State University	USA
Truyol, Albert	Academy of Environment ENSMSE et ENSHG	France
Tsai, Chang-Lung	Chinese Culture University	Taiwan
Tsaur, Woei-Jiunn	Da-Yeh University	Taiwan
Tseng, Juin-Ling	Minghsin University of Science and Technology	Taiwan
Tsiligaridis, John	Heritage University	USA
Tu, Shu-Fen	Chinese Culture University	Taiwan
Ucal, Meltem	Kadir Has University	Turkey
Ulovec, Andreas	University of Vienna	Austria
Unalan, Halit Turgay	Anadolu University	Turkey

Vallejo, Marta	Heriot-Watt University	UK
Vallejo Gutiérrez, José Refugio	University of Guanajuato	Mexico
Varughese, Joe	Northern Alberta Institute of Technology	Canada
Vasilache, Simona	University of Tsukuba	Japan
Vázquez, Ernesto	Autonomous University of Nuevo Leon	Mexico
Vegh, Laura	Technical University of Cluj-Napoca	Romania
Velaga, Sreerama Murthy	GMR Institute of Technology	India
Venkateswarlu, Somu	KL University	India
Venu Gopal, S.	Vardhaman College of Engineering	India
Vimarlund, Vivian	Linköping University	Sweden
Vintere, Anna	Latvia University of Agriculture	Latvia
Vityaev, Evgenii E.	Sobolev Institute of Mathematics SB RAS	Russian Federation
Vizureanu, Petrica	"Gheorghe Asachi" Technical University of Iasi	Romania
Wada, Shigeo	Tokyo Denki University	Japan
Waghmare, Vishal	Department of Computer Science, Vivekanand College, Kolhapur	India
Wataya, Roberto Sussumu	Adventist University Center of Sao Paulo	Brazil
Wei, Wei	Zhejiang University	China
Wei, Xinzhou	New York City College of Technology	USA
Whatley, Janice	University of Salford	UK
Whitbrook, Amanda M.	University of Nottingham	UK
Wielki, Janusz	Opole University of Technology	Poland
Wolfengagen, Viacheslav	Institute for Contemporary Education JurInfoR-MSU	Russian Federation
Wu, Tung-Xiung (Sean)	Shih Hsin University	Taiwan
Wu, Wen-Yen	I-Shou University	Taiwan
Xochicale Rojas, Hugo A.	DeSiC - Desarrollo de Sistemas de Cómputo	Mexico
Yang, Fengfan	Nanjing University of Aeronautics and Astronautics	China
Yang, Hung Jen	National Kaohsiung Normal University	Taiwan
Ye, Xin	California State University San Marcos	USA
Yoon, Changwoo	Electronics and Telecommunications Research Institute	South Korea
Yussupova, Nafissa I.	Ufa State Aviation Technical University	Russian Federation
Zafar, Sherin	University Faridabad	India
Zargayouna, Mahdi	Inrets Institute and Paris-Dauphine University	France
Zaridis, Apostolos	University of the Aegean	Greece
Zaveri, Jigish	Morgan State University	USA

ADDITIONAL REVIEWERS FOR THE NON-BLIND REVIEWING

Abdulrahaman, Ribwar	Koya University	Iraq
Acosta, Patricia	Universidad de las Americas	Ecuador
Acosta Guzmán, Ivan Leonel	Universidad de Guayaquil	Ecuador
Adamopoulou, Evgenia	National Tecnhical University of Athens	Greece
Adekunle, Yinka	Babcock University	Nigeria
Aderhold, Daniel	Universidad Peruana de Ciencias Aplicadas	Peru
Ahn, Dohee	Chung-Ang University	South Korea
Akdeniz, Rafet	Namik Kemal University	Turkey
Al-Masri, Alaaeddin	An-Najah National University	Palestine
Alsaqqar, Awatif	Aurok University	Iraq
Alvarado, Luz Deicy	Universidad Distrital Francisco José de Caldas	Colombia
Armas, Jimmy	Universidad Peruana de Ciencias Aplicadas	Peru
Armoush, Ashraf	An-Najah National University	Palestine
Barbosa, Cátia	Federal University of Minas Gerais	Brazil
Barbosa, Cátia Rodrigues	Universidade Federal de Minas Gerais	Brazil
Bauer, Thomas A.	University of Vienna	Austria
Belardi, Aldo Artur	Centro Universitário FEI	Brazil
Benova, Eleonora	Comenius University	Slovakia
Berleant, Daniel	University of Arkansas at Litte Rock	USA
Bernardi, Ansgar	German Research Center for Artificial Intelligence	Germany
Bernardino, Jorge	Institute of Engineering of Coimbra	Portugal
Bezhani, Eda	University Aleksander Moisiu	Albania
Blackmore, Chris	The Open University	UK
Bönke, Dietmar	Reutlingen University	Germany
Buchelli Perales, Orivel Jackson	Universidad Nacional de Trujillo	Peru
Buonopane, Gerald	Seton Hall University	USA
Burcham, Joan	Arkansas State Univesity	USA

Bustos García De Castro, Pablo	Universidad de Extremadura	Spain
Cantu, José	Universidad Autonoma de Nuevo Leon	Mexico
Casagni, Michelle	MITRE	USA
Cashel-Cordo, Peter	University of Southern Indiana	USA
Castañeda, Pedro	Universidad Peruana de Ciencias Aplicadas	Peru
Castek, Jill	University of Arizona	USA
Chen, Jong-Chen	National Yunlin University of Science and Technology	Taiwan
Chen, Zhikui	Dalian University of Technology	China
Collar, Emilio	Western Connecticut State University	USA
Costa, Ivanir	Universidade Nove de Julho	Brazil
Crepeau, John	University of Idaho	USA
Cunha, Izabella	Federal University of Minas Gerais	Brazil
Darwish, Mahmoud	Navajo Technical University	USA
Dave, Leena	RTI International	USA
De Magalhães, Candida Alzira	Universidade Federal de Roraima	Brazil
Decker, Tim	University of Siegen	Germany
Demaidi, Mona	An-Najah National University	Palestine
Demstichas, Kostas	Institute of Communication and Computer Systems	Greece
Denicol, Alexandre	Intellectos	Brazil
Dhiman, Rohtash	Deenbandhu Chhotu Ram University of Science and Technology	India
Dhir, Vijay	Sant Baba Bhag Singh University	India
Do Nascimento Morais, António J.	Open University	Portugal
Drews Jr., Paulo	Universidade Federal do Rio Grande	Brazil
Drumm, Christian	FH Aachen University of Applied Sciences	Germany
Duque, Néstor	Universidad Nacional de Colombia	Colombia
Egesoy, Ahmet	Ege University	Turkey
Egoavil Ayala, Miguel Sebastian	Universidad Peruana Cayetano Heredia	Peru
El Breidi, Farid	University of Southern Indiana	USA
Espejo, Raul	Syncho Reserach Ltd.	UK
Fang, Wen-Chang	National Taipei University	Taiwan
Fazlagic, Jan	Poznan University of Economics and Business	Poland
Fertalj, Kreso	University of Zagreb	Croatia

Figueiredo, Josiel	Federal University of Mato Grosso	Brazil
Florescu, Gabriela	National Institute for Research and Development in Informatics	Romania
Franco, José Ricardo Queiroz	Universidade Federal de Minas Gerais	Brazil
Gardea, Carlos	National Autonomous University of Mexico	Mexico
Ghosh, Joydeep	Indian Institute of Technology Bombay	India
Gimenez, Edson	Instituto Nacional de Telecomunicações	Brazil
Gregus, Michal	Comenius University	Slovakia
Ham, Chan	Kennesaw State University	USA
Hilário, Ronderson	Federal University of Minas Gerais	Brazil
Hinojosa, Moises	Universidad Autonoma de Nuevo Leon	Mexico
Hjelseth, Eilif	Norwegian University of Technology	Norway
Hofmann, Sara	University of Bremen	Germany
Hong, Jinglan	Shandong University	China
Hong, Seongtae	Sangmyung University	South Korea
Hosain, Shazzad	North South University	Bangladesh
Ismail, Yasser	Southern University and A&M College	USA
Ison, Ray	The Open University	UK
Ivanovs, Andrejs	Riga Stradinsh University	Latvia
Jacobs, Gloria	University of Arizona	USA
Jenčová, Edina	Technical University of Košice	Slovakia
Jencova, Edina	Faculty of Aeronautics of the Technical University of Kosice	Slovakia
Jiang, Wuhua	HeFei University of Technology	China
Jilek, Miroslav	Czech Technical University in Prague	Czech Republic
Kali, Yassine	Ecole de Techologie Superieure	Canada
Kämper, Klaus-Peter	FH Aachen University of Applied Sciences	Germany
Katrib, Miguel	University of Havana	Cuba
Khan, Farhan	National University of Sciences and Technology	Pakistan
Krishna, Rama	National Institute of Technical Teachers Training and Research	India
Lastre Aleaga, Arlys Michel	Universidad Tecnológica Equinoccial	Ecuador
Lee, Chung-Wei	University of Illinois at Springfield	USA
Lee, Meng-huang	Shih Chien University	Taiwan
Li, Jie	Shanghai Maritime University	China
Li, Ruqiong	Shanghai Normal University	China
Lin, Wayne	TakMing University of Science and Technology	Taiwan

Lisitsyn, Pavel	St. Petersburg State University	Russian Federation
Lopez Garay, Hernan	Universidad de Ibagué	Colombia
Maciá, Francisco	Universidad de Alicante	Spain
Marrone, Dan	Farmingdale State College	USA
Mauricio, David	Universidad Nacional Mayor de San Marcos	Peru
Maxey, Christopher	University of Maryland	USA
Meeson, Reginald	Institute for Defense Analyses	USA
Meister, Darren	Ivey Business School	Canada
Melgarejo, Miguel	Universidad Distrital Francisco José de Caldas	Canada
Miklos, Jorge	Paulista University	Brazil
Modlic, Borivoj	University of Zagreb	Croatia
Molina Beltran, Ferney Alberto	Universidad Nacional	Colombia
Mujumdar, Sudesh	University of Southern Indiana	USA
Müller, Karl H.	Steinbeis Transfer Center New Cybernetics in Vienna	Austria
Murzaku, Ines	Seton Hall University	USA
Myers, Margaret	Institute for Defense Analyses	USA
Nag, Abhijit	The University of Memphis	USA
Nedjalkov, Mihail	Bulgarian Academy of Sciences	Bulgaria
Nunes, Daniel	Instituto Nacional de Telecomunicações	Brazil
Ogbonna, Chibueze	Babcock University	Nigeria
Okada, Hiraku	Nagoya University	Japan
Oliveira, Allan	Federal University of Mato Grosso	Brazil
Oliveros, Jacobo	Benemérita Universidad Autónoma de Puebla	Mexico
Ott, Elfriede	Ostfalia University of Applied Sciences	Germany
Pawlak, Mirosław	Adam Mickiewicz University	Poland
Perez Vielma, Maira	National Autonomous University of Mexico	Mexico
Perlis, Donald	University of Maryland	USA
Peter, Timm-Julian	University of Siegen	Germany
Pettenpohl, Heinrich	Fraunhofer ISST	Germany
Porto, Marcelo Franco	Universidade Federal de Minas Gerais	Brazil
Prasad, P. M. K.	GVP College of Engineering for Women, Visakhapatnam	India
Qamhieh, Manar	An-Najah National University	Palestine
Qian, Yu	Cortexica Company	UK
Rahman, Rummana	North South University	Bangladesh
Rana, Faisal	American university of Dubai	United Arab Emirates
Ravi, Kishore Kumar	Indian Institute of Technology Kharagpur	India

Reis, Arsénio	University of Trás-os-Montes e Alto Douro	Portugal
Resende Faria, Diego	Aston University	Spain
Richards, Matthew	The Boeing Company	USA
Rico-Ramirez, Miguel Angel	University of Bristol	UK
Rioga, Danielle	Federal University of Minas Gerais	Brazil
Roushdy, Mohamed	Ain Shams University	Egypt
Rozevskis, Uldis	University of Latvia	Latvia
Ruiz-Pinales, José	University of Guanajuato	Mexico
Rus Mansilla, Francisco	University of Málaga	South Sandwich Islands
Saad, Maarouf	Ecole de Techologie Superieure	Canada
Sahd, Lize-Marie	Stellenbosch University	South Africa
Saini, Himanshi	Deenbandhu Chhotu Ram University of Science and Technology	India
Saini, Manish	Deenbandhu Chhotu Ram University of Science and Technology	India
Salem, Sameh A.	National Telecom Regulatory Authority	Egypt
Samiah, Abdul	National University of Sciences and Technology	Pakistan
Sánchez, Francisco Javier	Universidad Autónoma Metropolitana Iztapalapa	Mexico
Sánchez Suárez, Elio Edwin	Universidad de Guayaquil	Ecuador
Sayed, Samir	National Telecom Regulatory Authority	Egypt
Serkovic, Laura	Universidad Nacional Autónoma de México	Mexico
Sexton, Natasha	Stellenbosch University	South Africa
Shahini-Hoxhaj, Remzie	Universiteti i Prishtines	Kosovo
Silva Balarezo, Mariana	Universidad Catolica de Trujillo	Peru
Singh, Amardeep	Punjabi University	India
Singh, Karan	Jawaharlal Nehru University	India
Singh, Sudhansu Sekhar	KIIT University	India
Smoot, Chris	Institute for Adanced Studies on Climate Change	USA
Sobrado, Eddie	Pontificia Universidad Católica del Perú	Peru
Stöcker, Pamela	FH Aachen University of Applied Sciences	Germany
Subedi, Kul	University of Memphis	USA
Tarhan, Ayça	Hacettepe University	Turkey
Tartaraj, Azeta	University Aleksander Moisiu	Albania
Tommasino, Pasquale	Sapienza University	Italy
Trifiletti, Alessandro	Sapienza University of Rome	Italy
Tripathi, Kumud	Indian Institute of Technology Kharagpur	India

Tsiligaridis, John	Heritage University	USA
Valdivia, César	Pontificia Universidad Católica del Perú	Peru
Velandia, Hernando	Universidad de Pamplona	Colombia
Verzilin, Dmitrii	Lesgaft State University of Sport and Health	Russian Federation
Villarreal Valerio, Julian Anibal	Universidad Nacional Mayor de San Marcos	Peru
Viskup, Pavel	Tomas Bata University	Czech Republic
Walker, Daniel	Tsunami Memorial Institute	USA
Wang, Jun-Ren	National Taiwan Sport University	Taiwan
Weber, Lyle	The King's University	USA
Wei, Xinzhou	New York City College of Technology	USA
Wesley, Joan	Jackson State University	USA
Woodcock, Timothy	Texas A and M University	USA
Xia, Guang	HeFei University of Technology	China
Yoon, Changwoo	Electronics and Telecommunications Research Institute	South Korea
Yoon, Seokhyun	Dankook University	South Korea
Yu, Jaehoon	Osaka University	Japan
Zavala-Rio, Daniel	Instituto Tecnológico y de Estudios Superiores de Monterrey	Mexico
Žibala, Dace	Rīga Stradiņš University	Latvia
Ziegler, Christian	Karlsruhe Institute of Technology	Germany

HONORARY PRESIDENTS OF PAST CONFERENCES
Bela Banathy
Stafford Beer
George Klir
Karl Pribram
Paul A. Jensen
Gheorghe Benga

HONORARY CHAIR
William Lesso
(1931-2015)

PROGRAM COMMITTEE CHAIRS
Michael Savoie
C. Dale Zinn

GENERAL CHAIR
Nagib Callaos

ORGANIZING COMMITTEE CHAIRS
Belkis Sánchez
Andrés Tremante

CONFERENCES PROGRAM MANAGER /
PROCEEDINGS PRODUCTION CHAIR
María Sánchez

OPERATIONAL ASSISTANTS
Jaime Noguera
Kilian Méndez

Number of Papers Included in these Proceedings per Country
(The country of the first author was the one taken into account for these statistics)

Country	# Papers	%
TOTAL	88	100.00
United States	13	14.77
Peru	9	10.23
Germany	8	9.09
Japan	8	9.09
Latvia	8	9.09
Brazil	5	5.68
Mexico	5	5.68
Ecuador	3	3.41
Egypt	3	3.41
Taiwan	3	3.41
Austria	2	2.27
Canada	2	2.27
Poland	2	2.27
Belgium	1	1.14
China	1	1.14
Colombia	1	1.14
Costa Rica	1	1.14
Croatia	1	1.14
Czech Republic	1	1.14
Iraq	1	1.14
Italy	1	1.14
Norway	1	1.14
Pakistan	1	1.14
Paraguay	1	1.14
Russian Federation	1	1.14
Saudi Arabia	1	1.14
South Africa	1	1.14
South Korea	1	1.14
Spain	1	1.14
United Arab Emirates	1	1.14

Foreword

Our purpose in the 23rd World Multi-Conference on Systemics, Cybernetics and Informatics (WMSCI 2019) is to provide, in these increasingly related areas, a ***multi-disciplinary forum, to foster interdisciplinary communication*** among the participants, and to support the sharing process of diverse perspectives of the same trans-disciplinary concepts and principles.

Systemics, Cybernetics and Informatics (SCI) are increasingly being related to each other in almost every scientific discipline and human activity. Their common trans-disciplinarity characterizes and communicates them, generating strong relations among them and with other disciplines. They work together to create a whole new way of thinking and practice. This phenomenon persuaded the Organizing Committee to structure WMSCI 2019 as a multi-conference where participants may focus on one area, or on one discipline, while allowing them the possibility of attending conferences from other areas or disciplines. This systemic approach stimulates cross-fertilization among different disciplines, inspiring scholars, originating new hypothesis, supporting production of innovations and generating analogies; which is, after all, one of the very basic principles of the systems' movement and a fundamental aim in cybernetics.

WMSCI 2019 was organized and sponsored by the International Institute of Informatics and Systemics (IIIS, www.iiis.org), member of the International Federation of Systems Research (IFSR). The IIIS is a ***multi-disciplinary organization for inter-disciplinary communication and integration***, which includes about 5,000 members. Consequently, a main purpose of the IIIS is to foster knowledge integration processes, interdisciplinary communication, and integration of academic activities. Based on 1) the transdisciplinarity of the systemic approach, along with its essential characteristic of emphasizing *relationships* and *integrating* processes, and 2) the multi-disciplinary support of cybernetics' and informatics' concepts, notions, theories, technologies, and tools, the IIIS has been organizing multi-disciplinary conferences as a platform for fostering inter-disciplinary communication and knowledge integration processes.

Multi-disciplinary conferences are organized by the IIIS as support for ***both intra-*** and ***inter-disciplinary*** communication. Processes of intra-disciplinary communication are mainly achieved via traditional paper presentations in corresponding disciplines, while conversational sessions, regarding trans- and inter-disciplinary topics, are among the means used for inter-disciplinary communication. Intra- and inter-disciplinary communications might generate *co-regulative cybernetic loops*, via negative feedback, and *synergic* relationships, via positive feedback loops, in which both kinds of communications could increase their respective effectiveness. Figure 1 shows at least two cybernetic loops if intra- and inter-disciplinary are adequately related. A necessary condition for the effectiveness of Inter-disciplinary communication is an adequate level of **variety** regarding the participating disciplines. *Analogical thinking and learning processes* of disciplinarians depend on it; which in turn are potential sources of the creative tension required for cross-fertilization among disciplines and the generations of new hypotheses. An extended presentation regarding this issue can be found at www.iiis.org/MainPurpose.

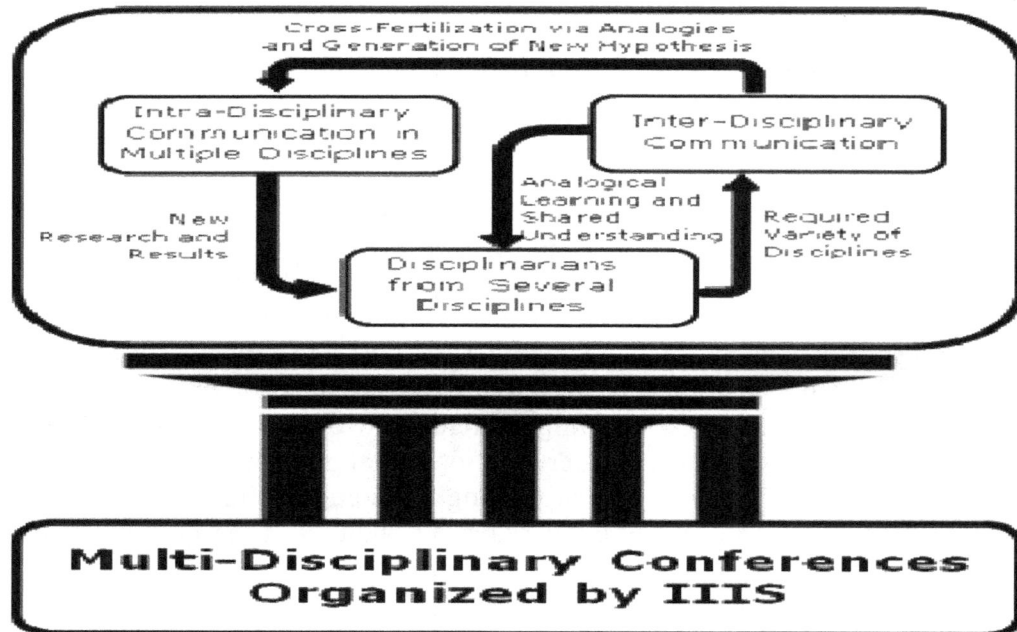

Figure 1

In the specific case of Systemics, Cybernetics and Informatics (SCI), the IIIS is an organization dedicated to contribute to the development of the Systems Approach, Cybernetics, and Informatics potential, using both: knowledge and experience, thinking and action, theory and practice, for:

a) The identification of synergistic relationships among Systemics, Cybernetics and Informatics, and between them and society.
b) The promotion of contacts among the different academic areas, through the transdisciplinarity of the systems approach.
c) The identification and implementation of communication channels among the different professions.
d) The supply of communication links between the academic and professional worlds, as well as between them and the business world, both public and private, political and cultural.
e) The stimulus for the creation of integrative arrangements at different levels of society, as well as at the family and personal levels.
f) The promotion of trans-disciplinary research, both on theoretical issues and on applications to concrete problems.

These IIIS objectives have oriented the organizational efforts of yearly WMSCI/ISAS/IMSCI/CISCI conferences since 1995.

On behalf of the Organizing Committee, I extend our heartfelt thanks to:

1. The 456 members of the different Program Committees, from 56 countries (including the PC members of the events organized in its context and jointly with WMSCI 2019). Almost all the members of the Program Committee are *authors or co-authors sessions' best papers in previous conferences*, i.e. papers selected by the respective audience as the best paper of the session in which they were presented.
2. The 748 additional reviewers, from 83 countries, for their *double-blind peer reviews*; and
3. The 232 reviewers, from 46 countries, for their efforts in making the *non-blind peer reviews*. (Some reviewers supported both: non-blind and double-blind reviewing for different submissions).

The names and affiliation of both kinds of reviewers are listed in these proceedings. We extend our gratefulness to all of them. The scholarly quality of the authors and the reviewers is what define the quality of the conference and its respective proceedings. Consequently, our gratitude is to the members of the programs' committees, both kinds of reviewers and the collaborating authors.

A total of 1537 reviews made by 980 reviewers, from 86 counties, (who made at least one review) contributed to the quality achieved in WMSCI 2019. This means an average of 8.49 reviews per submission (181 submissions were received). *Each registered author had access, via the conference web site, to the reviews that recommended the acceptance of their respective submissions*. Each registered author could also get information about: 1) the average of the reviewers' evaluations according to 8 criteria, and the average of a global evaluation of his/her submission; and 2) the comments and the constructive feedback made by the reviewers, who recommended the acceptance of his/her submission, so the author would be able to improve the final version of the paper.

In the organizational process of WMSCI 2019, about 181 articles were submitted. These pre-conference proceedings include about 88 papers that were accepted for presentation from 30 countries (41 countries taking into account the presentations in collocated events). I extend our thanks to the invited sessions' organizers for collecting, reviewing, and selecting the papers that will be presented in their respective sessions. The submissions were reviewed as carefully as time permitted; it is expected that most of them will appear in a more polished and complete form in scientific journals. This information about WMSCI 2019 is summarized in the following table, along with the other collocated events:

Conference	# of submissions received	# of reviewers that made at least one review	# of reviews made	Average of reviews per reviewer	Average of reviews per submission	# of papers included in the proceedings	% of submissions included in the proceedings
WMSCI 2019	**181**	**980**	**1537**	**1.57**	**8.49**	**88**	**48.62%**
IMSCI 2019	**88**	**439**	**974**	**2.22**	**11.07**	**41**	**46.59%**
WMSCI & IMSCI	**269**	**1419**	**2511**	**1.77**	**9.33**	**129**	**47.96%**
CISCI 2019	**118**	**572**	**1205**	**2.11**	**10.21**	**65**	**55.08%**
TOTAL	**387**	**1991**	**3716**	**1.87**	**9.60**	**194**	**50.13%**

All submissions were peer reviewed by the two-tier reviewing methodology of the International Institute of Informatics and Systemics (IIIS, www.iiis.org). As it might be noticed, from the table above, *9.6 reviews were made, in average, for each submission we received.* After the conference is over, the names of the reviewers will be published on the IIIS web site along with the titles of the papers each reviewer reviewed. This means that what had been a double-blind review, up to the conference, is transformed to single-blind review, after the conference is over. In this way, each author would have information about the names of the reviewers of his/her submission, but not vice-versa. Likewise, each author would know how many reviewers reviewed his/her submission and relate it to the average, being informed in the above table, of 9.6 reviews per paper.

Our two-tier reviewing methodology meet two different objectives of peer-review: 1) to improve the paper via non-anonymous reviewers (non-blind reviews) and 2) to improve the acceptance/non-acceptance decision of the Organizing Committee via traditional anonymous reviewers (double-blind reviews) A recommendation to accept, made by non-anonymous reviews, is a *necessary* condition, but it is *not a sufficient* one. A submission, to be accepted, should also have a majority of its double-blind reviewers recommending its acceptance. These two necessary conditions generate a more reliable and rigorous reviewing than any of those reviewing methods, based on just one of the indicated methods, or just on the traditional double-blind reviewing.

We extend our gratitude to the invited sessions' organizers: Dr. Shigehiro Hashimoto and Dr. Natalja Lace; as well as to the special track co-chairs and the co-editors of these proceedings, for the hard work, energy and eagerness they displayed preparing their respective sessions. We express our intense gratitude to Professor William Lesso (1931-2015) for his wise and timely, adequate and valuable tutoring, for his eternal energy, integrity, and continuous support and advice, as the Program Committee Chair of past conferences (since 1981), as well as for being a very caring old friend and intellectual father to many of us. We also extend our gratitude to Professor Belkis Sánchez, who brilliantly managed the organizing process.

Our gratitude to Professors Bela H. Banathy, Stafford Beer, George Klir, Karl Pribram, Paul A. Jensen, and Gheorghe Benga who dignified our past WMSCI conferences by being their Honorary Presidents. We also extend our gratitude to the following scholars, researchers, and professionals who accepted to deliver plenary workshops and/or to address the audience of the General Joint Plenary Sessions with keynote addresses.

We would like also to extend our gratefulness to Professor Shigehiro Hashimoto for his yearly support in the last 20 years as well as for his editorial work for the journal; as well as to Professor Grandon Gill, Dr. Jeremy Horne, Professor Thomas Marlowe and Professor Matthew E. Edwards for their continuous advice and support in the conferences they participated in, along the last 12 years; as well as in the conferences they were not able to participate in. Their advices and the kind of care they provided us with are highly valued and appreciated.

We also extend our gratitude to the following scholars, researchers, and professionals who accepted to deliver plenary workshops and/or to address the audience of the General Joint Plenary Sessions with keynote addresses.

Workshops and Conversational Sessions

Professor Thomas Marlowe, Seton Hall University, USA, Department of Mathematics and Computer Science, Program Advisor for Computer Science, Doctor in Computer Science and, Doctor in Mathematics.

Professor Stuart A. Umpleby, The George Washington University, USA, President of the Executive Committee of the International Academy for Systems and Cybernetics Sciences, Former President of The American Society of Cybernetics.

Professor Matthew E. Edwards, Alabama A&M University. USA, Professor of Physics and, Former Dean, School of Arts and Sciences, Director of IHSEAR: Institute of Higher Science Education Advancement, and Research.

Professor Tatiana Medvedeva, Siberian State University of Transport. Russia, Department of World Economy and Law Former Head of the Scientific and Practical Center for Business and Management.

Dr. Bruce E. Peoples, Innovations LLC, USA, Founder and CEO, Formerly at Université Paris 8, France, Laboratoire Paragraphe, Chair Emeritus of an ISO/IEC Standards Committee, Generated over 50 Invention Disclosures, 15 Patent Applications and 11 Patent Awards.

Professor William Swart, East Carolina University, USA, FMR. Dean of Engineering and Technology at New Jersey Institute of Technology, Provost and Vice President for Academic Affairs at East Carolina University, Researcher and Consultant at NASA's Space Shuttle.

Professor Richard Self, University of Derby, UK, The School of Computing and Mathematics, Senior Lecturer in Analytics and Governance.

Professor Thomas Marlowe, Seton Hall University, USA, Department of Mathematics and Computer Science, Program Advisor for Computer Science, Doctor in Computer Science and, Doctor in Mathematics.

Professor Shigehiro Hashimoto, Kogakuin University, Japan, Councilor and Dean, Faculty of Engineering, Former Associate to the University President. Doctor of Engineering and Doctor of Medicine. Biomedical Engineering.

Professor Matthew E. Edwards, Alabama A&M University, USA. Professor of Physics and Former Dean of the School of Arts and Sciences. Director of IHSEAR: Institute of Higher Science Education, Advancement and Research.

Dr. Paul Page, Queen's University Belfast, UK, School of Electronics, Electrical Engineering & Computer Science, High Performance and Distributed Computing, Lecturer (Education) – Society & Community.

Professor Stuart A. Umpleby, The George Washington University, USA, President of the Executive Committee of the International Academy for Systems and Cybernetics Sciences, Former President of The American Society of Cybernetics.

Professor Tatiana Medvedeva, Siberian State University of Transport. Russia, Department of World Economy and Law Former Head of the Scientific and Practical Center for Business and Management.

Fr. Dr. Joseph Laracy, Seton Hall University, USA, College of Arts and Sciences, Department of Mathematics and Computer Science, Complex Systems, Differential Equations, and Dynamical Systems.

Dr. Russell Jay Hendel, Towson University, USA, Dept. of Mathematics. Researcher in Discrete Number Theory, the Theory of Pedagogy, Applications of Technology to Pedagogy, and the Interaction of Mathematics and the Arts.

Dr. David Cutting, Queen's University Belfast, UK, School of Electronics, Electrical Engineering and Computer Science, Course Director: BSc Software, Engineering with Digital Technology Partnership, Fellow of the Higher Education Academy.

Professor William Swart, East Carolina University, USA. FMR. Dean of Engineering and Technology at New Jersey Institute of Technology. Provost and Vice President for Academic Affairs at East Carolina University. Researcher and Consultant at NASA's Space Shuttle.

Professor Christian Greiner, Munich University of Applied Sciences, Germany, Associate Dean Applied Research, Professor at the Department of Business Administration.

Professor Mohammad Ilyas, Florida Atlantic University, USA, Department of Computer and Electrical Engineering and Computer Science, Former Dean of the College of Engineering and Computer Science; Member of Global Engineering Deans Council.

Mg. Philipp Belcredi, Comparative-Systemic Intervention, Austria, Owner and CEO, Former CEO of Pewag Chain. Inc.

Professor Wen-Chen Hu, University of North Dakota, USA, School of Electrical Engineering & Computer Science, Former (2010-2017) editor-in-chief of the International Journal of Handheld Computing Research (IJHCR).

Professor Thomas Peisl, Munich University of Applied Sciences. Germany, Professor of International Management and Strategy, Former Marketing Director at General Electric Europe.

Professor Maritza Placencia Medina, Departamento Académico de Ciencias Dinámicas de la Universidad Nacional Mayor de San Marcos, Peru, Facultad de Medicina, Centro de Investigaciones Tecnológicas.

Professor Andrés Tremante, Florida International University, USA, Department of Mechanical and Materials Engineering.

Invited Sessions Organizers

Professor Shigehiro Hashimoto, Kogakuin University, Japan. Councilor and Dean, Faculty of Engineering, Former Associate to the University President. Doctor of Engineering and Doctor of Medicine. Biomedical Engineering.

Professor *Dr. oec* Natalja Lace, Riga Technical University, Faculty of Engineering, Economy and Management. Head of Department of Corporate Finance and Economics.

Many thanks to Drs. Sushil Archarya, Esther Zaretsky, and to professors Michael Savoie, Hsing-Wei Chu, Mohammad Siddique, Friedrich Welsch, Thierry Lefevre, José Vicente Carrasquero, Angel Oropeza, and José Ferrer, for chairing and supporting the organization of conferences and/or special events or tracks in the context of, or collocated with, WMSCI 2019, and previous conferences. We also wish to thank all the authors for the quality of their papers, the Program Committee members and the additional reviewers for their time and their contributions in the respective reviewing processes.

Our gratefulness is also extended to the organizations that provided scientific, academic, professional, or corporate co-sponsorships in this conference and/of previous ones. The following are among these organizations:

Google MITRE CORPORATION IASCYS The International Academy for Systems and Cybernetic Sciences THE STANDISH GROUP Innovations LLC Finanzas y Política Económica

SAINT LEO UNIVERSITY INVENTORS ASSISTANCE LEAGUE THOUGHTS TO PAPER IC3DT INTERNATIONAL CONSORTIUM OF 3D TECHNOLOGY IDEAMEXLAB Encuentros

Special Thanks to Dr. Jeremy Horne, Dr. Harvey Hyman, and Ms. Molly Youngblood Geiger (Google Partners Community Ambassador) for their efforts in helping us with the identification of above shown co-sponsors.

We extend our gratitude as well to professor Belkis Sanchez, Eng/Mg María Sánchez, Ms. Kilian Mendez, Mr. Jhonny Romero, Mr. Jaime Noguera, and Mr. Freddy Callaos for their knowledgeable effort in supporting the organizational process, maintaining the email lists, producing the hard copy and CD versions of the proceedings, developing and maintaining the software that supports the interactions of the authors with the reviewing process and the Organizing Committee, as well as for their support in the help desk, the promotional process, and their advising role in the promotion of the conference.

Professor Nagib C. Callaos, Ph. D.
WMSCI 2019 General Chair
www.iiis.org/Nagib-Callaos

VOLUME III

CONTENTS

Contents
                                                                                                i

Innovation and Technology Transfer in Emerging Economies - Invited Session Organizer: Elina Gaile-Sarkane and Inga Lapina (Latvia)

Čevers, Aldis; Gaile-Sarkane, Elīna (Latvia): "Indicators, Factors and Criteria for Assessing of the Customs Performance"   1

Babica, Viktorija *; Sceulovs, Deniss *; Rustenova, Elvira ** (* Latvia, ** Kazakhstan): "Digitalization of Public Procurement: Barriers for Innovation"   7

Grikke, Laura; Andersone, Ieva; Sceulovs, Deniss (Latvia): "Challenges of Sustainable Company Development: Case of Craft Business in Latvia"   13

Kasperovica, Ludmila; Lace, Natalja (Latvia): "Business Model Transformation and Business Viability. Case of Yellow Pages"   19

Pīlēna, Arta; Kavosa, Maija (Latvia): "A Control System for Strategy Implementation: A Case of a National Standardization Body"   25

Straujuma, Anita; Gaile-Sarkane, Elina; Ozolins, Modris (Latvia): "Alumni Segmenting for Fostering Innovation and Entrepreneurship in Universities"   31

Complexity: Complex Sciences and Systems

Alzate, Marco A.; Mejia, Marcela (Colombia): "Cognitive Cellular Automata for Image Segmentation: A Social Learning Metaphor "   37

Leybourne, Bruce *; Straser, Valentino **; Wu, Hong-Chun ***; Gregori, Giovanni ****; Bapat, Arun *****; Venkatanathan, Natarajan *****; Hissink, Louis ****** (* USA, ** Belgium, *** Taiwan, **** Italy, ***** India, ****** Australia): "Multi-Parametric Earthquake Forecasting the New Madrid from Electromagnetic Coupling between Solar Corona and Earth System Precursors "   43

Interdisciplinary Research, Education, and Communication (IDREC 2019)

Estrada-Domínguez, Jesús Eduardo; López-Lira Arjona, Alfonso; Hinojosa-Rivera, Moisés; Torres-Castro, Alejandro (Mexico): "Developing Innovation Technology Capacities in Large Manufacturing Firms from Mexico"   49

Gutiérrez Arenas, Rodrigo Alejandro; Salazar Guerrero, Evelyn; Martínez Alavez, Jacquelyn; Minami Koyama, Yukihiro (Mexico): "Experimental Paradigms in the Explanation of Mathematical Concepts"   55

Karulis, Miervaldis (Latvia): "Cluster and Factor Analysis of Satisfaction Perception of B-Learning of Medical Terminology"   59

Lara Gracia, Marco A. (USA): "Effect of Post-Panamax Containerships on Us Ports and Logistics Networks"   65

Laracy, Fr. Joseph R.; Marlowe, Thomas; Valdez, Edgar; Liddy, Msgr. Richard (USA): "Was Bernard Lonergan a Second-Order Cyberneticist?"   71

Placencia Medina, Maritza; Silva Valencia, Javier; Mechan Mendez, Víctor; Pando Álvarez, Rosa; Quintana Salinas, Margot Rosario; Carreño Escobedo, Jorge Raúl; Ascacivar Placencia, Yanelli Karen (Peru): "ALM Program: Ten Years of Educational Technology Interventions at the Faculty of Medicine at the Oldest National University in Perú"   76

Poszytek, Pawel (Poland): "The Framework of Teacher Competencies – An Evidence-Based Generic Model for Teachers' Training in Europe"   82

Rosenko, Svetlana I. *; Rezaev, Andrey A. ** (* Russian Federation, ** USA): "CommunicationS and Political Communication Today: New World, New Concepts, and Schemes "   88

Scholte, Tom (Canada): "Modeling Workplace Conflict with "Systems Theatre""   91

Ulloa Rubio, Bertha; Yupari Azabache, Irma Luz; Gálvez Carrillo, Rosa Patricia; Rodriguez Azabache, Julio Antonio; Wong Aitken, Higinio Guillermo (Peru): "Evaluation Model about Behavior, Quality Perception and Satisfaction of the Drinking Water Service in Trujillo- Peru"   97

Virtual Engineering

Heinz, Tim; Nelles, Oliver (Germany): "Data Distribution Assessment and Optimal Splitting of Data Sets"   103

Ulmer, Jessica *; Braun, Sebastian *; Lai, Chow Yin **; Cheng, Chi-Tsun **; Wollert, Jörg * (* Germany, ** Australia): "Generic Integration of VR and AR in Product Lifecycles Based on CAD Models"   109

Yassin, Amal *; Hefny, Mamdouh **; Elarif, Taha * (* Egypt, ** UK): "Augmented Reality Systems in Total Hip Arthroplasty"   115

Authors Index

121

Indicators, factors and criteria for assessing of the customs performance

Aldis ČEVERS
Riga Technical University, Faculty of Engineering Economics and Management
6 Kalnciema Street, Riga, LV-1048, Latvia

Elīna GAILE-SARKANE
Riga Technical University, Faculty of Engineering Economics and Management
6 Kalnciema Street, Riga, LV-1048, Latvia

ABSTRACT

The aim of the research is to analyze the most important elements of the customs performance assessment system and their applications. This topic is very actual because customs function and task priorities changes, customs services need to pay more attention to international threats. Similar tasks in different countries would be appropriate to use a similar strategic management methods. It is very important to develop a customs authority strategy, to set objectives, to organize the performance of functions and tasks, but without an appropriate performance assessment system, it will not be possible to judge the quality of the implementation of the strategy.

Keywords: capacity of public governance, effectiveness, assessment of operations, customs performance indicators, assessment criteria, factors of influence of customs operations.

1. INTRODUCTION

The broadest concept, which is widely used nowadays to characterize quality of work of a company, an institution or an organization is – governance. Governance has became an odd reality nowadays, which not only affects the place of the country in ranking charts and indexes, but also competitiveness of every company in the market and organization of operations of public governance. Nowadays important role is played both by institutional construction of the state and by the capacity of state administration in exercising of relevant core functions regarding integrated actions in defining the problem and coordination of implementing reforms, strategic planning, change management, communication about causes of state actions and achievable results.

As high the capacity as effective the operation and, to assess it, a comparative and methodical assessment of institution must be carried out.

Customs institutions possess various functions, quite rapid and wide amplitude of priority change, as well as dependency on external circumstances. At assessment such criteria as the following must be set apart and correctly interpreted: results of customs work; indicators as results of customs work and as pointers, which can be established within customs environment and outside of it; factors that affect results.

Maximum of those pointers must be studied, then most relevant and objective must be chosen and used to characterize stage of fulfillment of strategic aims, functions and objectives. It must be completely clear – how and why an indicator becomes a criterion,

in its turn the chosen criterions must correspond to the aim of assessment.

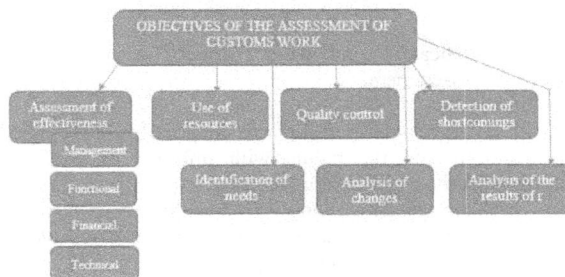

Figure 1. Objectives of the assessment of customs work.

The objective of the assessment is not always the functional outcomes of the institution or service. The government may be interested in the overall effectiveness of the institution, in certain situations it is important to assess the effectiveness of the use of resources at customs authorities, to identify shortcomings in the functioning of the service, to diagnose needs, to analyze the results of the reforms carried out. There is no universal method that serves all the objectives of the evaluation, special criteria should be selected that can most accurately describe the situation. The research has been carried out on the basis of theoretical aspects of strategic management, public administration and the customs matters. Author studied experience of various countries and international organizations recommendations of customs work planning, implementation and evaluation.

2. OUTCOMES AND INDICATORS

In theory and practice one can find several terms for indicators that are used for the assessment – indicators, criteria, factors. Each can be used in different ways.

The outcomes are the broadest term to define elements used in analysis and evaluation. The outcomes that result from reading the measurement or performing certain mathematical operations on their own will be accurate, but without a deeper analysis, without their place and significance in the finding process, this will not reflect the realities of the situation. Performance outcomes are to be classified for proper application (see Figure 2.). The outcomes used for evaluation can be variable and unchangeable, sensitive and unaffectable. Depending on the level of complexity, all outcomes can be divided in simple and complex. Qualitatively developed performance outcomes provide public administrations and the public with information about the planned objectives and those achieved within the allocated resources.

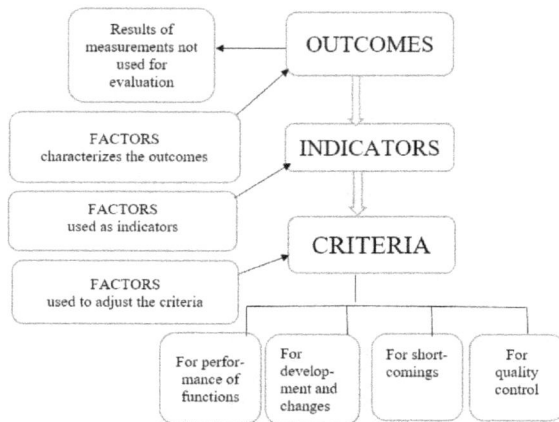

Figure 2. Indicators, indicators, factors and criteria for performance assessment.

Qualitatively developed performance outcomes provide public administrations and the public with information about the planned objectives and those achieved within the allocated resources. This approach is an internationally recognized good practice for public administration. The system of results and performance indicator outcomes provides the possibility to measure the extent of achievement of goals and, if necessary, to adjust actions (by increasing or reducing investment) in order to meet the needs of society as fully as possible. The results and performance outcomes illustrate the quality and volume of public services provided by public administrations [11].

Performance outcomes are the numerical values and characteristics of the investments and benefits that characterise or explain the extent of achievement of goals over a given period of time. Analytical outcomes measure the planned and achieved benefit-investment ratio.

Indicators are the basis for the evaluation process, which may also become evaluation criteria under certain methodologies. Indicator can be defined as a parameter or value that provides information on definite phenomenon. Indicators are usually designed for a specific goal. Their task is to accurately characterize the situation and to provide information to the decision maker. The development of indicators is a lengthy and always dynamic process, but unduly waste of time and resources in searching for other indicators, forgetting about the implementation of the plans themselves, should be avoided [11]. Good indicators are:
- applicable, if they reveal tasks and responsibilities of the body;
- useful because they allow to evaluate the activity;
- completely safe;
- verifiable because they can be easily calculated;
- repeatable [5].

In the field of customs, possible indicators vary widely in terms of origin, structure, type of calculation, degree of complexity, the objective and potential of using.

There are indicators demonstrating effective activity, and there are indicators showing unused potential as well as pointing to shortcomings in the work or the substantial external conditions. There are also a number of certain factors that can ensure operational efficiency.

Only the methodological, sequential and logical work with indicators can lead to maximum precise performance criteria determination.

Evaluation elements must appear already in planning documents. Institutional strategies should include the tasks to be performed, the criteria for evaluating their performance and the indicators the analysis of which will allow to objectively asses the criteria. Individual indicators may be used as assessment criteria, but based on justification.

The number of detected customs offenses is an performance outcome, it can become an indicator in the process of comparative analysis – e.g. the number of detected customs offenses has increased, but as a criteria it can be used taking into account the internal (e.g. resources allocated to this area of activity) and external factors (e.g. changes in the flow of goods) which influence the operation of customs.

3. SELECTION OF EVALUATION CRITERIA

According to definitions developed by the specialists, the **criterion** is a decisive, important indicator to assess, define and classify by. The determination of the criteria facilitates the research of the phenomenon, they are deduced from the subject, the ideal model of the process, which in its turn is the result of scientific research of that subject or phenomenon. The study of the origin of that concept also leads to conclusion that criteria implies a feature (or one of a number of features), by presence or the degree of which something is valued, determined, classified or qualified; the measure [7].

As stated in the Sustainable Development Strategy of Latvia, not only the accounting of invested resources should be implemented in efficiency assessment of the work of public administration, but mainly the measuring of the results (benefits) obtained assessing the cost efficiency of investments and using other assessment methods commensurable with the private sector. The strategy indicators mark the most important development aspects in order to inform the society in a clear form regarding the progress in particular development directions, allowing everybody to join the discussion with understanding, assess the correctness of the selected priorities, as well as to link the expected results with responsibility for the implementation of strategic tasks [8].

In order to assess the effectiveness of public administration, we need well-known evaluation criteria, since in society, subjectivist approaches to public-management phenomena are very common. The criteria for effectiveness are features, frontiers, side and manifestations of state administration, through the analysis of which you can determine the level and quality of management, its compliance with the needs and interests of society [19].

In creating the catalogue of assessment criteria and indicators for customs performance it is necessary to consider their different origins, methods of collection, reliability, objectiveness and use. When using performance indicators, for example, a distinction should be made between indicators illustrating performance from indicators illustrating performance of functions, and quantitative indicators from qualitative indicators.

Criterions for performance evaluation are established by methodological use of markers and indicators. The simplest way to formulate a criterion is to ask a question – whether a task has been completed, what goal has been achieved, any problem has been prevented, any system has been introduced?

Factors/indicators/criteria		
Factors (preconditions for successful drug fighting)	**Indicators** (outcomes to be used for evaluation)	**Evaluation criteria**
- the resources allocated to customs; - the number of employees involved; - distributed/used technical equipment; - the existence of a kinological service/level of organization; - organized cooperation in this field with other governmental organizations; - public support for the customs authority.	- the number of customs checks carried out (in the field of drugs); - the number of tests carried out by the kinological service; - the number of uses of technical means; - criminal proceedings initiated; - the number of actions taken jointly with the other institutions.	- cases of drug detentions and total quantities; - the number of persons detained in connection with the illegal movement of drugs; - violations detected as a result of cooperation measures; - decisions taken (number) on imposition of penalties; - decisions taken (number) on termination of record-keeping.

Table 1. Possible indicators and performance assessment criteria in the field of drugs.

This can be done only if the task is sufficiently precise. If the task is defined – to protect the company from narcotic drugs – then the criterion is easy to formulate – where there is or no narcotic substance in the customs territory illegally carried across the customs border. But this is already an evaluation methodology issue.

4. ROLE OF INTERNAL AND EXTERNAL FACTORS IN THE EVALUATION PROCESS

The factors or conditions may indicate a certain condition of the system and the presence of contributing or disturbing elements. In customs matters, they play a very important role: if the there are elements in the customs system such as the risk analysis system, the anti-corruption measures programme, the post-clearance audit system, the maximum use of possible information technology, this indicates a potentially good organization of work, which should give good results contributing to effective customs performance. At the same time, they can also be used as criteria for assessing the customs work; the indicators needed to evaluate the work and to define, compare and predict the results, can also be found here.

Without the environmental impact assessment, the measurements of results will not be true and may lead to the incorrect choice of criteria. The most important internal variable parameters of the management are the objectives, tasks, structure, technologies and personnel. The key factors for external environmental variables are the political process, economic situation, scientific progress, sociocultural changes, the impact of groups' interests [16].

Internal factors – the internal environment of the Customs and external factors related to processes in the country, society and international relations must be taken into account when applying the criterion.

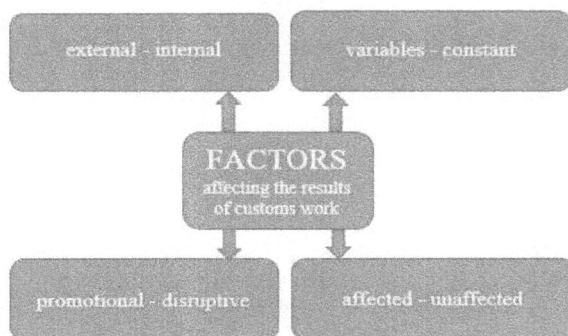

Figure 3. External and internal factors affecting customs work.

Factors that indicate the possibility of effective work, which also serves as a kind of indicator: the existence of a strategy, the quality of management, good workplace management, effective procedures, appropriate regulatory frameworks, the existence of adequate resources, the use of IT, risk management, highly qualified and motivated staff, management support, public support, well-organized internal and external cooperation, process control and regular evaluation of results.

Besides these internal and external indicators the results of the customs work depend from different supplement factors, related to the product itself, the location and type of movement, the choice of customs control methods, etc., such as the nature and special characteristics of the goods to be transferred, the country of origin of the goods, the value of goods, the control authorities, the border crossing point (land border, port or airport), the degree of risk defined in the process of risk analysis, application of the type and methods of control, etc.

5. INTERNATIONAL AND NATIONAL PRACTICES

Studies show that every state exercises development of these indicators and criterions, international organizations express their opinion about methods and elements of assessment, separate experts research these issues, however, a one-fits-all methodology, that would allow to fully and objectively assess the work of customs, has not been discovered yet.

The assessment system is affected by organizational model of the border enforcement agency. In the reports of work results of enforcement agencies in the US, the aspects of safety and defense dominate, in Estonia and Latvia customs agencies are deeply integrated within the state revenue service, therefore the assessment criterions are associated with collecting revenue. Russian criterions of assessment of customs agencies work are associated with prescribed aspects of effectiveness.

Criteria and indicators for evaluating the customs work can be found in national strategies, operational programs and plans, regional and international programs, guidelines of international organizations, business interest, public needs, customs reports on the results of its work, the description of the modernization projects, the quality management rules, the results of various diagnostics, survey results, and special methodologies.

The Customs Modernization Handbook issued by the World Bank, speaking on the diagnostics of customs authorities, indicates that a comprehensive diagnosis should use both quantitative and qualitative indicators and look at the effectiveness and efficiency of the institution, institutional design and management, and the institutional and economic environment of the customs administration [3].

Luc de Wulf points out that the performance indicators allow to assess the effectiveness of the customs work, to clarify the necessary reforms and their objectives, to carry out the monitoring of the implementation of reforms and to assess progress. Identification and systematization of these indicators allow a clear characterization of the reform objectives, both in terms of qualitative and quantitative indicators [3].

Several international organizations have worked in this direction including International Monetary Fund which identified several economic efficiency assessment criteria in the framework of the TTFSE (Trade and Transport Facilitation in Southeast Europe) program:
- the amount of the customs duties collected;
- the share of customs revenues in the total amount of tax revenues;

- wages and salaries (wage and salary fund of customs authorities in total) at a ratio of customs duties collected;
- the volume of trade turnover per one customs employee;
- number of declarations at a ratio of the number of customs employees;
- expenditure for the presentation of a single customs declaration.

Within the framework of the EU Customs Evaluation Project, the indicators reported by Member States on a quarterly basis were:
- number of import and export declarations;
- electronically entered declarations;
- documentary and physical control measures taken;
- simplified procedures.

In recent years (according to the 2013 report), the following additional indicators are compiled and analyzed:
- number of declarations;
- use of simplified procedures;
- number of electronically entered declarations;
- data from various electronic customs systems;
- customs value and customs duty;
- number and competence of customs officers;
- proportion of documentary control;
- proportion of physical control;
- the number of post-clearance controls (audit), the number of employees involved, the number of offenses detected;
- number of registered economic operators;
- number of simplified procedures and other customs permits.

At national level, indicators and criteria for assessing customs efficiency are most often grouped according to the main areas of customs activity. Lionel Pascal offers to WCO to use a small number of very clearly defined indicators in aims to evaluate:
- customs costs;
- implementation of the fiscal function;
- implementation of economic function;
- implementation of the protection function;
- implementation of the security function [9].

Belozerova S.V. and Belozerovs I.I. describing the problems of customs efficiency [17], expresses the opinion that the most important criterion of effective operation from the point of view of the participant of external economic relations is the speed of service (customs clearance, declaration). Professor Stephen Holloway in his turn mentions the following criterion as the most important for evaluating of customs operations, from the point of view of merchants:
- costs of processing trade and customs documentation;
- time taken to get trade documents approved;
- number of staff needed to process and handle trade documentation and customs;
- cargo clearance time;
- number of "security" actions [12].

According to Holloway, the model of Willis, Homel and Anderson should be used in border control [6]. High level results include reduction of customs clearance time and total export and import transaction costs, simplification of customs clearance process, identification of high risk cargo.

The specialists of the Russian Customs Academy are developing a methodology for using the Customs Efficiency Targeting Criteria offering a set of evaluation criteria and indicators [20]. It can be said that a certain system has been established, as it is based on one broader criterion, for calculation or determination of which a number of logically applied sub-criteria or indicators is required.

At national level, different approaches and methodologies of the the selection and application of indicators are emerging in the process of evaluating the results of customs work in practice. Even in countries with similar customs parameters, the indicators used and the approaches of their selection can be very different. Describing the development of performance evaluation in the Russian customs, which pays particular attention to the issue of efficiency, Alexei Gubin [1] points out that in assessment of customs performance results it is necessary to take into account various criteria and figures which are interrelated, such as the volume of controlled foreign trade, customs duties collected, criminal proceedings initiated, detected cases of illegal movements of goods, the structure of the customs service, the number of staff and the customs budget.

Following factors are indicated as factors that influence the performance of customs offices: level of customs payments, specifics of goods, specificity of transport, geographical structure of foreign economic relations participants, specificities of customs regimes to be served, location of customs offices [18].

In the EU countries, despite a common customs and foreign trade policy, the approach to assessing customs work is controversial. Frequently the evaluation problems are caused by too many disorganized indicators, lack of employee interest, willingness to use only financial indicators related to replenishment of the treasury, while neglecting other important functions. Too many indicators can break down the analysis: there are too many decision makers who are fighting for the quantity of measurements rather than quality, using the opportunities offered by new technologies.

Comparing European Standards for the Selection of Evaluation of Customs Performance, the author has identified significant differences, ranging from 10 indicators in 2 directions in Germany to 64 indicators in 5 functions in France [9].

By studying the positions of other countries in different regions of the world, the author finds out even more significant differences related to differences in their customs policies, the risks to be borne, peculiarities of customs service organization and other factors.

To a large extent, problems in the design of a common and generally applicable evaluation system are caused by a different approach to work planning and determination of objectives, directions and functions. For example, there are 4 strategic objectives and 7 performance criteria in the USA [14], 5 areas of activity and 14 criteria in the Jordan, but with a completely different approach and understanding of customs functions.

Prabodh Seth examines the practices of New Zealand, Jordan, South Africa, Japan and Egypt, as well as Mauritius, notes that revenue organizations around the world are using key performance indicators (*KPI*). They stem from strategic goals, with clearly defined criteria - what is achieved over a given period. For example, the Japanese customs service considers the promotion of trade as one of the most important goals and the time required for goods release is a critical indicator for assessing the results of customs work. Also, in Egypt, the reduced customs clearance time is the key indicator of success.

In the Baltic region, we can compare the approach of Estonia, Lithuania and Latvia to the selection and application of the criteria for assessing of customs work. This has been largely influenced by the different position of the customs service in the public administration system.

The assessment elements specified in the Strategic Development Plan [4] of the Estonian Tax and Customs Board lack the specifics and systems, the customs functions and tasks are not precisely specified, indicators are not set for all markers, the influencing factors are not considered. The performance indicators used in the Strategy Execution Assessment Document are general, customs and tax administration indicators are not differentiated, but separate of the them can be generally applied. The Lithuanian Customs Service's strategic planning document [2] does not specify markers or indicators that will be used as criteria for evaluating the implementation of the strategy. Exceptions are tasks that involve a measure that is a performance indicator itself. The performance indicators are set out in the annual customs performance report

In the Latvian situation, the strategic planning document [15] lacks precision. The activity is planned by defining the pillars, strategic goals, directions of action, performance results, performance indicators and their numerical values. The negative result is that the named performance indicators do not reflect all directions, functions and expenditures of customs activities. Also, in the activity reports, when evaluating the results of the SRS work, the created system is not applied correctly and precisely.

Research shows that:
- there is a very different understanding of customs functions and tasks in general;
- catalogs of indicators and criteria according to the purpose of evaluation are not created in evaluation of customs work;
- internal and external factors are not considered when setting criteria for assessment of customs work;
- in practice, a simplified approach has been observed – for evaluation are offered the results of work which do not correspond to the definition of an indicator or criterion;
- the lack of detailed and comprehensive systems for the assessment of customs performance could be due to the diversity of customs functions, the rapidly changing environmental conditions, the difficulty of reliable prediction or planning the results, the reluctance to show the system weaknesses;
- the evaluation system is influenced by the organizational model of the service and its degree of integration into the state administration system;
- not always the capacity of the customs service is in line with internal priorities and international obligations as well as with objective circumstances.

6. CONCLUSIONS

In order to create a systematic framework for the assessment of customs activities – a catalog of criteria, factors and indicators set up in accordance with the functions, tasks, competences and levels of activity to be performed, taking into account the internal and external environmental conditions, contributing and disturbing factors it is necessary to undertake definite actions in aims to identify and classify these elements (see Figure 4.).

In order to create a catalog of indicators of customs activity, indicators, internal and external environmental factors, guidelines are needed that correspond to the functions, tasks and directions of activity to be performed which can be used for the determination of evaluation criteria and development of methodology in the future.

It is necessary to understand which groups of indicators should be used for the evaluation of definite group of functions or activities and which are the most characteristic, it is necessary to evaluate even the performance of each employee – what task and function he/she performs by his/her activities – how important is his/her contribution to the implementation of the task or function

and to joint work result of the unit – whether the value of the work should be increased or lowered by the coefficient, taking into account the internal and external background.

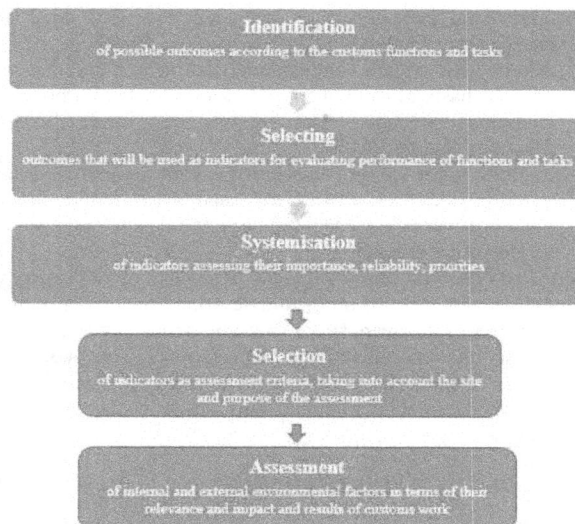

Figure 4. Classification of operations for the determination of elements of a customs work evaluation system.

There are several conclusions that can be drawn from studying the findings about the effectiveness of customs:
- The effectiveness of the customs service can be assessed from various aspects: efficiency of management, functional, technical, financial, operational efficiency, etc.;
- an effective customs service fulfills the specified tasks by performing the assigned functions according to requirements and priorities, using the available resources and favorable conditions, minimizing the risks and the impact of the unfavorable conditions;
- given the cross-border nature of customs matters, there are necessary generally acceptable definitions of customs effectiveness, its role in the context of the state, society, business, measurements and calculations of effectiveness, prerequisites for effectiveness determination and improvement;
- in assessing the effectiveness of the customs service, the specificities of public administration, customs tasks and functions, internal and external environmental conditions, current priorities should be taken into account;
- it is possible and necessary to evaluate the results of customs work using different methodologies for different levels of structural units, different tasks, processes and functions;
- The results of customs work will depend on good overall public administration, proper work organization, and level of capacity.

According to the above mentioned the following thesis for research, discussion and further examination can be imposed:
- by implementing the multiform functions, the assessment system must correspond with priorities and aims set by the strategic planning;
- pointers used in assessment must be extensive enough, taking into account the variety of functions and objectives carried out by customs and the aim of assessment, etc. conditions;

- when assessing pointers of customs work and its influencing factors, correct, objective and suitable indicators must be chosen, in order to create criterions for assessment and improvement of work;
- operational indicators and assessment criterions must be chosen accordingly to the purpose of assessment;
- reforms in the state administration are to be implemented only on basis of previous assessment with the purpose of enlarging the capacity of bringing into effect the set functions and objectives;
- In times, when the role of customs in carrying out the fiscal function decreases, the defense and safety issues arise, therefore ever larger integration of customs into the revenue service is not acceptable.

Internal and external safety is greatly dependent on the capacity of public governance. In order to assess the capacity of public governance, an assessment system must be created, by taking into account the functions, objectives and operational features of each institution. Capacity of customs agencies must correspond with internal priorities and international liabilities, as well as objective conditions.

7. REFERENCES

[1] Alexey Gubin. **Developing of Performance Measurement for Russian Customs Service.** http://incu.org/docs/Day_2_-_06._Alexey_Gubin_EN.pdf

[2] **Business strategy of the Lithuanian customs for 2011-2015.** http://www.cust.lt/web/guest/veikla/planavimodokumentai/strategija#en

[3] **Customs Modernization Handbook.** Editors Luc De Wulf, Jose B. Sokol. The World Bank, Washington, D.C., 2005, 356 p.

[4] **ESTONIAN TAX AND CUSTOMS BOARD 2013–2016.** http://www.emta.ee/sites/default/files/contacts-about-ETCB/structure-tasks-strategy/emta_eng.pdf

[5] **Ilgtspējīgas attīstības principi un indikatori pašvaldībās.** http://www.bla21f.net/projects/sail/latvia/bs4.pdf

[6] Katie Willis, Jessica Anderson and Peter Homel. **Measuring the effectiveness of drug law enforcement,** 2011

[7] **Letonika.lv.** Autoru kolektīvs Valentīnas Skujiņas vadībā: Inārs Beļickis, Dainuvīte Blūma, Tatjana Koķe, Dace Markus, Arvils Šalme; Zvaigzne ABC, 2000; © Tilde, 2009

[8] **Latvijas ilgtspējīgas attīstības stratēģija līdz 2030. gadam.** Latvijas Republikas Saeima. http://www.latvija2030.lv/upload/latvija2030_saeima.pdf

[9] Lionel Pascal. **Performance measurements: identifying appropriate methods for measuring and evaluating the performance of Customs.** http://incu.org/docs/Day_3_-_01_Lionel_Pascal_EN.pdf

[10] Prabodh Seth. **Performance Measurement in Customs.** http://incu.org/docs/Day_3_-_05_Prabodh_Seth_EN.pdf

[11] **Rezultātu un rezultatīvo rādītāju sistēmas pamatnostādnes 2008.-2013.gadam.** http://polsis.mk.gov.lv/LoadAtt/file18615.doc

[12] Stephen Holloway. **Measuring the Effectiveness of Border Management.** http://incu.org/docs/Day_3_-_02_Stephen_Holloway_EN.pdf

[13] **The Measurement of Results Project.**

[14] **U.S. Customs and Border Protection. Performance and Accountability Report.** Fiscal Year 2016. https://www.cbp.gov/sites/default/files/assets/documents/2017-Mar/FY-2016-CBP-PAR-508C.pdf

[15] **VID darbības un attīstības stratēģija 2017.–2019. gadam.** https://www.vid.gov.lv/sites/default/files/vid_darbibas_un_attistibas_strategija_2017-2019_1310.pdf

[16] Баранов Н.А. **Теория и методология анализа эффективности политико-административного управления.** http://nicbar.ru/adm_sist_lekzia3.htm

[17] Белозерова С. В., Белозеров И. И. Проблемы определения эффективности таможенного дела. **Сборник научных трудов СевКавГТУ.** Серия «Экономика». 2008. № 7.

[18] Косенко В.П., Опошнян Л.И. **Основы теории эффективности таможенного дела** М.: РТА, 2006.

[19] Седаков В.Г., Нарбинова М.М. **Теоретические проблемы оценки эффективности государственного управления.** http://www.vestnik-kafu.info/journal/3/91/

[20] Теория и методология таможенного дела. Сборник научных трудов. Проблемы совершенствования организации и деятельности таможенной службы. 1999. Москва: РИО РТА.

Digitalization of public procurement: barriers for innovation

Viktorija BABICA
Institute of Business Engineering and Management, Riga Technical University
Riga, Latvia

Deniss SCEULOVS
Institute of Business Engineering and Management, Riga Technical University
Riga, Latvia

Elvira RUSTENOVA
Department of Accounting and Finance, West Kazakhstan Agrarian Technical University
Oral, Kazakhstan

ABSTRACT

Digital transformation (DX) was introduced by the fourth Industrial Revolution. During the first decades of the new millennium DX provoked diffusion of digitalization of public procurement; that could contribute to achievement of enhanced efficiency, accountability, transparency, and participation of small and medium enterprises in tenders. Later the European Commission has emphasized the role of public procurement of innovation as a policy instrument to sustain smart and inclusive development, improve social welfare, provoke growth both of entrepreneurship and national competitive advantage. Despite the benefits provided by e-procurement, more than 60% of EU procurement procedures in 2017 used the lowest price as the only award criterion, excluding both innovation element and fair competition between suppliers. Thereby the existing system is lacking to compile with the tenets of public procurement policies. It was defined that effectiveness of e-procurement does not compile with efficiency of public procurement procedure; there exist barriers of purchasing innovation through e-procurement.

The study proved, public bodies lack of comprehensive approach of selection the awarding innovation proposal. This paper presents a research based model of a tender exhaustive award criteria to be adopted in the e-procurement system.

Keywords: Public procurement, Innovation, Digitalization, Award Criteria, E-procurement.

1. INTRODUCTION

Internet of Things, Artificial Intelligence, Big Data and Cloud computing became the major trailblazers of economic trends of the new millennium. By dint of global interconnectivity, real-time exchange of data and a fast growing IT environment it was possible to create a new paradigm of public procurement, which complements increase of the process transparency and forces organizations to enhance their potential of innovation to endorse competitiveness advantage [23].

Public procurement is being used by public bodies as a lever of economic, technological and social reform [20]. The interest in modernizing public procurement is linked to the justification of that public expenditures on purchasing goods and services annually represent 14% [9] of EU gross domestic product (GDP), that is a purchasing power, which if performed intelligently could significantly contribute to the EU sustainability and welfare through acquiring innovation, supporting technical transfer and knowledge management.

In the frames of the present study e-procurement is understood as "the application of digital tools by public institutions while implementing procurement process of purchasing goods or services, in order to improve efficiency, sustainability, and accountability of the process" [21].

It is considered, that transformation of public procurement through digitalization could lead to the achievement of what public bodies among EU are aiming to: reduce costs, increase effectiveness of the process, better transparency of the process [12], improve small and medium-sized enterprises' (SMEs) access to public procurement [17]. The present study seeks to prove if reforming public procurement could be a way to motivate, not inhibit, procurement of innovation and support for R&D.

This paper consists of five main sections. Section 1 provides a brief introduction of the main public procurement aspects related to the topic; section 2 reviews relevant literature on procurement and digitalization, definition of innovation, barriers of procurement of innovation, e-procurement correlation with purchasing of innovation, approaches of innovation evaluation; section 3 describes the used research methodology, presents data analysis and the study results. The final section consists of the conclusions and future research.

2. PROCUREMENT 4.0

Transformation of public procurement may adapt its perception of a purely administrative function to a more strategic one. Procurement 4.0 is a revolution driven by increasing digitalization, the use of cloud technologies and organizational process automation that transform traditional operations of public institution and the procurement function itself. It will establish an advantage by leveraging big data analytics for better decision-making, fostering innovation, and data integration to improve public procurement user experience and supplier performance. [12]

Public Procurement of Innovation (PPI)

Innovation Literature review of innovation concept served for development of the comprehensive definition of innovation as "a process, in which new or substantially improved product, idea, method or business process is launched, applied or acquired in a market or organization, creating new value for the consumer, a competitive advantage, and enhancing welfare of society". [e.g. 18, 37]

PPI The concept of public procurement of innovation is defined as "a procurement activity carried out by a public authority that leads to purchasing a good or a service which does not exist yet, but can be developed via R&D process within a reasonable period of time [5] or is new to the market [14]. PPI includes acquiring of new products, launching or implementation of new production methods, usage of new raw material supply sources and organizational approaches. This way PPI triggers to achieve better value for money [20]. PPI has been highlighted as a mechanism which may contribute to satisfaction of major social needs which cannot be met by traditional methods [24], and SMEs are perceived as the drivers of innovation in this setting [10] as they may be less conservative and more agile.

Compared to regular public procurement, PPI intends to create an arena of interaction between the public sector and potential and actual private sector suppliers [26].

Digital procurement

Electronic procurement has been announced as a mandatory mechanism for all types of public procurement since 2018 and it was expected that the initiative will not only simplify the entire procurement cycle for all parties involved, but also improve the efficiency of the procedure [13]. These policies are a response to the fact that public procurement, and PPI in particular, remain hard to enter for SMEs [7], because those have to face several barriers in tender processes.

Pros and cons Wen & Wei as benefits of public e-procurement marked efficiency, lower cost, and time saved per transaction, as well as agility, and enhanced accessibility of procurement information, faster evaluation, and increased quality of procurement process. Neupane et al. concluded that e-tendering is perceived to have the potential to improve transparency and accountability, which in turn, can reduce the probability of corruption in public tendering. Several studies as well prove that usage of digital instruments by public bodies could be used as anti-corruption tools [39].

Brun et al. examined five directions of benefits of e-procurement; such as improved transparency, decentralization, accountability, controlled process, supply based systematization and maverick-buying reduction. [1]

As a benefit of e-procurement OECD emphasizes reduction of direct interaction between public procurer and supplier. Digital technologies provide a competitive edge by improving the speed and quality of procurement, reducing risk and enhancing innovation. [36]. According to Vaidya reduction of costs is the mostly proved indicator of improved efficiency of public procurement after implementing digitization [2]. Gardenal claims that digitization of bureaucratic ways of tendering into more effective forms of organization may lead to better efficiency of the process [5].

Although many benefits of e-procurement proved to be exaggerated [4, 30]. E-procurement generated positive impact, when applied intelligently, is incontrovertible, but at the same time the granted benefits provoke bigger opportunities for corruption. The exact study stands that gains from digitalization of procurement process are controversial. It is not clear how e-procurement is able to enhance, not inhibit innovation.

Improved speed and agility of public procurement may reveal an outcome in increased lobbying and fraud. The reduced time spent for a tender, diminished costs and automatization give more opportunities for public buyers to call back and open tenders with specifications developed for exact supplier. Digitalization of procurement process may lead to increasing outreach and competition, but on the other hand make it easier for bid-rotation.

As well according to Aghion increased competition among suppliers, may provide more or fewer incentives to innovate depending on the market structure of a certain industry [4].

Efficiency of procurement process

OECD assess public procurement by Key Performance Indicators (KPIs) such as efficiency of the process, openness and transparency of the procurement process, professionalism of the procurers, contract management and supplier activity [22]. In case of Latvia state the procurement process does not correspond with the required level of transparency, as the number of criminal proceedings related to public procurement and the number of received applications for procurement procedure violations, in 2017, 15% of procurement procedures were contested [17]. The challenging applications suspend the termination of the procurement contract, therefore the challenge can significantly impede the implementation of important projects or the provision of public administration functions.

According to the Single Market Scoreboard [31], the public procurement can be evaluated by amount of tenders with single bids, contracts closed without a request for proposals, number of tenders used the lowest price criterion and the average speed of public procurement. The European Commission in the last public procurement directive emphasizes the need to enable SMEs to participate in tenders; the present paper argues that this does not reflect the effectiveness of the procurement, because in some EU states SME form biggest part of economically active enterprises.

The present study argues that the efficiency of procurement process should be also evaluated by the amount of R&D contracts and procurement of innovation; the mentioned efficiency indicators of the procurement process do not reflect the nature of the problem as, for example, the tenders that were closed after receiving single proposal may be over specified with technical requirements that do not promote competition.

Innovation in public e-procurement: triggers and barriers

Georghiou et al. claims that the communication between procurers and suppliers is "at the core of innovation procurement policy" [25]. Edler affirms that a systemic user-producer interaction would emphasize procurement of innovation [8]. Edquist affirms that the scope of public procurement limits interaction between procurement contracting authorities and suppliers leading to information and miscommunication related problems [5].

The study concludes, that lack of direct interaction between public procurement parties within the e-procurement procedure may inherit purchasing of innovation. The lack of flexibility or accessibility of a certain framework of a tender may lead into dead ends of an announced call for proposal.

According to Valovrita [38] public procurement of innovation intends on compulsory interaction between the parties, because information about unmet needs must be considered with the potential supplier. E-procurement use for collaboration or supplier management, has not been mention among the approach benefits [6]. Walker and Brammer [15] argues that there is evidence that e-procurement may prevent SMEs participation in the procurement processes. Communication between the parties may help to prove SMEs' innovation potential.

Shortage of procurement process

The classic public procurement system was criticized for allowance to apply the lowest price criterion, since 2018 when EU commission made it obligatory to implement e-procurement, it became easier to qualify bids by price. Uyarra et all. reported that main barriers of procurement process are lack of interaction with procurer, the use of rigid as opposed to outcome-based specifications, shortage of skills and capacity of procurers and a poor management of risk. Additional key concerns expressed by suppliers embedded low feedback on unsolicited ideas and cumbersome pre-qualification procedures and conditions. The present study claims that potential supplier evaluation should not affect awarded bid [8].

It was concluded that e-procurement process despite all the provided benefits do not overcome barriers for procuring innovation.

Despite of the mentioned above benefits provided by digitalization of the process, one goal of procurement strategy is missing – support for innovation. Purchasing innovation has been affected by flaws in development tender specification, social habits and biases such as behavioral, technological and organizational and by incomplete award criteria.

Tender award criteria

The majority of procurement procedures are being awarded based on the only award criterion - the lowest price [31]. Although the overall efficiency of e-procurement in the year of 2017 average number of tenders evaluated by the lowest price criterion has increased comparing to 2015 and 2016. Inconsistency of the dynamics has been provoked by the new and only award criterion presented in 2014 by the EU Commission – the most economically advantageous tender (MEAT). [14] That is a inclusive parameter, which can be defined by each contractor individually. MEAT includes three indicators: the best price-quality ratio, as sub criteria for quality European Commission offers the following non-financial indicators: quality, technical advantages, aesthetic and functional characteristics, accessibility, social and environmental characteristics, marketing opportunities; cost-effectiveness approach; life-cycle costing [11].

It is not clarified what should be understood by quality of an innovation bid, thus it was necessary to conduct a literature review to define indicators which could be used as a comprehensive evaluation of the quality of an innovation proposal.

Literature review: innovation evaluation criteria

Quality Brian determines that *quality* of a product is its ability to meet the needs of the consumer [33]. According to Jasinki quality or value of a bid should be determined by their viability, benefits, costs and associated risks [3]. Innovation should be able to create long-term stability, ensure return on investment, provide unique advantage and bear an added value, that leads to a sustainable and balanced development [2]. The basic quality criterion of innovation bid should be understood by proposal's sustainability, performance, durability and performance advantage. As quality still stands for an embracing criteria, the research was followed by defining of auxiliary evaluation criteria.

Risk resistance Frequently it is not possible to predict the result of innovation, its performance and user response precisely, thus if the result is intangible, there prevail certain risks, such as technological, organizational, societal, market, financial and risk of turbulence [32].

Financial effectiveness Hittmar et al. mentions the payback period and the discounted cash flow as the basic financial criteria [34]. Cost-effectiveness can be evaluated according to economy, efficiency and effectiveness provided by a bid.

Competitive advantage Innovation is the driving force of entrepreneurship. Effective innovation brings depending on its level, competitiveness at both international and local levels. Innovations can offer the following advantages: new financial sources for entrepreneurs, removal of barriers in legislation and taxation, new cooperation, support for the availability of skilled workers and facilitating the acquisition and assimilation of knowledge [27, 29].

Level of novelty The challenge of assessing innovation is the novelty of it. Regardless of whether the novelty can be measured, the main challenge is to define according to what to measure it [37]. The novelty level refers to a technological change from a pre-existing product. The degree of novelty should be appreciated from different perspectives: organizational, societal and marketability.

Effectiveness of innovation is seen as the ability to improve the service or work process, deliver the greatest value to customer, to solve organizational problems, and to address shortcomings.

According to the literature review of award criteria of innovation assessment the present study concludes that most criteria imply quantitative indicators, but those determine subjective estimate. The study argues that the successful procurement of innovation could be maintained by digital procurement, but requires strict monitoring to prevent the effect of ineffective subjectivity on the results.

3. RESEARCH

Conforming to the last Public Procurement Directive each public body is entitled to define award criteria that are considered the best for the certain tender. If for a common case such as obtaining office products application of the MEAT criterion is relevant, then if a tender allows submitting variants or comprises elements of innovation no criteria where price or costs is prevailing should be implemented.

The present study was conducted in order to define relevance of the certain set of award criteria (fig.1) to be implemented in the evaluation of a tender in public procurement of innovation.

The research was based on the expert method. It was essential to obtain various viewpoints of different economic sectors representatives. The research lasted from February to December 2018 and included 49 experts from 21 sector, among those were academic personnel, scientific workers, representatives of government bodies, high level managers and directors of private companies. Experts were interviewed about their opinion concerning the relevance of the proposed set of award criteria for innovation in their field of employment.

Evaluation of the award criteria was conducted by pair comparing of each of proposed criterion in case of predicting the potential for innovation success. The approach implemented permitted to define the importance of each criterion. No complete consensus was established due to industry differentials.

Findings
Information gathered through the interviews was analyzed by implementing the Analytic Hierarchy Process. Experts used 7-point scale for criterion comparison, where "1" stands for the equally important criteria, while "7" determines the very importance of one criterion. For each group of criteria, a normalized priority vector was determined according to Saaty methodology [36]. The Consistency Ratio was accepted up to 20% due to abstractness of the product evaluate by the proposed criteria.

Criterion of quality which stated for sustainability, performance, usability, potential decupling effect and eco-effectiveness was defined as the most important with the priority vector of 16.6%, followed by criteria of functionality (10.6%) and environmental impact (10.1%) (fig. 1).

Figure 1. Innovation evaluation criteria weight.

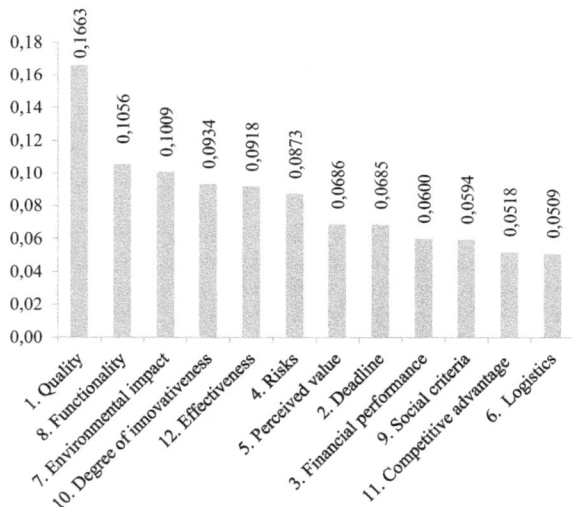

Source: Author's original.

To reduce the amount of criteria thus to simplify the awarding process it was concluded to group them depending on reciprocal coherence. Out of 12 possible award criteria were formed 4 groups: quality criteria set; the added value determinant criteria;

social benefit criterion; risk, costs and other non-financial criteria.

Evaluation Model
The purpose of the innovation bidding evaluation process is to determine which bid best meets the requirements of the call for proposal or which offer may provide the customer the greatest value. The bidding process and the selection of candidates are two independent processes.

For digital procurement system to correspond to the public procurement principles such as transparency, equality and fairness, and as procuring the best value for money is the main aim of public procurement [27] is crucial to implement the following award criteria model in the comprehensive tender evaluation (table 1).

Each step of the tender proposal evaluation model contains certain criteria, which are explained by sub criteria and indicators, procurer may decide if to follow all the steps of the model. If each step is successfully and objectively evaluated, then the assess of a bid embraces the all aspects of potential innovation influence on different systems and environments.

Table 1. Tender proposal evaluation model

Step	Criteria, sub criteria and indicator	
Step 1	Accordance with the obligatory requirements	
Step 2	Evaluation of quality	Sustainability
		Ecology
		Society
		Economy
		Performance (design)
		Technical
		Practical
		Esthetic
		Environmental impact
		Eco-design
		Resource consumption and emissions
		Functionality
		Productivity (effectiveness)
		Technical advantage
Step 3	Perceived value	Innovation measurement (assessment of changes according to:)
		The end-user
		Global
		Union
		Region
		Nation
		Organization
		Municipality
		Industry
		The competitive advantage of innovation
		Potential market share
		Financial strength
		Industry attractiveness
		Market stability
		Added value of the tender
		Conformity with long-term goals
Step 4	Risks, costs, logistics and other non - financial factors	Risks related with the proposal
		Threats
		Weaknesses
		Prevention
		Endurance
		Product life cycle cost
		Logistics
Step 5	Social impact	Social Return on Investment

Source: Author's original.

4. CONCLUSIONS

The aim of the study was to explicate the perceived benefits of public e-procurement such as increased transparency, savings for both participating parties, simplified and shortened process of procurement and better opportunities for SMEs to access to public procurement markets. Although it is not clear if simplified process do not provoke attempts of lobbying and bid-rigging.

Despite the useful and efficient opportunities that e-procurement can provide as a comprehensive digital platform, it has its downfalls. In light of EU Commission notice concerning support for innovation and R&D, it was examined what are barriers of innovation in within of e-procurement. It was concluded that public bodies lack of comprehensive tender award criteria model which could be used for procurement of innovation evaluation and be exhaustive, inclusive and fair. As well public procurement for innovation involves active communication between participating parties, which is eliminated by e-procurement system.

Bid price cannot reflect its innovation potential, also SMEs have less opportunities to compete with bigger rivals when only the lowest price criteria is implemented. Tender awarding process should involve full analysis of the merits of the bid. It is crucial to evaluate the proposal according to comprehensive criteria, which reflect the bid's quality, its potential impact to change, level of novelty and potential profitability. The approach will set it clear which of the eligible proposal may deliver the best value for money. The presented award criteria model should be embedded to the e-procurement platform for objective evaluation of bids.

Apart of the need to change proposal evaluation system, triggers for innovation should be implemented such as functional description of a tender and dialogue between suppliers and procurers.

As e-procurement system became obligatory less than a year ago, it should be analyzed if this change has affected statistics of purchasing of innovation and support for R&D. This matter is the basis for the author's further research.

5. REFERENCES

[1] C.W. Churchman, **The Design of Inquiring Systems**, New York: Basic Books Inc. Pub., 1971.
[2] J. Ivari, "A Paradigmatic Analysis of Contemporary Schools of IS Development", **European Journal of Information Systems**, Vol. 1, No. 4, 1991, pp. 249-272.
[1] A. Brun, S. Ronchi, X. Fan, "What is the Value of an IT E-Procurement System?", **Journal of Purchasing and Supply Management**, 16, 2010, 131-140.
[2] A. Cottam, J. Ensor, C. Band, "A benchmark study of strategic commitment to innovation", **European Journal of Innovation Management**, Vol. 4, 2001, pp. 88-94.
[3] A. H. Jasinski, "Barriers for technology transfer: the case of a country in transition", **Journal of Technology Management in China**, Vol. 4, 2006, pp. 119-131.
[4] A. Philippe, N. Bloom, R. Blundell, "Competition and Innovation: An Inverted-U Relationship", **The Quarterly Journal of Economics**, Vol. 120, No. 2, pp. 701-728.
[5] C. Edquist, J. M. Zabala-Iturriagagoitia, "Public Procurement for Innovation as mission-oriented innovation policy", **Research Policy**, 41(10), 2012, pp. 1757–1769.
[6] C. McCue, A. V. Roman, "E-Procurement: Myth or Reality", **Journal of Public Procurement**, Vol. 12, 2012, pp. 221-248.
[7] C. Nicholas, M. Fruhmann, "Small and medium-sized enterprises policies in public procurement: Time for a rethink?", **Journal of Public Procurement**, 14 (3), 2014, 328-360.
[8] E. Uyarra, E., Edler, J., Garcia-Estevez, "Barriers to innovation through public procurement: A supplier perspective" **Technovation**, 34(10), 2014, 631–645.
[9] European Commission, "Communication from the Commission to the European Parliament, the council, the European economic and social committee and the committee of the regions: Making public procurement work in and for Europe", 2017.
[10] European commission, "From the Commission to the European Parliament, the Council, the European Economic and Social Committee and the Committee of the Regions. A European agenda for the collaborative economy", 2016.
[11] European Parliament, Directive 2014/24/EU on Public Procurement, 2014.
[12] F. Bienhaus, A. Haddud, "Procurement 4.0: factors influencing the digitization of procurement and supply chains", **Business Process Management Journal**, 24(4), 965–984.
[13] G. Francesco, "A model to measure e-procurement impacts on organizational performance", **Journal of Public Procurement**, Vol. 13 Issue: 2, 2013, pp.215-242.
[14] Guidance on Public Procurement of Innovation, European Commission (2014)
[15] H. Walker, S. Brammer, "The relationship between sustainable procurement and e-procurement in the public sector", **International Journal of Production Economics**, 2012, 140.
[16] Informative e-procurement (online) European Commission home page [accessed 8 May 2019], Available: https://ec.europa.eu/gro wth/single-market/public-procurement/e-procurement_en
[17] Informative report of the Procurement Monitoring Bureau, 2017 [online]. LV PMB web page [accessed 8 May 2019]. Available: https://www.iub.gov.lv/lv/node/40
[18] J. Schumpeter, "The theory of economic development: an inquiry into profits, capital, credit, interest and the business cycle", **Harvard Economic Studies**, Vol. 46, 1934
[19] J. Stentoft Arlbjørn, P. Vagn Freytag, "Public procurement vs private purchasing", **International Journal of Public Sector Management**, 25(3), 2012, pp. 203–220.
[20] K. Vaidya, K., J. Campbell, "Multidisciplinary approach to defining public e-procurement and evaluating its impact on procurement efficiency", **Information Systems Frontiers**, 18(2), 2014, 333–348
[21] K. Vaidya, K., Sajeev, "e-Procurement initiatives in the public sector: Critical success factors that influence implementation success", **Journal of Public Procurement**, 5(4/5), 2006, 70-99.
[22] Key performance indicators of public procurement (2017) [online]. OECD homepage [accessed 7 May 2019]. Available at: http://www.oecd.org/fr/gov/ethique/procurement-key-performance-indicators.htm

[23] L. Downes, P. Nunes, **Big Bang Disruption: Strategy in the Age of Devastating Innovation**, UK: Harvard Business Review Press, 2014.

[24] L. Georghiou, J. Edler, E. Uyarra, "Policy instruments for public procurement of innovation: Choice, design and assessment. **Technological Forecasting and Social Change,** 86.

[25] M. Rolfstam, "Public procurement as an innovation policy tool: the role of institutions", **Science and Public Policy**, Vol. 36, 2009, pp. 349–360.

[26] M. Rolfstam, W. Phillips, "Public procurement of innovations, diffusion and endogenous institutions", **International Journal of Public Sector Management**, 2011, 452-468.

[27] P. Chatzoglou, D. Chatzoudes, "The role of innovation in building competitive advantages: an empirical investigation", **European Journal of Innovation Management**, Vol. 21, 2018, pp. 44-69.

[28] P. Davis, D. Mckevitt, "Supplier development and public procurement: allies, coachesand bedfellows", **International Journal of Public Sector Management**, Vol. 27, 2014, pp. 550 - 56.

[29] P. F. Drucker, "The discipline of innovation", **Harvard Business Review**, Vol. 63, 1985, pp. 67-72.

[30] P.F. Johnson, R.D. Klassen, "E- procurement", **MIT Sloan Management Review**, 2005.

[31] Public Procurement Scoreboard [online]. European Commission homepage [accessed 17 May 2019]. Available at: http://ec.europa.eu/internal_market/scoreboard/performance_per_policy_area/public_procurement/index_en.html

[32] Risk management in the procurement of innovation [online]. European Commission homepage [accessed 17 May 2019]. Available at: ec.europa.eu/invest-in-research/pdf/download_en/risk_management.pdf

[33] S. Brian, "Innovation overview and future challenges", **European Journal of Innovation Management**, Vol. 1, 1998, pp. 21 - 29

[34] S. Hittmar, M. Varmus, V. Lendel, "Proposal of Evaluation System for Successful Application of Innovation Strategy through a Set of Indicators", **Procedia Economics and Finance**, Vol. 26, 2015, pp. 17–22.

[35] S. Ronchi, A. Brun, "What is the value of an IT e-procurement system?" **Journal of Purchasing and Supply Management,** 16 (2), 2010, 131-140.

[36] T.L. Saaty and L.G. Vargas, "Models, Methods, Concepts & Applications of the Analytic Hierarchy Process", **International Series in Operations Research & Management Science**, 2012, pp. 13 – 54.

[37] U. Brentani, "Innovative versus incremental new business services: Different keys for achieving success", **Journal of Product Innovation Management**,18, 2001, 169–187.

[38] V. Valovrita, **Building Capacity For Public procurement of Innovation. Public procurement for innovation**. London, UK: Edwards Elgar Publishing, 2015, pp. 65 – 86.

[39] W. Wen, L. Wei, "Decision-making Analysis of E-procurement with the Rough Set Theory", **International Conference on Wireless Communications, Networking and Mobile Computing, Shanghai**, 2007.

Challenges of Sustainable Company Development: Case of Craft Business in Latvia

Laura GRIKKE
Institute of Business Engineering and Management, Riga Technical University
Riga, Latvia

Ieva ANDERSONE
Institute of Business Engineering and Management, Riga Technical University
Riga, Latvia

Deniss SCEULOVS
Institute of Business Engineering and Management, Riga Technical University
Riga, Latvia

ABSTRACT

The authors of the paper analysed international coffee trade, which is one of the most important factors for sustainable development of the industry, and also analysed the Latvian coffee roasters and their activities. The authors defined sustainable development in environmental, social and economic context, and established an implementation scenario of sustainable development in Latvian coffee roasters based on the importance of various criteria. The business model was approbated in Rocket Bean Roastery Ltd. The sustainable development model was confirmed by the company's financial calculations and the developed sustainable coffee supply chain.

The most important conclusions and suggestions of the research are that a sustainable business model of a coffee roaster has to be commercially successful, despite the growing effects of climate changes and volatile commodity prices, and should be a part of a sustainable society that is informed, knowledgeable and aware of the impact their purchases have.

Keywords: sustainable development, business model, craft business

1. INTRODUCTION

In the context of sustainability, international coffee market is one of the most analyzed markets today, as it currently faces a number of environmental, social and economic problems, such as the effects of climate change - pests, coffee tree diseases, decline in suitable coffee farmlands, low pay to coffee farmers for green coffee beans, low pay to workers and child labor, as well as fluctuations in green coffee prices and market intermediaries' speculations. Therefore new, innovative solutions are being sought to address these problems not only in coffee producing countries, but also involving players throughout the entire coffee supply chain.

The objective of the paper is to study and analyze sustainable development models and to develop a sustainable business model for coffee roasteries in Latvia according to the core values and sustainability criteria. The authors of the study put forward the following **hypothesis**: introduction of a sustainable development model in coffee roasteries in Latvia will improve the financial position of the company and reduce the negative impact of its operation on the environment and society.
To achieve the goal, the following **tasks** are defined:

- To know theoretical basis of sustainable development;
- To carry out analysis of sustainability of coffee production companies in Latvia;
- To analyse the sustainable development model for the trade of coffee beans;
- To develop a sustainable development model to facilitate development and growth opportunities for coffee roasters in Latvia;
- To approbate the model in the coffee company *Rocket Bean Roastery, Ltd.*.

The research has the following **limitations**: Due to the limits associated with amount of work, the coffee industry and the opportunities for sustainable development in this industry are chosen as the research sector. Coffee roasters in Latvia are the object of analysis – companies importing green beans for the post-processing and marketing. In the context of Latvia, these companies are also defined as coffee producers. The study does not cover companies that deal exclusively with distribution of international coffee brands in the territory of Latvia and are not roasters.

Conventional methods for the quantitative and qualitative data analysis of economics and management science have been employed during the preparation of the research, including multi-criteria decision-making method (Analytic Hierarchy Process (AHP)), statistical data processing, data grouping, inductive and deductive methods of data analysis.

2. SUSTAINABLE DEVELOPMENT

In view of the rapid deterioration of the climate, decrease of natural resources, in particular the availability of energy and water, and the growing gap between developing and developed countries, a solution must be sought to reduce the growth of such factors. The concept of sustainable development is not new, its origins date back to the second half of the 20th century, but nowadays the importance of sustainability has grown considerably both in society and in the international political context and it has gained a new form of expression.

Based on the 2030 Agenda for Sustainable Development adopted at the United Nations Sustainable Development Summit in New York on 25 September 2015, [1] the Latvian

Sustainable Development Strategy for 2030 was developed defining the key long-term goals of the state and society towards a unified goal of balanced and sustainable development of Latvia. The concept of sustainable development was defined clearly and extensively: "Sustainable development is an integrated and balanced development of the society's well-being, the environment and the economy that meets the current social and economic needs of the population and ensures environmental compliance and the preservation of biodiversity without compromising the needs of future generations."[2] The strategy set the goals and objectives to achieve in several priority sectors – the development of the Latvian cultural space, human capital, the paradigm shift in education, innovative and eco-efficient economy, nature, spatial development perspective, governance and public participation.

According to the authors of the paper, the described definitions of sustainable development do not have any significant differences in their wording, but they have several common features that are visible in all definitions of sustainable development, namely:
• Desired public status – a society that people want to keep and live in, because it corresponds to their desires and needs;
• Long-term ecosystem status – an ecosystem that retains its ability to support the existence of people and other living creatures;
• Balance between present and future generations, taking into account the needs of the present generation.

The concept of sustainable development is defined in different sources, but the term 'sustainable business' is a new and unspecified concept. Contemporary trends in sustainable economic development theory are based on the need and importance of preventing an irrational increase in the use of natural resources, given the growing global competitiveness in business and the rapidly growing profits of multinational companies and corporations.[3] Based on this and the above-mentioned information, sustainable business can be defined as "discovery and use of economic opportunities in the development and realization of a product or service for a company's ecologically and socially sustainable operation."[4] Shepherd and Patzelt (2011) define sustainable entrepreneurs as entrepreneurs whose companies or organizations integrate both what needs to be sustained in the long term (nature, environment, communities) and what needs to be developed (profits, and economic and other benefits for society and business).

Sustainable business is also often referred to as 'green', social, environmental or eco-business, but these terms overlap in the context of sustainability.

According to the authors of the paper, the concept of sustainable development not only determines how society develops, but above all, it is a set of views on how to ensure long-term prosperity and quality of life. It is based on the principles of democracy, gender equality, solidarity and the rule of law, as well as respect for human rights. In order to achieve the highest possible results in sustainable development, it is necessary to ensure the country and society as a whole with a dynamic economy, full employment, a high level of education, good medical care, environmental protection in a safe environment for people, respecting cultural, racial and gender differences.

3. COFFEE PRODUCTION COMPANIES IN LATVIA

Considering the Latvian climate and business environment, the Latvian coffee market is dominated by companies importing roasted coffee beans, coffee capsules, coffee pads or other kinds of coffee ready for sale and use from other countries, mostly Italy. The major retail chains contract with foreign coffee manufacturers and import coffee brands such as Illy, Nespresso, Paulig, Löfbergs Lila and others. The coffee market can be divided into two separate segments: the retail market, where coffee is purchased in large quantities, not only for consumption at home, and the public catering market or HoReCa, where coffee is for out-of-home use – in restaurants, cafes and bars, offices, and other public places.
Overall, coffee supply and diversity in Latvia is high, exceeding the indicators of other Baltic countries. In the Latvian coffee market, the competition among the largest coffee importers is considered to be quite intense. Entrepreneurs wishing to start a business must take into account not only the retailers' requirements for civil liability, but also the difficulties in concluding contracts with large, international manufacturers without ensuring the possibility of large sales.[5]
Coffee producers or roasters have a much smaller market share in Latvia than coffee importers – the amount of coffee produced in Latvia is only 3-4% of the coffee market, and competition between the coffee roasters is not great. It is considered that to coffee producers belong also those businesses that import green coffee beans and roast them in Latvia, rather than distributing coffee for sale to retail chains. According to the NACE classifier: economic activity 10.83 Processing of tea and coffee, 33 companies are currently registered in Latvia, of which only 11 companies import green coffee beans, and roast and process them in Latvia. [6] The authors of the paper are of the opinion that the number of coffee roasters in Latvia is so small for a number of reasons: first, coffee beans are not Latvian agricultural products because climate conditions are not suitable for coffee cultivation; secondly, raw materials (green coffee beans) are to be transported from coffee growing countries, which is a relatively time-consuming process; and thirdly, the coffee roasting process is not cheap – large financial investments in the company's fixed assets (mostly roasting equipment) are required.

For these and other reasons, several companies choose to distribute internationally recognized and well-known coffee brands by signing a distribution agreement rather than starting their own production. Coffee roasting, in turn, is the business of enthusiasts of the industry and the product.

4. SUSTAINABLE DEVELOPMENT MODEL FOR THE TRADE OF COFFEE BEANS

At a first glance, a model of sustainable business development may not seem to be profit oriented but to address social and environmental issues, which are the primary operational aspects. However, the most recent definitions of a business model by various authors are based on a number of interdependent factors and a set of activities that form the concept of business, including profit making, without which the company cannot exist.

Amit and Zott defined a business model as a system of interdependent activities that determine how a company is doing business with its customers, partners and suppliers.[7] Casadesus-Masanell un Zhu [8]defined a business model as finding new logics in doing business, which will bring value to stakeholders by focusing on new ways of generating income and defining the value that the company will deliver to customers, suppliers, and partners. Markides [9] wrote about fundamentally different business models in already existing companies that, in order to have a new business model, need to expand their current economic activities, either by attracting new customers in the market, or by encouraging existing customers to consume more business products.

Taking into consideration the latest business model definitions, the authors of the paper can make conclusions and offer their own business model definition in the context of sustainability – a business model is a set of interrelated and interdependent activities that consist of well-organized, monitored internal processes in the company for the purpose of providing value to the environment – society and the economy in general, while taking into account the company's impact on the environment. The company must develop a business model that ensures the competitiveness of the company while following the principles of operation and being part of a sustainable society. Taking into consideration such a definition of a business model, the authors prepared a sustainable development model for coffee producers in Latvia.

According to the authors of the paper, a perfect sustainable development model for coffee producers has the following characteristics:
• The business model must be commercially successful – the company must be aware of the value of the product and how to profit from it;
• The company must operate in the perspective of future – i.e., the company will continue to operate successfully despite climate changes, rising and volatile prices of raw materials and energy;
• The company must be part of a sustainable society – to be able to define the business model as sustainable it must be based on specific external conditions. At the same time, these conditions must coincide with a prosperous national economy that ensures social progress within the environmental capacity.

However, in reality, such values cannot coexist or they can exist only in a highly structured environment that has evolved over the long term, both within the company and in the country in which the company operates. In addition, future prospects are difficult to predict accurately taking into consideration climate changes, which are inevitable, and it is difficult for an individual company to mitigate their impact. The company's efforts to be part of a sustainable society can be useless as they may not deliver the expected results and profits in the context of the business environment of the country. In the framework of this study, the authors developed a sustainable business model for coffee producers in Latvia, which can have a positive impact on processes in the environment as well as bring a profit.

In order to introduce the concept of sustainability in the company and change the company's current practices, which would have a positive impact on the development of the company and the surrounding factors, it is necessary to evaluate the current business model of the company, thus gaining an understanding of the company's operating principles and possibilities of changing them taking into consideration sustainability factors. One of the most current and frequently used business models in both large and small companies worldwide is the Business Model Canvas (Osterwalder, 2018)

[10], which is mostly used in the start-up phase of new businesses. The authors of the paper believe that within the framework of this study, the model can be the first tool to be used to transform the business model or to create a sustainable development model.

The authors of the paper created three dimensions of the value proposition within the framework of the research – economic, environmental and social value, which responds to a number of issues such as product value / contribution to the company, environmental / ecosystem value, and impact on the environment, and value to the client and society as a whole. The authors also enhanced the costs and income structure blocks, adding two additional business impact factors. Factors with a negative / minus sign or negative impact on the environment and society were added to the costs block, while in the income block, the canvas was complemented by factors with a positive / plus sign or positive impact on the environment and society.

As a result, when designing a business model, the company takes into account and plans not only the course of activities and the resources needed, but also understands and plans the potential business outcomes in financial, environmental and social terms. Canvas development provides a structure for the model but it is not complete, because it does not envisage the development of specific criteria or goals in time frames. Further analysis is needed to determine the most important criteria to characterize the sustainability of coffee producers. By summarizing and evaluating the factors obtained in the SWOT analysis, the authors of the paper selected the factors according to their importance. The most important factors that coffee producers in Latvia should pay attention to are: climate changes (coefficient 4.75), increasing coffee production costs (4.25), unpopularity of Latvian brands (4), certified, organic coffee, or direct trade labels (3.8), building close relationships with coffee suppliers (3.6) and diversified products (3.5).

These and other factors derived from the analysis were divided into three groups by the authors of the paper, taking into account the distribution of sustainable development dimensions, which will be further defined as criteria for the model development. Environmental, social and economic criteria were defined. The main environmental criteria for coffee production are: certified, organic coffee, or direct trade labels, environmentally friendly packaging, and mitigation of climate changes. The social criteria are high quality coffee products, stable, long-term company relationships with suppliers, the Latvian coffee producer must be a coffee culture enthusiast and a knowledgeable industry specialist, as well as educate society about the coffee industry. Whereas, many more criteria were determined in the context of the national economy in Latvia and are as follows: stable demand for coffee in the market, reduction of production costs, product diversification for customer attraction, enhancing brand recognition, export of products and attraction of financial support.

In order to determine the importance of these criteria and to choose the most important criteria for all the Latvian coffee producers, the authors used the method of Analytical Hierarchy Process (AHP), developed by the American mathematician Thomas L.Saati in 2008 [11], defining priorities among the existing criteria to make a more successful decision on the solution of an existing problem / issue in an organized way.
When calculations were made for all criteria and sub-criteria, the authors obtained the following assessment that was used as

the basis for a sustainable development model of Latvian coffee roasters. The percentage in brackets is expressed in terms of the percentage of each criterion calculated.

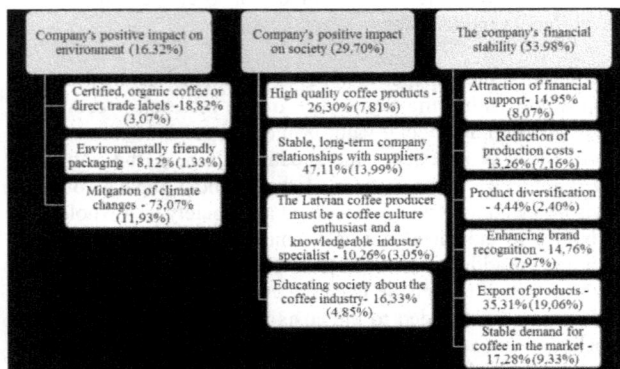

Fig. 1 The intensity indices of the importance criteria and sub-criteria

The results obtained – the intensity indices of the importance criteria and sub-criteria – show that for coffee growers, mitigation of the effects of climate changes is still the most important factor, which has a significant impact on many interrelated factors such as yields, production costs, price of coffee beans, etc. It is also worth noting that this criterion is one of the UN sustainable development goals – to take urgent measures to combat climate changes and their impact – not only in the coffee sector but also in other agricultural sectors.

Stable, long-term relationships with coffee suppliers are defined as the second most important sub-criterion. Maintaining such relationships is very important in the coffee sector because, as already mentioned, such relationships benefit the coffee grower / supplier as well as the coffee roaster. So, long-term co-operation agreements are concluded agreeing upon the price of coffee beans and ensuring direct co-operation without intermediaries, which is more advantageous for coffee producers in time and financial terms. The third most important sub-criterion in the sustainable development model is the export of products, which is especially important in the context of Latvia where the domestic market is small.

5. MODEL APPROBATION IN THE COFFEE ROASTERY

Taking into consideration several studies both on the international coffee industry in general and Latvian coffee producers, the authors developed a model based on the business model canvas principle. Rocket Bean Roastery Ltd., which is one of the newest players among Latvian coffee producers, was chosen as a pilot coffee roaster as the authors of the paper believe that it needs a sustainable development model to continue successful operations in the future.

The HAM method helped to identify the most important criteria in the environmental, social and economic dimensions of the sustainable development model, thus the authors of the paper defined the following indicators as the most important criteria and sub-criteria for the particular coffee producer Rocket Bean Roastery: • The company's financial stability (53.98%) – stable market demand (9,3%) and identifying new export markets (19.1%); • The company's impact on society (29,70%) – stable, long-term relationships with suppliers (14%); • The company's impact on the environment (16.32%) – support for farmers,

suppliers of green coffee beans in the coffee-producing countries affected by climate changes (11.9%).

By combining these factors and implementing significant changes in the company, the roaster, according to the authors, would operate on the principles of sustainable development, which would help to stabilize its positions in the Latvian and foreign markets in the long term. The focus of the company's business planning should be on ensuring the financial stability of the company; for this roaster, identification of new export markets and stable demand for coffee should be the priorities. Whereas, the company's impact on external factors – the environment and society – in the coffee sector is closely linked, which means that the criteria for enhancing long-term relationships between the roaster and the supplier, and supporting farmers affected by climate changes are complementary and mutually beneficial to the processes in the industry.

Although international initiatives and system development are needed to mitigate the effects of climate changes, coffee roasters in Latvia can influence their operations and consumer habits in various ways, which would result in a positive impact on the environment and coffee growing conditions. Ways of mitigating climate change effects in the context of Latvian roasters are, according to the authors, as follows:

• Eco-friendly packaging – consumer habits in coffee consumption play a major role in determining the ecological footprint of the coffee industry. The currently popular coffee capsules, designed to preserve the smell and taste of coffee, leave a much larger ecological footprint considering the amount of emissions generated when producing the metal capsules. Companies that distribute capsules should look for ways in which the buyer can transfer the used product for recycling, e.g. special recycling facilities for coffee capsules. For packaging of beans or ground coffee products, it would be better to choose paper or cardboard.

• Training and knowledge transfer – in the coffee culture and growing knowledge transfer between growers and roasters, as well as between roasters and distributors or consumers is a very important factor, because without this knowledge transfer, it is impossible to produce and sell high quality products. Many big roasters have developed training programs for coffee plantations, which describe the coffee harvesting process and selection of the best coffee beans to ensure high quality. Product distributors need to organize more specific training on proper preparation of coffee, while knowledge transfer would enhance consumer awareness of the origin of the product and its quality, which influence the price of coffee.

• Long-term relationships with coffee suppliers (which also include an appropriate fee / bonus for the coffee grower) – in the coffee sector, the most active participants are the owners of small coffee plantations (small farmers), who do not have financial means for the adaptation of coffee plants to climate changes (change of the plantation site or diversification of coffee tree types), therefore, a coffee roaster should be advised to establish long-term market relationships with a farmer on favorable terms, which would provide for and guarantee a better payment – above the market price.

A business model consists of four interlocking elements that, taken together, create and deliver value. The most important to get right, by far, is the first. Every successful company already operates according to an effective business model. By systematically identifying all of its constituent parts, executives can understand how the model fulfills a potent value proposition in a profitable way using certain key resources and key processes. With that understanding, they can then judge how well the same model could be used to fulfill a radically different CVP — and what they'd need to do to construct a new one, if need be, to capitalize on that opportunity. In any business, a fundamental understanding of the core model often fades into the mists of institutional memory, but it lives on in rules, norms, and metrics put in place to protect the status quo (for example, "Gross margins must be at 40%"). They are the first line of defense against any new model's taking root in an existing enterprise [12].

To have a concentrated and clear view of the factors of the sustainable development model for the Latvian coffee company,

Rocket Bean Roastery Ltd., the authors created a sustainable business model canvas for the coffee producing company, determining the economic, social and environmental value of the product, as well as forecasting the company's long-term impact on the environment and society. A detailed business canvas can be seen in Figure 2.

Main cooperation partners	Main activities	Economic value	Customer relations	Main market segments
• Coffee growers – suppliers of green coffee beans; • Coffee brewing tool rental firms; • Landlords of industrial premises • Coffee equipment engineers; • Developers of brand guidelines and ad-makers	• Responsible, transparent purchase of raw materials; • Employee training; • Roasting and packing of coffee; • Marketing and advertising activities, branding; • Quality control.	Coffee products roasted in Latvia, and their preparation equipment – brewing tools. **Environmental value** Coffee products purchased and roasted ensuring quality control and transparency, coffee products with guaranteed quality, environmentally friendly packaging and a bonus for the coffee grower.	• Customer training on the coffee market and processes, raising socially responsible awareness; • Establishing a close circle / club of clients; • Regular support for brand distributors.	• High-income customers who support a product manufactured in Latvia, demand quality and excellent coffee taste, are knowledgeable about the coffee market and are aware of the value of the product. • Distributors – cafes, restaurants and bars that value quality and products roasted in Latvia and are aware of the coffee market processes and the value of the product.
	Main resources • The factory / premises; • Green coffee beans without defects; • *Loring Smart Roast Kestrel35* coffee roasting equipment; • Coffee brewing tools; • Qualified workforce with knowledge of the coffee making process.	**Social value** High quality *100% Arabica* coffee products with a well-known origin and special preparation and taste for use at home and outside.	**Distribution channels** • Coffee cafe-roasters; • Sales outlets of distributors; • Pop-up outlets (coffee vans); • E-shop *esmilukafiju.lv*; • Off-site events focusing on sustainability in the context of the environment and society.	

Cost structure	Income structure
• Production costs of the product sold, such as raw materials, customs and excise duties, packaging, utilities; • Sales costs such as transport costs, advertising and marketing, employee training, employee wages; • Administration costs, such as office expenses, administration salary, representation.	• Coffee products sold in the coffee cafe roaster; • Rental of equipment for distributors and purchase of coffee products from roasters; • Income from exported goods in Europe where there is high demand for quality coffee; • Coffee industry training membership fees from distributors and consumers.
Negative environmental impact	**Positive environmental impact**
• Emissions from the coffee roasting process (but their impact is small and insignificant).	• Technical assistance to coffee growers (bonus, training) who are directly affected by the effects of climate changes and need resources to mitigate them; • Quality control and transparency at all stages of the chain,

	especially in the process of harvesting and processing coffee cherries; • Use of environmentally friendly packaging.
Negative social impact • Coffee products are only available to a specific customer segment that is able and willing to buy expensive coffee products.	**Pozitive social impact** • The consumer is aware of the sustainability processes in the coffee sector, gains an understanding of the price of coffee; • Promoting the awareness of a socially responsible society – an individual with his / her decision to purchase a product can also indirectly influence the living conditions of the coffee grower; • Belonging to a particular group of people who favor responsible purchases that deliver more value.

Fig.2. A sustainable development model for the company Rocket Bean Roastery Ltd.

According to the authors, implementing such a sustainable development model in the coffee roasting company could, in the long term, ensure the principles of sustainability and minimize the impact on the environment and society while ensuring the financial stability of the company. In the long term, when sustainability factors in the environmental and social context become more and more important, the company will be able to gain a competitive edge and attract more responsible and brand loyal customers with the core values of its activities, described in detail in this research.

6. CONCLUSIONS

In the context of sustainability the coffee industry is one of the most seriously endangered sectors as it is currently facing a number of environmental, social and economic challenges, such as temperature changes, coffee tree diseases, reduced amount of land suitable for coffee farming, low payment to coffee growers, green coffee bean price fluctuations and marketing intermediaries' speculations that significantly affect the regularity of the harvest season and the yield of coffee, as well as availability of farmland.

For Latvian coffee roasters to be able to ensure financial stability and growth that would have a positive impact on the environment and society in the long term, the authors recommend using the model of sustainable development worked out in this study, which can be used to determine the existing type of business activities and to improve the processes on the basis of sustainability criteria and their importance.

Coffee roasters should build close, transparent market relationships with green coffee bean suppliers in the long term, excluding marketing intermediaries.

Direct, fair trade in the long term will allow coffee roasters to keep track of the origin of coffee, quality control, and pay the coffee growers accordingly, while coffee growers will get regular customers and become aware of the importance of quality because for higher quality they will receive higher payments. The hypothesis is confirmed.

7. REFERENCES

[1] **Ilgtspējīga attīstība** [tiešsaiste] Vides un reģionālas attīstības ministrija [skatīts 2019.gada 4.martā]. Pieejams:http://www.varam.gov.lv/lat/darbibas_veidi/ilgtsp ejiga _attistiba/

[2] Latvijas Republikas Saeima (2010). **Latvijas ilgtspējīgas attīstības stratēģija līdz 2030. gadam**. Rīga: 6.lpp.

[3] Rashitovna Gainullina, Y. (2016). **Formation Of Innovative Approaches To The Designing Of A Three-Pronged Concept Of Sustainable Development Of Economic Systems In The Age Of Globalization.**

Kazakhstan: Journal of Internet Banking and Commerce, vol. 21, no. S6, pp.11

[4] Cohen, B., Winn, I. M. (2007). **Market imperfections, opportunity and sustainable entrepreneurship**. Journal of Business Venturing 22., pp.32.

[5] **Kafijas tirgus uzraudzība** (2015). [tiešsaiste]. Konkurences padomes noslēguma ziņojums, Rīga [skatīts 2017.gada 12. aprīlī]. Pieejams: http://www.kp.gov.lv/documents/feda 48d7516957309aa604b26dfc3ead897242 3e

[6] NACE klasifikators [tiešsaiste]. Lursoft datu bāze [skatīts 2019.gada 17.maijā]. Pieejams: https://nace.lursoft.lv/10.83/ companies?vr=3&o=20

[7] Amit, R., Zott, C. (2012). **Creating value through business model innovation**. MIT Sloan Manag. Rev. 53 (3), pp.41-49., pp.43.

[8] Casadesus-Masanell, R., Zhu, F. (2013). **Business model innovation and competitive imitation.** Strategic Management. J. 34 (4), pp.464-482., pp.472

[9] Markides, C. (2006). **Disruptive innovation: in need of better theory**. J. Prod. Innov.Manag. 23 (1), pp.19.-25.

[10] Osterwalder, A., Pigneur, Y. (2009). **Business Model Generation.** The Netherlands: Self Published. pp.54.-56.

[11] Saati, L.T. (2008). **Decision making with the analythic hierarchy process**. Int. J. Services Sciences, Vol. 1, No. 1, pp.86.-87.

[12] Johnson, W.M., Christensen, C.M., Kagermann H. (2008). **Reinventing Your Business Model** Harvard Business School Publishing Corporation, Dec. pp. 58.-67.

Business model transformation and business viability. Case of Yellow pages.

Ludmila KASPEROVICA, Natalja LACE
Faculty of Engineering Economics and Management, Riga Technical University
6 Kalnciema Str., Riga, LV-1048, Latvia

ABSTRACT

The article discusses the theoretical aspects of the digital transformation impact on business models. The empirical study examines the evolution of the Yellow Pages (YP) industry, which was significantly transformed by the impact of technological progress. Studying the evolution of the elements of the YP business model, the authors conducted a thorough analysis of secondary information sources, using scientific literature, industry expert reports, published materials from industry conferences and other sources. The aim of the study was to analyse what factors and risks should be taken into account in order to keep the positive financial results of business and what aspects of profit retention could be useful for other sectors as well.

Keywords: business model, business ecosystem, digital platforms, digital transformation, disruptive innovation, pricing strategies, Yellow Pages.

1. INTRODUCTION

The development of IT technologies and introduction of the Internet offer the society new opportunities which, however, are not easily identified as traditional stereotypes are broken. The introduction of the Internet created the conditions for transforming people's behavior and types of communication by moving physical things to a virtual environment. The business ecosystem has supported the process of turning competitors into collaborative partners. Innovations offered by digitization can be used not only as innovative tools for the sustainable development of a company, but also as destructive innovation, replacing existing products with alternative solutions [3].

The authors studied the impact of destructive innovations through the evolution of a particular YP industry business model, including the transformations of the elements of value proposition and value creation as well as their effects on the attainment of positive financial outcomes. Following the successive consideration of each element of the business model, the authors analyzed how companies in the industry were able to adapt to the new competitive conditions in the global market, which completely disrupted the long-standing industry standard. The authors were looking for the answers to the following questions: (1) How does the disruptive innovation transform the business model? (2) How does the transformation of business model elements and their interactions form a new viable BM? (3) What risk factors could be generalized and taken into account in order to retain positive financial outcomes in the business?

The research is based on the theoretical analysis of scientific literature on the development of external environment and technologies on business model transformation, as well as on the publications of industry leaders, experts, associations, conference materials and Website companies.

2. LITERATURE REVIEW

The Internet and digitalisation is more than just another technology, it is something of a new, powerful communication tool [12]. With the advent of the Internet, companies have constantly been trying to discover new ways of expanding collaboration, organizing economic activities through virtual and real world interaction [22]. Consumer products, refrigerators, televisions, telephones are equipped with digital features that connect and that are connected to the Internet. The technologies are no longer just for data input and output, they enter the human life at an extraordinary pace, changing their behavior and various phenomena [24]. The existence of a virtual world opens up new opportunities for new marketing channels that are more efficient than the print media [22].

The organisation's strategy is no longer confined to the internal view of the company, but focuses on the business environment, the ecosystem [13]. The business ecosystem consists of individuals, organizations, public authorities, as well as rules that ensure the company interacts with customers, competitors, media, and others [16].

However, the exchange of services in the ecosystem is not effective without a service platform that helps to collect and distribute resources as a result of their effective work. Platforms bring together several consumer groups and create value only on the basis of mutual interest of consumer groups. „*With two-sided network effects, the platform's value to any given user largely depends on the number of users on the network's other side. Value grows as the platform matches demand from both sides*"[7].

Digital technologies have had a significant impact on the economy, changing the way businesses interact with each other and with their customers. They created not only an innovative environment in which companies operated at a higher level - faster, cheaper, smarter, but also they developed many new business opportunities. The Internet has enhanced both the speed of information gathering and the availability of a significant amount of information [12].

Innovative development can work in two ways, for example, in pertinence to the innovation in enterprise sustainable development by improving existing products that can be sold at higher prices and attracting more customers or by destructive innovation [3]. Destructive innovation offers an alternative to existing products that are much cheaper and simpler to use, and partially or fully replace existing products. Destructive innovations do not try to create better products, they introduce new products that are not currently available on the market. At the same time, while for one business, it can be destructive innovation, for another one it can be productive as it can promote sustainable development [3].

In recent years, the concept of a business model has become the subject of a growing number of both academic and practitioner studies [1], [2], [4], [9], [26]. Scholars from different research areas have recognized the potential of new business models in promoting competitive advantages of enterprises [4].

Scholars confirm that a business model can be a source of competitive advantage [2]. Thomas Clauss [4] summarising definitions given by scholars, considers business models as templates of how enterprises run and develop their businesses at holistic and system-levels. Many scholars consider that a business model integrates three main business dimensions – the value proposition, value creation and value capture [4]. The value proposition dimension contains a portfolio of solutions for customers and ways of how they are offered. The value creation domain defines how and by what means enterprises create value along the value chain. Value capture defines how value propositions are converted into revenues [4].

There is an increasing consensus that the business model innovation is key to enterprise performance [9]. Digitalization is a new source for business model innovations; therefore, it results in a higher degree of enterprise competitiveness. The main objectives of digital transformation are the obtaining of new data and using these data to reimagine old processes. A more data-oriented approach creates an opportunity for gaining new knowledge and reimagining business models. While the concept of digital transformation has been discussed for many years, the digital transformation of a business model is still disputable. Topical issues here are how to digitally transform business models, and what kind of tools should be considered [17].

In the phase of business model digital transformation, the investment in R&D plays an important role in keeping Value Capture at a positive level [5].

3. METHODOLOGY

To determine today's dominant business standard in the YP industry, its evolution over the past 25 years, the current status and forecasts of future trends have been explored. The authors have studied the YP industry conference information, publications by industry associations, such as SIINDA (Search & Information Industry Association https://www.siinda.com), LSA (The Local Search Association https://www.thelsa.org), EASDP (eadp.org/), publications of the industry leaders in several Internet resources and documents of the World Economic Forum. The Annual Reports for the world's largest YP companies published in 2018 were studied in detail - Yellow Pages Limited (Canada) and European Directories Midco S.a.r.l., which includes more than 30 group companies in Europe. In order to determine the new sources of the revenue stream, the research of modern business niche products in the Internet resources has been studied. The data was discovered using the internet browser Google search for keywords, such as the internet business directories and yellowpages. Twenty five companies, which have being operating in America and the European market, have been selected. The products most frequently replicated in business offers were selected.

4. RESEARCH RESULTS

YP Business Development Trends

The YP business started in 1886 in America. These were books, printed on cheap yellow paper with telephone and address lists, ranked by company names and sorted by their type of activity in a particular local area. YP is a particularly important marketing channel for small and medium-sized businesses that are unable to organize large marketing campaigns. Books have traditionally been published once a year and distributed free of charge to the largest number of users who need to purchase the products or services offered by the ads [8]. YP is not a registered trademark, but the term has become a symbol of the industry and is used by companies in several countries of the world.

The specificity of the industry supported a small number of market players in each individual region [19]. In 90 years, with the growth of the Internet, publishers transferred their databases to the Internet by creating a variety of online media directories. Business directories with yellowpages.xx have been created in more than 75 countries worldwide. The introduction of the Internet impacted the increase of the number of information users and opened new marketing channels for advertisers.

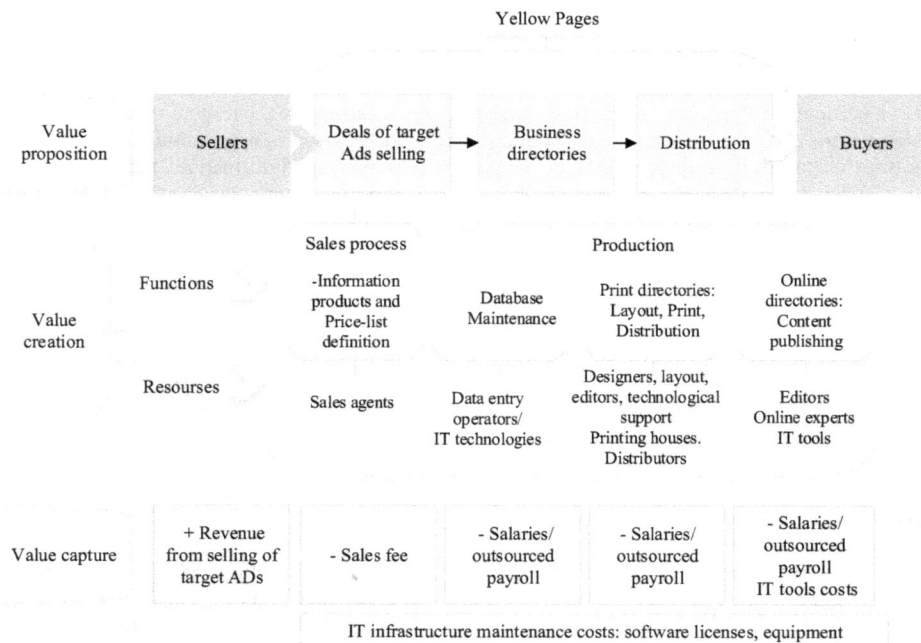

Figure 1 The core business model of YP

With the advent of the Internet, since the beginning of the 2000s, the dominant platform providers have been Google, Yahoo, Bing [7] which have joint the internet business ecosystem in the determinor capacity.

As a result, the number of market participants has increased significantly, breaking the standards of the YP sector monopoly. Google and other search platform providers have influenced the directory business and transformed it [3].

Since 2009, a number of major YP market players have begun to report financial difficulties or initiated bankruptcy procedures.

YP Business Model Evolution

As a result of the YP business analysis, the key elements of the Business Model have been identified by the authors. The core business model of YP is shown in Fig. 1. The original YP Business model is relatively simple, specifially, YP customers pay for ads that are highlighted among competitors' free entries. Books were printed in long-run and distributed free of charge for information users, who could potentially create a clients portfolio for advertisers. The higher volumes of books ensured that the more popular distribution channels were used and the higher was the demand for advertisers.

The development of the Internet has radically affected the YP business model's disruptive and transforming dimension of the "value proposition". As a result, the newly created business model is much more valuable than the original one. Both the original and newly created business models are shown in Fig. 2. The new business model shares the value gained among the members of the business ecosystem - partners, customers and information users [11]. New opportunities for the element innovation of the "value creation" dimension were opened owing to the development of technologies. Taking into account that the value of the information product increases with the increase in the number of its users; digital transformation of the business model opens a wide range of opportunities for "value captures" for companies in the industry.

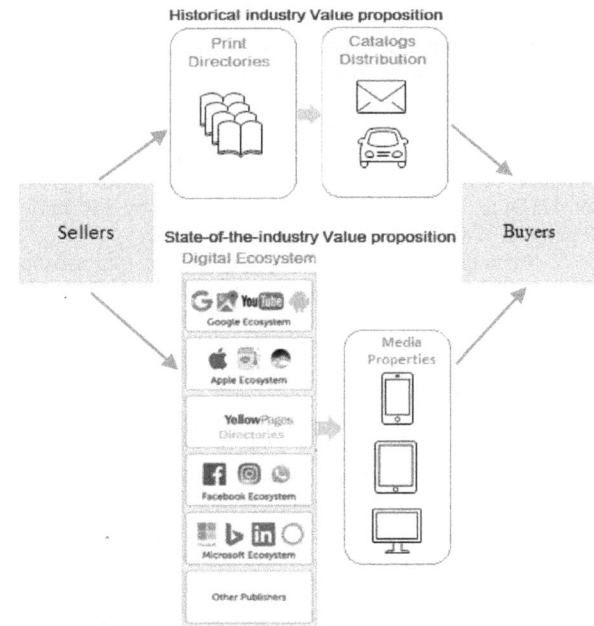

Figure 2. Evolution of YP business model (Source: [23] and authors)

An information product of the YP business can be easily converted into a digital format. The role of printing companies is diminishing and will no longer be needed when the media become fully electronic. Thousands of digital copies can be made by clicking a button and quickly sent over the internet [10].

Value proposition

The key elements of the dimension „ value proposition" of the business model and their development over the last 25 years are shown in the Table 1. The evolution period of theYP business model has split into three time periods, corresponding to 1 - before the Internet, 2 – the Internet entry stage, 3 – the entry of dominant platforms. The following labels have been used for the meaning of each element within the appropriate timeframe: P - primary, E- equivalent, M - minor. These labels will also be used to track the evolution of business model elements in other subchapters.

Table 1

The key elements of the dimension „value proposition" of the business model and their development

Elements	Period		
	1	2	3
1. Advertising customer	P	P	P
2. Target ADs components			
Business address	P	P	P
Fixed-line telephone Number	P	E	M
Mobile telephone Number		E	P
Logo	P	P	P
WEBsite, E-mail		E	P
Industry	P	P	E
Market products, Price-lists		E	P
Customer Reviews		M	P
Discount coupons. Marketing actions. Keywords. Payment options, Business hours		E	P
3. YP Media properties			
Print directories	P	P	M
Desktop		P	E
Laptop		M	P
Smartphone			P
4. Distribution channels of information products			
Distribution of print directories	P	P	M
Local Online Media Directories		E	P
Dominant provaiders platforms			P
Clients WEBsites			P
5. Information products			
Promotion products:			
Highlighted ads between the competitor entries in a printed directory	P	P	M
Sponsored listing in Local Online Media Directories		P	P
Digital marketing (Sponsored listing and Promote content) in dominant provider platforms		E	P
WEB presence products			

Infopages in YP online directories	P	P
Build and support clients WEBsite	M	P
Social media point of presence (Facebook, Linkedin, Twitter), Google my business profiles	M	P

Advertising Customers: The YP business model is viable in case of a large number of customers and it is essential that customers repeat their order year after year. According to Google, evaluating the sales cycle, the probability of retaining and reselling the product to existing customers is 60% - 70% of the total turnover, while attracting new customers probability is only 5% to 20% of the total turnover. According to ReachLocal, nowadays the success of retaining existing customers is achievable by investment in customer support and service [25].

Targeted ads: An enterprise's Data units have been modified over time. Initially the basic information about the record consisted of an address and a phone number. At the beginning of the 90s, the mobile phone number was added to information, which gradually replaced the stationary phone number. With the introduction of the Internet, contact information moved to a virtual environment where no human physical presence was required, which is why the company's website and e-mail were added.

Compared to the printed edition, the Internet does not limit the number of pieces of information and allows traders to publicize the assortment, descriptions, instructions and price lists of all offered items. The advantage of the Internet also makes it plausible to publish the most up-to-date information in real time and to announce the current events, such as sales promotion, changes in working hours and new price lists.

With the increasing number of information sources and pieces of information, it has become risky to present incorrect information compiled by intermediaries in a complex web ecosystem. Inaccurate or outdated information can result in dissatisfied users and lost sales [15].

YP Media Properties: After 100 years of existence of YP business, technology and the extensive use of the Internet cause changes in consumer habits. The amount of information that was previously available only in the printed directories has increased rapidly and transformed into the internet environment; the new technologies have outcompeted traditional print media. The printed YP catalogs are no longer available in many European states, such as Ireland, Finland, Denmark and Poland. Consistently with the experts' views, in the countries where such YP directories are still accessible, as in Belgium and Austria, their turnover share constitutes up to 10%, the exceptions being countries, such as Germany, Italy and France, in which the distribution of the printed directories continues to be viable.

With the development of the Internet, the number of devices where you can get information online has been expanding. Cell phones are transformed into Smart phones that provide the Internet connection and therefore information transmission possibilities. According to the LSA research, the popularity of devices used to access the Internet is ranked as follows: laptop 65%, smartphone 61%. desktop - 55% and tablet - 40%.

Distribution channels of information products: Under the influence of destructive innovations, the company's ability to recognize new knowledge and apply it for commercial purposes becomes crucial for business sustainability [5]. The introduction of the Internet opened up a great potential for increasing the number of information users, which cannot be achieved by increasing the print versions of catalogs. The number of printed copies is replaced by an increase in the Internet traffic and distribution channels - with popular web sites. Digital information contents have the advantage of information in a print edition. There is no need to wait a year until the new catalog is issued to correct obsolete data, current information is published instantaneously.

Customers of any company are the source of life for the company, which is why they must be protected by all means. "It is better to develop competencies that will make money in the future rather than stick to the skills that enabled the past to function successfully [3].

The platform concept has come across several sectors as a disruptive innovation from a totally unexpected perspective. The Google search platform has acted as a disruptive innovation for many types of catalogs including the YP business [3]. Google is defined as a search [20] dominant [14] platform across several categories of existing platforms. On the one hand, digital service platforms are supported by a large number of users; on the other hand, the development of the YP Internet resources, which bring together a large number of companies and increase networking users, which ultimately ensures the sustainability of Google platforms.

Information products: The specifics of the YP business, knowledge and IT infrastructure have been created and a large customer portfolio allows the YP business model to integrate new services into it. In addition to the distribution channels for their products, the advertising promotion can be expanded by publishing information products on dominant third-party search platforms. The production of WEB presence products can become a source of additional revenues.

The analysis of websites of the largest market players points to the most common Digital Marketing products - Google ADs, Search Engine Optimization (SEO), Pay-Per-Click programme (PPC), Social media advertising Management and Online reputation management. WEB presence products include developing of e-commerce, online store solutions, Website Fulfillment, Social media point of presence (Facebook, Linkedin, Twitter), Google My Busines, Google WEB and other Google opportunities.

According to "LSA 2019 Prediction", there are rapid changes in existing digital products and new innovative products are replacing existing ones. The popular SEO product based on the keyword ranking optimization is rapidly being replaced by the Voice search. People are interested not only in gaining relevant selections for their demand, but also in obtaining answers to their questions. Research has shown that investing in the Voice Search eCommerce could now boost Amazon's annual sales by $1.8 billion USD, and by 2022 the sales could grow by $40 billion USD per year [18].

Principles of revenue generation: Information products are intangible and may be classified as 'goods of experience', as potential consumers usually need to benefit from them in order to understand its quality [21]. Thus, pricing of products for two-sided networks is highly complex. The seller's price for the promotion of his product will always be higher, as more users are involved in searching for the products offered [7].

The YP business model is designed to charge for the following services: Advertising in YP print and online media, Developing WEB presence products and Digital marketing services on third-party platforms.

Historically, a one-time fee for advertising published in printed and online media was collected from customers. The fee for each item of information was requested separately. Now the market requires regular support and cash is collected as a regular monthly service fee. Informative product offerings combine both the promotion products and WEB presence product development. The products are packed in different proportions and are not available separately [21]. The expected value of packing makes it possible to achieve higher volumes of sales, greater economic efficiency and a greater profit per product than can be achieved if the same products are sold separately [10]. The evolution of pricing principles within the YP business model is shown in Table 2.

Table 2

The evolution of pricing principles

Pricing principles	Period		
	1	2	3
One-time fee for advertising	P	P	M
One-time fee for the development of the WEB presence product		P	M
Regular fee for the development of the WEB presence product and advertising of regular support			P

Revenues are collected in small amounts from a large number of customer orders. When selling information products, it is important to create a balance between the offered prices and the number of potential customers; it is also important to control the sales performance [21].

Value creation and cost structure

The value of the supply chain is a series of activities that generate and create value over time by increasing the total value of the company [10]. The key steps in the YP business value delivery are the sales process of an information product, the creation and maintenance of an information database, the development of the information product and the dissemination of it. The sequential execution of these steps is ensured by the interaction of external and internal resources. Technology development is seen as an important factor that affects the value chain [10].

Sales: Historically, customer communications and revenues were provided by a direct sales team. Sales agents sign contracts with customers for advertising placement for the next year's printed edition. Direct sales were active in attracting new customers. At the moment, the greatest emphasis in retaining existing customers is put on telemarketing, but in the future online client sites have to be developed.

The creation and maintenance of an information database: To ensure the delivery of information relevant to the user's search, there must be a sufficient number of information units. The volume and accuracy of the database is the greatest business value. Information products may become irrelevant in a short time period [10]: 60% of local business information may be changed in 24 months [15]. Thus, maintenance of the database is a systematic and regular process, which should be based on the use of actual data gathering methods (Table 3).

Table 3

Trends in the development of data maintenance techniques

Database maintenance methods	Period		
	1	2	3
Physical inspection of addresses and search of them in independent print sources	P	P	M
Manual data search in the Internet resources		E	P
Tools and automation based on data collection from other Internet ecosystem resources			P

The cost of maintaining a database is not dependent from the amount of advertising sales revenues. In order to attain the best quality of the database at a lower cost, it is important to create a balance between the use of technology and manual data processing. To do it, it is possible to deploy own resources or

outsource. In order to make such decisions, it is necessary to follow the development of technologies at a high professional level, to know the state of current technologies in the industry and to choose the most suitable method of maintenance of the database from the variety of possibilities offered. Technological developments should be monitored not only for data collection, but also for their reliability, control and substitution.

Development of an information product, development of IT infrastructure: Digital transformation has fundamentally transformed the process of developing and delivering of the YP information product. Although for several years the information products have been distributed in a physical format (book/CD), digitization technologies have significantly increased the number of information users and reduced the cost of information dissemination [21].

The digital innovations of the YP business model has impacted almost every stage and elements of the value creation. The CRM systems (Salesforce, net-linx, Vendasta) support sales functions; the volume and quality of the database maintenance can be enhanced with the techniques of the Web crawler search engine technology. Computer storage capacity doubles every two years, reducing the cost of storing data [10]. The distribution of informative products is also supported by several tools for implementing the SEO campaign - Ahrevs, Silktide, Bootsability, Fairrank; Google, Facebook ADs Campaigns: Adplorer, publoCity, MatchCraft, Aquisio; WEBsite Building Tools: Wordpress, Mono Solutions, Joomla, Duda.

Value capture

The digital transformation of the YP business model has changed the composition of revenues and costs and their share in total profits or loss structure (Table 4). The labels used for resource definition are the following: Staff (ST), Technology (IT), Commercial agents (Ag), Printing houses (PR) Distributors (DIS).

Table 4

Profit or loss composition

Revenue and costs positions		Period		
		1	2	3
Revenues by product group				
Print media directories		P	E	M
Local Online Media Directories			E	P
New media: Digital marketing			M	P
WEB presence products				P
Costs	Resources			
Sales fee	Ag	P	P	P
Database maintenance costs	ST/IT	P	P	P
Layout of print directories	ST/IT	P	E	M
Print costs	PR	P	E	M
Distribution of print directories	DIS	P	E	M
YP Online Media Directories infopages produstion costs	ST/IT		P	P
Digital marketing and WEB presence production costs	ST/IT		M	P
IT infrastructure maintenance	ST/IT	M	P	P
Gross profit				

Risks of value capture

Revenues: In order to provide the infrastructure for business existence, the required level of turnover must be achieved. As a result of the digital transformation of the business model, the strategic task of YP companies is to balance the decrease in turnover from historical products (printed directories) with the new digital marketing turnover. As noted in the 2018 reports, Yellow Pages Limited (Canada) and European Directories Group reported a 10% to 20% total decrease of turnover over the previous year. The increase of the digital media turnover up to 10% was not able to replace the 30% - 40% decrease in turnover of historical print directories [23],[6]. In turn, the sharp competition in the digital marketing does not allow to reasonably predict the amount of revenue from new business types.

Introduction of IT technology. Risks associated with achieving a positive financial result are seen by companies in: 1) implementing IT technologies, significant additional costs associated with investment in IT, modification of existing products and the development of new products and technologies; 2) non-availability to improve their information technology systems and to develop new types of products in a timely and effective manner [23],[6].

5. CONCLUSIONS

The authors concluded that creating a viable and profitable business model under the conditions of affecting digital transformation is possible only if all elements of the business model interact with each other. It is important to reveal the importance of each element of the business model within a certain period of time in order to leave behind the old, unprofitable elements of the value proposition, thus, aiming to reduce the resources needed for the creation of value. As a result of the analysis of the evolution of the elements of the YP business model, the authors identified some important issues that must be taken into account when creating a profitable BM:

• Conduct research to promptly discover the potential for the development of the business model or the effects of disruptive technology on the existing business model
• Replacing the falling revenues from the old businesses with the revenues from new sources.
• Introducing new, market-driven products, reviewing the cost structure and creating a cost-balanced pricing policy.
• Revising the level of digital maturity of the company.
These factors can also be applied to any business model of other industry under the conditions of digital transformation.

6. REFERENCES

[1] A. Batocchio, A. Ghezzi, (2016). **A method for evaluating business models implementation process**. Business Process Management Journal, 22(4), 712–735.

[2] C.M. Christensen, (2001). **The past and future of competitive advantage.** MIT Sloan Management Review, 42, 105–109.

[3] C.M. Christensen, M.E. Raynor, (2003). **The Innovator's Solution: Creating and Sustaining Successful Growth**. Boston: Harvard Business School Press.

[4] T. Clauss, (2017). **Measuring business model innovation: conceptualization, scale development, and proof of performance**. R and D Management, 47(3), 385–403.

[5] W. M. Cohen, D. A. Levinthal, (1990). **Absorptive Capacity: A New Perspective on Learning and Innovation.** Administrative Science Quarterly, 35(1), 128–152.

[6] **Consolidated Financial Statements 2018 European Directories Mido S.a. r. l., Luxembourg.** Retrieved from http://www.europeandirectories.com

[7]T. Eisenmann, G.Parker, M.W.Van Alstyne, (2006). **Strategies for two-sided markets**. Harvard Business Review, 84(10), 1–11.

[8] E. Hyvönen, K. Viljanen, (2002). **Yellow Pages on the Semantic Web. Towards the Semantic Web and Web Services**, Proceedings of XML Finland 2002 Conference, (october 21-22), 3–14.

[9] IBM, 2006. **Expanding the Innovation Horizon**. The Global CEO Study 2006. IBM Business Consulting Services, 1–61.

[10] R.P. Joseph, R. P. (2018). **Digital Transformation, Business Model Innovation and Efficiency in Content Industries: A Review.** The International Technology Management Review, 7(1), 59–70.

[11] P. Kita, I. Šimberova, (2018). **An overview of business models in the Czech chemical industry, a sustainable multiple value creation perspective.** Entrepreneurship and sustainability issues, 5(3).

[12] G.T. Lumpkin, G. G. Dess, (2004). **E-Business Strategies and Internet How the Internet Adds Value.** Organizational Dynamics, 33(2), 161–173.

[13] R.F. Lusch, S. Nambisan, (2015). **Service Innovation: A Service-Dominant Logic perspective.** MIS Quarterly, 39(1), 12.

[14] A. Moazed. **Platform Business Model – Definition. What is it? Explanation**. Applico. (2016, May 1). Retrieved from https://www.applicoinc.com/blog/what-is-a-platform-business-model/ - dominant platforms

[15] J. Morsello, G. Sterling, (2018). **Local Listings Management out of Chaos**. Local Search Association Materials, 14.

[16]H. Rubenstein, (1996). **The death of competition: Leadership and strategy in the age of business ecosystems** - By James E. Moore, Harper Business, 1996. Book Review and Commentary by Herb Rubenstein, President, Sustainable Business Group, 21, 2640–2650.

[17]D. Schallmo, C.A. Williams, L. Boardman, (2017). **Digital Transformation of Business Models — Best Practice, Enablers, and Roadmap.** International Journal of Innovation Management, 21(8), 1740014-1-17.

[18]G. Shaoolian. **Why Voice Search Will Dominate SEO In 2019 And How You Can Capitalize On It**. Forbes (2018, December 27).

[19] Thumbtack Journal. (2015, October 7). **How Do The Yellow Pages Still Make Money?** Retrieved from https://www.thumbtack.com/blog/how-do-the-yellow-pages-still-make-money/

[20] M. Uenlue, **The Platform business model, Innovation Tactics**, (2017, June 26). Retrieved from https://www.innovationtactics.com/platform-business-model-complete-guide/

[21] S. Viswanathan, G. Anandalingam, (2005). **Pricing strategies for information goods**. Saadhana, 30(June), 257–274.

[22] M. Wasko, R. Teigland, D. Leidner, S. Jarvenpaa. (2017). **Stepping into the Internet: New Ventures in Virtual Worlds**. MIS Quarterly, 35(3), 645.

[23] **Yellow Pages Limited Annual Report 2018 and Presentations.** Retrieved from https://corporate.yp.ca/en/investors/overview/

[24] Y. Yoo, (2010). **Computing in Everyday Life : A Call for Research on Experiential Computing**. MIS Quarterly, 34(June), 213–231.

[25] W. Young, **Top 10 insights on local marketing at LSA17, Search Engine Land**, (2017, March 27). Retrieved from https://searchengineland.com/top-10-insights-local-marketing-lsa17-271648

[26]C. Zott, R.H. Amit, L. Massa, (2011). **The business model: Recent developments and future research**. Journal of Management. 37(4), 1019-1042

A Control System for Strategy Implementation:
A Case of a National Standardization Body

Arta PĪLĒNA and Maija KAVOSA
Riga Technical University, Faculty of Engineering Economics and Management
Kalnciema iela 6, Riga, LV-1048, Latvia

ABSTRACT

Effective control of strategy implementation in today's dynamically changing operating environment is becoming increasingly important to ensure sustained success of organizations. The aim of this paper is to analyze the importance of implementing an effective control system for strategy implementation. To ensure a comprehensive analysis of the characteristics of a control system in an organization, the authors perform an evaluation of a control system model for strategy implementation in a national standardization body. Research methods such as analysis of the relevant scientific literature, as well as logical analysis is performed. Based on both the theoretical research and analysis of the organization the authors identify the importance and main aspects of an effective control system for strategy implementation.

Keywords: strategic management, control system, sustained success, quality management, standardization.

1. INTRODUCTION

Organizations develop strategies to gain a competitive advantage, attract customers and improve the operations, products and services of the organization. The need for strategy development and implementation in all organizations is still emphasized, despite the rapid and often unforeseen changes not only in the external but also in the internal operating environment [12]. In order to ensure the implementation of strategic plans the strategy development stage should be followed by actions that ensure the implementation of planned activities, traceability of the results achieved and monitoring of the organization's operational environment and conditions affecting the achievement of the planned results [22]. Therefore it is necessary to introduce control mechanisms that allow to evaluate the degree of implementation of the strategy and to timely identify deviations from the planned results.

The implementation of the strategy can be compared to the PDCA cycle, thus the strategy development phase should be followed by its implementation, the comparison of the results achieved with the set objectives, as well as the improvement of the strategy and its implementation measures to ensure the adaptation to changes in the external and internal environment of the organization. Therefore, in order to achieve the objectives set in the strategy, an effective control mechanism – a control system – is needed to ensure a continuous monitoring of the implementation of the strategy, identification of the necessary adjustments and improvements and ongoing feedback on the effectiveness of the strategic management process. To ensure the implementation of the strategy, it is complemented by a strategic management process that promotes continuous monitoring of the internal and external environmental factors of the organization, as well as the planning of the organization's activities and resources to achieve its strategic objectives, contributing to the organisation's ability to achieve sustained success [19], [25].

The scientific aim of the research activities is to evaluate the theoretical aspects of the strategic management and control system in order to analyze the characteristics of a control system for strategy implementation and to evaluate the control system model of a national standardization body.

The methodology is based on comparison and analysis of literature and views published by various authors about strategic management and characteristics of a control system for strategy implementation, at the same time defining the activities to be carried out within the framework of the research.

The basic information on the strategic management is given in Section 2. In Section 3 the authors introduce the basic information on the role of the control system for strategy implementation, while in Section 4 the authors describe the results of the evaluation of the control system model for its implementation in the national standardization body. In Section 5 the authors offer their conclusions.

2. STRATEGIC MANAGEMENT AND ACHIEVING SUSTAINED SUCCESS

Strategic management can be defined as an effective and efficient use of existing production resources (natural resources, human resources, capital, infrastructure, raw materials, etc.) with the aim of maintaining long-term operation of the organization, gaining a competitive advantage and increasing the profit of the organization. The process of strategic management includes planning, organization, coordination, application and control of the organization's future activities [22]. The foundation of the strategy is the organization's vision of its future position as well as its mission and values. In order to ensure coherence of the activities with the set guidelines, the strategic directions and action plans should be based on the vision and values of the organization therefore improving the organization's ability to achieve the set objectives and leading the organization to fulfilling the planned financial results [5], [22].

Taking into account the constantly changing operating environment of organizations, the analysis of their context and the changing needs of the parties involved should be performed regularly to ensure the implementation of the required processes and the acquisition of resources necessary for the effective operation of the organization [16]. In order to ensure the traceability of changes and to facilitate their implementation, there is a need for continuous monitoring of requirements as well as identification of actions to be implemented in case of change, including employee involvement, clear task definition, tools for monitoring and controlling the implementation of the strategy [21], [3]. To ensure this, the integration of existing functions and processes is needed, contributing to the full progress of the strategic objectives at all levels of the organization [14].

After examining the literature on strategic management, the main activities of the strategic management process towards sustained success were reviewed (see Table 1).

Table 1. The main activities of the strategic management process – supporting research [created by authors]

Activity	Purpose	Key references
Effective management of human resources	To ensure the effectiveness of activities by involving specialists with appropriate knowledge, access to information, and analytical skills to make the right decisions	Rostoka et al. (2019); Radomska (2014); Mjakuškina et al. (2016).
Meeting the needs and desires of the stakeholders	To meet the long-term needs and expectations of the parties involved continuously	LVS EN ISO 9004:2018; Latham (2014); Yang et al. (2011).
Holistic approach of improving the performance of the organization	To discover ever more effective ways to create useful products and services	Lentjušenkova et al. (2016).
Innovation in the functions and processes of the organization	To ensure that all the activities of the organization are consistent with strategic guidelines and development trends	Latham (2014).
Quality management	To establish an appropriate environment and culture in the organization, a foundation for innovation and development, as well as continuous identification of the stakeholders' needs which are directly related to the organization's sustainable development	Rebelo et al. (2016); Jasiulewicz-Kaczmarek (2014); Todorut (2012).
Responsibility of top management	To ensure that the organization's activities include planning, implementation, monitoring, evaluation, improvement and innovation at all levels, in the context of intense global competition	Hyväri (2016).
Leadership	To ensure the development of a strategic plan, as well as assigning executive and supervisory responsibilities to responsible persons, while ensuring a constant review of strategic directions in line with changes in the organization's operating environment	Slavik et al. (2015); Dogan (2015).
Involvement of the participants in the processes of strategy development, communication and implementation	To contribute to the organization's consideration of different ideas, experiences and attitudes and ensuring a common understanding of the organization's activities and orientation towards the achievement of the set objectives	Wittek-Crabb (2012); Baumgartner et al. (2017); Engert et al. (2016).

From the analysis of the texts the authors conclude that the process of strategic management consists of continuous activities – analysis, decision-making and implementation – that are necessary for the implementation of the strategy, thus achieving sustained success is also due to the organization's ability to follow sustainability principles in its operations. In order to implement the principles of sustainable development in strategic management, a review of the strategic management process is necessary, assessing its participants, the methods used and the content of the strategy, including the organization's operational guidelines, key values and objectives.

3. A CONTROL SYSTEM FOR STRATEGY IMPLEMENTATION

The increasing complexity and dynamics of the business environment is evolving the importance of risk management as it is becoming increasingly important in planning and evaluating the performance of an organization. It is used to mitigate the undesirable effects of risks and to benefit optimally in situations where risk-taking is desirable [8]. A risk-based approach is therefore considered a best practice technique that ensures the establishment of priorities and the allocation of necessary resources that can ensure the effective mitigation of risks affecting the organization's performance [27].

In order to monitor the organization's operational aspects, as well as to assess whether those aspects on which the strategy is based remain valid, a continuous monitoring should be performed to avoid exceptional deviations from the strategy implementation plan [23]. The evaluation of the strategy should facilitate the review of the expected results, assessment criteria, objectives and values, as well as the identification of alternative strategies thereby ensuring dynamic adaptation to change [5]. Internal control mechanisms provide an important contribution to increasing the value of the organization, the sustainability of management activities and the reliability of the organization's performance reports [28]. Since sustainability concepts are not changing as such, it is important to emphasize that their use is expanding in areas that are not previously affected [10]. Controls are based on the identification of risks and measures required to mitigate and monitor their likelihood of occurrence, as well as to regularly evaluate the performance of the organization against predefined criteria [28].

Control systems are considered to be strategy implementation tools needed to manage change in the organization in response to changes in its environment, while providing feedback on the effectiveness of the strategic management process. These are the objective setting, measurement and feedback systems used by managers to assess whether the organization is achieving the desired direction and implementing the strategy successfully [23]. This emphasizes the importance of the development of managers' competences to ensure the comprehensive analysis of the business environment since control of strategy implementation includes reviewing and monitoring the strategic directions and planned activities, while evaluating the overall topicality of the strategy and additional circumstances affecting the performance of the organization [29], [23]. If deviations from the planned results are observed, it is necessary to change the strategy, its implementation activities and control mechanisms [23].

To ensure the effectiveness of the strategic management process, the control system should provide a regular analysis of the internal and external environment to identify timely changes that are essential to achieving the organization's objectives. Various methods of strategic management and analysis of the organization, such as analysis of strengths and weaknesses, opportunities and threats, can be used to identify these conditions [6]. Based on the identified factors that influence the operation of the organization, changes in the strategy, organization processes and functions can be introduced while maintaining the continuity of the organization's activities and the pursuit of planned results [5].

Since the evaluation of measurable indicators relevant to the organization is essential for operational planning and monitoring of achievement of planned results, in addition to the traditional performance measurement and monitoring functions of the organization, the control system should define the boundaries of the organization's operations in line with strategic directions, provide the basis for defining and evaluating the key performance indicators of the organization, and promote the identification of deviations from the strategic objectives previously set [5], [23]. In order to facilitate the achievement of the outcomes of the strategy, the organization's management and employees should be continuously informed of the level of implementation of the strategy and the actions to be taken [5]. As an element of the control system in assessing and ensuring the performance of an organization in accordance with the applicable requirements, as well as identifying good practice examples and improvement opportunities internal audit is often used to provide information on the organization's compliance to the requirements, while also gaining assurance of the employee awareness of the organization's context and processes [28].

According to the requirements of ISO 9001, an organization shall periodically perform a management review, focusing on the organization's operational issues, such as changes in external and internal factors, customer satisfaction and feedback from stakeholders, process performance and degree of achievement of quality objectives [15]. Thus, based on an organization's performance analysis, the management review could provide the basis for continuous improvement of the organization's performance and contribute to the effectiveness of strategic management. By identifying deviations from the set requirements and strategic objectives, it is necessary to implement actions that eliminate the causes of deviations, as well as to make decisions about necessary changes in the strategy, organizational activities or the control system. Therefore a correlation can be drawn with the quality management principles and the requirements of ISO 9001, which require a response to the identified non-conformities, the assessment of the need for action to eliminate the causes, as well as the evaluation of the effectiveness of the implemented corrective actions [5]. Consequently, strategy implementation control measures can therefore be aligned with the PDCA cycle common in quality management, adjusting its stages to the strategic management process (see Figure 1).

A control system for strategy implementation therefore should include mechanisms for the analysis of the context of the organization, setting measurable objectives and implementing instruments for monitoring the achievement of the defined results, as well as implementing actions for improving the performance of the organization and ensuring adaptation to the changes of the environment by changing the strategy and the control mechanisms for its implementation.

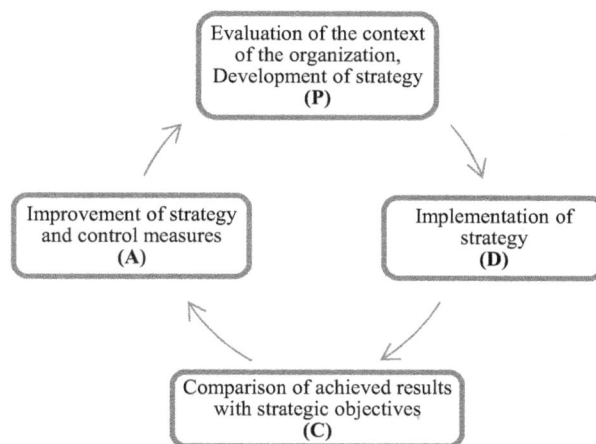

Figure 1. The cycle of stages for strategy implementation [created by authors]

After analysing the information from the control system study in the context of strategic management, the authors can conclude that control systems are among the main strategy implementation tools needed to manage change in the organization in response to the environmental changes in order to provide feedback on the effectiveness of the strategic management process. Thus, there is a need to develop a mechanism for monitoring the performance of the organization and its influencing factors.

4. EVALUATION OF THE CONTROL SYSTEM MODEL FOR STRATEGY IMPLEMENTATION IN A NATIONAL STANDARDIZATION BODY

Standardization plays an important role in the international conformity assessment system by providing uniform conditions, promoting a common understanding of the criteria to be assessed, and contributing to the reliability of results [7]. Moreover, in the view of changing market needs and scientific developments, continuous improvement of standards and standardization processes is being implemented [20]. That indicates that the actions of national standardization bodies should also be focused on continually improving their processes, products and services. The organization in question is the Latvian national standardization body – "Latvian standard" Ltd (LVS). It is a state-owned corporation with 100% holding in the Ministry of Economics of the Republic of Latvia. LVS implements the state policy in the field of standardization, contributing to the quality infrastructure in Latvia, and it operates for the common good of society by providing standardization products and services to businesses and society. LVS is a member of European and international standardization bodies – CEN, CENELEC, ISO, IEC and has a sales contract with ETSI. The core business processes of LVS are the development of standards and their dissemination.

LVS has implemented a certified quality management system according to ISO 9001:2015 therefore control mechanisms applicable to achievement of quality objectives are already implemented. Considering that both the quality system and the implementation of the strategy are based on the understanding of the stakeholder needs and expectations, risk-based thinking, as well as the analysis of external and internal environmental factors, it is possible to link these control mechanisms and integrate them into organizational processes to ensure the achievement of both strategic and quality objectives. The control system model for strategy implementation of LVS is visualized in Figure 2.

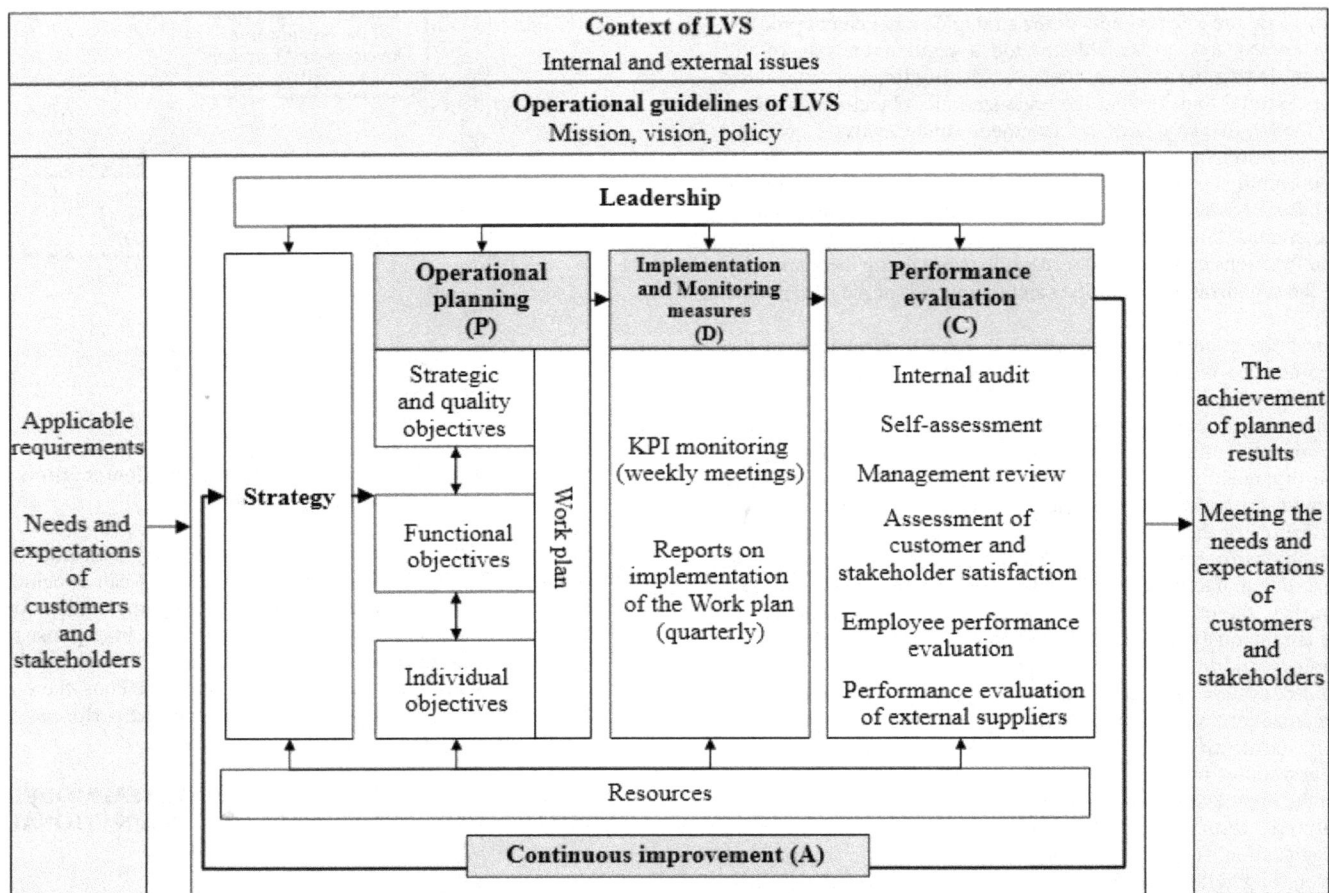

Figure 2. Control system model for strategy implementation in "Latvian Standard" Ltd [created by authors]

The model of the control system was developed based on the PDCA cycle, the interaction of the organizational elements of the structures covered by ISO 9001:2015 and ISO 9004:2018 and adapted to the specificity of LVS. It includes a number of interrelated blocks that reflect organizational aspects and processes relevant to strategic management. When evaluating the control system model of LVS, the specifics of the activities of LVS should be taken into account, emphasizing the importance of achieving the planned results and satisfaction of the parties involved, as well as the theoretical considerations for monitoring the implementation of the strategy and the necessary elements of the control system. Given that LVS is a national standardization body, the control system for strategy implementation should also include the measures required by membership requirements of European and international standardization organizations.

The activities of LVS should be based on the context of the organization, therefore there is a need for continuous improvement of processes for continuous monitoring, review and evaluation of internal and external conditions to ensure that the organization is able to respond to changes in its operating environment in a timely manner. The in-depth review of internal and external conditions has so far taken place in the quality system management reporting meetings, but a more regular flow of information will ensure that timely reactions to the identified changes are performed. In order to ensure a continuous understanding of these changes, an effective flow of information

is needed not only with external stakeholders, but also between employees.

The role of the top management of LVS is essential to ensure operational efficiency and employee motivation. Top management's responsibility should include regular review of the strategy and operational guidelines of LVS, identification of necessary changes and decision-making on their implementation. The initiative to introduce a control system should come from top management to define the most appropriate solutions for planning and evaluating performance by appointing responsible employees for the implementation of these activities. Top management should ensure that the employees of LVS are aware of the organization's operational guidelines and promote an organizational culture based on them. Top management should also be able to gain employee motivation to engage in LVS process improvement activities and, if necessary, seek solutions to possible resistance resulting from changes in existing operations.

By defining the tasks to be performed according to the strategic directions and quality objectives at several control levels, it will be possible to ensure a more effective control of the implementation of the strategic plan, as well as a common understanding of the progress of LVS in the implementation of the strategy. According to the specifics of the activities of LVS and applicable requirements, the following performance evaluation measures should be maintained:

- Internal audit – in addition to the existing requirements, the employees' understanding of the strategy of LVS and their performance in its implementation, as well as the newly introduced control mechanisms for monitoring performance indicators should also be assessed;
- Self-assessment – the self-assessment required by CEN-CENELEC should be carried out at specified intervals and regular monitoring of the implementation of the planned improvement measures should be performed. The self-assessment should provide the basis for determining good practices and opportunities for improvement;
- Customer and stakeholder satisfaction assessment – it is possible to expand the range of customer survey respondents by launching customer satisfaction assessment activities not only for regular but also one time customers. It is also necessary to maintain regular communication with the Ministry of Economics and the National Standardization Council to ensure that LVS is aware of their expectations and to promote cooperation in the development of national standardization processes;
- Employee performance evaluation – regular evaluation of employee performance is required to identify skills to be developed and assign tasks for future periods. The evaluation system would thus enable direct managers to define the results to be achieved, measure the performance, identify the competence to be developed, and objectively plan and develop more appropriate employee training and development programs.
- Measuring the performance of external suppliers – to ensure that external products and services that affect the operation of LVS and the satisfaction of the parties involved meet the requirements of LVS, a clear identification of the requirements to be set and an explanation of the operational guidelines to external suppliers is needed. Attracting external suppliers whose performance and innovations coincide with the vision of improving the performance of LVS and facilitating continuous improvement should be pursued.
- Management review – the procedure for organizing the existing management review process should be continued by involving all LVS employees to ensure awareness of the performance of LVS and their contribution to strategy implementation and the improvement of the quality system. It is possible to increase the number of management review meetings by addressing the current issues of the strategic management and quality management system efficiency.

Taking into account the specificity of the strategic management process and the actions and knowledge required to achieve strategic objectives, timely resource planning and attraction is required:

- People – when planning the activities to be implemented, it is necessary to carry out evaluation of the existing human resources capacity, taking into account the changing workload and the competence necessary for the efficient execution of processes;
- Infrastructure – given the crucial importance of an advanced information technology infrastructure and its efficient use in optimizing the internal processes of the standardization system, there is a need for continuous identification of necessary changes in the software and technical support. When innovations are introduced, their impact should be continuously monitored and evaluated, taking into account internal and external circumstances, associated risks and environmental impacts. With the introduction of new technologies, primary planning activities should include identification of the needs and expectations of the stakeholders. Considering the copyright protection of standardization documents and the processing of personal data in standardization processes, consideration should be given to integrating the requirements of ISO/IEC 27001 into the existing quality system to improve information security management;
- Process environment – conditions for the motivation of the employees to achieve the set strategic and quality objectives should be ensured. Increasing employee mobility and promoting an environment where the employees are informed about the progress of LVS in achieving the set results should also be considered. It is recommended to put visualization tools at workplaces, such as the meeting room, to illustrate the current information and development progress. In order to develop LVS as a sustainable organization, it is necessary to consider the implementation of activities that would reduce the impact of LVS on the environment, and to promote a working culture in which the employees pay attention to issues related to the possibilities of reducing the consumption of natural resources;
- Organizational knowledge – taking into account the specificity of LVS, it is necessary to maintain the existing knowledge transfer and preservation measures, supplementing them with a clear definition of what results need to be achieved. Taking into account the aspiration to increase employee mobility, in addition to face-to-face training, it is recommended to develop training materials and courses in the electronic environment.

On the basis of the research, it could be observed that in order to implement the elements of the control system in the activities of LVS, there is a need for quality system improvement measures that are oriented towards increasing the ability of LVS to achieve sustained success, as well as integration of the strategic objectives at all levels and activities of LVS. Also, it is necessary to create awareness among the employees of LVS about continuous improvement as a tool for long-term success, a source of learning and an opportunity to implement the necessary changes for development and work organization. A culture must be introduced where learning integrates both employee competence and overall organizational competence, thus moving towards achieving the strategic objectives and enhancing the reputation of LVS as an institution capable of providing professional services. Thus, it is possible to predict that effective implementation of the elements included in the control system model will ensure continuous improvement of the operations of LVS, fulfilment of applicable requirements, achievement of the set objectives, as well as increase of satisfaction of customers and stakeholders.

5. CONCLUSIONS

The strategic management process consists of continuous activities that are necessary for the implementation of the strategy, thus achieving sustained success is also due to the organization's ability to follow sustainability principles in its operations. Control systems are among the main strategy implementation tools needed to manage change in the organization in response to the environmental changes in order to provide feedback on the effectiveness of the strategic management process. By maintaining an effective strategic management process, the organization can achieve sustained success and ensure satisfaction of customers and stakeholders. Achieving sustained success in an organization is closely linked to quality assurance and management: meeting the requirements set for the organization, fulfilling the needs and expectations of the parties involved, as well as ensuring continuous improvement. Therefore, it is important for the organization to include the basic principles of quality management to maintain a functioning control system and to apply the tools of evaluation and improvement of the organization. The control system model for strategy implementation in "Latvian Standard" Ltd covers the main factors influencing the actions of a national standardization body. The existing means of performance evaluation and promotion of improvement acts as an essential basis for the implementation of measures for strategy implementation, therefore an integration of these measures are necessary to ensure the achievement of planned results and sustained success.

6. REFERENCES

[1]   A. V. Todorut, A. V. "Sustainable Development of Organizations through Total Quality Management", **Procedia - Social and Behavioral Sciences**, Vol. 62, 2012, pp. 927-931.

[2]   A. Witek-Crabb "Sustainable Strategic Management and Market Effectiveness of Enterprises", **Procedia – Social and Behavioral Sciences**, Vol. 58, 2012, pp. 899-905.

[3]   A. Zeps "Strategic Solutions for Sustainable Development and International Excellence of Organizations" Summary of the Doctoral Thesis. Riga: Riga Technical University, 2016, p. 47.

[4]   C. C. Yang, K. J. Yang "An integrated model of value creation based on the refined Kano's model and the blue ocean strategy" **Total Quality Management and Business Excellence**, Vol. 22, Issue 9, 2011, pp. 925-940.

[5]   F. R. David, F. R. David "Strategic Management: A Competetive Advantage Approach, Concepts and Cases, 16th edition" Essex: Pearcson Education Limited, 2017, p. 680.

[6]   G. R. Jones, C. W. L. Hill (2013). "Theory of Strategic Management with Cases, Tenth International Edition" Florence: South-Western College Publishing p. 817.

[7]   H. J. de Vries, B. Nagtegaal, S. Veenstra, "Business Need and Opportunities for Transatlantic Harmonization of Standards and Conformity Assessment", **Standards Engineering**, Vol. 69, Issue 2, 2017, pp. 1 -11.

[8]   H. K. Mohammed, A. Knapkova "The Impact of Total Risk Management on Company's Performance", **Procedia – Social and Behavioral Sciences**, Vol. 220, 2016, pp. 271-277.

[9]   I. Hyväri "Roles of Top Management and Organizational Project Management in the Effective Company Strategy Implementation", **Procedia - Social and Behavioral Sciences**, Vol. 226, 2016, pp. 108-115.

[10]   I. Mežinska, I. Lapiņa, J. Mazais "Integrated management systems towards sustainable and socially responsible organisation", **Total Quality Management & Business Excellence**, Vol. 26, Issue 5-6, 2015, pp. 469-481.

[11]   J. R. Latham "Leadership for Quality and Innovation: Challenges, Theories, and a Framework for Future Research", **Quality Management Journal**, Vol 21, Issue 1, 2014, pp. 11-15.

[12]   J. Radomska "Operational risk associated with the strategy implementation", **Management**, Vol. 18, Issue 2, 2014, pp. 31-43.

[13]   J. Slavik, A. Putnova, A. Cevakoba, "Leadership as a tool of strategic management", **Procedia Economics and Finance**, Vol. 26, 2015, pp. 1159-1163.

[14]   L. S. Dias, M. G. Ierapetritou "From process control to supply chain management: An overview of integrated decision making strategies", **Computers and Chemical Engineering**, Vol. 106, 2017, pp. 826-835.

[15]   **LVS EN ISO 9001:2015 -** Quality management systems - Requirements (ISO 9001:2015) Retrieved from https://lvs.lv/lv/library/read/95806

[16]   **LVS EN ISO 9004:2018 -** Quality management - Quality of an organization - Guidance to achieve sustained success (ISO 9004:2018). Retrieved from https://www.lvs.lv/lv/library/read/139230

[17]   M. F. Rebelo, G. Santos, R. Silva "Integration of management systems: towards a sustained success and development of organizations" **Journal of Cleaner Production**, Vol. 127, 2016, pp. 96-111.

[18]   M. Jasiulewicz-Kaczmarek "Is Sustainable Development An Issue For Quality Management?", **Foundations of Management**, Vol. 6, Issue 2, 2014, pp. 51-66.

[19]   M. Mišanková, K. Kočišová, "Strategic Implementation as a part of strategic management", **Procedia - Social and Behavioral Sciences**, Vol. 110, 2014, pp. 861-870.

[20]   M. Mĺkva, V. Prajová, B. Yakimovich, A. Korshunov "Standardization – One of the Tools of Continuous Improvement", **International Conference on Manufacturing Engineering and Materials (ICMEM 2016)**, June 6-10, 2016. Nový Smokovec: Elsevier Ltd., pp. 329-332.

[21]   M. Stříteská, L. Jelínková "Strategic Performance Management with Focus on the Customer", **Procedia – Social and Behavioral Sciences**, Vol. 210, 2015, pp. 66-76.

[22]   N. Dogan "The Intersection of Entrepreneurship and Strategic Management: Strategic Entrepreneurship", **Procedia - Social and Behavioral Sciences**, Vol. 195, 2015, pp. 1288-1294.

[23]   N. E. Wanjohi "Strategic Control Systems in Strategy Implementation and Financial Performance of Bamburi Cement Limited, Kenya" University of Nairobi, 2013, p. 75.

[24]   O. Lentjušenkova, I. Lapiņa "The Transformation of the Organization's Intellectual Capital: from Resource to Capital", **Journal of Intellectual Capital**, Vol. 17, Issue 4, pp. 610-631.

[25]   R. J. Baumgartner, R. Rauter "Strategic perspectives of corporate sustainability management to develop a sustainable organization", **Journal of Cleaner Production**, Vol. 140, 2017, pp. 81-92.

[26]   S. Engert, R. J. Baumgartner "Corporate sustainability strategy - bridging the gap between formulation and implementation", **Journal of Cleaner Production**, Vol. 113, 2016, pp. 822-834.

[27]   S. Mjakuškina, I. Lapiņa "Evaluation of Market Surveillance Implementation and Sustainability", **Flexible Systems Management**, Australia, Ultimo, 4-6 December, 2016. Singapore: Springer, 2016, pp. 257-269.

[28]   T. Danescu, M. Prozan, R. D. Prozan "The valances of the internal audit in relationship with the internal control – corporate governance", **Procedia Economics and Finance**, Vol. 26, 2015, pp. 960-966.

[29]   T. Ņikitina, I. Lapiņa "Creating and Managing Knowledge towards Managerial Competence Development in Contemporary Business Environment", **Knowledge Management Research and Practice**, Vol. 17, Issue 1, 2019, pp. 96-107.

[30]   Z. Rostoka, J. Locovs, E. Gaile-Sarkane "Open Innovation of New Emerging Small Economies Based on University-Construction Industry Cooperation", **Journal of Open Innovation: Technology, Market, and Complexity**, Vol. 5, Issue 1, 2019, pp. 1-17.

Alumni Segmenting for Fostering Innovation and Entrepreneurship in Universities

Anita STRAUJUMA
Researcher, Faculty of Engineering Economics and Management of Riga Technical University
Kalnciema 6, Riga, LV1048, Latvia

Elina GAILE-SARKANE
Professor, Faculty of Engineering Economics and Management of Riga Technical University
Kalnciema 6, Riga, LV1048, Latvia

Modris OZOLINS
Researcher, Faculty of Engineering Economics and Management of Riga Technical University
Kalnciema 6, Riga, LV1048, Latvia

ABSTRACT

This research describes principles of alumni segmenting that foster innovation and entrepreneurship in universities (further HERI (Higher Education and Research Institutions)). It is based on previous research, which describes that among many other ways of mutual interaction, all alumni are university lifetime customers [41]. Customers have very important role in fostering organization's innovation capacity – for a sustainable advancement organizations must manage knowledge to, from and about customers [15]. Customer engagement requires deep knowledge and vision on advancement of customers from initial involvement to a deeper and more meaningful cooperation which involves co-creation and innovation that set the base for entrepreneurship in HERI. Article describes the case of Riga Technical University how alumni engagement has resulted in various organizational developments that support innovations and entrepreneurship.

Keywords: alumni relations, alumni segmenting, customer segmenting, kay account management.

1. INTRODUCTION

Customer segmentation divides customers in groups that have similar needs, resources and interests in relation to a particular product or service. Segmentation is central concept within marketing and organizations use segmentation to better respond to customer needs increase their satisfaction [7, 13, 19, 22, 23]. "Customer needs are desires, wants, or cravings that can be satisfied by means of the attributes or characteristics of a product – a good or service" [18]. Customer segmentation is typically described by marketing-driven demographic groups that are derived by making surveys on a significant part of customer base to learn about their lifestyle, needs, preferences, behavior, values, living standards etc.. Based on this research, number of segments are identified and organization customers are assigned to respective segments [5, 19]. There are some general concepts of customer segmentation but in particular industries, the segmentation can become very specific. Alumni segmentation in HERI is an important tool to reach the goals of alumni relations and there are different approaches according to the goals, richness of available data and resources. Most of the research is connected to fundraising activities. Another type of engagement where alumni segmenting is often studied is mentoring. Grouping alumni into particular categories that share similar

characteristics helps to gain greater mutual understanding and improve organization's needs to serve the alumni better and to foster their positive and accumulative engagement with the university.

Key account management (KAM) is a field of research, investigating and designing techniques for better relationships with most valuable customers of the organizations. Those customers that are vital for the existence of this organization – losing them would mean getting into serious difficulties. This research paper regards HERI alumni as lifetime customers [41] and applies key account management principles in alumni segmenting to provide long-term alumni engagement in HERI for fostering the innovation.

2. CUSTOMER SEGMENTATION IN KEY ACCOUNT MANAGEMENT

The foundation and core for KAM activities is selecting the right customers [25, 27, 29, 33, 34].

Table 1 Categorizing key customers. Adopted from [27]

	Star	Strategic	Status	Streamline
Description	Strategic customers of the future	The most innovative and important prospects	Strategic customers of the past	Customers who constantly query the price, negotiate on everything
Attractiveness	High	High	Low	Low
Relative business strength now	Low	High	High	Low
Life cycle stage	Start-up/development	Deep, close relat.	Maturing	Mature
Strategic approach	Invest for growth	Strategic investment	Proactive support	Manage for cash

At first, the task seems to be trivial and straight connected to the financial gains. However, the KAM is about strategic decisions – aligning choice of strategic customers to the strategy of the organization. And that is not always reflected directly in short term financial results [27] . KAM requires clear customer segmenting rules that support the long-term strategic goals. It must be taken into account that the term relationship is by a definition a two-way road thus the selection of key customers also involves their perception of the organization. This approach divides the key customers into four segments: Star, strategic, status and streamline key customers (see Table 1.).

3. ALUMNI SEGMENTATION

Most common and basic segmentation of alumni is according to their age and study field. The deeper analysis helps to discover and exploit coherence between alumni personal attributes and experience [42]. Such as finite-mixture model framework based on monetary value of annual contributions [4;8] or mixture of demographic and involvement attributes [10].

There are several other approaches how universities segment alumni – by level of their engagement, by gender, ethnicity, year of graduation etc. – the method is chosen in relation to the planned activities and services (alumni relations, career, mentoring, fundraising) [2;6;36;37].

In typical university structure, alumni relations go hand in hand with fundraising activities although it varies – some institutions merge the functions but some keep them separate advocating "first friendrising, then fundraising" principle. Mentoring function also varies in university structures – sometimes it is a task of career center, often it is one of alumni relations functions. However, these three activities that are connected to alumni are being studied separately or interdependently. Table 1 summarizes how different fields of research that are connected to alumni relations segment alumni – e.g. research articles on fundraising describe alumni segmentation according to gender, religious beliefs, age, etc. At the same time research articles by different authors on mentoring do not describe gender or religious beliefs segmenting but rather age, study field, career stage, etc..

Table 1 Alumni segmentation attributes, research and fields of application (F- Fundrising, AR - Alumni Relations, M - Mentoring) (developed by authors)

Segmentation attribute	Research	F	AR	M
Gender	[3, 39]	X	X	
Religious beliefs	[44]	X		
Age	[3, 16, 31, 39]	X	X	X
Study field	(Durango-Cohen, Torres and Durango-cohen, 2013)	X	X	X
Graduation year (era)	[9]	X	X	
Career stage	[38]	X	X	X
Satisfaction with study experience	[1, 35, 42]	X	X	
Motivation	[40]	X	X	X
Level of involvement/ engagement (champions, friends, acquaintances)	[9, 43, 44]	X	X	X
Financial contribution	[4, 9, 16]	X		
Alumni (family) revenue data	[1]	X		
Needs and interests	[28]	X	X	X
Overall civic engagement	[17, 30, 39, 42]	X	X	X
menting looking at dynamics:				
Annual contributions patterns over the years	[8, 9]	X		
Mixture of demographic and involvement attributes	[10, 14]	X	X	X

Few authors review segmentation according to the level of activity. The basic division [32] describes four obvious levels: active contributors, non-contributors, potential contributor journeys, everyone else. A deeper analysis distributes types of activities and proves that groups of alumni have same engagement patterns as when they were students [42]. There is rare theoretic research on segmenting alumni according to their knowledge, talent or co-creation capacity. Some alumni mentoring program companies [20] advice to segment alumni in talent communities:

- New graduates & interns
- Future talent pools
- Critical & high potential talent
- Future women leaders
- High potential alumni
- Consulting alumni

Research of business organizations reviews customers' co-creation capacity [45]. Successful alumni segmenting sets a basis for further strategic engagement of alumni in HERI development. Necessity of alumni knowledge management (KM) is one of main alumni relations drivers besides the financial interests of HERI.

4. TRIPLE HELIX MODEL OF ALUMNI SEGMENTATION

The proposed method for alumni segmenting involves three components just like in geometric concept and triple helix model of innovation. The proposed components are:

1. Finances
2. Knowledge
3. Cocreation capacity

Just like in the long race for right DNA structures scientists have been discussing whether DNA is double or triple stranded and what impact is from triplex structures [21], universities continue to search for golden combination of alumni segmentation to make the relationship work with full potential. The typical segmentation of finances (fundraising) and knowledge (partly mentoring) needs the binding element – co-creation capacity.

In each segmentation component four subgroups emerge – streamline, status, star and strategic (Table 2). The concept is adapted from key account management. There the customers are segmented according to their attractiveness (Low/high) and organization's relative business strength as seen by the customer (low/high).

Table 2 Triple helix alumni segmentation in HERI (developed by authors)

Segm. levels	Description	Examples
Finance		
Streamline	Alumni, who constantly query the price, negotiate on everything. Want to see rapid return on investment. Manage for cash.	Alumni association member paying membership fees.
Status	Strategic alumni of the past. Mature relationship.	Alumni who have donated individually for university projects.
Star	Strategic alumni of the future. Relationship is just developing.	Alumni actively promoting university fundraising projects; owners of companies that are potential sponsors.
Strategic	High net worth alumni. The most innovative and important ones. Deep, close relationship.	Owner/CEO of large company regularly sponsoring strategic projects.
Knowledge		
Streamline	Alumni ready to cooperate on business basis, giving discounts or other favorable conditions.	Share experience in seminars, must be paid for that (gives discount); owners of training companies; consultants; experts.
Status	Strategic alumni of the past. Mature relationship.	Mentors; guest lecturers.
Star	Strategic alumni of the future. Relationship is just developing. Has needed expertise for common projects.	Publicly recognized opinion leader from industry
Strategic	The most innovative and important ones. Deep, close relationship. Common projects.	Scientist working in large company.
Cocreation capacity		
Streamline	Beneficiaries of alumni activities, interested to stay close to university	Active participant of alumni events.
Status	Strategic alumni of the past. Mature relationship.	Alumni association board member; lobby.
Star	Strategic alumni of the future. Relationship is just developing.	Publicly recognized opinion leader with a potential to promote higher education.
Strategic	The most innovative and important ones initiating and managing common projects.	Advisory board; involved in valorization.

Such segmentation helps alumni relations practitioners to engage alumni meaningfully according to their interests, resources and level of activity. An illustrative example of benefits for such engagement is as follows. Large university is not homogenous. It has complex structure and alumni have sometimes radically different interests and views. If alumni relations address all alumni without segmenting, those who are not interested in particular activities, evaluate alumni relations operations as unsuccessful and annoying and stop engaging and following alumni relations news. In addition, if there are some active alumni who would like to invest their time and finance and alumni relations do not offer them appropriate opportunities, they will find other organizations where to invest their energy and resources. Such Triple helix segmentation divides alumni in three strategically most important segments and additionally in each of these segments allows engaging alumni according to their level of activity. Alumni upgrade to next level of activity must be one of alumni relations deliberate tasks that must be carried out by recognizing alumni potential and offering alumni development opportunities. The triple helix alumni segmentation will set up basis for alumni knowledge management according to their engagement segment and level of activity.

5. IMPACT OF THE ALAUMNI TRIPLE HELIX MODEL ON FOSTERING INNOVATION AND ENTREPRENEURSHIP IN UNIVERSITIES

Riga Technical University (RTU) has undergone through dynamic changes during last 10 years. Adding valorization to the two existing main strategic pillars – research and education and turning towards the 3-rd generation university [46] to serve industry needs have been among them. Development of an appropriate innovation ecosystem have been acknowledged highly as one of the necessary pillars. In order to utilize alumni incentives in investing, knowledge sharing and co-creation, number of strategic activities have been launched by RTU.

In order to strengthen industry – academia links, and engage graduates into cooperation, Alumni relations have been identified as a vitally important strategic direction. As a result, RTU Alumni Association was established in 2012. In 2019 it was recognized as important player in fostering joint business – academia initiatives.

In 2013 RTU was evaluated by Institutional Evaluation Programme of European University Association. International experts highly recognized valorization initiatives of the university, as well as high recognition of university efforts by employers.

In order to 2016 the RTU Design Factory (DF) was opened as a co-creation space where creative ideas of scientists and students, turn into prototypes, which later become products and enter the market in collaboration with industry. Since that, RTU DF is serving as a hub for linking industry with academia and solving business challenges. University alumnus had supported development of the DF financially.

In 2019 a new for Latvia "Industrial Doctorate" cooperation initiative was launched as a joint incentive between Riga Technical university and LMT - a leading mobile telecommunications operator in Latvia, in order to develop pioneering solutions based on cutting-edge wireless technologies.

The different initiatives mentioned above served as alumni engagement instruments. They have resulted in strengthening university reputation. Since 2017 RTU have been included in the number of the leading international ratings like The Times Higher Education World University Rankings, QS World ranking and U-Multirank. (Table 3 and Table 4).

Table 3 QS and THE rankings (2019) of the leading Baltic technical universities

Universi-ties	Rankings			Scores of separate indicators (cooperation with industry)	
	QS World Ranking	Times Higher Edu-cation (THE) Rankings	QS Employ-ability Rankings	THE World Rankings - Industry Income (score)	QS World Rankings - Employer Reputation (score)
RTU	751-800	801-1000	301-500	50.7	23.9
VGTU*	581-590	-	301-500	-	36
KTU**	751-800	1000+	-	37.5	21.2
Taltech***	601-650	601-800	301-500	45.5	21.3

VGTU – Vilnius Gegiminas Technical University, Lithuania;
**KTU – Kaunas Technical University, Lithuania;*
***Talcech – Tallinn Technical University, Estonia*

RTU has the same overall QS World rank as KTU, which is not as high as for VGTU and Taltech, but what regards QS Employability ranking, all Baltic technical universities are ranked identically. If we compare Times Higher Education ranking, RTU is taking a place between Lithuanian and Estonian competitors. However, if we compare separate indicators characterizing cooperation with industry, RTU is taking the leading positions.

Table 4 U-Multirank (2018) of the leading Baltic technical universities

Univer-sities	Knowledge Transfer						Regional Engage ment
	Income from pri-vate sour-ces	Co-publi-cations with indus-trial part-ners	Patents awar-ded (size-norma-lized)	Indus-try co-patents	Spin-offs	Publi-cations cited in patents	Student intern-ships in the region
RTU	C*	C	C	E	A	D	B
VGTU	A	D	D	E	A	D	B
KTU	C	D	E	N/A**	A	D	B
Taltech	B	B	B	D	D	C	N/A

U-Multirank compares university performance across a range of different indicators grading them from "A" (very good) to "E" (weak)
** N/A - data not available*

Data in the Table 4 show that indicators, which are related to industry – academia cooperation, vary between countries. The weakest indicator for all the countries are issuing the joint patents. The number of spinoffs, which at certain extent characterize level of entrepreneurship, is showing the best performance in three of the universities compares.

Entrepreneurship refers to an individual's ability to turn ideas into action and is therefore a key competence for all, helping people to be more creative and self-confident in whatever they undertake [11]. Therefore, more and more countries acknowledge that entrepreneurship education should become a basic feature in education systems. The need to facilitate employability and new business creation is outlined in the Rethinking Education communication and the Entrepreneurship 2020 Action Plan by the European Commission [12]. To strengthen study process by creating entrepreneurship competences, RTU in cooperation with Rotterdam university of Applied Sciences in the Netherlands, South-Eastern Finland University of Applied Sciences in Finland and Anglia Ruskin University in UK is working on designing a new Product Development and Entrepreneurship study course for engineering students. The studies were performed as a part of ERASMUS+ KA2 project, to validate the theoretical detections EntreComp [26]: the Entrepreneurship Framework was set as a benchmark for emerging and demanded skills in the labour market (Lapina and Nikitina, 2019). Three focus groups that consisted of 5 start-up entrepreneurs, alumni of the universities were considered as an identification method to recognize the sets of knowledge, skills and competences for further analysis. Based on that the new upgraded entrepreneurship teaching methodology will be developed. Alumni groups of the partner institutions have already committed to contribute their expertise in designing the best possible methodology.

8. CONCLUSIONS

This work indicates value of alumni engagement in HERI activities. As alumni directly and indirectly are involved with HERI after they graduation, among other roles as investors, students and employers they are life-long customers. The research demonstrated that key account management principles can be applied in HERI alumni relations management. Authors applied key account management customer segmenting principles in development of new alumni segmenting model which takes into account not only alumni interests but also their capacity to engage with HERI. Alumni grouping into particular categories that share similar characteristics helps to engage them in sustainable way. It allows to approach them according to their interests and capabilities and upgrade their involvement from small interactions up to strategic involvement in HERI projects and decisions. Riga Technical University case demonstrates scale and diversity of alumni engagement for advanced innovations and entrepreneurship.

9. REFERENCES

[1] Baade, R. A. and Sundberg, J. O. (1996) 'What determines alumni generosity?', **Economics of Education Review**, 15(1), pp. 75–81. doi: 10.1016/0272-7757(95)00026-7.

[2] del Barrio-García, S. and Luque-Martínez, T. (2009) 'The value of client perceptions in university strategic planning: an empirical research study', **Industry and Higher Education,** 23(6), pp. 423–436. doi: 10.5367/000000009790156391.

[3] Belfield, C. R. and Beney, A. P. (2000) 'What Determines Alumni Generosity? Evidence for the UK', **Education Economics**, 8(1), pp. 65–80. doi: 10.1080/096452900110300.

[4] Le Blanc, L. A. and Rucks, C. T. (2009) 'Data mining of university philanthropic giving: Cluster-discriminant analysis and Pareto effects', **International Journal of Educational Advancement**. Palgrave Macmillan, 9(2), pp. 64–82. doi: 10.1057/ijea.2009.28.

[5] Böttcher, M. *et al.* (2009) 'Mining changing customer segments in dynamic markets', **Expert Systems with Applications**, 36(1), pp. 155–164. doi: 10.1016/j.eswa.2007.09.006.

[6] Chi, H., Jones, E. L. and Grandham, L. P. (2012) 'Enhancing mentoring between alumni and students via smart alumni system', **Procedia Computer Science. Elsevier Masson SAS**, 9, pp. 1390–1399. doi: 10.1016/j.procs.2012.04.153.

[7] Cuadros, A. J. and Domínguez, V. E. (2014) 'Customer segmentation model based on value generation for marketing strategies formulation', **Estudios Gerenciales**. Universidad ICESI, 30(130), pp. 25–30. doi: 10.1016/j.estger.2014.02.005.

[8] Durango-Cohen, E. J. and Balasubramanian, S. K. (2014) 'Effective Segmentation of University Alumni: Mining Contribution Data with Finite-Mixture Models', **Research in Higher Education**, 56(1), pp. 78–104. doi: 10.1007/s11162-014-9339-6.

[9] Durango-Cohen, E. J., Torres, R. L. and Durango-cohen, P. L. (2013) 'Donor Segmentation : When Summary Statistics Don ' t Tell the Whole Story', **Journal of Interactive Marketing**. Elsevier B.V., 27(3), pp. 172–184. doi: 10.1016/j.intmar.2013.04.002.

[10] Durango-Cohen, P. L., Durango-Cohen, E. J. and Torres, R. L. (2013) 'A Bernoulli-Gaussian mixture model of donation likelihood and monetary value: An application to alumni segmentation in a university setting', **Computers and Industrial Engineering**. Elsevier Ltd, 66(4), pp. 1085–1095. doi: 10.1016/j.cie.2013.08.007.

[11] EUR-LEx Publications Office (2007) **Promoting entrepreneurship in schools and universities**.

[12] Europäische Komission (2008) 'Entrepreneurship in higher education, especially within non-business studies', **Final Report of the Expert Group**, p. 10.

[13] Floh, A. *et al.* (2014) 'Customer segmentation using unobserved heterogeneity in the perceived-value-loyalty-intentions link', **Journal of Business Research**. Elsevier Inc., 67(5), pp. 974–982. doi: 10.1016/j.jbusres.2013.08.003.

[14] Gaier, S. (2005) 'Alumni satisfaction with their undergraduate academic experience and the impact on alumni giving and participation', **International Journal of Educational Advancement**, 5(4), pp. 279–288. doi: 10.1057/palgrave.ijea.2140220.

[15] Gebert, H. *et al.* (2003) 'Knowledge-enabled customer relationship management: integrating customer relationship management and knowledge management concepts', **Journal of Knowledge Management**. doi: 10.1108/13673270310505421.

[16] Grant, J. H. and Lindauer, D. L. (2014) '**The Economics of Charity Life-Cycle Patterns of Alumnae Contributions**', 12(2), pp. 129–141.

[17] Harrison, W. B., Mitchell, S. K. and Peterson, S. P. (1995) 'Alumni Donations and Colleges' Development Expenditures: Does Spending Matter?', **American Journal of Economics and Sociology**, 54(4), pp. 397–412. doi: 10.1111/j.1536-7150.1995.tb03243.x.

[18] Hill, C. W. L. and Jones, G. R. (2007) **Strategic management: An integrated approach, Strategic Management An Integrated Approach**.

[19] Hsu, F. M., Lu, L. P. and Lin, C. M. (2012) 'Segmenting customers by transaction data with concept hierarchy', **Expert Systems with Applications**. Elsevier Ltd, 39(6), pp. 6221–6228. doi: 10.1016/j.eswa.2011.12.005.

[20] Insala (2015) **How to Increase Alumni Engagement With Segmentation**. Available at: http://www.insala.com/Articles/how-to-increase-alumni-engagement-with-segmentation.asp (Accessed: 21 May 2019).

[21] Jain, A., Wang, G. and Vasquez, K. M. (2008) '**DNA triple helices: Biological consequences and therapeutic potential**', Biochimie, pp. 1117–1130. doi: 10.1016/j.biochi.2008.02.011.

[22] Jonker, J. J., Piersma, N. and Van Den Poel, D. (2004) 'Joint optimization of customer segmentation and marketing policy to maximize long-term profitability', **Expert Systems with Applications**, 27(2), pp. 159–168. doi: 10.1016/j.eswa.2004.01.010.

[23] Kim, S.-Y. *et al.* (2006) 'Customer segmentation and strategy development based on customer lifetime value: A case study', **Expert Systems with Applications**, 31(1), pp. 101–107. doi: 10.1016/j.eswa.2005.09.004.

[24] Lapina, I. and Nikitina, T. (2019) 'Today's Business and Entrepreneurship Development: Knowledge Dynamics and Competences of Managers and Entrepreneurs', in **IFKAD**.

[25] Laurin, E. (2017) **Box paradox: how key account management contributes to business model innovation**. Stockholm School of Economics.

[26] MCCALLUM, E. *et al.* (2018) **EntreComp into Action. Get Inspired. Make it Happen. A user guide to the European Entrepreneurship Competence Framework**. Luxembourg. Available at: https://ec.europa.eu/jrc/en/publication/eur-scientific-and-technical-research-reports/entrecomp-action-get-

inspired-make-it-happen-user-guide-european-entrepreneurship-competence.

[27] McDonald, M. and Woodburn, D. (2007) **Key Account Management. Second. Burlington**, USA: Elsevier.

[28] Meer, J. and Rosen, H. S. (2009) 'Altruism and the Child Cycle of Alumni Donations', **American Economic Journal: Economic Policy**, 1(1), pp. 258–286. doi: 10.1257/pol.1.1.258.

[29] Millman, T. F. (1996) 'Global key account management and systems selling', **International Business Review**, 5(6), pp. 631–645. doi: 10.1016/S0969-5931(96)00031-5.

[30] Monks, J. (2003) 'Patternss of giving to one's alma mater among young graduates from selective institutions', **Economics of Education Review**, 22(2), pp. 121–130. doi: 10.1016/S0272-7757(02)00036-5.

[31] Olsen, K., Smith, A. L. and Wunnava, P. V. (1989) 'An Empirical Study of the Life-Cycle Hypothesis with Respect to Alumni Donations', **The American Economist**, 33(2), pp. 60–63. doi: 10.1177/056943458903300207.

[32] Palmer, H. (2016) **SEGMENTATION AND JOURNEY PLANNING FOR UNIVERSITY ADVANCEMENT – A MODEL**. Available at: https://hollypalmerconsulting.com/2016/08/07/segmentation-and-journey-planning-for-university-advancement-a-model-part-1/ (Accessed: 21 May 2019).

[33] Pardo, C. (1997) 'Key account management in the business to business field: The key account's point of view', **Journal of Personal Selling and Sales Management**, 17(4), pp. 17–26. doi: 10.1080/08853134.1997.10754107.

[34] Pardo, C., Salle, R. and Spencer, R. (1995) 'The key accountization of the firm: A case study', **Industrial Marketing Management**, 24(2), pp. 123–134. doi: 10.1016/0019-8501(94)00039-Y.

[35] Pearson, J. (1999) 'Comprehensive Research on Alumni Relationships: Four Years of Market Research at Stanford University', **New Directions for Institutional Research**, 1999(101), pp. 5–21. doi: 10.1002/ir.10101.

[36] Rattanamethawong, N., Sinthupinyo, S. and Chandrachai, A. (2017) 'An innovation model of alumni relationship management: Alumni segmentation analysis', **Kasetsart Journal of Social Sciences.** Elsevier Ltd. doi: 10.1016/j.kjss.2017.02.002.

[37] Rattanamethawong, V., Sinthupinyo, S. and Chandrachai, E. A. (2015) 'An Innovation System that Can Quickly Responses to the Needs of Students and Alumni', **Procedia - Social and Behavioral Sciences**. Elsevier B.V., 182(182), pp. 645–652. doi: 10.1016/j.sbspro.2015.04.801.

[38] Rawski, M. J. (2011) '**The Seven Essentials of Highly Engaged Alumni**'.

[39] Ronca, J. M. (2014) 'Characteristics of Alumni Donors Who Volunteer at their Alma Mater Author (s): David J . Weerts and Justin M . Ronca Source : **Research in Higher Education** , Vol . 49 , No . 3 (May 2008), pp . 274-292 Published by : Springer Characteristics at their Al', 49(3), pp. 274–292.

[40] Schofield, P. and Fallon, P. (2012) 'Assessing the viability of university alumni as a repeat visitor market', **Tourism Management**, 33(6), pp. 1373–1384. doi: 10.1016/j.tourman.2011.12.021.

[41] Straujuma, A. and Gaile-Sarkane, E. (2018) 'ALUMNI KNOWLEDGE MANAGEMENT MODEL FOR SUSTAINABLE HIGHER EDUCATION AND RESEARCH INSTITUTION MANAGEMENT Methodology of Research Alumni – university customers', **Journal of Business Management**, 15(1691–5348), p. 77.-89. doi: https://doi.org/10.32025/RIS18011.

[42] Weerts, D. J. and Cabrera, A. F. (2017) 'Segmenting university alumni using a person-centered methodology', **International Journal of Nonprofit and Voluntary Sector Marketing**, 22(3), pp. 1–10. doi: 10.1002/nvsm.1577.

[43] Weerts, D. J., Cabrera, A. F. and Sanford, T. (2010) 'Beyond giving: Political advocacy and volunteer behaviors of public university alumni', **Research in Higher Education**, 51(4), pp. 346–365. doi: 10.1007/s11162-009-9158-3.

[44] Weerts, D. J. and Ronca, J. M. (2009) 'Using classification trees to predict alumni giving for higher education', **Education Economics**, 17(1), pp. 95–122. doi: 10.1080/09645290801976985.

[45] Windler, K. *et al.* (2017) 'Identifying the right solution customers: A managerial methodology', **Industrial Marketing Management**. Elsevier Inc., 60, pp. 173–186. doi: 10.1016/j.indmarman.2016.03.004.

[46] Wissema, J. G. (2009) 'Chapter 5: Technostarters', in **Towards the Third Generation University : Managing the University in Transition.**

Cognitive Cellular Automata for Image Segmentation:
A Social Learning Metaphor

Marco A. ALZATE
Universidad Distrital Francisco José de Caldas
Bogotá, Colombia

Marcela MEJIA
Universidad Militar Nueva Granada
Bogotá, Colombia

ABSTRACT

Cognitive agents have the ability to perceive their environment and act on it according to models of reality built through memory, intelligence and language. Interacting cognitive agents interchange information about their models in order to build a collective knowledge of their reality (social learning). In this paper we use this distributed cognitive system paradigm to solve a segmentation problem in image processing from the complex systems engineering approach. We build a cognitive cellular automata where each pixel in the image is a cognitive agent. Social learning is achieved by stigmergic and direct communication among agents. Our results outperform typical segmentation methodologies for granular material. Our social cognitive learning metaphor exemplifies a complex systems engineering approach for more general applications.

Keywords: social learning, image processing, cellular automata, granular material, political formation, nature/nurture.

1. INTRODUCTION

In recent decades, there has been an enriching feedback between Science and Engineering. On the one hand, engineering design processes have been inspired by biological, physical, psychological, ecological and sociological phenomena (among many others) to solve computationally difficult problems [1]. On the other hand, engineering experimentation with these inspired processes has shed some light on the explanation of the corresponding scientific phenomena [2]. Here we explore a potential similar synergistic relationship between neuropsychology, sociology and complex systems engineering, related to the design of distributed cognitive dynamic systems.

Psychology and neurology study the cognitive abilities of human beings, that is, the ability of man to perceive his environment and act on it according to mental models that arise from perception/action cycles mediated by memory, attention, intelligence and language [3]. Sociology studies the collective phenomena produced by human beings, that is, the behavior of human beings when they are living together in a shared habitat, giving rise to culture and history [4]. The complexity sciences study systems that exhibit emergency and self-organization, that is, systems composed of many parts that, when interacting, give rise to new macroscopic qualities of the system in the form of spontaneous structures, more as an effect of the interactions than an effect of the functional contribution of the parts [5]. There is no doubt, then, that neuropsychology, sociology and the engineering of complex systems have many pending dialogues.

Sociological phenomena arise from the interaction of human beings. Arguably, these phenomena are emergent characteristics produced by self-organization through cognitive interactions [6]. This idea can inspire engineering procedures for complex systems. Our purpose in this paper is to present a basic example of a distributed dynamic cognitive systems design, and to discuss it in the context of neuropsychology and sociology, as a social learning process among cognitive agents.

The engineering problem in question corresponds to the segmentation of a noisy pavement image into two classes of regions, asphalt and gravel (Figure 1) [7]. The social metaphor is the formation of liberal and conservative opinions as a society evolves from childhood to maturity. Each pixel is classified as gravel or asphalt like each individual in the society becomes liberal or conservative. Each pixel begins with an initial gray level, so that dark pixels are likely to become asphalt and light pixels are likely to become gravel. Similarly, there could be natural genetic conditions that make children likely to become liberals or conservatives. However, the local environment also determines how some dark pixels could belong to gravel areas and light pixels to asphalt regions, as family values, education and friends help to determine political tendencies of a teenager. Finally, a careful model based classification should help to refine the final decision of whether a pixel should be classified as gravel or asphalt, as mature citizens use more rational criteria and discussions with fellow citizens to decide a particular behavior.

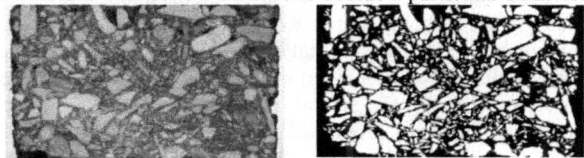

Figure 1. (a) Original pavement image. (b) Asphalt and gravel segmentation

This paper use the metaphor of political opinion formation to classify pixels in pavement images. Initially, the pixels are dark or light indicating some "childhood tendencies", although they are not very clear about their positions. Then, "teenager pixels" tend to get closer to similar pixels and to take distance from different pixels just by imitation of their closer friends, without too much communications nor rationalization. Finally, "mature pixels" build a model of their environment and interchange information among neighbor pixels in order to make a rational decision of its own classification as asphalt or gravel. We believe this process is close to that of liberal or conservative opinion formation in a society as its members grow nurturing from nature tendencies.

The paper is organized as follows. After this brief introduction, a first social learning approach to segmentation is presented in section 2. This approach leads to the cognitive cellular automata model presented in section 3. This model works in two phases: a "teenager" cellular automata in which each pixel tries to get closer to similar neighbor pixels and move away from different neighbor pixels (as presented in section 4), and a "mature" cellular automata where pixels interchange knowledge to decide their own class (as presented in section 5). Section 6 presents some results and section 7 conclude the paper.

2. SOCIAL COGNITIVE APPROACH

The gravel/asphalt image segmentation is not an easy problem. We built a simple drawing program to allow a human being to segment an image manually, so several graduate students tried to do it. The results are uncertain in the sense that different students obtained very different segmentations for the same image, and even the same student obtained different segmentations at different times for the same image. Anyway, this manual process, depicted in Figure 2, gives better results than common automatic segmentation procedures.

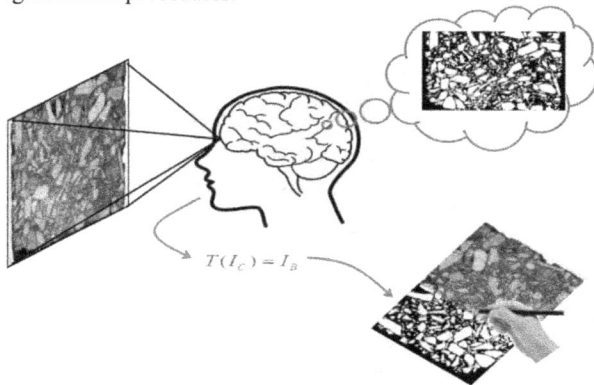

Figure 2. Manual segmentation of the images

We consider the graduate student is a cognitive system: She perceives the color image, I_C, and uses all her relevant knowledge acquired during her undergraduate studies in engineering and all her previous experience with similar problems in order to obtain a binary image, I_B, as a transformation of the original color image, $I_B = T(I_C)$. This mental binary model reflects her interpretation of the original color image, generating a sequence of actions to capture the mental image on the computer screen through the drawing program. This perception/action cycle, mediated by a mental model of reality, is what we call the cognitive process. The notorious differences among segmentations of the same image by different students show that the mental process through which action is decided from perception through intelligence, memory and attention can be very different from one student to another, although all of them are good segmentations (Figure 3).

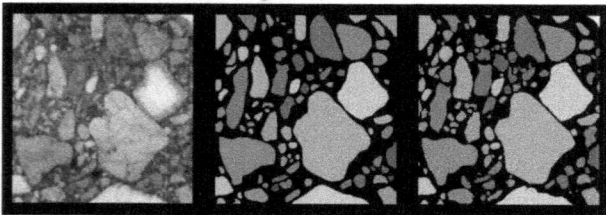

Figure 3. Different students produce different segmentations

Neuropsychology have taught us a lot about this internal decision process that controls the perception-action cycle [8]. The great neuroscientist J.Fuster considers it as a flow of information between the cognitive agent and its environment, from sensory organs to motor effectors that change the environment, which leads to new perceptions and new actions, until some goal is achieved [9]. Dr. Fuster finds that the perception/action cycle is physically represented by "cognits" (subnetworks of cortical neurons that are constructed during Hebbian learning, forming a hierarchical structure of perception/memory/action) [10]. This fundamental idea has inspired many engineers, as formalized in the work of Dr. Simon Haykin [11], to build the Theory of Dynamic Cognitive Systems. It uses statistical signal processing, stochastic control, information theory, statistical learning and game theory to simulate the cognitive abilities of the human being (perception, memory, attention, intelligence, language, action), according to neuroscience.

The fact that several students obtain very different segmentations for the same color image can be attributed to different reasons. For example, at the most basic perception, some students have better vision than others. More psychologically, different aspects of the image can be interesting to focus attention, so the student concentrates on some visual stimuli while ignores others (e.g., those more interested in plastic arts are more careful delineating the gravel). In the action part of the cycle, some students have better fine motor skill than others. The mood of the students also has a great influence. However, if they work on the images segmented by other students, the results tend to converge on a much more satisfying segmented image. The process is depicted in Figure 4. This leads us to the second theme of our approach: social learning.

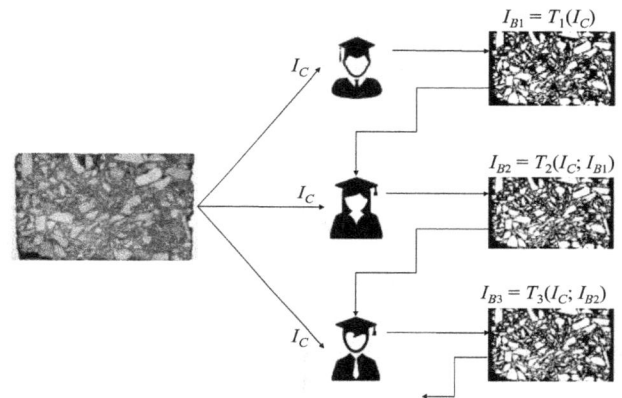

Figure 4. Social interaction for better segmentation

First, student 1 applies her own transformation T_1 to the original image I_C and obtains the first segmented image, I_{B1}. This segmented image is given to student 2, along with the original image I_C, in order for her to apply her own transformation T_2 and obtain the second estimation of the segmented image, I_{B2}. This process is repeated with several students, each generating a new segmented image form the original image and the segmented image of the previous student. At each iteration, the students not only add minute details, but also shrink or stretch some gravel, joint different gravels in a bigger one, separate a single gravel into two smaller ones, etc. Many times, they reverse the changes made on previous iterations by other students. Although there is not a final consensus on which is the correct segmentation, each iteration leads to a more acceptable segmentation, so students get more satisfied each time, as shown in the sequence of iterations of Figure 5.

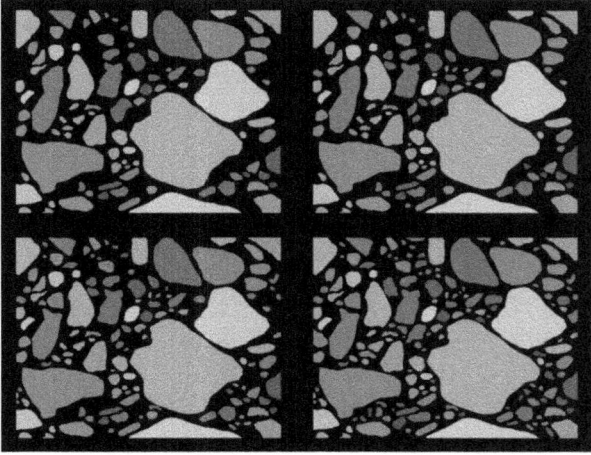

Figure 5. Segmentation refinement through social learning

Social psychology have taught us a lot about this social learning process that controls the distributed consensus among rational agents [12]. Recently, this kind of processes have attracted research interest in engineering for distributed estimation in sensor networks, consensus algorithms in robotic networks, distributed machine learning, synchronization in mobile ad hoc networks, cooperation emergence in cognitive radio networks, etc. [13] In particular, the topic of opinion dynamics over social networks, where agents can communicate only with a local group of agents, but beliefs are propagated through the network, is gaining more importance for its potential effects (good or bad) on democracy [14]. In our case, each student weights its own opinion on the correct segmentation with that of the previous student, which brings a summary of the opinions of all previous students. Presumably, the nth student builds the following estimation:

$$I_{Bn} = T_n(I_C; I_{Bn-1}) = I_{Bn-1} + A_n \cdot (T_n(I_C) - I_{Bn-1})$$

where A_n is a matrix of 0's and 1's, the same size as the image, choosing for each pixel her own independent classification, $T_n(I_C)$, or that of the previous estimation, I_{Bn-1}. Consensus is achieved if A_n tends to a zero matrix as n increases [15]. In our case, most students reach a zero matrix after a few iterations, but some of them keep making very small changes in conflictive regions of the image (although most entries of their matrices reaches the value zero).

In this paper we explore how social learning among distributed cognitive agents can lead to an acceptable solution to the difficult problem of gravel/asphalt segmentation in pavement images. Instead of human cognitive agents perceiving the image and acting on it, we consider each pixel in the image as a cell in a cellular automata that becomes the cognitive agent in the distributed learning system.

3. THE COGNITIVE AGENT AND ITS ENVIRONMENT

The agent is the pixel, a cell in a cellular automata, which can perceive and act on a small neighborhood of the image, an array of 31×31 pixels around it. Each element of the array (each pixel) can take a particular gray level value between 0 and 255. A pixel with a zero value is black, a pixel with a value 255 is white and other values correspond to intermediate gray levels between black and white. The cell agent compute a bit according to its 31×31 neighborhood, so that a new I_B image is built, in the same domain of I_G but with co-domain $\mathbb{Z}_2 = \{0, 1\}$, where the pixels in zero state correspond to asphalt and the pixels in state 1 correspond to gravel.

The agents have simple perception/action capabilities: They can perceive the gray value of each pixel in its 31×31 neighborhood and they can change their own gray value.

In order to decide what action to take, we consider the whole image as a society that evolves with time according to local social interactions among the members. A pixel being asphalt o gravel is like a person being liberal or conservative. In a first stage, the agents are not very clear about their positions, but they like to get closer to similar agents and to take distance from different agents, without too much communications nor rationalization, just by imitation of their closer friends. This way, they form a segregated society of teenagers with many tribes in a continuum of political positions, which are easy to discretize in a number of groups with some liberal or conservative tendencies.

In a second stage the agents get more rational (more mature?) and polarize the society into two types of pixels according to a more elaborated procedure: They communicate among them and evaluate the maximum-a-posteriori probability of being part of one group or another according to their perceptions, the communication with neighbor agents, their experience as teenagers, and their own believes. For this second stage, those agent that did make up their minds early in time become references for other doubtful agents in the rational stage.

4. A SOCIETY OF TEENAGERS

In the first stage, each agent considers the range of gray values within its neighborhood. If all of them are very similar, the agents moves to the average, wanting to belong. If there are significant differences, however, they timidly moves toward those a little bit closer to them. As this process is repeated in a cellular automata of local interactions, different tribes are formed. The algorithm is as follows.

Given the gray image in the neighborhood of an agent, I_G, it can compute the maximum, the minimum, the average and the range of the gray levels:

$$mx = \max_{(x,y)} I_G(x, y)$$
$$mn = \min_{(x,y)} I_G(x, y)$$
$$\mu = \frac{1}{N} \sum_{(x,y)} I_G(x, y)$$
$$r = (mx - mn) / mx$$

where (x,y) runs over all pixels in its neighborhood. The quantity r talks of the homogeneity (low r) or heterogeneity (high r) of the ideas in the neighborhood. If it is low, the agent wants to belong and changes its gray level closer to the mean:

$$I_G(x) \leftarrow r \cdot I_G(x) + (1-r) \cdot \mu$$

The lower r, the closer the agent gets to the mean in a single step. If r is high, there are different ideas in the neighborhood and the agents gets closer to the people that enforce its own ideas:

$$I_G(x) \leftarrow \begin{cases} r \cdot mn + (1-r) \cdot I_G(x) & \text{if } I_G(x) < \mu \\ r \cdot mx + (1-r) \cdot I_G(x) & \text{if } I_G(x) \geq \mu \end{cases}$$

The higher r, the closer the agent gets to the corresponding local extreme in a single step. Figure 6 shows a sequence of interactions of this cellular automata in a profile of pixels. Sharp transitions are emphasized and small transitions are smoothed out, discriminating among local peaks and valleys of gray intensity, as local tribes for teenagers to hang out with.

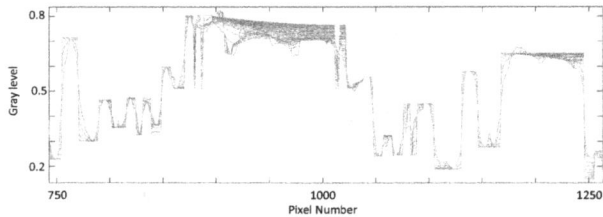

Figure 6. Iteration of the simple cellular automata "Look like my group and differentiate myself from other groups"

Figure 7 shows an image and the result after the initial "teenagers" cellular automata. Conservative agents are clearly defined as deep dark pixels but there is a huge range of liberal agents that go from dark to light distributed in more or less irregular groups.

Figure 7. Results after the initial "teenagers" cellular automata

To help them take a decision, we use local Otsu thresholding, add regional maxima and then apply simple image opening. The centers of dilated local maxima of the distance to zero transform shows regions of liberal concentration, true gravel. We chose circles around those points with the distance to nearest zero as the radio, and make those circles grow over the binarized image in order to determine true gravel regions. Similarly, we use the complements to determine true asphalt regions. The rest of the image are those agents that did not take a final decision during its youth, so they will make up their minds at a mature age, in the next stage of the society.

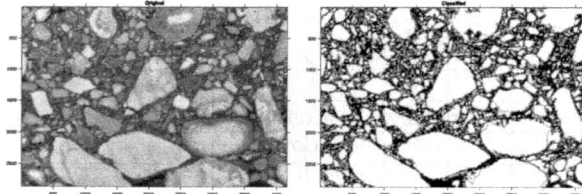

Figure 8. Classification of the pixels in three states

5. A Society of mature agents

A mature agent recognizes that his own class is a matter of probabilities. Indeed, for a given image processed in the teenager society, it is easy to estimate the gray level distribution for each class of pixel. Figure 9 shows the distribution corresponding to Figure 8.

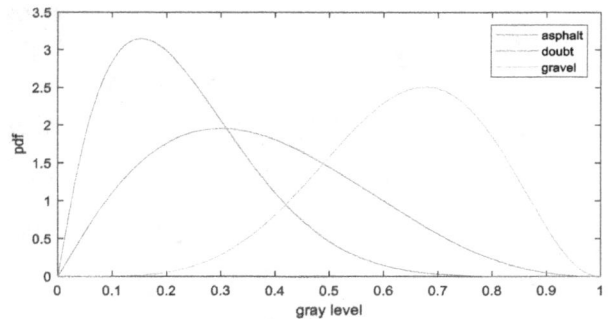

Figure 9. Global distribution of the gray level for each class of pixels

Figure 9 also shows that its own gray level is not enough criteria for an agent to decide its class, so it needs to develop better cognitive capabilities:

Perception: Each agent is capable of perceiving the state of each pixel in its 31×31 neighborhood.

Attention: Among this 961 observed values, each agent pays more attention to closer data as it computes a 21-dim vector of features: its own gray level, the mean, standard deviation, maximum and minimum in a 3×3 neighborhood, the mean, standard deviation, maximum and minimum in a 7×7 neighborhood, the mean, standard deviation, maximum and minimum in a 15×15 neighborhood, and the mean, standard deviation, maximum and minimum in a 31×31 neighborhood. These features of the neighborhood form a vector $\underline{d} \in \mathbb{R}^{17}$, which becomes the state of the agent, as it represents the perceived and processed information. However, since this data is highly redundant, each agent extracts the three principal components, giving a 3-dimensional state vector (Figure 10).

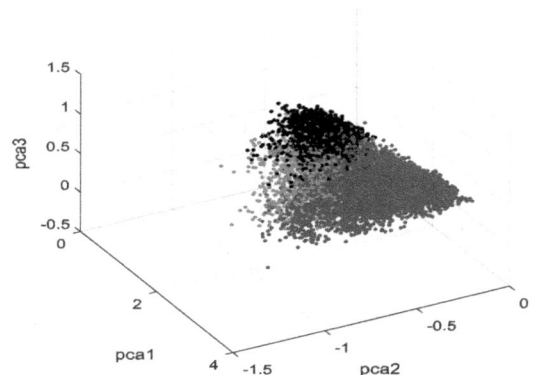

Figure 10. Three principal components of the 21-dim feature vector

Intelligence: Besides being able to compute its vector state form the perceived pixel values, the agent keeps a model of the world to help it understand its perception and decide how to act in its world. The world is interpreted as a mixture of Gaussians, where the state $\underline{d}$ obey to one of two different Gaussian distributions, one for asphalt pixels with mean vector $\underline{\mu}_a$ and covariance matrix Σ_a, and another one for gravel pixels with mean vector $\underline{\mu}_g$ and covariance matrix Σ_g. The iterative estimation of these parameters is the individual learning process that leads to social learning and the emergency of an acceptable segmentation. The agent is rational in the sense that, given the perceptions, it tries to maximize the likelihood by adapting its beliefs.

Memory: Each agent keeps track of its world model through the parameters $\underline{\mu}_a$, Σ_a, $\underline{\mu}_g$ and Σ_g. Indeed, these parameters are the code that summarizes what the agent has learned so far.

Action: Each agent is capable of increasing or decreasing its own gray level according to its perceptions and its model of the world. At the nth iteration, it computes its probability of being gravel, $p_g(n)$, and adds to its own gray level the quantity $\beta_n \cdot (p_g(n)\text{-}0.5)$, where β_n is a learning rate parameter that decreases with time. By changing their gray value, agents act on its world according to their beliefs.

Language: The agents communicate indirectly among them stigmergically through their own action, since increasing or decreasing its gray level affects the environment (the perceptions) of the neighbor agents. But they also are capable of communicating their own state to each of its 31×31 neighbors in a single broadcast message. This is a local communication capability for a limited amount of information (that required to compute the next estimate of $\underline{\mu}_g$, $\underline{\mu}_a$, Σ_g, Σ_a and a_g). However, this iterated interaction eventually propagates the information over the whole image, given rise to the emergent segmentation of gravel and asphalt.

Now we describe the probabilistic rational behavior of the agents according to their cognitive capabilities. On the space of $N = 3$ principal components, the agents use a Gaussian mixture model (GMM). The fundamental idea is to assume that the probability density function of the features has the following form:

$$f\left(\underline{d}\middle|\underline{\mu}_a,\Sigma_a,\underline{\mu}_g,\Sigma_g,a_g\right) = a_g f_g\left(\underline{d}\middle|\underline{\mu}_g,\Sigma_g\right) + (1-a_g) f_a\left(\underline{d}\middle|\underline{\mu}_a,\Sigma_a\right)$$

where $\underline{d} \in \mathbb{R}^3$ is the vector of principal components and

$$0 \le a_g \le 1$$

$$f_g\left(\underline{d}\middle|\underline{\mu}_g,\Sigma_g\right) = \frac{1}{\sqrt{(2\pi)^N |\Sigma_g|}} \exp\left(-\frac{1}{2}\left(\underline{d}-\underline{\mu}_g\right)^T \Sigma_g^{-1}\left(\underline{d}-\underline{\mu}_g\right)\right)$$

$$f_a\left(\underline{d}\middle|\underline{\mu}_a,\Sigma_a\right) = \frac{1}{\sqrt{(2\pi)^N |\Sigma_a|}} \exp\left(-\frac{1}{2}\left(\underline{d}-\underline{\mu}_a\right)^T \Sigma_a^{-1}\left(\underline{d}-\underline{\mu}_a\right)\right)$$

$\underline{\mu}_g$ and $\underline{\mu}_a$ are also vectors in $\mathbb{R}^3$ that correspond to the expected values of the features in the gravel and asphalt pixels, respectively. Σ_g and Σ_a are matrices in $\mathbb{R}^{3\times3}$ that correspond to the correlation matrices of the features for the asphalt and gravel pixels, respectively. The agent estimates $\underline{\mu}_g$, $\underline{\mu}_a$, Σ_g, Σ_a and a_g through a simple procedure: The 31×31 neighborhood is segmented into a binary image I_S through teenager cellular automata, and the estimations are obtained averaging over each kind of pixel:

$$a_g = \frac{1}{N_P} \sum_{(x,y)} I_S(x,y)$$

$$\mu_g = \frac{1}{N_P \cdot a_g} \sum_{(x,y)} I_S(x,y)\underline{d}(x,y)$$

$$\mu_a = \frac{1}{N_P \cdot (1-a_g)} \sum_{(x,y)} \left(1-I_S(x,y)\right)\underline{d}(x,y)$$

$$\Sigma_g = \frac{1}{N_P \cdot a_g} \sum_{(x,y)} \left(\underline{d}(x,y)-\mu_g\right)\cdot\left(\underline{d}(x,y)-\mu_g\right)^T I_S(x,y)$$

$$\Sigma_a = \frac{1}{N_P \cdot (1-a_g)} \sum_{(x,y)} \left(\underline{d}(x,y)-\mu_a\right)\cdot\left(\underline{d}(x,y)-\mu_a\right)^T \left(1-I_S(x,y)\right)$$

where $N_P = 961$ is the total number of pixels in the neighborhood,

(x,y) runs over the 31×31 neighborhood, and $\underline{d}(x,y)$ is the state of the cell in the position (x,y) of the neighborhood. Based on these estimates of $\underline{\mu}_g$, $\underline{\mu}_a$, Σ_g, Σ_a and a_g, the cell computes the probability of being gravel for each neighbor pixel using Bayes' rule:

$$P\left(G\middle|\underline{d}(x,y)\right) = \frac{a_g f_g\left(\underline{d}(x,y)\middle|\mu_g,\Sigma_g\right)}{a_g f_g\left(\underline{d}(x,y)\middle|\mu_g,\Sigma_g\right) + (1-a_g) f_a\left(\underline{d}(x,y)\middle|\mu_a,\Sigma_a\right)} \quad (1)$$

where (x,y) runs over all pixels in its neighborhood. This probability goes through one step of refinement for re-estimating the parameters:

$$a_g = \frac{1}{N_P} \sum_{(x,y)} P\left(G\middle|\underline{d}(x,y)\right)$$

$$\mu_g = \frac{1}{N_P \cdot a_g} \sum_{(x,y)} \underline{d}(x,y) P\left(G\middle|\underline{d}(x,y)\right)$$

$$\mu_a = \frac{1}{N_P \cdot (1-a_g)} \sum_{(x,y)} \underline{d}(x,y)\left(1-P\left(G\middle|\underline{d}(x,y)\right)\right)$$

$$\Sigma_g = \frac{1}{N_P \cdot a_g} \sum_{(x,y)} \left(\underline{d}(x,y)-\mu_g\right)\cdot\left(\underline{d}(x,y)-\mu_g\right)^T P\left(G\middle|\underline{d}(x,y)\right)$$

$$\Sigma_a = \frac{1}{NP \cdot (1-a_g)} \sum_{(x,y)} \left(\underline{d}(x,y)-\mu_a\right)\cdot\left(\underline{d}(x,y)-\mu_a\right)^T \left(1-P\left(G\middle|\underline{d}(x,y)\right)\right)$$

Finally, these new parameters are used to re-estimate the probability of the pixel to be gravel, as in equation (1). This is just one step of the EM algorithm [16], but the agent does not iterate it until convergence, because this is simply an intermediate opinion to be shared with the neighborhood, in order to emerge a global opinion, the segmented image. Indeed, this probability represents the belief of the agent about its own classification. It tries to enforce this belief on its neighborhood by adding to its own gray level the quantity $\beta \cdot (P(G|\underline{d}(x,y))\text{-}0.5)$, where β is a learning rate parameter that can be decremented with time.

This process completes the perception/action cycle of each cognitive agent, which becomes a single step of the mature cellular automata. This cellular automata algorithm is repeated until convergence. Then, as the last step, we repeat the post-processing of the teenager cellular automata: local Otsu thresholding, regional maxima, image opening, distance transform, and region growing.

6. SEGMENTATION RESULTS

Figure 11 shows the evolution of $P(G|\underline{d}(x,y))$, the local probability of each pixel to be gravel, during 15 steps of the cellular automata, which bring the automata close to equilibrium. Once the pixels have agreed on the probability of being gravel, the simple post-processing is performed, leading to the result shown in Figure 12.

We have used several segmentation methods, not pretending to be exhaustive, but only to have something to compare with. As shown in Figure 13, we use an adaptive Otsu's method, a k-means approach with the same parameters in $\mathbb{R}^{17}$, a neural network with these 17 inputs trained with the manually segmented images, and a GMM/EM method. Recently we submitted a paper with a "committee of experts" method in which the four methods of Figure 13 are added and post-processed with several heuristics [18]. Classification results are not as satisfactory as those of the two phase cellular automata, and time processing is several times bigger than that of the two phase cellular automata.

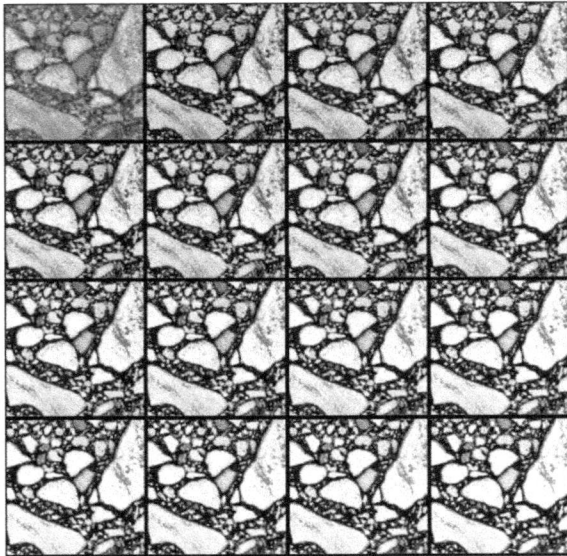

Figure 11. Evolution of social learning among cognitive agents

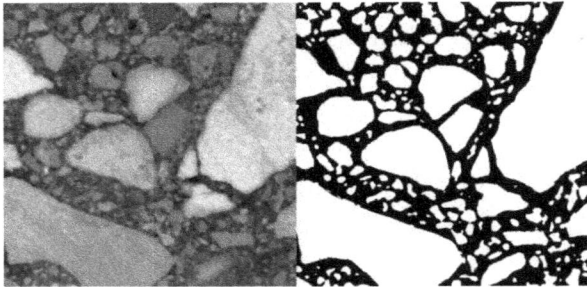

Figure 12. Final classification through cognitive social learning cellular automata

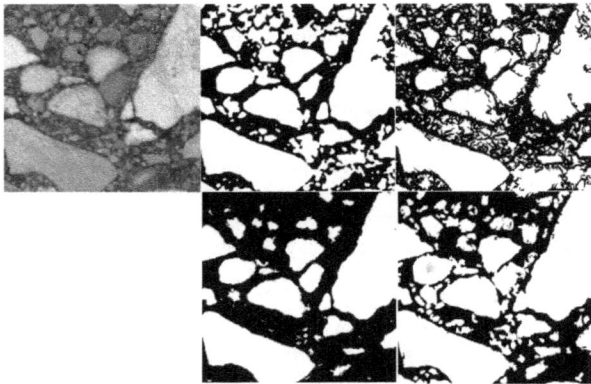

Figure 13. Segmentation by (a) adaptive Otsu, (b) 2-means on $\mathbb{R}^3$, (c) Neural network and (d) GMM/EM

As a final comparison, when the iteration with several graduate students starts with the output of the cognitive social learning cellular automata, the number of iterations and modifications is drastically reduced: The performance of our cognitive classifier got close to the human classifier.

7. CONCLUSIONS

Cognitive cellular automata is an interesting approach to complex systems engineering, since it can be applied as a mathematical model of a great number of complex systems in science and engineering. In this paper we used a simple model of social learning and opinion formation as an inspiration for granular segmentation. Using two stages of cognitive cellular automata, one resembling teenager's tribe formation and another resembling mature opinion formation, we obtained a good asphalt/gravel classifier in pavement images. The results are better than traditional segmentation algorithms and the method requires less computation time. As a future work, we will consider opinion changes, so that we can track variations of class in dynamical distributed systems. Such changes could be used as inspiration for many engineering problems, such as collaborative access in cognitive radio networks.

The authors would like to thank Dr. Oscar Javier Reyes, from the Geotecnica research group at Universidad Militar, for all the technical support he gave us during the elaboration of this research project.

8. REFERENCES

[1] J. C. Wooley and H. S. Lin, "Catalyzing Inquiry at the Interface of Computing and Biology", National Research Council, 2006.

[2] L. Pasotti and S. Zucca, "Advances and Computational Tools towards Predictable Design in Biological Engineering". Computational and Mathematical Methods in Medicine. 2014: pp. 1–16.

[3] J. M. Fuster, "The cognit: A network model of cortical representation", International Journal of Psychophysiology Vol. 60, No. 2, May 2006, pp. 125–132

[4] A. Bandura, "A social cognitive theory of personality". In L. Pervin (Ed.), "Handbook of personality" 2nd ed., pp. 154-196. Guilford Publications, New York, 1999.

[5] P. Érdi, "Complexity Explained", Springer-Verlag, Heidelberg, 2008.

[6] T. S. Smith and G. T. Stevens, "Emergence, Self-Organization, and Social Interaction: Arousal-Dependent Structure in Social Systems", Sociological Theory, Vol. 14, No. 2, 1996, pp. 131-153.

[7] A. Mejía, O. Reyes, J. Useche, "Técnicas de Inteligencia Artificial Utilizadas en el Procesamiento de Imágenes y su Aplicación en el Análisis de Pavimentos". Revista de la Escuela de Ingeniería de Antioquia, Vol 16, pp. 189-207, 2019

[8] R.B.Mars, J.Sallet, M.F.Rushworth, and N.Yeung, "Neural Basis of Motivational and Cognitive Control", MIT Press, Cambridge, 2011

[9] J.M.Fuster, "Upper processing stages of the perception-action cycle" TICS Vol 8, No. 4, pp. 143-145

[10] J.M.Fuster, "Prefrontal Cortex in Decision-Making: The Perception-Action Cycle", In book: Decision Neuroscience an Integrative Perspective (Chapter 8), Academic Press, London, 2016.

[11] S. Haykin, "Cognitive Dynamic Systems", Cambridge University Press, 2012.

[12] A. McAlister, C. A Perry and G. Parcel, "How Individuals, Environments, and Health Behaviors Interact: Social Cognitive Theory". Health Behavior and Health Education:

Multi-parametric Earthquake Forecasting the New Madrid
From Electromagnetic Coupling between Solar Corona and Earth System Precursors

Disclosure: An expanded version of this paper was previously published in New Concepts in Global Tectonics Journal, v. 7, no. 1, pp. 3-25, March. 2019 http://users.neo.registeredsite.com/3/4/0/21850043/assets/NCGTJV7N1S.pdf

by
Bruce Leybourne, Ms., IEVPC – CEO, Sebastian, Florida, USA
Valentino Straser, Department of Science and Environment, UPKL Brussels
Hong-Chun Wu, Institute of Labor Occupational Safety and Health, Formosa Scientific Center, Taiwan
Giovanni Gregori, PhD., Professor, Istituto di Acustica e Sensoristica O. M. Corbino (INM-CNR), Roma, Italy
Arun Bapat, PhD. Former Head Earthquake Engineering - Central Water and Power Research Station (CWPRS), Pune, India
Natarajan Venkatanathan, PhD., Electrical and Electronics Engineering, SASTRA University, Thanjavur, Tamil Nadu, India
Louis Hissink, Research Director-IEVPC, Chief Editor-NCGT Journal, NSW, Australia

Acknowledgement: In recognition of Dr. Dong Choi's tenacious research as past Director of International Earthquake and Volcano Prediction Center (IEVPC) and from his persistent efforts as Chief Editor of New Concepts in Global Tectonics (NCGT) Journal toward the goals of this paper we honor his memory by including him as an honorary Co-Author posthumously.

ABSTRACT

Forecasting large earthquakes M ≥ 6.0 with satellite monitoring and Radio Direction Finding techniques of Electro-Magnetic (EM) precursors associated with earthquakes are possible. International Earthquake and Volcano Prediction Center (www.ievpc.org) consider phenomena driving earthquakes within a framework of strong solar EM coupling with the entire Earth system, through EM induction driving ionosphere-air-earth currents. Catastrophic earthquakes have repeatedly stricken the New Madrid Seismic Zone during the last 4 major solar hibernation cycles since 1400 AD. Research suggests another cycle of strong magnitude 6.0 to 8.0 earthquakes in the New Madrid region during the upcoming (~2021-2057), solar minimum period. The 1811–12 earthquakes, occurred in the midst of Dalton Solar Minimum (1793-1830), causing many types of ground failures including lateral spreading and ground subsidence by soil liquefaction across the Mississippi River flood plain and tributaries over 15,000km². Studies by USGS and damage assessments by FEMA estimate damages to infrastructure approaching $600 billion. Common denominators between seismic precursors associated with a solar EM driver are found by analyzing data on ionization phenomena in areas under tectonic stress such as: Outgoing Long-wave Radiation (OLR); Total Electron Content (TEC); atmospheric effects, such as Jet Stream and other meteorological phenomena related to earthquake clouds and lights.

Keywords: *Earthquake Forecasting, Radio Direction Finding, Solar EM Coupling, Solar Minimum/Hibernation, New Madrid Seismic Zone, Seismic Precursors, Stellar Transformer, Outgoing Long-wave Radiation, Total Electron Content, Jet Stream Precursors, Earthquake Clouds and Lights.*

1. RECURRING NEW MADRID EARTHQUAKES

Historic New Madrid earthquakes have occurred during every solar minimum, four in a row, since 1400 AD (Fig. 1). And catastrophic New Madrid earthquakes such as occurred in 1811–1812 were associated with the Dalton Minimum affected the larger New Madrid Seismic Zone (Fig. 1 & 2). Understanding the common denominator between analyzed seismic precursors with an associated solar EM driver should be of major concern.

Studies by USGS and damage assessments by FEMA within the past decade estimate damages to infrastructure within the New Madrid Seismic Zone approaching over $600 billion worth of damage [1].

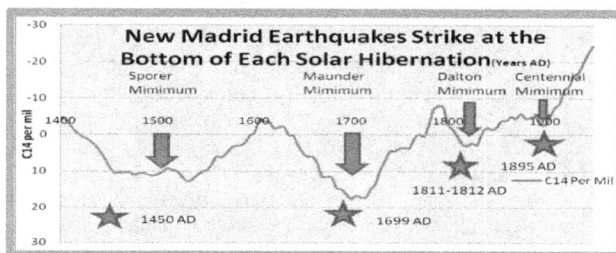

Fig. 1. Solar Activity Deduced from C¹⁴ Proxy Variation. History of New Madrid earthquakes compared to solar minimums or "solar hibernations" from 1400-1950 AD. Major New Madrid earthquakes as red stars. Source: [2] Data: [3].

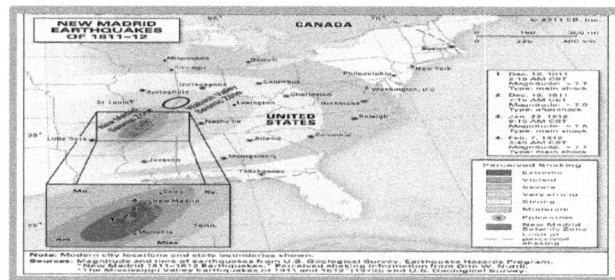

Fig. 2. New Madrid Seismic Zone (NMSZ) earthquakes of 1811-12. Base map cited from Encyclopedia Britannica, Inc. Wabash Valley Seismic Zone is added [4].

2. SOLAR RELATIONSHIPS

Historic records comparing earthquake to solar cycles (Fig. 3) show convincingly an increase in quake and volcanic activities during the solar low cycles throughout the globe [5]. The solar cycles linked to this anti-correlation are theoretically caused by solar induction cycle variations of magnetic fields among celestial bodies within our solar system. When the induction cycles are interrupted during disruptive solar events, violent internal discharges can occur within our planet resulting in large magnitude earthquakes, mentally conceptualized as lightning from below. This is feasibly explained by Gregori [6], who attributed to the Earth's core being a leaky capacitor or a battery; when solar activity is high, the Earth's core is charged, whereas when the Sun's activity is in low phase, the core in turn discharges energy.

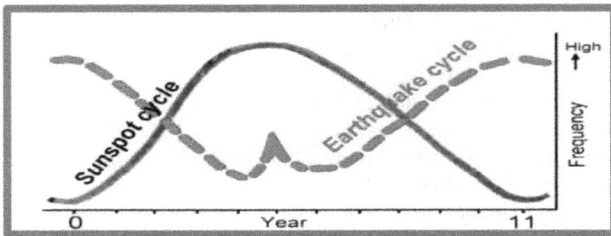

Fig. 3. Anti-correlation between the solar and earthquake cycles [5].

IEVPC understands and monitors precursor signals associated with these disruptive solar events, and on this basis has developed innovative methods of earthquake forecasting. Based on the next arrival of a major prolonged solar low or solar hibernation cycle, which may last until 2050 AD or more. Another series of large earthquakes are expected to strike the New Madrid region [2]. It has also been found that seismic energy transmigrates northward synchronized with the recent accelerated north magnetic polar movement during the declining solar cycle in the Central America-Caribbean area [4] (Fig. 4). This is confirmed by sudden increased earthquake activity since 1990 when the solar cycle 22 peaked and a longer solar cycle started, which includes the 11-year solar cycles 23, 24 and likely 25 and 26. Increased energy inputs from the southern hemisphere expand northward as explained from the mid-ocean ridge coupling to ridges encircling Antarctic (increased radial induction) with increased space weather events as explained by Stellar Transformer concepts [7]. A combination of these facts may well explain the historic devastating New Madrid earthquakes that occurred during every solar minimum, four in a row, since 1400 AD.

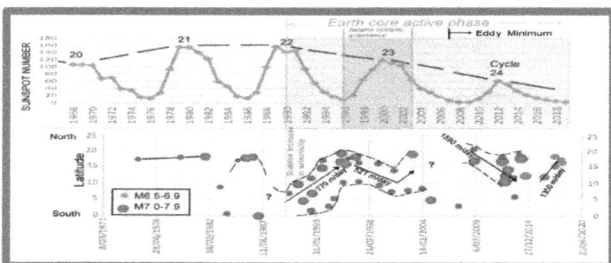

Fig. 4. Solar cycles and earthquake propagation trend in Central American Pacific coast [4.] Note a general trend when earthquakes move northward as the solar cycle is in decline, but southward when the solar cycle rises.

The *Stellar Transformer Concept* [7] contends that simple step down energy induction occurs between Sun and Earth, much like the transformer process that steps down your household energy from higher voltage transmission lines sourced from the power company. The Sun would represent a large coil from the power company, while the Earth represents the smaller coil to your home. The larger coil element generally excites current into the smaller coil element by induction of step down energy. Layers within the Earth hold and release charge acting as

condensers, or capacitance layers. To simplifiy understanding of the relationships, solar coronal holes aligned with the Sun's north-south polar axis can be considered as axial induction elements, while those aligned with the equator are considered radial induction elements. These dark coronal holes on the Sun represent the induction current elements of our *Solar Stellar Transformer* (Fig. 5), charging/discharging the Sun from elements within the arm of our spiral galaxy and thereby the Solar System including Earth, via electro-magnetic wavelength and frequency response, in an Electric Universe framework [8].

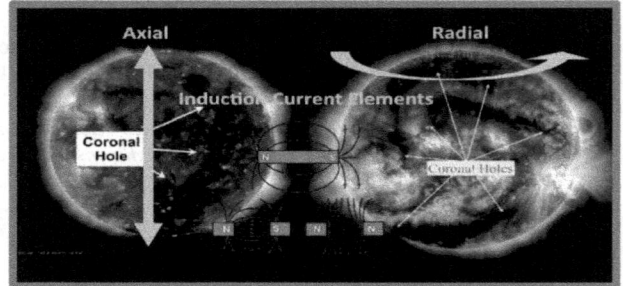

Fig. 5. Solar Stellar Transformer Induction Current Elements Coronal holes express induction elements in axial vs. radial orientations determining axial vs. radial affects on Earth systems. Polarity determines attractive/repulsive force determining charging/discharging relationships [7].

3. SEISMICITY & TECTONIC FRAMEWORK

The arrival of another solar minimum is in harmony with the increased seismic activity in the Caribbean and offshore Central America along Pacific coast, and Mexico, as represented by a large M = 7.5 earthquake offshore Honduras on 10 January 2018. Further support comes from the extremely high water temperature of the Gulf of Mexico observed in March 2018, which followed the earthquake [4]. Energy release from the Earth's outer core dramatically increases during the major solar low cycles indicated from the "Earth core active phase" [4] and seismo-volcanic quiescence [11, 12]. IEVPC studies show a link between deep and shallow earthquakes, originally established by Blot [11], as the Energy Transmigration (ET) concept. Transmigration rates of thermal energy towards the surface from deep-seated earthquakes are on the order of 0.15km/day. The ET concept allows forecast of strong shallow quakes, magnitude 6.5 or greater several years in advance, based on the appearance of strong deep-seated earthquakes. Within the upper mantle, energy transmigration generally takes place in two modes [12]. 1.) One mode surfaces through inclined fracture zones of the Wadati-Benioff zone [13], a planar zone of seismicity corresponding with a down-going slab driven by mantle convection [14]. 2.) Second mode enters sealed porous zones of mantle low seismic velocity lenses or channels [15] and transmigrates laterally until finally rising through fracture systems. These slanted fractures and lateral low velocity lenses provide conduits for outer core-derived EM energy propagating as "lightning from below", emitting long wavelength radio signals at very low frequency in the band above 20kHz, manifesting about 20 hours before an earthquake within the epicenter area [16]. Thus thermal joule energy released from large shallow EM seismic precursor activity may trigger large ground fault earthquakes fairly rapidly. Detecting EM and geomagnetic seismic precursors has rarely been implemented for forecasting, as earthquakes are simplistically considered the result of grinding plate motions within the Plate Tectonic paradigm, and their true EM nature (solar ***EM induction***[1] triggering "lightning from below") has been ignored by most tectonic theories until Earth Endogenous Energy by Gregori [6] revealed a plasma core construct with anode tufts or sea-urchin spines. The resultant EM propagation has previously been considered the result of a piezoelectric effect. The piezoelectric effect is considered a release of electric energy from motion or sudden fracturing of rock, but detection of radio precursors from EM propagation before earthquakes points to problems of interpretation with this argument.

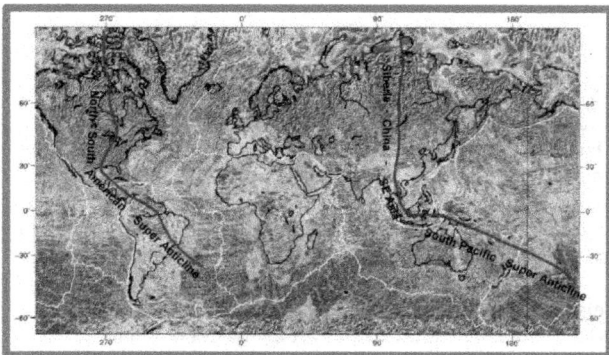

Fig. 6. World Magnetic Anomaly Map [17] - **Antipodal Archean Origin Super-Anticlines** (brown lines) [18, 19]. These anticlines have been repeatedly reactivated during Proterozoic and Phanerozoic. Note that the Caribbean Sea and the Mississippi Valley are situated on the axis of the anticline.

Earthquakes occurring in the NMSZ originate within a unique tectonic settings strongly related to the global-scale geological structure of the North-South American Super-anticline (NSAS) that runs from South America, via the Caribbean and Mississippi Valley, to the Canadian Shield [18, 19] (Fig. 6). It's a fundamental geological structure formed in the Archean stage, the beginning of the Earth's formation. Another antipodal super-anticline extends from SW Pacific, via SE Asia and South China, to Siberia. These anticlinal structures have influenced the subsequent development of the Earth by repeated magmatic and tectonic activities throughout the Phanerozoic, especially since Mesozoic. Earthquake and volcanic energies in the Central America come from the outer core under the Caribbean Sea and transmigrate to the Pacific coast through the oceanized horst structures, one of which now forms the Cayman Trough [4]. The direction of energy movement is controlled by the level of thermal energy input into the Caribbean dome from the outer core, which is inversely correlated with the solar cycle. During the declining solar cycle, earthquake and volcanic swarms move northward, but during the rising cycle, southward. This energy transmigration cycle pattern explains why the catastrophic New Madrid earthquakes have occurred exclusively during the major solar minimums. Bearing the above in mind, a very

strong earthquake in the offshore Caribbean north of Honduras (M = 7.5) along the Cayman Tough on 10 January 2018 caught our attention, because of this seismic energy link to the New Madrid Seismic Zone through the (brown line) NSAS (Fig. 6). This earthquake occurred at the *Radial-Axial indution* junction of this global-scale NSAS and the E-W trending Cayman Fault. The seismic energy of this quake is considered to have derived from the outer core through gigantic Archean fracture systems developed in the mantle deep under the Caribbean [4].

RADIO DIRECTION FINDING (RDF) [16]

The Radio Direction Finding (RDF) Network, developed by the Radio Emissions Project [20] allows 24/7 monitoring of a wide bandwidth of the Earth's background electromagnetic emissions to trace radio anomalies in seismically active areas for a "crustal diagnosis" in real time, on a global scale [16]. By combining RDF information of appropriately spaced antennae array stations (of some tens of km) one can locate the source of EM emission by triangulation and discriminate source direction, position, and distance from the station. The system provides data on the temporal variation of frequency, magnitude, and source intensity. During the experimentation with the Radio Emissions Project strong and precise radio emissions were detected preceding destructive earthquakes worldwide [21, 22]. The station began to provide the first data on the origin of electromagnetic signals in March 2017. On 2 February 2018 monitoring of the United States began in the New Madrid from the station in Lariano Rome, Italy, (Fig. 7). Pre-seismic crustal emissions of radio waves are detected with RDF at very low frequency in the band above 20kHz manifesting about 20 hours before an earthquake revealed 57 earthquakes M ≥ 2.5, including earthquakes of magnitude 3.3 and 4.4 in December 2018. In this case the "dark purple" azimuth was kept under strict control focused on the New Madrid Fault 8,500 km away from the monitoring station in Italy [16] (Fig. 7).

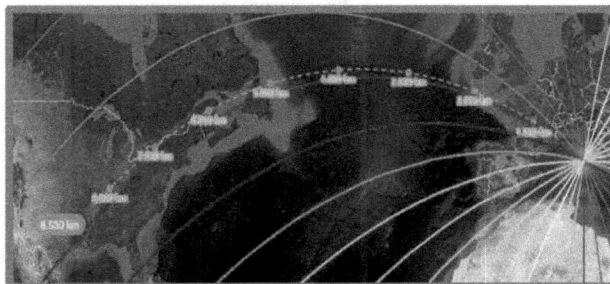

Fig. 7. World Mapping RDF System of the Radio Emissions Project - 8500 km indicated by violet azimuth in NW direction to monitor New Madrid Fault area from RDF monitoring station in Lariano (Rome, Italy) [16]. Source: Google Maps.

The radio-anomalies frequency is inversely proportional to the average electromagnetic frequency of seismic magnitude signals. The periods during many electromagnetic emissions always precede earthquakes of a strong or greater intensity than the average of the period. Groups of signals or single very intense signals preceded the occurrence of earthquakes. It is also evident that solar activity has an important influence on the electromagnetic emissions detected with the RDF system. The study in this case has found that these emission concentrations in a given period of time somewhat follow the Sunspot Number inversely proportional to solar activity (Fig. 8).

---

[1] *Electro-Magnetic* or *Magnetic Induction* is the production of an electromotive force, or voltage, across an electrical conductor in a changing *Magnetic* field. The induction characteristics are determined by current alignments between layers in the Earth and polarity relationships between of the Earth, Sun and other planets. The alignment and polarity determine the attraction or repulsive forces in Plasma Core physics and determine charging and discharging forces on our planet.

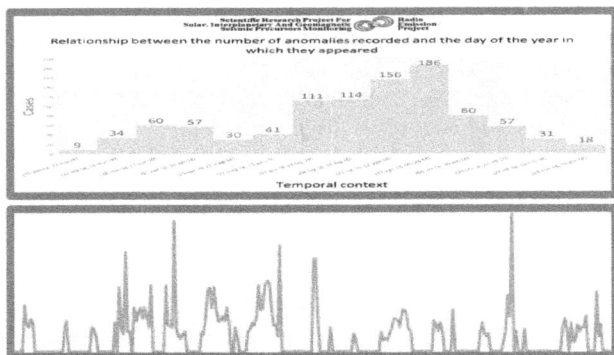

Fig. 8. Inversely Proportional number of radio-anomalies time series [16] (upper inset) follows the number of Sunspots (lower inset). Source: http://www.sidc.be.

OTHER SIGNIFICANT PRECURSORS

Understanding the common denominator between analyzed seismic precursors with an associated solar EM driver should be of concern. The comparison is carried out by collecting data on ionization phenomena in areas under tectonic stress such as: Outgoing Long-wave Radiation (OLR); Total Electron Content (TEC); atmospheric effects, such as Jet Stream and other meteorological phenomena related to earthquake clouds and lights. For example: the Jan. 16, 1995 Kobe earthquake was preceded by earthquake lights [23]; similar observations were reported from Mexico and other seismic regions of the world [24, 25].

Outgoing Long-wave Radiation

Average maximum local temperatures within the potential earthquake zones are higher than normal by 5-7°C, gradually increasing over few days. Usually a rise in the range of 7-12°C or more indicates an imminent earthquake. The temperature rise can be observed ~3-4 days before earthquakes. Outgoing Long wave Radiation (OLR) measurement, a satellite-based measurement can be used as an effective tool to identify the earthquake preparation zones. Atmospheric and surface phenomena like anomalous Outgoing Long-wave Radiation (OLR) normally appear 5 to 30 days before the occurrence of moderate and big earthquakes. Preliminary analysis of a recent Peru earthquake occurring on September 25, 2013 with M = 7.0 is shown (Fig.13) [26]. The appearance of anomalous transient radiation can be correlated with the tectonic stress and thermodynamic processes in the atmosphere. OLR measures radiation from ground, lower atmosphere, and clouds together. An algorithm calculates the OLR, at 8 to 12 μm [27]. An anomalous OLR flux can be defined as change in energy index (dE_index), which signifies the statically defined maximum change in the rate of OLR for a given location and time specific spatial locations and predefined times [28]. The appearance of the short lived OLR anomaly is observed before the occurrence of the Peru earthquake (Fig. 13). Short-lived anomalies appeared thrice before the occurrence of the earthquake on September 25, 2013. An example of first anomaly appeared on September 07, 2013, and it lasted till September 10, 2013. The intensity of the daily current field OLR value slowly increased from September 07, 2013 and it reached peak value on September 10, 2013 (Fig. 13a, b, c & d). The OLR anomaly started disappearing from September 10, 2013 "night", and it was completely disappeared on September 11, 2013, which was recorded by NOAA satellite during "day" pass (Fig. 13e).

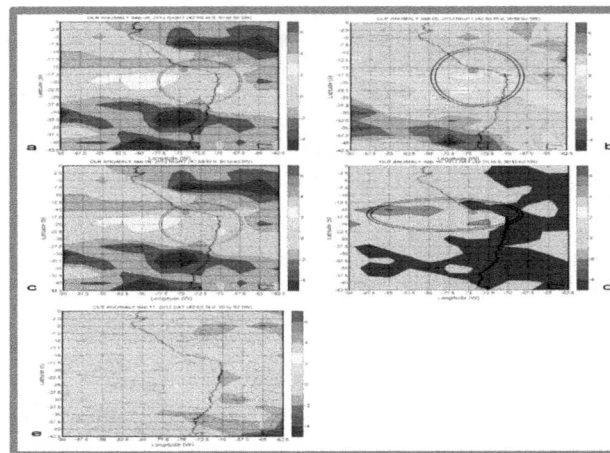

Fig. 13 (a, b, c, d & e): OLR Anomaly evolution for the first time observed before the earthquake occurred at 50km S of Acari, Peru (15.882°S, 74.543°W) on September 25, 2013. The regions with anomalies are circled and epicenter was marked by red concentric circle [26].

Seismo-Electro-Magnetic

When the temperature of any magnetic body increases, the magnet starts losing its magnetic properties. The magnetism decreases as the temperature rises. The temperature at which the magnet entirely loses its magnetism is known as the Curie temperature or Curie point. This effect is extensively manifested at sub-surface temperature level. About 3 to 5 days before the occurrence of an earthquake the rise is sharp and rapid and it peaks on the day of earthquake. As a result of the rise in sub-surface temperature in the hypo-central region, the geomagnetic field declines. The reduction in the magnetic field adversely affects the transmission and propagation of electric and electromagnetic signals coined the Seismo-Electro-Magnetic Effect [29]. It affects radios, telephones and televisions. If a radio station is transmitting a signal at a particular frequency, say 1000 kHz, then the same will be received about ten to twenty hours before the occurrence of the earthquake at 1100, 1200, 1300.... 1900, 2000 kHz, or more. In the case of televisions, there are repeated audio, visual and spectral disturbances. The number of disturbances goes on increasing till the occurrence of the earthquake. It has been seen that these effects are manifested about two to three days in advance and are observed intensely about ten to twenty hours before the earthquake. Thus radio broadcasting may go to higher frequencies, while landlines and inflight communications can be disturbed within the epicenter area 3-4 days beforehand, television broadcast within 15 hours of an event. While mobile phones within 30-40 km of an event may become non-functional within 100 minutes of an event.

Jet Streams

IEVPC case studies show many M ≥ 6.0 earthquake locations were identified with Jet Stream precursors (Fig. 14). In fact, the interruption of velocity flow-lines that cross above an earthquake epicenter occurs 1–70 days prior to the event, with duration 6–12 hours, at ~100 km average distance between Jet Stream's precursor and epicenter [30]. Satellite observation found possible atmospheric disturbances in jet stream velocity before the powerful M = 8.3 Chile Earthquake on 16 Sep. 2015. The jet stream was interrupted at the epicenter on 13 June 2015 at 06:00 UTC (Fig. 14), 96 days prior to the major M = 8.3 Chile Earthquake, and the epicenter deviation was less than 80 km. The prediction posted on 2015/06/14 had the time range from 2015/06/13 to 2015/07/13, in Central Chile at the location (32.3S, 71.6W) and magnitude M > 5.5. The actual event was an M = 8.3 about two months later than predicted on 2015/09/16 - 22:54:33 UTC in Central Chile at location (31.570°S, 71.654°W) at a depth of 25.0 km [30, 31, 32, 33].

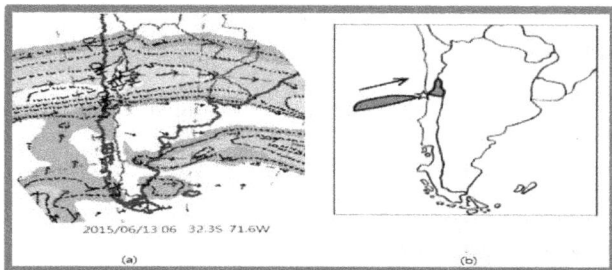

Fig. 14. The anomalous behavior of jet stream: (a) The original jet stream map (S.F. State University), (b) The jet stream at a speed of 130 knots (234km/hour) was interrupted at the epicenter on 13 June 2015 at 06:00 (UTC). The epicenter was located at the interrupted region [30].

CONCLUSIONS

Many sound reasons support Solar EM induction model for New Madrid seismicity. This paper and related references document scientific grounds for linking deep geological structure of the Caribbean Sea to its northern area, the New Madrid Seismic Zone. The following points were documented. 1). The latest gigantic earthquake, January 2018 magnitude 7.5 offshore north Honduras, occurred at the junction of one of Earth's most fundamental structures, the North-South American Super-anticline and the E-W Cayman deep fault, recalling the relationships of *Axial vs. Radial induction.* 2). The quake occurred above a major low velocity lens at 400 to 500 km depth, which is considered an energy transmigration volcanic surge channel likely filled with ionized liquid and gas. 3). The low velocity lens shallows northward to Gulf of Mexico and appears to extend to the New Madrid Seismic Zone, where a distinctive low velocity lens is developed at the top of the mantle. 4). Seismic activity has dramatically increased since 1990, especially since 2007. These years are significant, because the former is the starting year of a one-order longer solar cycle, and the latter the starting year of the current Solar Minimum. 5). A comparison of Central American earthquakes and solar cycle shows that during the declining years of solar cycles, seismic energy transmigrates northward, and during the rising period southward. 6). These facts explain the damaging New Madrid earthquakes that exclusively occurred during the last four major solar minimums. 7). There are strong scientific grounds to forecast another series of major earthquakes in the New Madrid Seismic Zone during the current solar minimum.

In the light of the now confirmed start of a prolonged, solar hibernation for the coming 30 years or so, which are comparable to Dalton Minimum or worst case, a Maunder Minimum ("Little Ice Age"), a repeat of the 1811-12 earthquakes should be expected. The window of highest risk for another major New Madrid earthquake extends roughly from 2021 through 2038. Seismic and volcanic activities in the Caribbean may foretell energy release in the New Madrid region with a delay of only a few years. This warning is further emphasized by the fact that earthquake activity has increased

dramatically in recent years in the Caribbean, as represented by the M = 7.5 northern offshore Honduras earthquake in January 2018. We consider this gigantic quake is a harbinger of the coming New Madrid quake. Based on IEVPC's innovative geologic/tectonic expanded electro-dynamic model, within an Earth Endogenous Energy [6] and Stellar Transformer [7] framework, understanding of the Earth's interactions with space weather can be improved. This provides an understanding of some common electromagnetic denominators associated with earthquakes and their seismic precursors. Methods have been individually verified as valid for earthquake forecasting. http://www.ievpc.org/earthquake-papers.html.

REFERENCES

[1] Elnashai, A.S., et al., **Impact of New Madrid Seismic Zone earthquakes on the Central USA**, volume 1. MAE Center Report No. 09-03, October, 2009.

[2] Casey, J.L., Choi, D.R., Tsunoda, F. and Humlum, O., **Upheaval! Why catastrophic earthquakes will soon strike the United States?** Trafford Publishing, 332p, 2016.

[3] Reimer, P. J., Baillie, M. G. L., Bard, E., Bayliss, A., Beck, J. W., Blackwell, P. G., Bronk Ramsey, C., Buck, C. E., Burr, G. S., Edwards, R. L., Friedrich, M., Grootes, P. M., Guilderson, T. P., Hajdas, I., Heaton, T. J., Hogg, A. G., Hughen, K. A., Kaiser, K. F., Kromer, B., McCormac, F. G., Manning, S. W., Reimer, R. W., Richards, D. A., Southon, J. R., Talamo, S., Turney, C. S. M., van der Plicht, J., & Weyhenmeyer, C. E., **IntCal09 and Marine09 radiocarbon age calibration curves, 0-50,000 years cal BP**. *Radiocarbon, 51*(4), 1111-1150, 2009.

[4] Choi D.R., Casey, J.L., Leybourne, B.A. and Gregori, G.P., **The January 2018 M7.5 offshore North Honduras earthquake: its possible energy link to the New Madrid Seismic Zone, Mississippi Valley**, *New Concepts in Global Tectonics Journal*, Mar. v.6, no. 1, pp. 21-36, 2018.

[5] Choi, D.R. and Maslov, L., 2010. Earthquakes and solar activity cycles. *NCGT Newsletter*, no. 57, p. 85-97.

[6] Greogry, G.P., **Galaxy-Sun-Earth relations**. *Beiträge zur Geschichte der Geophysik und Kosmischen Physik*, Band 3, Heft 4, 471p, 2002.

[7] Leybourne, B.A., **Stellar Transformer Concepts: Solar Induction Driver of Natural Disasters - Forecasting with Geophysical Intelligence**, *Journal of Systemics, Cybernetics and Informatics*, Orlando, FL, V. 16, N. 4, pp. 26-37, ISSN: 1690-4524, 2018.

[8] Thornhill, W. and Talbott, D., *The Electric Universe*, Mikamar Publishing, p. 132, May 24, 2007.

[9] Choi, D.R., **The January 2010 Haiti seismic disaster viewed from the perspective of the energy transmigration concept and block tectonics**. *NCGT Newsletter*, v. 54, p. 36-44, 2010.

[10] Tsunoda, F., Dong R. Choi, Kawabe, T., **Thermal energy transmigration and fluctuation.** *NCGT Journal*, v. 1, no. 2, p. 65-80, 2013.

[11] Blot, C., **Volcanisme et sismicité dans les arcs insulaires. Prévision de ces phénomènes.** *Géophysique*, v. 13, Orstom, Paris, 206p, 1976.

[12] Choi, D.R., **The great 17 July 2017 offshore Kamchatka earthquake, its link to deep energy source, and geological significance.** *NCGT Journal*, v. 5, no. 3, p. 379-390, 2017.

[13] Benioff, Hugo, **"Seismic evidence for the fault origin of oceanic deeps"**. Bulletin of the Geological Society of America. *Geological Society of America.* 60 (12): 01 Dec., 1949, pp.1837–1866, 1949. doi:10.1130/0016-7606(1949)60[1837:seftfo]2.0.co;2.

[14] Holmes, A., **Principles of Physical Geology (3 ed.)**. Wiley. pp. 640–41. ISBN 978-0-471-07251-5, 1978.

[15] Meyerhoff, A.A., Taner, I., Morris, A.E.L., Agocs, W.B., Kamen-Kaye, Bhat, M.I., Smoot, N.C., Choi, D.R. and Meyerhoff-Hull, D. (ed.), **Surge tectonics: a new hypothesis of global geodynamics**, Kluwer Academic Publishers, 323p. 1996.

[16] Straser, V., Cataldi, D., and Cataldi, G., **Electromagnetic Monitoring of the New Madrid Fault U.S. Area with the RDF – Radio Direction Finding of the Radio Emissions Project**, *NCGT Journal*, v. 7, no. 1, 2019.

[17] Korhonen, J.V., Fairhead, J.D., Hamoudi, M, Hemant, K., Lesur, V., Mandea, M., Maus, S., Purucker, M., Ravat, D., Sazonova, T. and Thebault, E., **Magnetic anomaly map of the World** (and associated DVD), Scale, 1:50,000,000, 1st edition, Commission for the Geological Map of the World, Paris, France, 2007.

[18] Choi, D.R., **An Archean geanticline stretching from the South Pacific to Siberia**. *NCGT Journal*, v. 1, no. 3, p. 45-55, 2013.

[19] Choi, D.R. and Kubota, Y., **North-South American Super-Anticline**, *NCGT Journal*, v. 3, no. 3, p. 367-377, 2015.

[20] Cataldi, D., Cataldi, G. and Straser, V., **SELF and VLF electromagnetic emissions which preceded the M6.2 Central Italy earthquake that occurred on August 24, 2016**. European Geosciences Union (EGU), General Assembly 2017. Seismology (SM1.2)/Natural Hazards (NH4.7)/Tectonics & Structural Geology (TS5.5), 2017. Also: The 2016 Central Italy Seismic sequence: overview of data analyses and source models. *Geophysical Research Abstracts* Vol. 19, EGU2017-3675.

[21] Straser, V., Cataldi, G. and Cataldi, D., **Radio-anomalies: a tool for earthquake and tsunami forecasts.** European Geosciences Union (EGU) General Assembly 2015, Natural Hazard Section (NH5.1), Sea & Ocean Hazard - Tsunami, Geophysical Research Abstract, vol. 17, Vienna, Austria, 2015. Harvard-Smithsonian Center for Astrophysics, High Energy Astrophysics Division, SAO/NASA Astrophysics Data System.

[22] Straser, V., Cataldi, G. and Cataldi, D., **SELF and VLF electromagnetic signal variations that preceded the Central Italy earthquake on August 24, 2016.** *NCGT Journal*, vol. 4, no. 3, p. 473-477, 2016. Harvard-Smithsonian Center for Astrophysics, High Energy Astrophysics Division, SAO/NASA Astrophysics Data System.

[23] Tsukuda, T., 1992. **Sizes and some features of luminous sources associated with the 1995 Hyogo-Ken Nanbu earthquake.** *J. Phy. Earth*, v. 45, p. 73-82.

[24] King, C.Y., 1983. **Electromagnetic emission before earthquake.** *Nature*, v. 301, p. 377.

[25] Lomnitz. C., **Fundamentals of earthquake prediction**, 326p. New York, 1994.

[26] Venkatanathan, N., and Natyaganov, V., **Anomalous Outgoing Longwave Radiation Observations Preliminary Results of September 25, 2013 (M7.0) Peru Earthquake.** *New Concepts New Concepts in Global Tectonics Journal*, v. 1, no. 4, p. 5 – 10, 2013.

[27] Gruber A. and Krueger A., **The status of the NOAA outgoing long wave radiation dataset.** *Bulletin of American Meteorological Society*, v. 65, p. 958–962, 1984.

[28] Ouzounov, D., Pulinets, S., Romanov, A., Romanov, A., Tsybulya, K., Davidenko, D., Kafatos, M. and Taylor, P., **Atmosphere-ionosphere response to the M9 Tohoku earthquake revealed by multi-instrument space-borne and ground observations: Preliminary results.** *Earthquake Science*, v. 24, no. 6, p. 557-564, DOI: 10.1007/s11589-011-0817-z, ISSN: 1674-4519, 2011.

[29] Bapat, A., **Role of Telecom in Seismic Surveillance.** *Proc. Nat. Sym. On Developments in Geophys.* Banaras Hindu Univ., Varanasi, p. 129 – 132, 2003.

[30] Wu, H.C., **Anomalies in Jet Streams that Appeared Prior to the 16 September 2015 M8.3 Chile Earthquake,** *New Concepts in Global Tectonics Journal*, V. 3, No. 3, pp. 407-408, September 2015.

[31] Wu, H.C., Tikhonov, I.N. and Cesped, A.R., **Multi-parametric analysis of earthquake precursors.** *Russian Journal of Earth Sciences*, v. 15, no. 3, 2015. doi:10.2205/2015ES000553.

[32] Wu, H.C. and Tikhonov, I.N., **Jet streams anomalies as possible short-term precursors of earthquakes with > 6.0.** *Research in Geophysics*, Special Issue on Earthquake Precursors, v. 4, no. 1, p. 12–18, 2014. doi:10.4081/rg.2014.4939.

[33] Wu, H.C. and Tikhonov, I.N., **The earthquake prediction experiment on the basis of the jet stream's precursor.** 2014 AGU Fall meeting, NH31A-3844.

DEVELOPING INNOVATION TECHNOLOGY CAPACITIES IN LARGE MANUFACTURING FIRMS FROM MEXICO

Jesús Eduardo Estrada-Domínguez
Universidad Autónoma de Nuevo León
Monterrey, Nuevo León/México

Alfonso López-Lira Arjona
Universidad Autónoma de Nuevo León
Monterrey, Nuevo León/México

Moisés Hinojosa-Rivera
Universidad Autónoma de Nuevo León
Monterrey, Nuevo León/México

Alejandro Torres-Castro
Universidad Autónoma de Nuevo León
Monterrey, Nuevo León/México

ABSTRACT

In Mexico, innovation has developed disproportionately among its states. For its part, the state of Nuevo Leon has carried out activities in favor of innovation which have been differentiated as an innovative state in comparison with the other entities that make up our country. However, several experts with a greater number of research centers and a high budget devoted to science, technology and innovation activities have paid less attention to human resources. The present investigation seeks to demonstrate that factors have a positive impact on the technological innovation capacity of human capital. The above, based on the premise that the level of innovation, both of nations and industries, is directly related to the ability of human resources to innovate. It is important to clarify that when referring to the term technological innovation, it is limited to the development of new or improved products or processes. The research proposes four factors such as creativity, the ability to absorb knowledge, knowledge about innovation and technical knowledge in engineering, which are expected to be directly and positively related to the technological innovation capacity of individuals.

Key Words: Innovation, R&D, Creativity, Innovation Capacity

1. INTRODUCTION

The present research proposes a strategic model focused on defining those factors that have a positive impact on the capacity of human resources to develop new or improved products or processes, known in the literature as technological innovations (Akman & Yilmaz, 2008). To carry out the above, several factors have been proposed, related to this capacity and which are listed below: Knowledge about innovation, creativity, technical knowledge and the ability to absorb knowledge.

In this study, the capacity for technological innovation is established as a dependent variable, which refers to the development of new or improved products or processes. Regarding the independent variables, these correspond to creativity, the capacity to absorb knowledge, knowledge about innovation and technical knowledge in engineering, among which we expect to find some positive and significant relationship.

Annually, the World Economic Forum, through its global competitiveness report, performs an analysis in which it measures the competitiveness of 140 economies based on 12 pillars. These proposed pillars are: Institutions, Infrastructure, Macroeconomic environment, health and primary education, education and higher education, efficiency of the goods market, efficiency of the labor market, Financial market development, technological preparation, market size, business sophistication and, finally, innovation.

Based on the study conducted by the World Economic Forum, it has been found that there is an identified problem that focuses on the low capacity of technological innovation within our country compared to other nations in Latin America and the world.

This is striking because Mexico, even with the large amount of economic resources it has, has not managed to consolidate itself as an innovative nation and is well below the level desired in research, development and technological innovation.

Figure 1 shows a graphic representation of our country in 2016 with respect to the 12 pillars as the key to competitiveness, considered by the World Economic Forum where pillar number 12 corresponding to innovation is the second lowest this country.

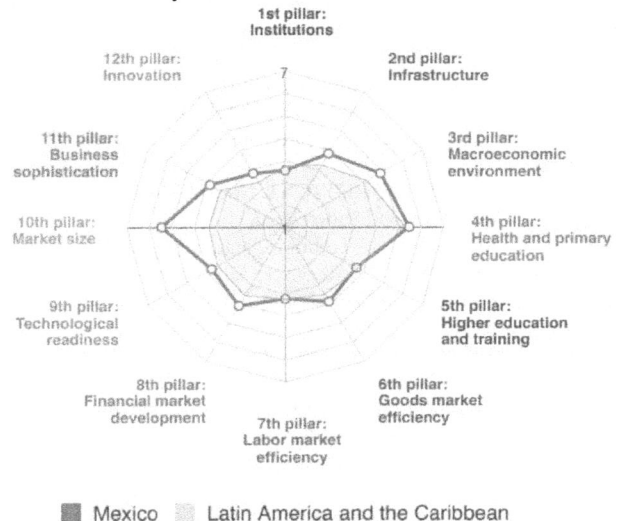

Figure 1. Pillars of Mexico in competitiveness 2017
Source: Global Competitiveness Report

It is important to note that, to measure the level of innovation, corresponding to pillar number 12, the World Economic Forum has been based on the following factors:

1) Innovation capacity
2) The quality of scientific research institutions
3) R & D expenditure by companies
4) University-Industry collaboration on R & D issues
5) Public policy oriented to advanced technology
6) The preparation of scientists and engineers
7) International patent applications (PCT)
8) The protection of industrial property

Despite the large number of initiatives in favor of innovation, such as the creation of research centers, economic incentives in R & D and the large number of graduates in engineering and exact sciences, a minimum advance has been achieved in terms of innovation. Therefore, the proposal of this research is to focus on the most important element of the innovation process, the human resource, since this resource is the one who intervenes during the whole process and without their knowledge it would not be possible to develop new products and processes.

Although Nuevo León is one of the states of Mexico with the greatest technological development and economic stability, little attention has been paid to the most important resource in the innovation process, the human resource. Given the importance of this resource, this research will focus on those factors that have a positive impact on the technological innovation capabilities of these resources, so that future efforts make even greater efforts to develop them.

The general objective of the research is to determine the characteristics that allow human resources to develop the capabilities of technological innovation in the large manufacturing companies of Nuevo León, what will allow to contribute knowledge for the development of new or improved products or processes in the companies of the industrial sector, to generate a model in particular those dedicated to manufacturing located in the city of Monterrey and its metropolitan area.

Therefore, the general research hypothesis is the following: Creativity, the capacity to absorb knowledge and technical knowledge in engineering are characteristics that positively influence the development of the technological innovation capabilities of the human resource.

The next section aims to analyze the general aspects of the factors that make up the independent variables and the dependent variable of the research through the review of the literature.

2. THEORETICAL FRAMEWORK
Capacity of technological innovation
The concept of technological innovation capacity stems from the theory of resources and capabilities, which emphasizes that knowledge should be valued as the most valuable resource that organizations can possess (Zack, 1999), this being a fundamental resource in the process of innovation.

Recently several researchers have mentioned that the vision of skills can be applied to innovate and to increase the number of large companies that focus on developing an ability to be innovative (Börjesson, Elmquist, & Hooge, 2014). This has been argued because the innovation capabilities of companies are important both for their competitiveness (Björkdahl & Börjesson, 2012) and for their growth (O'Connor, 2008).

One of the most important intangible resources within organizations is knowledge, which is often considered as an essential element in innovation capacities (Keskin, 2006). In the change management literature, the acquisition and application of knowledge has been identified as an important activity to properly understand the process of technological innovation.

Regarding the concept of innovation capacity, the systematic review of literature allows as a first instance to find the existence of a set of definitions and approaches that reveal the complexity of said concept, which are shown in table 1.

Table 1. Review of the concept Innovation Capacity.

Authors	Definition (CI)
Lawson & Samson (2001)	Ability of the firm to continuously transform ideas and knowledge into new products, processes and systems for the benefit of the firm
Barbosa (2014); Cakar y Erturk (2010)	It is the ability to mobilize the knowledge possessed by the employees and the combination thereof, to create new knowledge, resulting in innovation products or processes.
Pen, Shroeder y Shah (2008)	It is the strength or ability of a set of practices of the organization to develop new products or processes

Source: Self made

With the above, a specific definition of the concept of innovation capacity is proposed, which consists of the ability or ability to generate and develop new or improved products and processes. Likewise, these processes and products will be used as a unit of measurement for the present investigation highlighting the importance of knowledge within this same process.

Unlike the concept of invention, innovation is defined as a process that leads to the creation of new or improved products, processes and services for its commercialization which allows to advance, compete and differentiate successfully in the market (Baregheh, Rowley, & Sambrook, 2009). That is, innovation is the application of an invention on a significant scale, followed by commercial success. For its part, technological innovation is one that focuses solely on products and processes (Mothe & Nguyen, 2010).

The ability to develop new ideas and innovations is one of the organizations' main priorities (Porter & Stern, 1999). Since the knowledge economy became important, intense international competition and considerable technological progress have made innovation increasingly the center of competitiveness. Innovation is the mechanism by which organizations produce new products, processes and systems needed to adapt to changing markets, technologies and modes of competition. (Dougherty & Hardy, 1996).

Functional capabilities allow a company to develop its technical knowledge (Amit & Schoemaker, 1993). The integrative capabilities allow firms to absorb knowledge from external sources and combine the different technical skills developed in the different departments of the company (Cohen & Levinthal, 1990). For its part, innovation capacity is proposed as a higher order integration capacity; that is, the ability to mold and manage multiple capacities (Fuchs, Mifflin, & Miller, 2000).

Organizations that possess this capacity for innovation can integrate the capabilities and key resources of your company to stimulate innovation successfully. Regarding the factors that influence the capacity for innovation, several determinant elements such as culture, management capacity, organizational climate, human talent and knowledge management were found in the literature. For Smith (2001); the role of people and knowledge in the process of generating and developing innovation capabilities is preponderant, so in this study will be analyzed those factors related to human talent.

Creativity

Creativity can come from small million employee acts that accumulate in continuous improvement significantly or alternatively, which can result in a radical idea that transforms the business strategy or even to create new business. Therefore, organizations should promote creativity at all levels. Creativity requires divergent thinking and requires being driven by knowledge (Lawson & Samson, 2001).

Creativity, which can be defined as the capacity to produce new works, has been considered as the starting point and root of innovation (Lin & Liu, 2012). Creativity has always been at the heart of business, but its importance is now more evident than ever, taking into account that currently the execution capacities are widely related and the life cycles of the new offers are very short; that is, the companies that offer their products and services are in a very changing environment where everyone seeks to satisfy the needs of the consumer as quickly as possible before the competition does it for them (Escribá & Montoro, 2012).

As such, creativity has become the most highly valued intangible resource in the occupations and variety of tasks within industries (Shalley & Gilson, 2004). Likewise, it has been proven that directing creative efforts is fundamental to achieving innovation management (Oke, 2007) and is also recognized as one of the most important leadership responsibilities for future success (Yukl, 2013).

In general, creativity is associated with an individual that generates a novel idea, which plays the role of seed, root and starting point of innovation (Lin & Liu, 2012). On the other hand, innovation reflects a collective effort aimed at the implementation of creative ideas (Giannopuolou, Gryszkiewicz, & Barlatier, 2014). Here is the relationship between creativity, which refers to the generation of ideas, and innovation, which is conceptualized as the application of ideas. Therefore, it becomes vital to have creative people to carry out the innovation process.

It is essential that the human resource is creative to carry out the innovation process effectively. It should be mentioned that companies do not usually innovate in isolation, but rather in collaboration with other organizations to acquire, develop and exchange different types of knowledge, information and other resources (Fagerberg, 2005).

Due to the close relationship between the concepts of creativity and innovation, it is necessary to define both concepts, as well as to establish their differences. Creativity is often defined as the generation of new and useful ideas to transform them into value (Giannopuolou, Gryszkiewicz, & Barlatier, 2014). For its part, innovation is a word from the Latin *innovare*, which means "to do something new" (West & Farr, 1990). Innovation can refer to a process or the results of a process (Oddane, 2008). The result of this process can be classified as product innovations or process innovations, that is, a change in the way things are created (Bessant & Tidd, 2011).

Through the literature search on the concept of creativity, and for the purposes of the present investigation, this concept will be defined as an internal process which is carried out in the mind of everyone for the generation of ideas based on the knowledge to transform them into value.

According to Applied Research Studies, it is possible to appreciate the concepts of creativity and innovation associated with the production of new and useful products or processes. In the literature, different researchers tend to distinguish creativity and innovation through dichotomies such as process vs. product (Lumsden, 1999) and thinking vs. doing (Amabile, 1996).

Burnside (1990) mentions that creativity is the generation of novel (new) and useful ideas, while innovation refers to the implementation of said ideas, and innovation as the selection of such ideas, development and marketing.

Creativity can also be defined as a mental behavior which generates search processes and discover new and unusual solutions, but with meaning, in different areas of life (Villa & Poblete, 2007). Based on this definition, and in an exhaustive investigation, Dueñez (2013) elaborated items to measure the creativity of individuals with pressure. These items have been taken and adapted in the present investigation to measure the creativity variable, which are shown below:

Do you use the information given to generate new ideas?
Do you deepen your ideas from different approaches?
Do you establish a variety of alternative ideas?
Do you use the ideas of others by amplifying them or transforming them in an original way?
Do you develop an original project approach with a high level of elaboration?

Despite the importance of creativity, this is not enough in itself, it needs to be implemented in innovation; adopt new ideas and turn them into actions. For this, it requires the application of existing knowledge and the development of new knowledge. Ideas are the food of innovation and the latter represents a much tougher proposal than creativity.

Knowledge Absorption Capacity

In recent decades, the concept of absorption capacity (ACAP) has received considerable attention in the literature. Based on the work of Cohen and Levinthal, researchers have shown that ACAP influences innovation (Tsai, 2001), business performance, intra-organizational transfer of knowledge and inter-organizational learning (Gupta & Govindarajan, 2000). ACAP is defined as the ability of the company to identify, assimilate and exploit the knowledge acquired from external sources which facilitates the accumulation of knowledge and its subsequent use (Cohen & Levinthal, 1990). For their part, Zahara and George expand ACAP to four dimensions, which are acquiring, assimilating, transforming and exploiting (Zahra & George, 2002).

Basically, the capacity of absorption of a company lies in the acquisition of information, its assimilation and its application for commercial purposes, which are part of the capacity for innovation. The absorption capacity is related to the level of knowledge of the company. For this, we must focus, first, on knowledge, that intangible, rare and inimitable resource.

The acquisition refers to the ability of a company to identify and obtain knowledge from external sources. Assimilation refers to the ability of a company to develop useful processes and routines to analyze, interpret and understand the knowledge acquired externally (Szulanski, 1996). On the other hand, transformation refers to developing and refining those routines that facilitate the combination of existing knowledge with acquired knowledge and assimilate it for future use (Zahra & George, 2002). Finally, exploitation denotes the capacity of a company to improve, expand and use its existing routines, competencies and technologies to create something new based on transformed knowledge (Haro-Dominguez, Aranda, Montes, & Moreno, 2007).

Having described the various dimensions in which ACAP is composed, we will proceed to identify the items that will be used to measure this variable, which have been obtained from the research of Flatten & Zahara (2011).

Table 2 shows the proposed items, which are divided into the four dimensions that make up the absorption capacity.

Table 2. Measurement items for ACAP

Dimension	Items
Acquisition	- The search for relevant information about our industry is a daily practice in our company - The management of our company motivates the staff towards the use of information sources within our company. - The management of our company motivates the staff towards the use of sources of information external to our company
Assimilation	- In my company, ideas and concepts are communicated to all areas of the company. - The management of my company emphasizes the support between different areas of the company for the solution of problems. - In my company there is an efficient flow of information (if an area obtains external knowledge, it communicates with other areas quickly.
Transformation	- The staff of my company can structure and use the knowledge external to the organization - The staff of my company can absorb external knowledge, adapt it for future purposes and have it available - The staff of my company successfully links existing knowledge with new knowledge external to the organization
Exploitation	- The management of my company is involved in the development of new products - My company regularly adapts technologies according to the new acquired external knowledge - My company can work more effectively by adopting new technologies from an external source

Source: López-Lira Arjona's research

The research carried out by both López-Lira Arjona and Flatten and Engelen offers a useful tool with which to evaluate companies. The proposed measures allow comparing the ACAP of one company with those of others, providing a basis to determine where additional investments should be made to update and improve the use of ACAP. Managers can leverage their businesses creatively by conceiving and exploring ways to integrate the four dimensions of ACAP. Strategic heterogeneity, an important source of competitive advantage, results from the efforts of managers to configure their companies to create varied and new products, systems and processes that distinguish their company from that of the competition. Like other intangible resources, ACAP requires managerial attention and sustained investment.

Technical Knowledge in Engineering

With what has been seen up to this moment, without a doubt, the skills, aptitudes and knowledge have an important impact on the life opportunities of both organizations and individuals. Without these factors, both people and companies could not compete in a globally connected and increasingly complex world. Undoubtedly, social and economic transformations have been carried out, which in turn have caused changes in the demand for skills.

With manufacturing and other low-skilled tasks in the increasingly automated service sector, the need for repetitive skills and routines is decreasing, while the demand for information processing capabilities and other high-level cognitive and interpersonal skills is growing.

Technical knowledge is a fundamental part of the innovation process. It must be remembered that one of the factors with which the World Economic Forum measures innovation is the number of engineers available in the country. At this point something happens that is striking because our country is currently the eighth nation with the largest number of engineers internationally. This data can be seen in table 3.

Table 3. Ten countries with the highest number of engineers graduated annually

Rank	Country	Annual number of engineering graduates
1	Russia	454,436
2	U.S.	237,826
3	Iran	233,695
4	Japan	168,214
5	Korea	147,858
6	Indonesia	140,169
7	Ukrania	130,394
8	Mexico	113,944
9	France	104,746
10	Vietnam	100,390

Source: World Economic Forum 2015/UNESCO

This data attracts attention because the main actor in the development of technological innovations should be a human resource with the qualities and skills of an engineer or with some scientific profile.

The technical knowledge will be defined in this research as those skills and abilities in exact sciences which allow a greater understanding of both physical and chemical phenomena for the approach and resolution of problems.

This is where the questions arise about the performance of graduates in the industry that both develop their technical skills during their professional career with which they seek to meet the demand demanded in the workplace.

The items to be used in this section will be based on the skills of the graduate profile of the engineers established by ABET (Accreditation Board for Engineering) which are listed below:

- Ability to apply knowledge of mathematics, science and engineering.
- Ability to design and conduct experiments, as well as analyze and interpret data.
- Ability to design a system, component or process to meet the desired needs within realistic constraints, such as economic, environmental, social, political, ethical, health and safety, manufacturability and sustainability.
- Ability to identify, formulate and solve engineering problems.
- Ability to use the techniques, skills and modern engineering tools necessary for the practice of engineering.

These skills will be formulated as a question with the purpose of constructing the items for measurement. Once each of the variables has been developed together with the items, the measurement instrument will be elaborated.

3. METHODOLOGY

The type of research is exploratory and descriptive as it investigates and describes the phenomenon that is investigated; It is correlational because it aims to find the relationships between two or more variables at a given time and is explanatory because it allows to explain the phenomenon studied.

It is a non-experimental investigation, since the variables were not deliberately manipulated; that is, the independent variables were not intentionally modified, what was basically done was a perception analysis with quantitative results of the obtained data.

As Kerlinger (1979, p.116) points out, "Non-experimental or ex post-facto research is any investigation in which it is impossible to manipulate variables or randomly assign subjects or conditions." In fact, there are no conditions or stimuli to which the subjects of the study are exposed. The subjects are observed in their natural environment, in their reality.

The investigation is of the transactional type, since data was collected in a single moment, in a single time range or specific period. Its purpose was to describe the variables and analyze their incidence and interrelation at a given time. In this sense, the relationship between each of the independent variables and their causal effect on the dependent variable was measured in terms of the development of technological innovation capabilities in the large industries of the manufacturing sector.

The population of this study was the large companies in the manufacturing sector of the state of Nuevo Leon, specifically those located in the city of Monterrey and its metropolitan area, since this is the third state with the greatest contribution to Mexico's GDP. In the present investigation based on data from the National Statistical Directory of Economic Units (DENUE) which is administered by the INEGI, the population shown is of a total of 280 large manufacturing companies only in the selected municipality.

It is important to mention that the frame of reference allows the physical identification of the elements of the population, as well as the possibility of enumerating them and, therefore, proceed to the selection of the sample elements.

The study subjects are the heads of the areas of research, development and innovation, or some area to order, since the information requested requires certain specific knowledge of both the subject and the company.

4. PRELIMINARY CONCLUSIONS

Despite the great efforts that have been made, the state of Nuevo Leon still needs to raise the awareness of both companies and higher education institutions about the importance of innovation. As mentioned before, this is a determining factor for the economic development of a nation, as well as its level of prosperity. While it is true that Nuevo León is currently one of the states with the most technological development and research, there is still much to be done. It is necessary to develop technological innovation capabilities in the personnel of this nation more competitive internationally.

REFERENCES

Akman, G., & Yilmaz, C. (2008). Innovative capability, innovation strategy and market orientation: an empirical analysis in Turkish software industry. *International Journal of Innovation Management*, 69–111.

Amabile, T. (1996). *Creativity in Context: Update to the Social Psychology of Creativity.* Boulder: WestView Press.

Amit, R., & Schoemaker, P. (1993). Strategic assets and organisational rent. *Strategic management journal*, 33–46.

Baregheh, A., Rowley, J., & Sambrook, S. (2009). Towards a multidisciplinary definition of innovation. *Management Decision*, 1323 - 1339.

Bessant, J., & Tidd, J. (2011). *Managing Innovation: Integrating Technological, Market and Organizational Change.* Chichester: Wiely & sons.

Björkdahl, J., & Börjesson, S. (2012). Assessing firm capabilities for innovation . *International Journal of Knowledge Management Studies*, 171-184.

Börjesson, S., Elmquist, M., & Hooge, S. (2014). The challenges of innovation capability building: Learning from longitudinal studies of innovation efforts at Renault and Volvo Cars. *Journal of Engineering and Technology Management*, 120-140.

Burnside, R. (1990). *Improving corporate climates for creativity.* Chichester: Wiley.

Cohen, J., & Levinthal, D. (1990). Absorptive capacity: A new perspective on learning and innovation. *Administrative Science Quarterly*, 554-571.

Dougherty, D., & Hardy, C. (1996). Sustained production innovation in large, mature organisations: Overcoming innovation-to-organisation problems. *Academy of Management Journal*, 1120–1153.

Escribá, E., & Montoro, S. (2012). creativity and innovation in the firm. *International Journal of manpower*, 244-248.

Fagerberg, J. (2005). Innovation: a guide to the literature. En J. Fagerberg, *Innovation: a guide to the literature* (págs. 1-26).

Fuchs, P., Mifflin, K., & Miller, D. W. (2000). Strategic integration: Competing in the age of capabilities. *California Management Review*.

Giannopuolou, E., Gryszkiewicz, L., & Barlatier, P. (2014). Creativity for service innovation: a practice-based perspective. *Managing Service Quality*, 23-44.

Gupta, A., & Govindarajan, V. (2000). Knowledge flows within the multinational accumulation: The case of R&D. *Strategic Management journal*, 473-496.

Haro-Dominguez, d. C., Aranda, D., Montes, J., & Moreno, R. (2007). The impact of absorptive capacity on technological acquisitions engineering consulting companies. *Technovation*, 417-425.

Keskin, H. (2006). Market orientation, learning orientation, and innovation capabilities in SMEs: An extended model. *European Journal of innovation management*, 396-417.

Lawson, B., & Samson, D. (2001). Developing Innovation Capability in organisations: A dynamic capabilities approach. *International Journal of Innovation Management*, 377-400.

Lin, C., & Liu, F. (2012). A cross-level analysis of organizational creativity climate and perceived innovation. *European Journal of Management*, 55-76.

Lumsden, C. (1999). Evolving creative minds: stories and mechanisms. En C. Lumsden, *Evolving creative minds: stories and mechanisms* (págs. 153-168). Cambdridge.

Mothe, C., & Nguyen, T. (2010). The link between non-technological innovations and technological innovation. *European Journal of Innovation Management*, 313 - 332.

O'Connor, G. (2008). Major Innovation as a Dynamic Capability: A Systems Approach*. *Journal of product innovation management*, 313-330.

Oddane, T. (2008). *Organizational conditions for innovation: a multiperspective approach to nnovation in a large industrial company.* Trondheim: Thesis for PhD degree.

Oke, A. (2007). Innovation types and innovation management practices in service companies. *International Journal of Operations & Production Management*, 564-587.

Porter, M., & Stern, S. (1999). *The New Challenge to America's Prosperity: Findings from the Innovation Index.* Washington D.C: Council on Competitiveness.

Shalley, C., & Gilson, L. (2004). What leaders need to know: a review of social and contextual factors that can foster or hinder creativity. *The Leadership Quarterly*, 33-53.

Szulanski, G. (1996). Exploring internal stickiness: Impediments to the transfer of best practice within the firm. *Strategic Management journal*, 27-43.

Tsai, W. (2001). Knolwedge transfer in interorganizational networks: Effects of network position and absorptive capacity on business unit innovation and performance. *Academy of Management journal*, 996-1004.

Villa, A., & Poblete, M. (2007). *Aprendizaje basado en competencias.* Bilbao: Universidad de Deusto.

West, M., & Farr, L. (1990). Innovation at work. En M. West, & L. Farr, *Innovation at work* (págs. 3-13). Chichester: Wiley.

Yukl, G. (2013). *Leadership in Organizations.* Boston: Pearson.

Zack, M. (1999). Developing a Knowledge strategy. *California Management Review*, 125-145.

Zahra, S., & George, G. (2002). Absorptive capacity: A review, reconceptualization, and extension. *Academy of Management Review,*, 185-203.

Experimental paradigms in the explanation of mathematical concepts

Rodrigo Alejandro GUTIÉRREZ ARENAS
Instituto de Física, Universidad Nacional Autónoma de México, UNAM
México City, México

Evelyn SALAZAR GUERRERO
Facultad de Ingeniería, Universidad Nacional Autónoma de México, UNAM
México City, México

Jacquelyn MARTÍNEZ ALAVEZ
Facultad de Ingeniería, Universidad Nacional Autónoma de México, UNAM
México City, México

Yukihiro MINAMI KOYAMA
Facultad de Ingeniería, Universidad Nacional Autónoma de México, UNAM
México City, México

ABSTRACT

Nowadays, one of the best ways to achieve that students acquire interest in learning something new, is to show them the future functionality of that knowledge. Engineering is a fascinating area of study because through knowledge of mathematical concepts, the physical phenomena that give rise to multiple applications in different areas are analyzed, but it's only possible to analyze the theory in the classroom.

As mentioned above, it's important that engineering students relate mathematical concepts to experimental subjects such as physics and chemistry. Students achieve a significant learning of mathematics using these as tools of explanation by manipulating instruments, parameter analysis and the comparison of results obtained, that allow to identify that the variables or symbols used together.

This is one of the main goals of project PE111218 Design of laboratory experiments to strengthen mathematical learning concepts in basic sciences, started at the beginning of 2018, where a group of teachers work on designing experiments that will be implemented in theoretical courses of mathematics for students of the first semesters at the School of Engineering of Universidad Nacional Autónoma de México, UNAM.

The project will last two years in which it's intended to have a set of experiments that will be available to teachers of different courses in the areas of basic sciences. The experiments will be applied to different groups of students, carrying out opinion polls both to teachers and students to perform comparative analyses and evaluate the possibility of achieving good learning in students with these experiments.

It's also of vital importance to show students the use of existing specialized software that allows to verify results immediately and to analyze hypothetical situations in which they could have some feedback of what can happen when changing some of the parameters used in the experiments or the data obtained.

In this work we will mention three experiments that are currently in development and the result that we obtained by carrying them out with some pilot groups.

Keywords: Engineering education, basic sciences.

1. INTRODUCTION

Engineering students require different skills in the study of mathematics, also, understanding and mastering certain branches of physics will make them able to solve engineering problems where they identify, formulate and apply basic sciences. Therefore, it is desirable for teachers to mention that there is a close relationship between mathematical concepts in the engineering field.

During the first two years at UNAM's Faculty of Engineering more than 60% of the courses are math oriented, in which very few times applications are presented. In consequence, the challenge as teachers is, first of all, to research applications of the mathematical concepts that appear in the course programme or syllabus and to identify the best way of showing them to the students so that they achieve significant learning of those concepts.

In this context the Project "Design of laboratory experiments to strengthen mathematical learning concepts in basic sciences", encourages teachers and students to identify simple applications in which they see mathematical concepts of basic sciences and can be seen as an explanation of a physical phenomenon that can measure, quantify or visualize. In the same way it encourages students to use specialized software so that they could be able to corroborate results mathematically calculated and identify the advantages of parameter modifications and early design techniques. But in addition emphasize, that the analytical theoretical knowledge very useful for analysis of the results.

Working with university students in the firsts years of engineering programs is to confront a frequent question: is that useful for me? And taking into account that they are quite curious to know why and how the world works, they are also suspicious of the usefulness to solve exercises or memorize definitions, formulas and concepts. For math teachers it's not easy to use phrases like "you'll see it later" or "in your later course you will see in greater detail", etc. For them this is not enough as Gutiérrez manifests in [1]: "Their mental activity is intense and independent and they have a critical position in the knowledge of their teachers. They are attracted to generalizations, by the search of general principles and laws, to which particular facts are due and inclined by individual reflection", therefore we must show applications of mathematical concepts that appear in our subject.

One of the theories of adult learning [2], it's the Knowles' Andragógica theory. This theory mentions four assumptions:
1. They are self-taught
2. They have accumulated experience which is a source of learning.
3. They are attentive to learning when learning can help them cope with the tasks and problems of their lives.
4. They need to develop skills to work with theoretical knowledge [1].

These four points give us the guideline to propose these experiments for students to develop research skills, teamwork and results analysis, unlike students who do not.

Next we will describe three experiments that have been carried out with students, we will mention the methodology that is carried out in each one of them, as well as the results that we have obtained when doing them.

2. METHODOLOGY

The proposal of the experiments, is in charge of the professors who participate in the project that teach different subjects of basic sciences, the proposal goes from choosing the concept to developing the experiment, to investigate the linkage that has this concept with some physical phenomenon or some later subject and considering the necessary basic knowledge with which the students count to be able to understand it.

The format of each one of the experiments goes from the approach of a previous questionnaire in which the student is asked to carry out a simple research where it is contextualized of the phenomenon and the instruments to be used in the development of the experiment, after that work teams are formed that by the characteristics of the groups in the School of Engineering, usually happen to be of different careers, which enriches the learning of the team members. Already formed teams the teacher gives the explanation showing the student linking the theory with the experimental. At the end you will be asked to each team to submit a report of the experiment where expresses its conclusions and make comments. It is also performed a survey of opinion.

One of the experiments that has been carried out with the students is the titled "Application of the differential equations in electrical circuits", in which from a RLC circuit the student is shown in an oscilloscope the signal generated by the circuit.

Image 1. Students visualizing RLC Circuit response

The mathematical model that describes the system is a differential equation of second order, which the students have solved in their theory class and have also visualized three possible types of solution of the differential equation, with this experiment the students relates the type of system response damped, subdamped or overdamped, with the type of roots that they obtain in the resolution of the differential equation and also they visualize it in the screen of the oscilloscope.

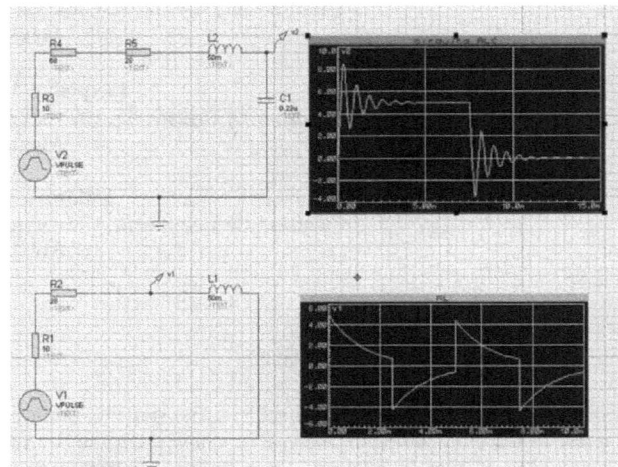

Image 2. Students relates the type of system response with the type of roots

The second experiment proposed was the solution of differential equations using a computer algebra system (CAS). Nowadays computer algebra systems like Mathematica or Maple are quite common in the classroom. Teachers that give math related courses must take advantage of those computer algebra systems. The approach given in this experiment is that the student could solve easily problems that usually require a lot of work in the classroom (on the board, for example). This approach encourages the student to not be afraid of long and difficult problems.

Usually when you are trying to design a solution for a real-life engineering problem, the mathematical expressions, in this case differential equations, are quite difficult to solve because they are completely and absolutely symbolic. A typical differential equations course favors only numbered oriented differential equations to solve, for example the initial value problem:

$$y'' + 4y = 0$$
$$y(0) = 1 \quad y'(0) = 1,$$

has a solution:

$$y(t) = \frac{1}{2}\sin 2t + \cos 2t,$$

in contrast a design oriented initial value problem:

$$y'' + \frac{k}{m}y = 0$$
$$y(0) = y_0 \quad y'(0) = v_0,$$

with a solution:

$$y(t) = y_0 \cos \sqrt{\frac{k}{m}}\, t + v_0 \sqrt{\frac{m}{k}} \sin \sqrt{\frac{k}{m}}\, t$$

The two former differential equations represent the same problem: an harmonic oscillator but with two different approaches. The first one emphasizes only on the solution as a mechanization of method used to solve it, meanwhile the second one takes into account the physics of the problem (k is the spring constant, m the mass and y the position of the mass). The second approach allows the student to see what happens to the solution if one or both of the parameters are modified (k or m).

The pedagogic reasons on why the traditional differential equation course prefers the first type of differential equations are clear. For a student it's easier to solve them and to comprehend the solution methods, but the main problem is that the students and teachers tend to stay in those kind of examples, always using as an excuse the amount of work to try to solve the design oriented problems.

In that context, if we want to use experiments to explain mathematical concepts we require that students are capable to understand the physical implication of the parameters involved in the modelling of physical phenomena. Using CAS as tools to balance the concepts seen in class widen the vision of the students, and allow them tackle more difficult problems without the fear of hard work. It is important to acknowledge that first the student must know how to solve the mathematical problems by hand to understand completely all the nuances the solution method has. This kind of approach must be done at the end of each topic or at the end of the course.

Students of the School of Engineering have particular characteristics such as disposition for teamwork, capacity for analysis, synthesis and adaptation to new situations, as well as creative spirit; therefore is important to exploit these characteristics in order to benefit the learning of mathematical concepts that in the beginning may seem abstract, but with the help of experimentation, teamwork and results analysis can land concepts studied through simple applications.

A subject of great importance in the study of Engineering is linear algebra because is the basis of the study of vector spaces, linear transformations, internal product and linear operators, which are the core of the study of applications of digital signal processing, electronic circuits, approximation of mathematical models and their solution by least squares, cryptography, Fourier analysis, modulators, computer animations, among many other applications.

The Study of linear algebra in the School of Engineering in the second semester of the career requires an analysis and understanding of basic concepts to interact with the subsequent concepts so as to advance with more knowledge complexes in the course are counted with previous solid knowledge. However, the general and abstract character of many algebraic concepts require a detailed explanation of their meaning, which is why a special experiment was developed to address one of the elementary concepts of linear algebra: binary operation.

The concept of binary operation is generally explained, that is, it addresses finite and infinite sets, as well as usual symbols or new symbology that represents the generic character of the

operation. In the experiment "Implementation of binary operations with logic gates" identifies that the binary operations not usual represented with abstract symbols are used in the operation of the logic gates which are the basis of the digital electronics and through which complex circuits are developed, digital clocks and messages in digital displays, so then, you can link the concepts learned in linear algebra with subjects of later semesters where they are analyzed with depth the nature of the phenomena studied.

Image 3. Students building the logic gates

In this experiment we work with a set of two elements that are 0 and 1, so that the truth tables indicate the results of operating these elements according to the type of gate that is used, in this case the ignition of a LED (light emitting diode), it shows an application of digital electronic gates where binary operations are used, and it is also possible to develop more complex functions with the combination of the first ones.
The material used is very simple so it can be implemented in the classroom, required push buttons, LEDS, resistors, wires caliber, breadboard, battery and battery connector.

The development consists of assembling the logic gates AND, NAND, OR y NOR through the wiring of basic electronic circuits.

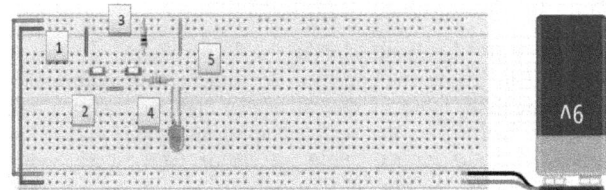

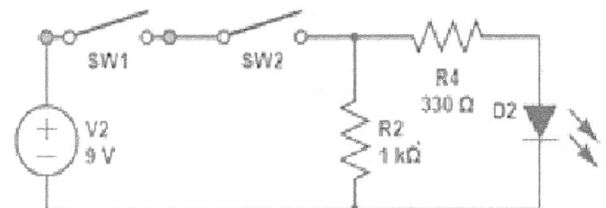

Image 4. Diagram of the logical floodgate AND

And once connected each circuit proceed to perform the experiment, pressing each of the push button according to the different binary combinations possible and scoring the results in the table of truth, being that the push button pressed is considered as 1 logical and without pressing as 0 logical, in the same way the LED on is logical 1 and off is logical 0, so with the results the floodgate is identified to later indicate if the binary operation complies with the properties: lock, commutativity and existence of the identical element.

Push Button 1	Push Button 2	LED
0	0	0
0	1	0
1	0	0
1	1	1

Table 1. Results of the experiment with the first logic gate

Based on the development of the experiment and the achievement of results, the students identify that the concepts used in the course of linear Algebra are applied in binary operations in the logic floodgates of the circuits so they show disposition and liking for this activity.

Linear algebra students are thankful that from the first sub-topic of the syllabus they are given the application of abstract concepts and mathematical generalizations. They participate in building of the logic gates with enthusiasm so the clear instructions on the part of the teacher are indispensable for their correct arming. When students relate the results of the binary operation with the LED illumination they are amazed that they understand that it is a reality that abstract concepts have applications in the design of logic floodgates that in turn are applied in digital electronics.

3. RESULTS

Students have stated that it is very useful to carry out these experiments because they immediately identify the application that mathematics has in physical phenomena.

It is necessary to mention that the experiments are more interesting for some students than for others, this assumes in some of the cases to which the career that they are studying has not direct bearing on the realized application, however it is emphasized that in the field of labor will work with multidisciplinary groups for which it is important that they know applications diversity because the field of engineering is very rough.

4. CONCLUSIONS

Without a doubt, the approach of these experiments has proved to be an extra job for the teachers who participated in the project because they are extracurricular activities; however it has been worthwhile since we have managed to promote logical thinking in students as well as the development of indispensable competencies that will serve them throughout the race.

Indirectly we generate in the students motivation to continue studying the mathematics from another point of view, like a tool

that has an application and not simply like formulas that will not serve them later.

Students who have participated in the experiments are a sample of curious students and interested in learning more about what is seen in the classroom, as it is also an extra-class work for them.

We would like these experiments to be disseminate to all the students who take the basic science subjects, but currently only has reached a few, due to the infrastructure that is counted to carry out the experiments, as well as the little interest that they show some colleagues in presenting this type of activity to their students. At the first disadvantage we are employed, since we try to propose remote experiments, in which a physical place is not needed to be able to realize them, for the second if it is a little more complicated and we consider that participating in this type of congresses we can disseminate and make known the results that have been achieved as well as the material generated for use in improving student learning.

5. ACKNOWLEDGEMENTS

Research carried out thanks to the program UNAMDGAPA-PAPIME PE111218 "Design of laboratory experiments to strengthen mathematical learning concepts in basic sciences" (Diseño de prácticas de laboratorio para fortalecer el aprendizaje de conceptos matemáticos en ciencias básicas).

6. REFERENCES

[1] M. Gutiérrez, "El aprendizaje de la ciencia y la información científica en educación superior", **Anales de documentación**, No. 5, 2002, pp. 197-212.

[2] R. Hacker y M. Harris, Adults learning of science for scientific literacy: some theoretical and methodological perspectives. **Studies in the Education of Adults.** 24(2): 217-224, 1992.

Cluster and Factor Analysis of Satisfaction Perception of B-learning of Medical Terminology

Miervaldis KARULIS

Language Center, Rīga Stradiņš University, 16 Dzirciema Street, Riga, LV 1007, Latvia

ABSTRACT

This study was dedicated to exploration of student perception of satisfaction of b-learning. The aim was to evaluate student satisfaction attributes (objective and subjective) in the b-learning setting of the study courses: Medical Terminology in Latin and English and to reveal homogenous groups of students of different study programmes Dentistry, Medicine, Nursing, Occupational Therapy, Physiotherapy and Public Health with respect to their satisfaction of b-learning at Rīga Stradiņš University. A cross-sectional study was carried out involving 418 students in the years of 2018 and 2019. The survey comprised 6 domains: information quality, system quality, service quality, use, user satisfaction and net benefits. Satisfaction attributes (10) were evaluated according to students' objective (fulfillment) and subjective (perception) aspects. For each attribute an index was created, which was used to reveal homogeneity of student groups. A two-step cluster analysis, factor analysis and non-parametric tests were performed using IBM SPSS Statistics 20. The results indicated a high rate of satisfaction of e-learning (46% - 67%), while the cluster analysis segregated 3 groups of students of different study programmes with respect to their responses. The exploratory factor analysis revealed 4 factors. The obtained results can be taken into account when creating personalized b-learning courses and conducting further surveys.

Keywords: B-learning, Satisfaction, Perception, Cluster analysis, Factor analysis, Medical Terminology.

1. INTRODUCTION

Learning Management Systems (LMS) have been extensively used in higher education institutions for the last two decades. LMS involve learning platforms that effectively use Information and Communication Technology, among which MOODLE is one of the most popular. These learning platforms are an integral part of distance learning. Besides they have been successfully incorporated in blended learning (b-learning) or partially online courses providing a choice of learning style. Online education or e-learning has led to significant changes in how students learn and how they are taught. Mahande and Jasruddin [1] define E-learning as a dynamic learning environment through the use of the Internet to improve the quality of learning.

Higher education policy makers worldwide are focusing on integrating e-learning systems into all study programs, while fully respecting student's interests and satisfaction. The teaching staff of Language Center of Rīga Stradiņš University have been implementing b-learning in several courses of Medical Terminology in the e-learning environment (MOODLE) for the last three years, hence, an increased interest

in achieving higher levels of student satisfaction with b-learning.

The aim of the present study was to evaluate the student satisfaction and perception (objective and subjective) in the b-learning setting of the study courses: Medical Terminology in Latin and English and to reveal homogenous groups of students of different study programmes and courses. The findings of the study should be taken into consideration when improving b-learning courses for particular groups of students.

2. E-LEARNING SATISFACTION MODELS

In 1989, Davis [2] propounded the Technology Acceptance Model (TAM), which is based on 4 factors: perceived usefulness, ease of use, attitudes, and intention regarding user acceptance of technology. TAM has been widely accepted among researchers. Much research has been conducted on student satisfaction with e-learning in attempt to find its influencing factors. Satisfaction becomes key for its success. The Latin word "satis" means sufficiently, well enough and adequately. According to Sary and Herlambang [3] "satisfaction is a pleasant or unpleasant emotional state that is displayed in a positive attitude toward various activities and responses to the external environment", or Zaheer, Babar, Gondal and Qadri [4] define satisfaction "as a person's attitude or feelings associated with various factors that are affecting a particular situation". In the educational setting, Avgerinou [5] points out that satisfaction is "the perceived value of the learner with educational experiences", but the authors in [4] consider students' satisfaction as "perception developed from the perceived value of education and experience gained". As a result, satisfaction can lead to students' higher motivation, engagement, and success. TAM and its modifications have been extensively used in measuring satisfaction of e-learning, for instance, Zaili, Moi, Yusof, Hanfi and Suhaimi [6] examine the influencing factors, Sunkara and Kurra [7] focus on the personalization factors of e-learning and Roach and Lemasters [8] deal with the level of satisfaction with e-learning in comparison to traditional one. For e-learning satisfaction research, the authors of [9, 10] describe the application of the Kano Model, which involves two aspects of the attribute: an objective (fulfillment) and subjective (perception of satisfaction). To identify critical elements of b-learning the researchers of [9] use five attributes: system quality, service quality, information quality, use and net benefit, which were previously included in the Kano model quality attributes.

3. MATERIALS AND METHODS

To evaluate student satisfaction and perception of e-learning, a cross-sectional study was carried out in December, 2018, and

January, 2019 at Rīga Stradiņš University, when 418 local and foreign students of the first and second study year of the study programmes of Dentistry, Medicine, Nursing, Occupational Therapy, Physiotherapy and Public Health (Table 1) were interviewed using the questionnaire, comprising a list of 10 statements with 5 multiple categorical answers (a respondent had to choose only one of them) (Table 2) and an open-ended comment. The slightly modified statements were borrowed from the study in [9], but the survey procedure was simplified by abandoning the Kano two-dimensional model, which caused difficulties for respondents to be "consistent" in giving answers resulting in a low response rate [9]. To find out homogeneity of student groups, a cluster analysis and statistical tests were performed. Factor analysis was performed to find a simpler model based on a few concepts. The descriptive and inferential assessment of students' responses, two-step cluster and factor analysis procedures, and tests were processed using IBM SPSS Statistics 20 (a significance level of 95%).

Table 1. Demographic profile of the students

			Dentistry	Medicine	Nursing	Occupa-tional Therapy	Physio-therapy	Public Health	Total
					Study Programme				
Students	Local	Count	32	196	16	15	11	21	291
		% within Students	11.0	67.4	5.5	5.2	3.8	7.2	100.0
		% within Study Program	76.2	62.6	100.0	100.0	100.0	100.0	69.6
	Foreign	Count	10	117					127
		% within Students	7.9	92.1					100.0
		% within Study Program	23.8	37.4					30.4
	Total	Count	42	313	16	15	11	21	418
		% within Students	10.0	74.9	3.8	3.6	2.6	5.0	100.0
Gender	Male	Count	11	92		3	2	1	109
		% within Gender	10.1	84.4		2.8	1.8	0.9	100.0
		% within Study Program	26.2	29.4		20.0	18.2	4.8	26.1
	Female	Count	31	221	16	12	9	20	309
		% within Gender	10.0	71.5	5.2	3.9	2.9	6.5	100.0
		% within Study Program	73.8	70.6	100.0	80.0	81.8	95.2	73.9
	Total	Count	42	313	16	15	11	21	418
		% within Gender	10.0	74.9	3.8	3.6	2.6	5.0	100.0
Study Course	Medical Terminology in Latin	Count	42	180	16	15	11	21	285
		% within Study Course	14.7	63.2	5.6	5.3	3.9	7.4	100.0
		% within Study Program	100.0	57.5	100.0	100.0	100.0	100.0	68.2
	Medical Terminology in English	Count		133					133
		% within Study Course		100.0					100.0
		% within Study Program		42.5					31.8
	Total	Count	42	313	16	15	11	21	418
		% within Study Course	10.0	74.9	3.8	3.6	2.6	5.0	100.0

4. RESULTS

Most of the students (>50%) (Table 2) were satisfied with the availability of interactive e-study environment at any time and place, its technical stability and reliability as well as the availability of instructions how to perform e-assignments.

The response "*I consider important*" received the highest frequency for the attribute of easy to use and user-friendy interface of the e-study environment, but the least for availability of interactive e-study environment at any time and place. The students' perception of availability of audio/video resources and use of mandatory (graded) exercises and tests in the e-study environment received "*I can accept*". The response "*I do not care*" was given more frequently to availability of audio/video resources in the e-study environment and a variety of communication options (on-site: in pairs, groups - and on-line: Internet). Stydents were more dissatisfied with availability of audio/video resources in the e-study environment, but least satisfied with availability of instructions how to perform e-tests with examples in the e-study environment and instructions how to perform e-tests with examples in the e-study environment.

Table 2. Distribution of students' responses by percentage

	I am dissatisfied; %	I do not care; %	I can accept; %	I consider important; %	I am satisfied; %
Q1 Technical stability and reliability in the e-study environment	2.4	1.4	3.1	32.1	**61.0**
Q2 Easy to use and user-friendly interface of the e-study environment	1.7	2.4	9.6	**37.1**	49.2
Q3 Lecturer's instructions how to use the e-study environment	1.0	9.3	7.7	32.5	49.5
Q4 Availability of audio/video resources in the e-study environment	**5.0**	**15.3**	**12.5**	30.1	37.1
Q5 A variety of communication options (on-site: in pairs, groups - and on-line: Internet)	1.7	**13.6**	11.2	27.3	46.2
Q6 Possibilities of knowledge self-assessment in the e-study environment	2.4	6.0	7.6	33.5	50.5
Q7 Use of mandatory (graded) exercises and tests in the e-study environment	2.6	6.0	**11.2**	30.4	49.8
Q8 Blended learning (combination of traditional learning with an interactive e-study environment)	0.7	8.6	8.4	30.4	51.9
Q9 Availability of instructions how to perform e-tests with examples in the e-study environment	0.7	7.9	8.6	26.8	**56.0**
Q10 Availability of interactive e-study environment at any time and place	1.0	4.8	4.5	23.2	**66.5**

The two-step cluster analysis was conducted to find out whether there are different groups of students with similar satisfaction and perception. Three clusters (Table 3) were segregated using the attributes as evaluation fields. The segregation yielded in the silhouette coefficient (within the range of 0.5 – 1.0) measuring both a good cohesion and separation with the outlier treatment of 8%.

To better highlight the differences between clusters, Table 3 shows only the percentage above 50, which describes the distribution of responses among clusters. Most of the responses "*I am dissatisfied*" and "*I do not care*" were given by the foreign students (cluster 1) who studied the course "Medical Terminology in Latin". The exception was the attribute Q6, for which the highest response "*I am satisfied*" rate was given within this cluster and 30% among the clusters. The local students were segregated between two clusters according to the study courses. In cluster 3, the response "*I am dissatisfied*" dominated for the attributes Q5, Q6, Q7 and Q10. In cluster 2, the responses varied (for each attribute less than 50%), except for the attribute Q2, for which the response "*I am dissatisfied*" was the most frequent (45%) among clusters.

Table 3. Distribution of students' responses among clusters

	Cluster 1 29.7%	Cluster 2 33.5%	Cluster 3 36.8%
Students	Foreign 100%	Local 50%	Local 50%
Gender	Male 50%, Female 25%	Female 45%	Male 50%, Female 30%
Study Programme	Medicine 35%	All	Medicine 50%
Study Course	Latin 50%	Latin 50%	English 100%
Q1	I am dissatisfied (80%) I do not care (50%)		I can accept (50%)
Q2	I do not care (55%)		
Q3	I am dissatisfied (75%)		
Q4	I am dissatisfied (55%) I do not care (50%)		
Q5	I do not care (55%)		I am dissatisfied (50%)
Q6		I do not care (50%)	I am dissatisfied (60%)
Q7	I do not care (50%)		I am dissatisfied (55%) I can accept (50%)
Q8	I am dissatisfied (70%) I do not care (50%)		I can accept (50%)
Q9	I do not care 50%)		
Q10	I do not care (65%)		I am dissatisfied (70%)

In order to assess whether there were differences between student groups, study programs and courses on the one hand and the frequency of the respective response on the other hand, the index for each attribute was introduced, which was expressed as a percentage of one-type given response on all attributes by each respondent. Table 4. summarizes the Mann-Whitney U test results of p-values, which indicates a statistically significant (p<0.05) difference in almost all responses, except "*I can accept*", between local and foreign students. Statistically significant differences also exist between student groups, genders and study courses with respect to the response " *I do not care*". In Table 5, p-values indicate statistically significant differences between the students of the following study programmes: Dentistry – Medicine, Dentistry – Public Health, Public Health – Nursing and Public Health – Occupational Therapy with respect to the response " *I am satisfied* ". In Table 6, p-values indicate statistically significant differences between the students of the following study programmes: Dentistry – Public Health, Medicine – Physiotherapy, Medicine – Public Health, Occupational Therapy – Physiotherapy and Physiotherapy – Public Health with respect to the response " *I can accept* ". No statistically significant differences were confirmed among the students with respect to the rest of responses.

Table 4. Mann-Whitney U test results on differences in responses between students groups, gender and study courses (**p-values**, asymp. sig., 2-tailed)

	I am dissatisfied	I do not care	I can accept	I consider important	I am satisfied
Students (local, foreign)	**0.012**	**0.000**	0.157	**0.008**	**0.000**
Gender	0.179	**0.034**	0.332	0.392	**0.015**
Study Course	0.327	**0.003**	0.513	0.542	0.222

Table 5. Mann-Whitney U test results on differences between two study programmes (**p-values**, asymp. sig., 2-tailed)

I am satisfied	Dentistry	Medicine	Nursing	Occupational Therapy	Physio-therapy
Medicine	**0.015**				
Nursing	0.446	0.394			
Occupational Therapy	0.460	0.387	0.968		
Physiotherapy	0.791	0.382	0.765	0.917	
Public Health	**0.002**	0.088	**0.033**	**0.037**	0.128

Table 6. Mann-Whitney U test results on differences between two study programmes (**p-values**, asymp. sig., 2-tailed)

I can accept	Dentistry	Medicine	Nursing	Occupational Therapy	Physio-therapy
Medicine	0.195				
Nursing	0.496	0.953			
Occupational Therapy	0.178	0.557	0.711		
Physiotherapy	0.105	**0.029**	0.078	**0.019**	
Public Health	**0.006**	**0.020**	0.140	0.232	**0.004**

A principal components and principal axis factoring analysis with both the varimax and direct oblique (delta 0) rotation were conducted to assess underlying variables. All the analyses provided 4 extracted factors containing the same items (Table 7). The maximum likelihood (varimax) analysis confirmed goodness-of-fit of the model: 4 factors ($\chi2$ = 12.083, df = 11, p = 0.357), which explained 66.155% of the total variance (principal components analysis, varimax).

Table 7. Rotated component matrix (principal components, varimax)

	Factor Loading			
	1	2	3	4
Q9	0.719			
Q7	0.712			
Q6	0.698			
Q3	0.693			
Q4		0.811		
Q5		0.747		
Q1			0.819	
Q2			0.631	
Q10				0.906

5. DISCUSSION

The student satisfaction rate was around 50% and above (Table 2) for almost all the attributes; the students were more satisfied with the delivery aspects of those courses than the content aspects, which was stated by Roach and Lemasters [8]. Each attribute contributed differently to satisfaction, which is in line with several other studies [1, 3, 4, 6, 8, 11, 12, 13, 14]. For instance, Strong, Irby, Wynn and McClure [11] and Cole, Shelley and Swartz [13] found that the most cited reasosn for satisfaction – convenience; for dissatisfaction – lack of interaction. The findings of the authors in [4] showed that students (more than 21,000 respondents in the study) were highly satisfied by the e-learning education; highest score – instructor support, lowest score – tutorial support. Sary and Herlambang [3] noticed a positive correlation between student satisfaction and the effectiveness (target achievement, adaptability, satisfaction and responsibility) of the implementation of the e-learning, which corresponds to the results of the present study (mostly related to the response "I consider important").

The attribute of availability of audio/video resources in the e-study environment is contradictory for it received the highest response rates of "I do not care" and " I am dissatisfied". This coincides with the results of the study [8] and can be attributed as content weakness. However, the response "I do not care" may imply that these resources are abundantly available in other sources. The same can be addressed to communication options.

Considering that the differences between the response frequencies for "I am satisfied"-"I consider important" and "I consider important"-"I can accept" are practically the same and fall within the range of 18% - 22% for such attributes as Q1, Q8 and Q7, it can be concluded that these attributes are evaluated by students as the key factors of b-learning. For the same reason of similar response frequencies for "I do not care"-" I am dissatisfied" (0.7% - 7.2%), one can assume that both the attributes Q2 and Q9 are treated negatively by those students who do not succed in b-learning.

The authors of the present study did not find any research performed on satisfaction of e-learning, using the cluster analysis, however, Bauk, Šćepanović and Kopp [9] hinted that different analytical methods in assessing the level of satisfaction should be recommended. This method can be easily used to identify groups of individuals that are similar to each other but different from others in other groups. The cluster analysis carried out in this study identified three clusters that were almost equally distributed. Surprisingly, all the foreign students in Cluster 1 were the most critical and indifferent to almost all the attributes. This fact can be consistent with Sunkara and Kurra's [7], which revealed the need for personalized and more adaptive and customized e-learning systems with possible support to satisfy the needs of learners including learning styles. Cluster 2 included local students who chose all the responses almost equally to all the attributes, but for the attribute Q6 the response "I do not care" dominated in this cluster. Possibly, each of those students could have different experience in b-learning, therefore not paying so much attention to self-assessment resources provided in e-study environment. The students of Cluster 3 seem to be more dissatisfied with the crucial aspects of e-learning, but they could accept the attributes Q1, Q7 and Q8, which may give the impression that they were forced to accept b-learning.

The satisfaction difference among the students of different study programmes is in line with the results of cluster analysis. These statistically significant differences existed between local and foreign students, genders and study courses with respect to the response "I do not care", possibly suggesting that other

factors influence student satisfaction of e-learning. Chandrasiri and Jayasinghe [12] discovered in the research that subjective norms or social influence had a direct impact on satisfaction. In addition, Pham L., Limbu, Bui, Nguyen and Pham H. T. [15] found the relationship between student satisfaction and student loyalty. Besides, phychological predispositions studied by Dziuban et al. [16] played an important role suggesting that other latent factors may exist.

Students expressed their b-learning perception of the attributes proposed in the survey, mainly based on their subjective judgments, which could be expressed as both an assessment of the learning experience they acquired and their willingness to expect something useful in this type of learning process. Therefore, such a student satisfaction should be seen in two ways: positive assessments and critical reviews.

Factor analysis was performed to find a simpler model based on fewer factors. The loading of Q8 was less than 0.4 and it was common to several other factors, therefore it was excluded, which is understandable for all the items included in the survey related to b-learning. The interpretation of the 4 factors is given in Table 8. It should be noted that further research is needed to find other items (not only one) for additional special advantages as attractive attributes of satisfaction perception of b-learning.

Generally, for successful implementation of b-learning in various courses of Medical Terminology, the 4 factors should be considered as the underlying principles.

Table 8. Interpretation of factors

Items	Factors
Q9 Availability of instructions how to perform e-tests with examples in the e-study environment	Instructional provision
Q3 Lecturer's instructions how to use the e-study environment	
Q7 Use of mandatory (*graded*) exercises and tests in the e-study environment	
Q6 Possibilities of knowledge self-assessment in the e-study environment	
Q5 A variety of communication options (*on-site: in pairs, groups - and on-line: Internet*)	Provision of diverse communications
Q4 Availability of audio / video resources in the e-study environment	
Q1 Technical stability and reliability in the e-study environment	Technical support and convenience
Q2 Easy to use and user-friendly interface of the e-study environment	
Q10 Availability of interactive e-study environment at any time and place	Special advantages

6. CONCLUSIONS

1) Students considered the following attributes as the most satifying: availability of the e-learning environment at any time and place, its technical stability and reliability and instructions of its usage, but as the least satisfying – a variety of communication options and availability of audio/video resources since they are available in internet applications and forums.
2) Most of the students of the study course "Medical Terminology in Latin" (Cluster 1) considered the attributes in the following decreasing order: Q3- Q9-Q6-Q5-Q7-Q1-

Q2-Q4-Q8-Q10, which indicates their greater demand (must-be) for these attributes of this order.

3) Most of the students of Cluster 2 and Cluster 3 considered the attributes in the same order, which indicates their greater satisfaction (attraction) with these attributes.

4) The study had some limitations: the Kano two-dimensional model was not used due to a complex understanding to provide answers and the number of satisfaction attributes was reduced to 10 for the same reason. Hence, some attractive satisfaction attributes were lost.

5) Statistically significant differences between local and foreign students, genders and study courses with respect to several responses on satisfaction of b-learning were proved.

6) Statistically significant differences between students of several study programmes with respect to several responses on satisfaction of e-learning were proved.

7) Four factors were found related to satisfaction perception of b-learning: instructional provision, provision of diverse communications, technical support and convenience, and special advantages.

8) It is necessary to explore continuously the stability of student satisfaction attributes of b-learning for they have an increasing impact on competitiveness in higher education.

7. REFERENCES

[1] R.D. Mahande, Jasruddin, "The Conceptual Model of User Satisfaction for E-Learning Edmodo on Undergraduate Students: A Preliminary Study", **Proceedings of the 1st International Conference on Computer Science and Engineering Technology Universitas Muria Kudus (ICCSET)**, Kudus, Indonesia, 2018, pp. 658-667, viewed 29 May 2019, <https://eudl.eu/doi/10.4108/eai.24-10-2018.2280533>

[2] F.D. Davis, "Perceived Usefulness, Perceived Ease of Use, and User Acceptance of Information Technology", **MIS Quarterly**, Vol. 13, No. 3, 1989, pp. 319-340, viewed 29 May 2019, <https://www.academia.edu/2036076/Perceived_usefulness _perceived_ease_of_use_and_user_acceptance_of_informat ion_technology>.

[3] F.P. Sary, O. Herlambang, "E-Learning Program Effectiveness on Students' Learning Satisfaction at Telkom Unversity Bandung", **Proceedings of the 1st Economics, Law, Education and Humanities International Conference (The First ELEHIC)**, Padang, Indonesia, vol. 2019, 2019, pp. 271-280, viewed 29 May 2019, <https://www.researchgate.net/publication/332116951_E-learning_Program_Effectiveness_on_Students'_Learning_S atisfaction_at_Telkom_University_Bandung>.

[4] M. Zaheer, M.E. Babar, U.H. Gondal, M.M. Qadri, "E-Learning and Student Satisfaction", **Proceedings of the 9th Annual conference of Asian Association of Open Universities (AAOU)**, Kuala Lumpur, Malysia, 2015, viewed 29 May 2019, <https://www.researchgate.net/publication/295400881_E-Learning_and_Student_Satisfaction>.

[5] M.D. Avgerinou, "Teacher vs. Student Satisfaction with Online Learning Experiences Based on Personality Type", **Proceedings of the 7th Pan-Hellenic Conference with International Participation, ICT in Education**, University of Peloponnese, Korinthos, Greece, Vol. I, 2010, pp. 223-231, viewed 29 May 2019,

[6] N. Zaili, L.Y. Moi, N.A. Yusof, M.N. Hanfi, M.H. Suhaimi, "The Factors of Satisfaction on E-Learning Usage Among Universiti Malaysia Kelantan Students", **Journal of Information System and Technology Management**, Vol. 4, Issue 11, 2019, pp. 73-83, viewed 29 May 2019, <http://www.jistm.com/PDF/JISTM-2019-11-03-06.pdf>.

[7] V.M. Sunkara, R.R. Kurra, "An Analysis of Learner Satisfaction and Needs on E-Learning Systems", **International Journal of Computational Intelligence Research**, Vol. 13, No. 3, 2017, pp. 433-444, viewed 29 May 2019, <https://www.ripublication.com/ijcir17/ijcirv13n3_09.pdf>.

[8] V. Roach, L. Lemasters, "Satisfaction with Online Learning: A Comparative Descriptive Study", **Journal of Interactive Online Learning**, Vol. 5, No. 3, 2006, pp. 317-332, viewed 29 May 2019, <https://www.ncolr.org/jiol/issues/pdf/5.3.7.pdf>.

[9] S. Bauk, S. Šćepanović, M. Kopp, "Estimating Students' Satisfaction with Web Based Learning System in Blended Learning Environment", **Education Research International**, Vol. 2014, 2014, pp. 1-11, viewed 29 May 2019, <https://www.researchgate.net/publication/261996039_Esti mating_Students'_Satisfaction_with_Web_Based_Learning _System_in_Blended_Learning_Environment>.

[10] G. Dominici, F. Palumbo, "How to Build an E-learning Product: Factors for Student/customer Satisfaction", **Business Horizons**, Vol. 56, No. 1, 2013, pp. 87-96, viewed 29 May 2019, <file:///C:/Users/User/Downloads/How_to_Build_an_E-Learning_Product_Facto.pdf>.

[11] R. Strong, T.L. Irby, J.T. Wynn, M.M. McClure, "Investigating Students' Satisfaction with eLearning Courses: The Effect of Learning Environment and Social Presence", **Journal of Agricultural Education**, Vol. 53, No. 3, 2012, pp. 98-110, viewed 29 May 2019, <http://www.jae-online.org/attachments/article/1687/53.3.98%20Strong.pd f>.

[12] G.D.T.D. Chandrasiri, J.N. Jayasinghe, "Factors Affecting the User Satisfaction for E-Learning Systems", **Proceedings of the 15th International Conference on Business Management (ICBM 2018)**, Colombo, Sri Lanka, 2018, pp. 1018-1031, viewed 29 May 2019, <http://dr.lib.sjp.ac.lk/bitstream/handle/123456789/8164/ Factors%20affecting%20the%20User%20Satisfaction%2 0for%20e-Learning%20Systems.pdf?sequence=1&isAllowed=y>.

[13] M.T. Cole, D.J. Shelley, L.B. Swartz, "Online Instruction, E-Learning, and Student Satisfaction: A Three Year Study", **International Review of Research in Open and Distance Learning**, Vol. 15, No. 6, 2014, pp. 111-131, viewed 29 May 2019, <https://www.researchgate.net/publication/279320409_O nline_Instruction_E-Learning_and_Student_Satisfaction_A_Three_Year_Stud y>.

[14] S. Ghazal, H. Al-Samarraie, H. Aldowah, ""I am still learning": Modeling LMS Critical Success Factors for Promoting Students' Experience and Satisfaction in a

Blended Learning Environment", **IEEE Access**, Vol. 6, 2018, pp. 77179-77201, viewed 29 May 2019, <https://www.researchgate.net/publication/328751422_I_am_still_learning_Modeling_LMS_Critical_Success_Factors_for_Promoting_Students'_Experience_and_Satisfaction_in_a_Blended_Learning_Environment>.

[15] L. Pham, Y.B. Limbu, T.K. Bui, H.T. Nguyen, H.T. Pham, "Does E-Learning Service Quality Influence E-Learning Student Satisfaction and Loyalty? Evidence from Vietnam", **International Journal of Educational Technology in Higher Education**, Vol. 16, No. 7, 2019, pp. 1-26, viewed 29 May 2019, <https://www.researchgate.net/publication/331021518_Does_e-learning_service_quality_influence_e-learning_student_satisfaction_and_loyalty_Evidence_from_Vietnam>.

[16] C. Dziuban, P. Moskal, J. Thompson, L. Kramer, G. DeCantis, A. Hermsdorfer, "Student Satisfaction with Online Learning: Is it a Psychological Contract?", **Journal of Asynchronous Learning Network**, Vol. 19, No. 2, 2015, viewed 29 May 2019, <https://www.researchgate.net/publication/282699144_Student_Satisfaction_with_Online_Learning_Is_it_a_Psychological_Contract>

Effect of Post-Panamax Containerships on US Ports and Logistics Networks

Marco A. LARA GRACIA
Department of Engineering, University of Southern Indiana
Evansville, Indiana 47712, USA

ABSTRACT

The expansion of the Panama Canal has had a remarkable impact at varying degrees in different sectors of the US economy including ports and logistics networks. This paper addresses impact on port infrastructure required to prepare US container ports located on the East Coast and the Coast of the Gulf of Mexico for the arrival of Post-Panamax containerships, which are vessels that due to their dimensions require US port authorities to deepen and widen the port's navigation channels for the safe transit of such big vessels and port operators to replace cranes used to load/unload shipping containers on/from containerships with bigger cranes. This paper also addresses the economic impact of Post-Panamax containerships in US logistics networks. Post-Panamax containerships are vessels that cross the Panama Canal after the completion of the Panama Canal expansion project.

Keywords: TEU, Panamax and Post-Panamax Containerships, Deep Draft, and Ship-to-Shore Cranes.

1. INTRODUCTION

1.1 Terminology
- TEU or Twenty-Equivalent Unit: A 20' shipping container.
- Panamax containership: A vessel that due to its dimensions can pass through the original locks of the Panama Canal.
- Post-Panamax containership: A vessel that due to its dimensions cannot pass through the original locks of the Panama Canal.
- Deep draft: Depth of a navigation channel.
- Ship-To-Shore (STS) crane: Specialized crane used to load/unload containers on/from containerships.

1.2 Panama Canal
France was the first country to attempt to build the Panama Canal. A team led by Ferdinand de Lesseps, builder of the Suez Canal in Egypt, started construction work in 1880 with the idea of building the Canal at sea level. Multiple difficulties including frequent heavy rain, which invariably resulted in deadly landslides, and lack of means and resources to fight and eliminate yellow fever and malaria, which caused thousands of workers to die, led to the collapse of the Ferdinand de Lesseps' construction project. By 1889, the death toll of French workers was 20,000 approx.

After years of losing money and human lives, the French offered the rights of the Canal and remaining equipment to the US for $109 million. The US rejected the offer and considered building their own canal in Nicaragua, an idea that was eventually discarded due to volcanic activity in the region. Eventually, the French dropped their offer to $40 million and the deal was finalized in 1904. The construction project started the same year.

The Panama Canal consists of a series of man-made artificial lakes and channels. At each end of the Canal there are three sets of locks. These locks make it possible to cross the isthmus at 87 feet above sea level on Gatun Lake. Each lock allows for the changing of the level of water to either raise or lower a vessel to the height of the next section of the Canal. The total length of the Canal is about 51 miles, with about 28.1 miles between the inner locks. On the Atlantic side are the Gatun locks, which consist of three lock chambers with a raise capacity of 85 feet. On the Pacific side there are the Pedro Miguel locks, which have one 31 foot chamber, and the Miraflores locks with two chambers of 51 foot lift combined. Miraflores locks are located near Panama City.

The Panama Canal officially opened on August 15, 1914. Inaugural passage was made by the SS Ancon vessel. Approximately 3.4 million cubic meters of concrete went into building the locks, 240 million cubic yards of dirt were excavated and removed, and 5,600 workers died between 1904 and 1913 [1]. The Panama Canal cost the US $375 million, which is equivalent to $8.6 billion in today's dollars [2].

The Panama Canal changed the navigation maps of shipping companies. Figure 1 shows that approximately 7,800 miles can be saved if a ship navigating from San Francisco to New York City travels through the Panama Canal [3]. Travel time, fuel, and CO_2 emissions can also be significantly reduced.

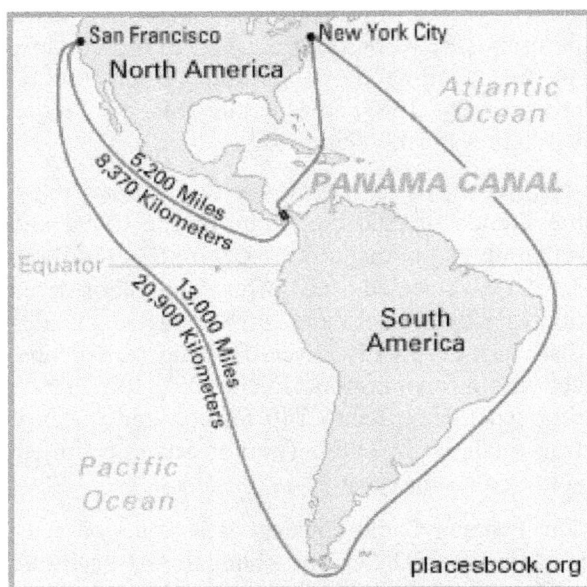

Figure 1. Distance saved in a Francisco - New York City trip through the Panama Canal [3].

1.3 Expansion of Panama Canal

The primary goal of the expansion project was to double its cargo capacity and allow for larger ships to pass through the canal. A secondary goal was to reduce the level of traffic in the Canal. By being able to accommodate larger ships, the number of smaller ships will decrease, while the cargo capacity will increase. The expansion was necessary as it was estimated that the Panama Canal lost 10-15% in revenue to the Suez Canal, where larger ships could pass through [4].

The expansion project included the construction of a new set of locks on both the Atlantic and Pacific sides of the canal, widening and deepening of existing channels, and raising the maximum level of Gatun Lake. The new locks, which are 1400 feet long, 180 feet wide, and 60 feet deep, can accommodate much larger vessels (Post-Panamax) than the original locks. In addition to building a new set of locks, the expansion project also required the construction of several new access channels. On the Atlantic side of the Canal, a single 2 mile channel was constructed, while on the Pacific side, two new channels, one 3.9 miles in length, and the other 1.1 miles in length were constructed. The total cost of the expansion project has been estimated at $5.25 billion.

Figure 2 shows the dimensions of the original and new locks (Post-Panamax locks) of the Panama Canal as well as the dimensions and carrying capacity of the Panamax and Post-Panamax vessels. A Panamax vessel is shown on the left side of Figure 2 whereas a Post-Panamax vessel is shown on the right side.

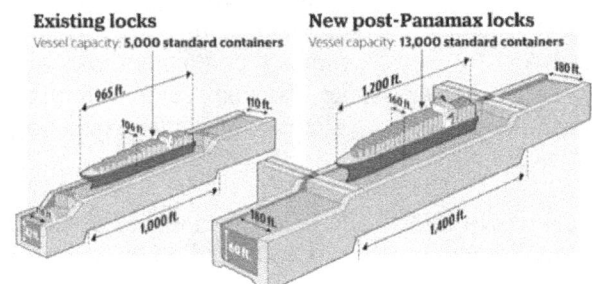

Figure 2. Panamax and Post-Panamax locks [5].

The expansion project began in 2009. On June 26, 2016, the containership COSCO, carrying 9,472 TEUs, made the inaugural passage of the expanded Panama Canal.

The expansion of the Panama Canal has substantially improved global commerce and connectivity. Currently, the Panama Canal currently serves 140 routes, connecting 1,700 ports and 160 countries. The main user of the Panama Canal is the U.S., which represents about 67 percent of the total cargo moving through the Canal. China is the second most frequent user of the Panama Canal, representing about 16 percent of the total cargo that transits the Panama Canal [6].

2. POST-PANAMAX CONTAINERSHIPS

The most notable difference between Panamax and Post-Panamax vessels is the carrying capacity, which is approximately 4,500 TEUs for Panamax containerships and 12,000 TEU's for a Post-Panamax containership. Figure 3 shows a detailed comparison of Panamax and Post-Panamax containerships.

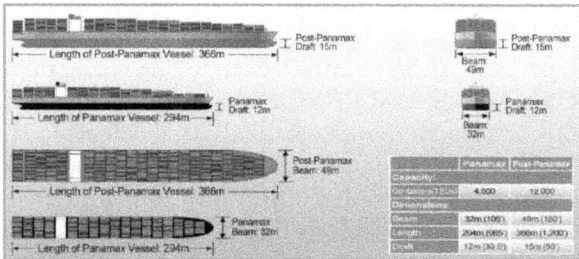

Figure 3. Comparison of Panamax and Post-Panamax vessels [7].

The Post-Panamax expansion has allowed the canal to grow in capacity from 341 million tons. in 2015 to 442 million tons. in 2017, as shown in Figure 4. Neo-Panamax (Post-Panamax) vessels account for 191 million tons of the FY 2018 total, or around 43% of tonnage, while the usage of the Panamax locks has seen a dip from 341 million tons in 2015 to 251 million tons in 2018. This is a result of the usage of Post-Panamax containerships and the retirement of older Panamax vessels [8].

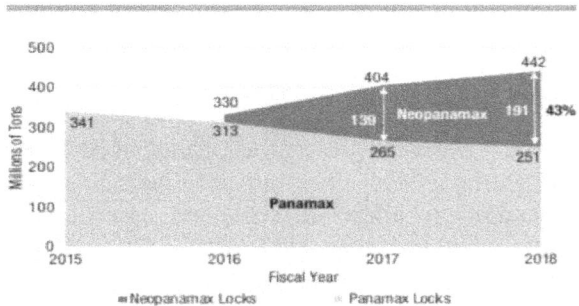

Figure 4. Comparison of Panamax and Neo-Panamax (Post-Panamax) locks in terms of tonnage [8].

Figure 5 illustrates that 18% of FY 2018 volume was through the new locks. This 18% of transits were responsible for 43% of canal tonnage [8].

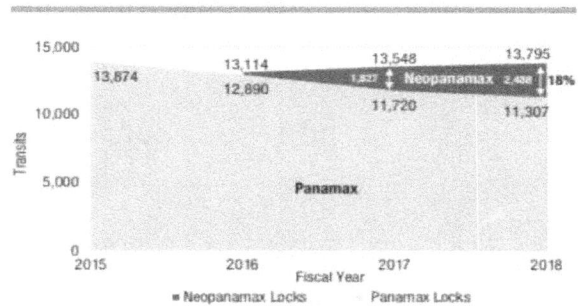

Figure 5. Comparison of Panamax and Neo-Panamax (Post-Panamax) locks in terms of transits [8].

The new locks are creating almost $500 million per year in revenues, and in FY 2018 brought in 46% of total tolls, as shown in Figure 6 [8].

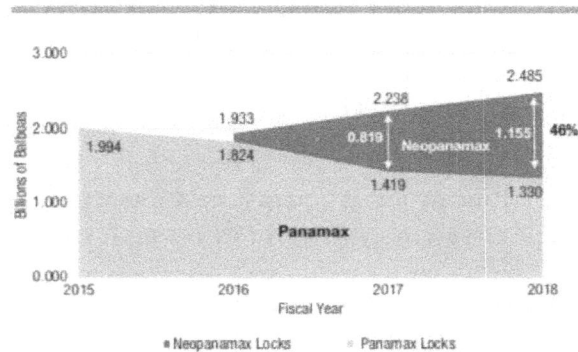

Figure 6. Comparison of Panamax and Neo-Panamax (Post-Panamax) locks in terms of toll revenue [8].

As of December 2018, over 5,000 Post-Panamax vessels had passed through the new locks of the Panama Canal [6]. 51% of the 5,000 vessels is from the container segment, liquefied petroleum gas represents another 26%, and liquefied natural gas vessels made up 10%. The remaining transits are a mixture of dry/bulk goods vessels, car carriers, and cruise ships. It is anticipated that by the end of year 2020, shipments of liquefied natural gas through the canal will increase fivefold to over 30 million tons. Combined these numbers indicate a very large increase in volume through the canal, and a significant increase in the amount of money coming into the economy of Panama [9].

It is expected that the number of Post-Panamax vessels that cross the Panama Canal will continue to grow, which is the trend since the inauguration of the Post-Panamax locks. Please see Figure 7 [10].

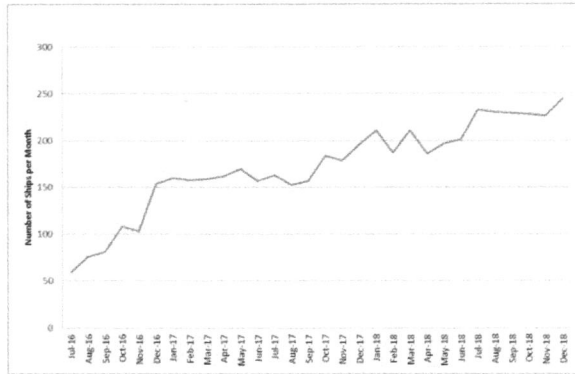

Figure 7. Transits of Post-Panamax vessels [10].

Post-Panamax vehicle carriers could carry approximately 30% more vehicles than Panamax vessels and Post-Panamax dry bulk carriers, tankers, and cruise ships could carry nearly twice the capacity of the corresponding Panamax vessels [11].

3. EFFECT OF POST-PANAMAX CONTAINERSHIPS ON US PORTS

3.1 Deepening and widening navigation channels and harbors of US Ports

Extensive work to deepen and widen navigation channels and harbors has been consistently required to allow Post-Panamax vessels to safely arrive at US ports located along the Coast of the Gulf of Mexico and the East Coast. Deepening a navigation channel or harbor is technically referred to as "increasing the deep draft of a navigation channel or harbor".

This paper reports projects undertaken to increase the deep draft of the navigation channels and harbors of the following ports:
- Charleston, South Carolina
- Savannah, Georgia
- Norfolk, Virginia
- Houston, Texas
- New-York/New Jersey.

The plan for the Port of Charleston is to be the deepest harbor on the U.S. East Coast [12]. To proceed with this plan, the South Carolina General Assembly set aside $300M for the project. In the fall of 2017, the US Army Corps of Engineers Charleston District was awarded the first of two construction contracts of $47M

and $213M to deepen the Charleston entrance channel. Dredging operations began in 2018. With a navigation channel depth of 52 feet, entrance channel depth of 54 feet, as well as enlarged turning basins, the Charleston harbor will be the deepest harbor on the US East Coast [12]. This enhancement in port's infrastructure will create the conditions ideal for the frequent arrival of Post-Panamax containerships.

The Savannah Harbor Expansion Project ("SHEP") was undertaken by the State of Georgia Government to deepen the 18.5 mile outer harbor to 49 feet at mean low water and the Savannah River channel to 47 feet [13]. $266M has been set aside by the State of Georgia to complete the project, which is expected to conclude in 2019. SHEP will allow the Savannah port to accommodate Post-Panamax containerships [13].

In 2018, via the Virginia Port Authority, Port Norfolk was approved a $350M dredging project to deepen its harbor to handle both Post-Panamax and Suez Canal vessels [14]. The project will deepen the Norfolk harbor from 50 feet to 55 feet and widen the navigation channel from 1,000 to 1,300 feet east of the Chesapeake Bay Bridge, which will allow unrestricted two-way traffic. After the expansion project is complete, Port Norfolk will be able to accommodate containerships of up to 22,000 TEU's, a significant increase from the 10,000-15,000 TEU containerships that currently utilize its harbor. Design work is expected to be completed in 2020, with construction to begin shortly thereafter [14].

In 2017, Houston finished dredging its Bayport and Barbours Cut container terminals to a 45-foot depth to allow the transit of considerably larger containerships [15]. Recently, the US Army Corps of Engineers Houston District started a project to widen a curve to allow larger containerships to safely enter and exit Bayport. Widening the curve from the Houston ship channel to Bayport will provide safely access for containerships measuring 1,160 feet long and 150 feet wide, compared to the current maximum of 1,096 feet long and 143 feet wide. Unlike the ports of Charleston, Savannah, and Norfolk, Houston funded its dredging project by using $80M of its own funds, foregoing federal matching funds for the deepening in order to speed completion of the work [15].

In 2016, the Port Authority of New York and New Jersey announced the completion of its $2.1B decade-old project, which started in 2005, aimed at dredging the New York-New Jersey port to a depth of 50 feet [16]. The project was undertaken in order to allow the East Coast's largest port to accommodate the size of Post-Panamax containerships. One of the unique contributors to the success of the project was the undertaking of certain sustainability efforts during the span of the project. For example, as a result of multiple lawsuits initiated by industry-environmentalists, sand dredged from the expanded channels was used to restore wetlands habitats at several marsh sites within Jamaica Bay, New York and Lincoln Park, New Jersey. In addition, approximately 900,000 cubic yards of sand and glacial till from the Port Jersey channel was used to restore shallow water fish habitat in an unused navigation channel south of the former Military Ocean Terminal in Bayonne, New Jersey [16].

In addition to the $2.1B project to dredge the navigation channel of the New York – New Jersey port, a $1.7B project was undertaken to increase the vessel navigational clearance of the Bayonne Bridge to allow the safe passage of Post-Panamax containerships under the bridge. Figure 8 shows a picture of the Bayonne Bridge.

Figure 8. The Bayonne Bridge under construction [17].

3.2 Increasing size of STS cranes

A Ship-To-Shore (STS) crane is a gantry crane used at container ports to load/unload containers on/from vessels. Depending on the size of the vessel and the number of STS cranes available more than one STS crane can operate on a vessel. Figure 9 shows a STS crane.

Figure 9. A Ship-to-Shore crane [18].

As shown in Figure 3, a Post-Panamax vessel is significantly wider than a Panamax vessel. The arrival of Post-Panamax vessels has forced port operators from the Gulf of Mexico and East Coasts to replace STS cranes used load/unload Panamax vessels with bigger cranes capable of loading/unloading bigger vessels (Post-Panamax containerships), which is a major investment.

4. EFFECT ON US LOGISTICS NETWORKS

Walmart Inc. began building massive distribution centers near major US ports in order to take advantage of the increased cargo volume provided by Post-Panamax containerships [19].

In the summer of 2018, Wal-Mart opened a $135M, 2.5M square foot distribution center in Mobile, Alabama. Merchandise brought into the Mobile distribution center arrive through the Port of Mobile in shipping containers. From there, goods move approximately 15 miles west along Interstate 10 to the Irvington facility via semi-tractor trailers before they are broken down and their products shipped to Walmart regional distribution centers across the US [19].

Harbor trucking companies are increasing their prices and charging their customers for excessive waiting times at congested container ports serviced by Post-Panamax containerships as US imports from Asia are the largest generator of truck moves for retailers [21].

Plans are underway for the Mississippi River to become home for the American Patriot Holding (APH) container vessel, which will able to handle up to 20,000 TEUs and will dock at a future 1,000-acre container port being planned at a new 4,200-acre complex in Plaquemines, Louisiana where the imported containers will be loaded onto APH container vessels to be shipped up the Mississippi River [22].

REFERENCES

[1] *Panama Canal History.* (2019). Retrieved 2019, from Canal de Panama: http://pancanal.com/eng/history/history/index.html

[2] Wagtendonk, A. v. (2014, Aug 15). *PBS News Hour.* Retrieved from PBS.org/NewsHour: https://www.pbs.org/newshour/world/panama-canal-helped-make-u-s-world-power

[3] Placesbook. (n.d.). Retrieved January 2019, from https://www. placesbook.org

[4] Brown, B. (2018). *Impact of the Panama Canal Expansion.* Retrieved 2019, from: https://www.theitosgroup.com/impact-of-panama-canal-expansion/

[5] Panama Canal Authority. (n.d.). Retrieved February 2019, from https://www.pancanal.com/eng/pr/press-releases /2018 /12/10/pr664.html

[6] Panama Canal Connects. (n.d.). Retrieved form https://maritime-executive.com/article /panama-canal-connects-1-700-ports

[7] Morrison, B. (2012). *Race-To-The-Top: East and Gulf Ports Prepare for Post-Panamax World.* Durham: Duke University

[8] http://pancanal.com/eng/general/reporte-anual/2018-AnnualReport.pdf

[9] https://worldmaritimenews.com/archives/ 266454/5000th-neopanamax-ship-transits-panama-canal/

[10] Transits. (n.d.) Retrieved January 2019 form http://www.pancanal.com/common/ maritime/advisories/

[11] Leigh B. Boske, P. (2017). *Panama Canal Utilization.* Austin: University of Texas at Austin.

[12] South Carolina Ports. (2019). *Harbor Deeping.* Retrieved from South Carolina Ports: http://www.scspa.com/cargo/planned-improvements/harbor-deeping/

[13] Georgia Ports Authority. (2016, June 30). Transportation by the Numbers: Two Ports Five Terminals. Savannah, GA, USA.

[14] Ashe, A. (2018, May 31). *Eyeing 19,000 TEU ships, Virginia ports get $350 million for deepening.* Retrieved from JOC.com: https://www.joc.com/port-news/us-ports/virginia-port-authority/eyeing-19000-teu-ships-virginia-ports-get-350-million-deepening_20180531.html

[15] Bonney, J. (2017, January 30). *Army Corps Expanding Houston Channel to allow larger ships.* Retrieved from JOC.com: https://www.joc.com/port-news/us-ports/port-houston/army-corps-expanding-houston-channel-allow-larger-ships_20170130.html

[16] JOC Staff. (2016, September 2). *NY-NY port completes 50-foot channel project.* Retrieved from JOC.com: https://www.joc.com/port-news/us-ports/port-new-york-and-new-jersey/ny-nj-port-completes-50-foot-channel-project_20160902.html

[17] The Bayonne Bridge, (n.d.) Retrievd from https://www.hdrinc.com/portfolio/bayonne-bridge-navigational-clearance-project

[18] STS Crane. (n.d.). Retrieved January 2019, from https://www.kalmarglobal.com

[19] AL.com. (2018, June 1). *Massive Walmart Distribution center opening Aug. 14th in Mobile County.* Retrieved from AL.com: https://www.al.com/news/2018/06/massive_ walmart_center_opening.html

[20] Houston Business Journal Staff. (2006, April 27). *Giant Wal-Mart DIstribution Center has an equally large impact.* Retrieved from Houston Business Journal: https://www.bizjournals.com/houston/stories/ 2006/05/01/focus6.html

[21] Houston Business Journal Staff. (2006, April 27). *Giant Wal-Mart DIstribution Center has an equally large impact.* Retrieved from Houston Business Journal: https://www.bizjournals.com/houston/stories/ 2006/05/01/focus6.html

[22] Desormeaux, H. (2019, Jan 2). *Blue Water report.* Retrieved from AmericanShipper.com: https://www.americanshipper.com/news/blue water-report-the-gateway-to-americas-heartland?autonumber=73107

Was Bernard Lonergan a Second-Order Cyberneticist?

Fr. Joseph R. Laracy   **Thomas Marlowe**
Department of Mathematics and Computer Science

Edgar Valdez   **Msgr. Richard Liddy**
Department of the Core Curriculum   **Center for Catholic Studies**
Seton Hall University, South Orange, NJ 07079, USA
{thomas.marlowe | joseph.laracy | edgar.valdez | richard.liddy}@shu.edu

ABSTRACT

In reading the early 20th century works that defined second-order cybernetics together with the works of their contemporary, the philosopher and theologian Bernard Lonergan, SJ, one is struck by the resonances and interplay between the two perspectives, especially in terms of the scientist/observer interacting with and reflecting upon the subject, as well as the differences and contrasts between the two views. In this short overview, we present the case that Lonergan can be understood in part as an early and illuminating figure for understanding and reflecting upon second-order cybernetics itself.

Keywords: Cybernetics, Bernard Lonergan, Generalized Empirical Method, Cognitional Theory.

1. INTRODUCTION

In reading the works of 20th century philosopher and theologian Bernard Lonergan, SJ, one may find echoes or even anticipation of major themes of second-order cybernetics [SOC]. Most important may be

- An emphasis on the process of knowledge and cognition, including a reexamination of the Thomistic experience-understanding-judgment view of human knowing, with the insistence on understanding the role of the observer as a key to valid knowledge;
- A call for method, accepted and employed, in theology and philosophy, comparing the scientific method on the one hand, and the structures of mathematics on the other, resulting in his Generalized Empirical Method;
- A need for reflection (Insight) in philosophy, science, mathematics, and social science;
- And an integration of the social, natural, and formal sciences into his work, sometimes as a topic or perspective, sometimes as a tool, and sometimes by analogy.

In this article, we present the view that Lonergan should be considered as a key figure in the development of, and for the modern understanding of, second-order cybernetics. We first review the development and major ideas in that field, then consider Lonergan, his work, and his approach, and in particular its interactions and implications for knowledge, cognition, learning, and insight, both in general, and for the formulation and examination of research models and approaches.

We then consider separately the views from both perspectives of the natural and biological sciences, the mathematical sciences, the social sciences, and philosophy (and theology). We then seek to codify the overlaps, contrasts, and interactions of the approach of Lonergan with that of second-order cybernetics. We present a perspective integrating Lonergan's views with cybernetics, while considering differences and conflicts, and then consider some broadly applicable (and some more narrowly applicable) lessons. Finally, we present our conclusions and suggest paths for using and further exploring this connection.

2. CYBERNETICS

First Order Cybernetics

The term "cybernetics" comes from the Greek word, κυβερνήτης, meaning steersman, governor, pilot, or rudder. The American mathematician, Norbert Wiener, first utilized the term *cybernetics* in his 1948 book on the study of control and communication in the animal and the machine [1]. This seminal work established foundations for what would become control theory, analog computing, artificial intelligence, neuroscience, and communication theory. The MIT professor also made lasting contributions to the mathematical theory of Brownian motion and the foundations of signal processing. Wiener's research on probability theory provided the basis for Claude Shannon's development of information theory [2].

The British psychiatrist, W. Ross Ashby, was another pioneer in the field of cybernetics. He developed the fundamental concepts of the homeostat, the law of requisite variety, the principle of self-organization, and the principle of regulatory models [3]. The Hungarian-American mathematician, physicist, computer scientist, John von Neumann, also made a contribution to cybernetics when he developed what are now referred to as Von Neumann cellular automata (CA). The purpose of his CA was to provide insight into the logical requirements for machine self-replication, eventually utilized in von Neumann's universal constructor (i.e., a self-replicating machine in CA environment) [4].

First Order (Engineering) Cybernetics survives as an interdisciplinary field focusing on the design, analysis, and control of dynamic systems at universities in countries such as Norway, the UK, and Russia. Through the IEEE Systems, Man, and Cybernetics Society and a few other learned societies, cybernetics research continues in the USA, albeit not nearly as pervasively as its founders would have hoped [5]. The field has largely deliquesced into computer science, decision and control engineering, artificial intelligence and (more recently) data science, robotics, and bioengineering.

Second Order Cybernetics

The Austrian-American physicist, electrical engineer, and philosopher, Heinz von Förster, is widely acknowledged as the father of second-order cybernetics. He founded the Biological Computer Laboratory (BCL), a research institute of the Department of Electrical Engineering at the University of Illinois in Urbana-Champaign. The BCL was a productive research community from 1958 until 1976 when von Förster retired. The focus of the research at the BCL was on self-organizing systems, bionics (i.e., the application of biological methods and systems found in nature to the study and design of engineering systems), and bio-inspired computing (i.e., analyzing, formalizing, and implementing biological processes using computers). See [6].

The American computer engineer and management scientist, Jay Wright Forrester, continued to develop second-order cybernetics with an emphasis on the modelling and simulation of complex systems. Forrester founded the System Dynamics research group at MIT which focused on the study of the non-linear behavior of complex systems over time using stocks, flows, internal feedback loops, table functions, and time delays. His first application domain was analyzing industrial business cycles [7].

Another significant figure in this space is the Austrian biologist, Karl Ludwig von Bertalanffy, who developed the field of general systems theory (GST). GST offered a universal theory of systems with applications in numerous domains. It emphasizes holism over reductionism and organism over mechanism [8]. Manfred Drack and David Pouvreau point out however that Bertalanffy had an "ambivalent relationship" with the traditional cybernetic community and preferred to emphasize the distinctions between the two approaches [9].

Lonergan was certainly aware of Bertalanffy's work. In *Method in Theology*, he favorably cites his 1968 book *General Systems Theory*. Like cyberneticists, Lonergan was concerned about reductionism in the sciences. He observes that reductionism was particularly evident in the human sciences. Lonergan writes,

> Reductionists extend the methods of natural science to the study of man. Their results, accordingly, are valid only in so far as a man resembles a robot or a rat and, while such resemblance does exist, exclusive attention to it gives a grossly mutilated and distorted view. General system theory rejects reductionism in all its forms, but it still is aware of its unsolved problems [10].

A traditional electrical engineer interested in complex systems, or "first-order" cyberneticist, studies a system as if it were a passive, objectively given object. On the other hand, a "second-order" cyberneticist, often studying an organism or social system, acknowledges that the system under study is an agent in its own right, interacting with the observer. However, it should be noted that there was no "schism" between the two "orders," at least early on: Heinz von Förster, for example, was also involved in the development of first-order cybernetics in the 1950s.

Von Förster attributes the origin of second-order cybernetics to the quest to develop a model of the human mind [11]:

> …a brain is required to write a theory of a brain. From this follows that a theory of the brain, that has any aspirations for completeness, has to account for the writing of this theory. And even more fascinating, the writer of this theory has to account for her or himself. Translated into the domain of cybernetics; the cybernetician, by entering his own domain, has to account for his or her own activity. Cybernetics then becomes cybernetics of cybernetics, or *second-order cybernetics*.

The Anglo-Irish cybernetician, Ranulph Glanville, president of the American Society of Cybernetics, 2009-2014, and a leading light in the "second wave of second-order cybernetics," combined a multidisciplinary and interdisciplinary perspective with a view of design as the creation of novelty as much as, or more than, problem solving, and saw design and cybernetics as opposite sides of the same coin [12]. He stressed the feedback-loop interaction of observer and system, and of action and understanding, and applied these philosophical perspectives to science studies, understanding scientific explanations as an interaction between nature and the observer.

Second-order cyberneticists tend to emphasize topics in epistemology, and in ethics. In their study of complex systems, they often focus on the qualities of autonomy, self-consistency, self-referentiality, and self-organization, and the interaction of system and observer.

3. BERNARD LONERGAN

Bernard Lonergan, S.J. was a twentieth century Canadian Jesuit philosopher and theologian whose work spanned the subfields of these disciplines while also incorporating and influencing work in the social and natural sciences. In his seminal work, *Insight*, Lonergan holds that a very common and basic supervening act of understanding is operative throughout and critical for all cognitional activity, and views learning as a structured interweaving of experience, understanding, and judging.

Turning our attention to this act allows us to understand some of the truths of particular fields of inquiry but more importantly it allows us to understand the dynamic process of understanding in general. Lonergan famously writes "thoroughly understand what it is to understand, and not only will you understand the broad lines of all there is to be understood but also you will possess a fixed base, an invariant pattern, opening upon all further developments of understanding." [13] This allows us to recognize the systematic unity of all cognition and prescribes for us an approach that can be employed for particular inquiries but also internalized as a disposition towards all possible knowledge. What results is what Lonergan calls the Generalized Empirical Method. This method can be understood as taking an empirical scientific approach to the experiences, insights and judgments of consciousness. As such it

> consists in determining patterns of intelligible relations that unite the data [of consciousness] explanatorily… However, generalized method has to be able to deal, at least comprehensively, not only with the data within a single consciousness but also with the relations between different conscious subjects, between conscious subjects and their milieu or environment, and between consciousness and its neural basis [14].

Because the data of the consciousness of the knower necessarily falls within the scope of inquiry, such method also gives rise to an ethical dimension that Lonergan calls self-appropriation.

Mathematics offers evidence of the necessity of this reflective process even in the most formal *a priori* domains. Mathematical formalizations cannot be separated from the process through which they are formalized and this involves "gradually acquiring the insights that are necessary to understand mathematical problems, to follow mathematical arguments, to work out mathematical solutions. This acquisition occurs in a succession of higher viewpoints." [15] The insights of higher-level mathematics are conditioned by the insights, experiences, and judgments of lower-level mathematics. A mathematician can generate analytic propositions seemingly at will that tend towards completeness, generality, and ideality. Such propositions, however, must be conjoined with data and consistency constraints that the formal element then structures, even if these exist only in some conceptual universe. Thus, even pure mathematics cannot merely begin with certain analytic propositions and run rampant. Rather there is a procedure of deductive inference that serves as a process of checking.

4. LONERGAN AND CYBERNETICS

Lonergan's cognitional theory aligns with the aims of second order cybernetics, because it is fundamentally reflective and systematic. While insight is the lynchpin, the system is structured by a kind of feedback loop formed through experiencing, understanding, and judging. Understanding and judging condition and form the knower's experience which leads to other insights and further understanding and judging. This loop is inseparable from the knower who experiences, understands, and judges. "So far I have been talking about events as if there were nobody there; but there is someone who senses, imagines, inquires, understands, formulates his understanding, asks whether it is so, grasps the sufficiency of the evidence, and makes the judgment." [16] For Lonergan, the reflective moment of understanding this cognitional process also changes what we can understand. That is, the epistemological awareness is crucial for further metaphysical content. This situates us as knowers within the functional unity we seek to know: being. An example often used to demonstrate the supervening nature of insights asks us to consider the next entry in the series OTTFFSS. The realization of the correct answer is not a result of further information or rearranging the entries. It is a "Eureka" about the relationship among the entries. This realization requires awareness of the knower because the intelligible relationship has to do with what the knower is seeking. As such it calls for a kind of thinking about thinking that influences thinking.

So Lonergan's cognitional theory is not only to be understood as systematic but also as seeking systematicity. In this way, he is seeking understanding on a systematic level yet within that system and thus interacting with it. In part, Lonergan sees himself as bringing this systematicity, which has been successful in mathematics and physics to philosophical and theological cognition,

> A single insight yields a conception, a definition, an object of thought; but from a cluster of insights, you build up a system of definitions, axioms, postulates and deductions…By way of contrast, St. Thomas' *Summa Theologiæ* and his *Summa contra Gentiles* are not simply systems. While those works do hold together, his method is not that of setting down definitions, axioms, and postulates, and then deducing. In fact, that is just what he does not do [17].

Though second order cyberneticists can find commonality with Lonergan, there are clear moments of departure. One such moment concerns the turn to second order. For Lonergan, the cognitional structure presumes that the knower is situated within being. This kind of Aristotelian empiricism does not hope or suppose that it would be better to inquire into being from outside it. That perspective outside of being is one Lonergan rejects as necessary for the kind of objectivity that is concerned with impartiality. Impartiality is possible by refining our attention to generalized empirical method, not by bypassing it altogether.

A second point of departure might be in the notion or conception of structure. Within cybernetics, the structure of the system has to be understood as abstracting something from the object of investigation. This abstraction can of course come without an evaluative judgment about the relative significance of what is abstracted out or with a judgment that deems that which has been abstracted as irrelevant or unimportant. But for Lonergan, structure is decidedly more ontologically pervasive. Insofar as something is, it is intelligible. Insofar as it is intelligible it is structured. In this strong sense, there are no accidents for Lonergan. Systematicity permeates all of being and the knower's attention to it is not a matter of abstraction but rather an admission of the isomorphism between being and our unrestricted desire to know.

5. SCIENTIFIC DISCIPLINES FROM THE TWO PERSPECTIVES

Science is an interaction among nature, the professional and academic community, and the individual scientist. Science evolves through the understanding and judgment of individual scientists, leading to modeling, theory formation, and interpretation, interacting both with experiment and the scientific community. The roles of the three, and in particular the relevant domains and attributes of nature, and the balance among the three, change as one traverses the spectrum from social science and economics through the biological sciences to the natural sciences, ending with the formal sciences—mathematics, logic, and theoretical computer science.

The dependence of the conclusions of the social sciences (including economics), not only on interaction with the subjects, but also with the observer scientist, is now well-accepted. But both SOC and Lonergan view observer interaction as key in the biological and natural sciences as well.

Most second-order cyberneticists, on the other hand, don't devote much attention to the formal sciences, nor see them as having any special role. Lonergan, on the other hand, looks very much to logic and mathematics. One reason Lonergan pays special attention to the formal sciences is to draw out the nature and significance of the empirical method.

What is empirical about the generalized empirical method is not that it takes for granted a material existence that gives rise to our ideas about the external world. This view can be forcefully rejected by many formal sciences. Lonergan rather takes as a given the data of consciousness, the content of our insights, experiences, and judgments. These data are within the knower, and as such are present in the cognition of all inquiry. As such, the formal sciences do not occupy a special epistemological position but serve a useful epistemological role. The privileged science for Lonergan is metaphysics because questions of meaning in general, and in particular a technique for determining and integrating meaning, require metaphysical equivalence. In this sense, Lonergan is pointing to the same notions as Horne [18] concerning the integration of *episteme* and *techne* but he situates those concerns within metaphysics. Lonergan seems to have accepted the 20th century terminology of logic as mere sets of rules for thinking.

6. LONERGAN AS A SECOND-ORDER CYBERNETICIST

In Lonergan's Generalized Empirical Method (GEM), a person engages in a discursive process between apprehension, insight, and judgment. Lonergan's notion of *insight* is the crucial link between simply perceiving data and true understanding. It is one thing to notice something and it is completely another to genuinely understand it. The GEM also includes the important processes of attention, imagination, and memory. Ultimately, the GEM should lead to decision and action.

Here we see a clear parallel with the cybernetic notions of observation, feedback/communication, and control of a dynamic system. Lonergan does not treat the process of human cognition as a static object simply to be observed. He acknowledges the dynamicity of the human mind and the importance of self-appropriation. His concern is not knowledge of an "abstract self." He hopes to lead a person in an experience of one's self-consciousness taking possession of itself.

An important aspect of cybernetics is the science of observing and describing dynamics as well as interacting in engineering and biological processes. Lonergan engages in an analogous quest for the human intellect in his development of the GEM. Both Lonergan and the second-order cyberneticist would certainly agree that science always involves the scientist.

Differences certainly exist between the work of Lonergan and most second-order cyberneticists. As a priest and professor of dogma at the Pontifical Gregorian University in Rome, Catholic theology was Lonergan's principle application domain. Unlike many cyberneticists, but closer to the second-wave practitioners [12, 19], Lonergan's main concern was not with artificial intelligence, autonomous craft, bionics, or cyborgs (i.e., beings with both organic and biomechatronic components), but rather with metaphysics and epistemology, with human beings as reasoning agents, and the role of reasoning in understanding the divine.

Lonergan also has, as noted above, a very different view of both the nature and the role of logic and mathematics. For him, these are, in addition to structures for formal deduction, models of conceptual reasoning and an epitome of the role of intuition. In contrast, the proponents of second-order cybernetics are on the whole less interested in the role or process of mathematical inquiry — the early second-order cyberneticists following their first-order predecessors (with the notable exception of Wiener) in tending to continue seeing mathematics primarily as an adjunct to science and engineering, and those in the second wave focusing on the biological and social sciences, and on design as a cognitive process, with mathematics as part of the analogy toolkit and infrastructure.

7. CONCLUSIONS, OPEN ISSUES, AND FUTURE WORK

There are strong similarities in perspective and approach between Bernard Lonergan and the contemporary founders and later researchers in second-order cybernetics. These argue that considering Lonergan in the context of second-order cybernetics, and perhaps even viewing him as one of its (though perhaps not well known) founders, provides useful insights on both its development and its continued value for the philosophy of both science (broadly understood) and cognition, and for the study of science itself.

On the other hand, there are significant differences. The priority given by Lonergan to epistemology and metaphysics distinguishes him from most in the field of SOC. As a priest-philosopher/theologian, questions of meaning in general, and in particular a technique for determining and integrating meaning, both for its own sake and to deal with important questions, were also significant concerns for Lonergan. For example, the American theologian, John Cush, writes,

> Lonergan witnessed the effects of the Great Depression as friends of his family experienced unemployment and even hunger. This was a life-changing experience for

Lonergan, and caused him to orient his natural interests in epistemology in a social-ethical direction, including the study of economics [20].

As mentioned above, it is known that Lonergan was aware of and at least to some extent approved of the work of von Bertalanffy, if not of later developments in SOC. However, Lonergan appears not to be as well known, neither to his contemporaries in the SOC community [21], nor to the current SOC community.

Further investigation will be needed to determine which if any of those contemporaries were aware of Lonergan, and if so, of the connection of the GEM to the SOC approach, in particular in respect of subject-observer interaction and of reflection. In addition, comparison of the view and treatment of the formal sciences by Lonergan and by the SOC community is of particular interest to the authors. Finally, we hope to contact current SOC practitioners to determine their awareness of and reaction to the work of Lonergan, and perhaps contact selected Lonergan scholars to pursue the reverse connection. Finally, we hope to further explore the above-mentioned references in *Method in Theology* to functional specialization and the influence of Karl Ludwig von Bertalanffy.

8. REFERENCES

[1] N. Wiener, **Cybernetics, Second Edition: or the Control and Communication in the Animal and the Machine**. Cambridge, MA: MIT Press, 1965.

[2] C. Shannon, A Mathematical Theory of Communication. **The Bell System Technical Journal**, Vol. 27, No. 3, July 1948, 379–423.

[3] W.R. Ashby, **An Introduction to Cybernetics**. London: Chapman and Hall, 1956.

[4] J. Von Neumann, A.W. Burks, **Theory of Self-Reproducing Automata**. Urbana: University of Illinois Press, 1966.

[5] J.R. Laracy, Addressing System Boundary Issues in Complex Socio-Technical Systems. **Systems Research Forum**, Vol. 2, 2007, pp. 19-26.

[6] H. von Förster and W.R. Ashby, Biological Computers. **Bioastronautics**. K. E. Schaefer (e.d), New York, Macmillan Co., 1964, pp. 333– 360.

[7] J. Forrester, **Industrial Dynamics**. Cambridge, MA: Productivity Press, 1961.

[8] L. von Bertalanffy, **General System Theory**. New York, George Braziller, Inc., 1969.

[9] M. Drack and D. Pouvreau, On the history of Ludwig von Bertalanffy's 'General Systemology', and on its relationship to cybernetics – part III: convergences and divergences. **International Journal of General Systems**, Vol. 44, No. 5, 2015, pp. 523-571.

[10] B. Lonergan, **Method in Theology**. Toronto: University of Toronto Press, 2003, p. 248.

[11] H. von Förster, **Understanding Understanding: Essays on Cybernetics and Cognition**. New York: Springer-Verlag, 2003, p. 289.

[12] R. Glanville, Try again. Fail again. Fail better: The cybernetics in design and the design in cybernetics. **Kybernetes**, 36(9/10), 1173–1206. doi: 10.1108/ 03684920710827238

[13] B. Lonergan, **Insight: A Study of Human Understanding**. Toronto, University of Toronto Press, 1992, p.22.

[14] **Ibid**. p.268.

[15] **Ibid.**, 336.

[16] B. Lonergan, **Understanding and Being**. Toronto University of Toronto Press, 1990, p.113.

[17] **Ibid.**, pp. 52-3.

[18] J. Horne, Preface and Chapter 1 (The Core), in J. Horne (ed.), **Philosophical Perceptions of Logic and Order**. IGI Global, June 2017.

[19] S. Umpleby, Second-Order Cybernetics as a Fundamental Revolution in Science . **Constructivist Foundations**, 11(3): 455–465. 2016. http://constructivist.info/11/3/455

[20] J. Cush, **John Courtney Murray as Contextual Theologian: An Interpretation Based on Bernard Lonergan and Robert Doran**. PhD Thesis, Pontifical Gregorian University, 2017, p. 91.

[21] N. Callaos, Personal Communication, 2017.

ALM Program: Ten years of educational technology interventions at the Faculty of Medicine at the oldest National University in Perú.

Maritza PLACENCIA MEDINA
Senior Professor - Universidad Nacional Mayor de San Marcos (UNMSM)
Lima, Perú.
Javier SILVA.VALENCIA
Medical Doctor – TeleSalud Unit UNMSM, Biomedical Informatician in Global Health– UPCH
Lima, Perú.
Víctor MECHAN MENDEZ
Senior Professor of Hematology – UNMSM
Lima, Perú.
Rosa PANDO ÁLVAREZ
Instituto de Investigaciones Clínicas –UNMSM
Lima, Perú.
Margot Rosario QUINTANA SALINAS
Instituto Centro de Bioquímica y Nutrición –UNMSM
Lima, Perú.
Jorge Raúl CARREÑO ESCOBEDO
Systems and Information Engineer - UNMSM
Lima, Perú.
Yanelli Karen ASCACIVAR PLACENCIA
Economista, Colaborador externo
Lima, Perú

RESUMEN

Due to its benefits to promote student participation, develop skills, and strengthen the relationship with the teacher; Active learning methodologies (ALM) must be a priority in the university system. However, its optimal and massive use is still low.

Since 2008, a program was initiated to facilitate the correct implementation of ALM in the Faculty of Medicine of the National University of San Marcos (UNMSM). In this paper, we explain holistically the interventions and results of multiple projects: Innovations in Problem Based Learning (PBL) and Information and Communication Technologies (ICT).

Significant achievements were made among students and empowering teachers in the use of computer databases and design of competency-based evaluation matrix. A virtual simulation laboratory was created, fostering a transdisciplinary exchange that strengthened the academic activity. We show the methodologies used and student perception in subjects such as Pharmacology, one of the most difficult in the medical career and which served as an intervention model.

Palabras clave: Teaching competences, Active Learning methodologies (ALM), ICT, PBL, medical education.

INTRODUCCIÓN

The achievement of active and meaningful learning is a priority in any current university system [1]. This learning occurs when the person interacts with their environment and elaborates personal representations and value judgments that allow them to make decisions based on reference parameters [2]. Achieving this requires not only having an instructional pedagogy, but incorporating contributions from other fields, in addition to educational research for constructivist and sociocultural learning.

However, the current system of university education is very diverse and fragmented [3], with traditional teaching predominating, centered on the unidirectional transfer of knowledge. To position active and meaningful learning, authors like Dee Fink [4] bet on key aspects such as teaching: "*how to learn, use the scientific method, perform self-learning and analyze the nature of the courses*".

Especially in careers such as Human Medicine which must have a high level of learning [5, 6], these innovations are more effective when associated with experiments, reflexive dialogues, self-evaluations and the application of ICTs [7, 8, 9]. The empowerment of medical students through ALM is a primary objective that requires a moral and ethical commitment for both teachers and students [10]. An empowered student is an element with a high value not only for its high level of knowledge but also because it becomes a reference when engaging in topics beyond those offered by the university.

At the National University of San Marcos (UNMSM), the oldest national university in Peru, various factors led to a lack of deepening of meaningful learning: Teachers with little predisposition to change, poor knowledge of the method and absence of authorities to promote the acquisition of competences; have avoided to a certain extent that the student can be more proactive when taught with innovative methodologies [11], such as problem-based learning (PBL) [12].

In the present work, the development of the multiple investigations carried out is presented in a holistic way: We begin by showing information about the reality found 10 years ago, then a global description of what has been developed, focusing on the objectives and general guidelines of the interventions. Some indicators of processes and results are shown, and finally, a discussion and future perspectives are presented.

*The Spanish version of this article was presented to the Ninth Ibero-American Conference on Complexity, Information Technology and Cybernetics: CICIC 2019.

DIAGNOSIS OF THE INITIAL SITUATION

During 2008, a cross-sectional and descriptive study was conducted through an anonymous survey to determine the student's perception of the organization, academic management and teaching-learning provided. The students were volunteers of the third year of Human Medicine (n = 30) and identified high points, deficient areas, and gaps where an intervention could be generated.

Resultados:
➢ 44% did not reach a high level of learning (According to the Bloom scale) [5]
➢ 37% attended theoretical classes by obligation.
➢ The technique of least use of learning was the problematization and integration of information
➢ 50% attended pleasant methodologies different from the traditional ones for overcoming and actively participating in it.

INTERVENTIONS FOR CREATING CONTENT

The information found was disseminated and in the following years, several isolated initiatives were carried out. In 2012, the same situational diagnosis was made again, this time to 59 students, to evaluate changes. The results found were all similar, including that 47% of students did not use electronic resources in their learning.

Thus, the design of structured interventions in the course of Pharmacology was initiated, whose objective was initially the systematic creation of own content based on three pillars:
➢ Problem Based Learning (**PBL**)
➢ Use of Virtual Simulation Software (**VSS**) and
➢ Information and Communication Technologies (**ICTs**)
Table 1 summarizes the initiatives in which educational resources were created according to the area and objectives set.

INTERVENTIONS FOR THE PROMOTION OF ACTIVE METHODOLOGIES

The development of the "ALM Program" involved creating learning that promotes analysis, reflection, and intuition with the development of science and research; besides generating pleasure to educate, to learn and to build knowledge.

Although each intervention pursued specific objectives, they all had three moments in common:
a) **Awareness stage**, which was a constant battle to raise awareness among students, teachers and faculty authorities to allow, generate and be part of the changes
b) **Creation of ad hoc resources** and
c) **Teacher training** for teaching using new resources and new technologies

ALM Program Overview

The program is the result of a gradual process initiated with teacher awareness activities in the use of ALM and the use of virtual simulation software to initially learn experimental pharmacology and research on medicinal plants.

The target audience was students of different years and teachers. To carry out the projects, a multidisciplinary team of doctors, researchers, teachers, administrative staff and student assistants was formed. The work methodology used was based on the one

brought by an International ALM course led by Dr. Hendrik Van

Table 1. Interventions for the creation of meaningful learning

Year	Objectives	(Area) and resource created	Training carried out
Pharmacology teaching with virtual simulators			
2012	Install softwares as an option to experiments.	(VSS) Creation of 4 guides for the use of software	Six trainings of respect for life, replacement of animals and virtual software
	Facilitate student-teacher access to new information	(TIC) Creation of a web portal Access to bibliography and information	
Inclusion of Active Methodologies			
2011	Create an educational platform for learning and as a support for interaction between students and teachers	(TIC) First virtual classroom of Pharmacology with self-learning material, tutorial support, and record of activities.	Two asynchronous trainings to create virtual classrooms and how to direct them.
2012	Increase meaningful learning through modules based on problem-solving and discussion	(ICT) Virtual classroom with e-books and didactic material of each class prepared by teachers	Three sessions to agree on PBL and common use of an evaluation matrix
		(ABP) Cases problems in 6 modules. Creation of a matrix to evaluate performance and achievement.	
Creation of a Virtual Simulation Laboratory			
2013	Consensus on the correct use of the environment and software	(VSS) Guidelines for student use of the Laboratory	Two trainings for teachers for correct use of laboratory hardware and software and how to use new resources to achieve meaningful instruction in the student.
	Create virtual environments for use within the laboratory	(TIC) Renewal of a website with a virtual classroom in open source software: access to a schedule, to teachers, access to bibliographic resources	
	Establish learning with new virtual simulators and more cases.	(VSS) Tutorials for solving problems with software and its practical application.	
Teaching new topics: Pharmacogenetics			
2011	Agree on learning by resolution and discussion of cases	(PBL) Design of 02 problem cases.	Training in cases: "Warfarin in genotypes CYP2C9 / VKORC1" and "Abacavir in genotypes HLA-B5701 in HIV"
2014	Establish pharmacogenetics learning through ALM	(ICT) Creation of a virtual classroom and use of email and Facebook as a learning tool.	

contents until 2014

Wilgenburg (University of Amsterdam) who provided the software used [13]. There, it was defined as "active participation of learning" to the review of knowledge (pharmacokinetics and pharmacodynamics) with respect to a practical result (pharmacological effect of drugs), continuing with the discussion of results for the consolidation of knowledge and the virtual presentation of knowledge.

Figure 1 summarizes in a timeline the interventions made during the 10 years and then its methodology and results are briefly exposed.

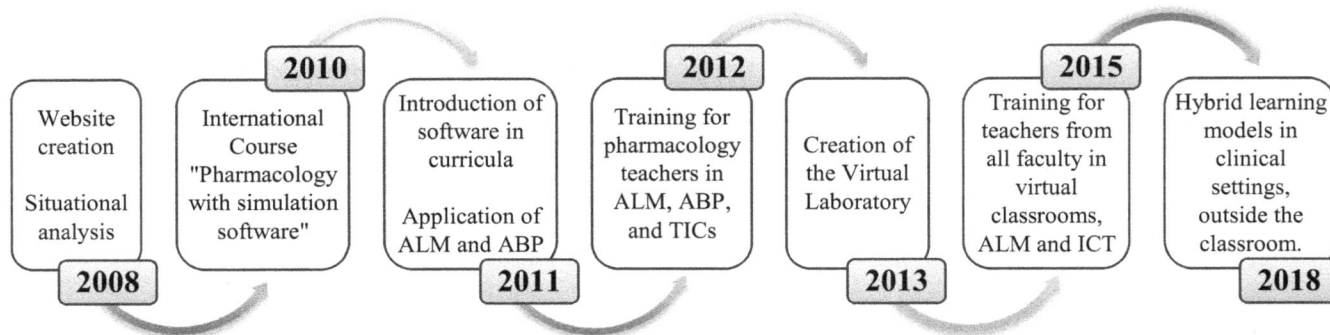

Figure 1: Timeline of the milestones during the ten years of educational technology interventions.

IMPACT OF ICT AND ABP IN THE ACADEMIC PERFORMANCE. YEARS 2010 TO 2012

By the year 2012, some methodologies such as PBL for self-learning had already been applied. It was proposed to compare the academic performance of 405 students, since 2010 (n = 139), 2011 (n = 132) and 2012 (n = 134).

Design and general description:

During 2010 there was no formal intervention, the teaching methodology used was the traditional one. In 2011, the use of ALM began and in 2012 the use of ALM methodologies with PBL was increased.

The intervention of the year 2012 involved laying the methodological foundations for achieving meaningful learning, which was improving year after year (see Figure 2). Extraordinary sessions were held with teachers in order to agree on the analysis of the case-problems raised and 7 sessions of PBL were conducted with interactive material in teams of 05 students and a facilitator teacher.

The materials were published in the virtual classroom, to allow learning to the rhythm of the student, who received a digital disc (DVD) with programmed practices, E-Books of Pharmacology and teaching materials prepared by teachers.

Results

No significant difference was found in the final averages of the course in the three years evaluated (p = 0.053). However, there was a significant increase in the scores for 2012 when evaluating the modules intervened separately (p = 0.001).

The general perception of the students in 2012 was that the applied ALM allowed them a higher level of learning (according to the Bloom scale), allowing them not only to remember and understand but also to analyze and synthesize the information..

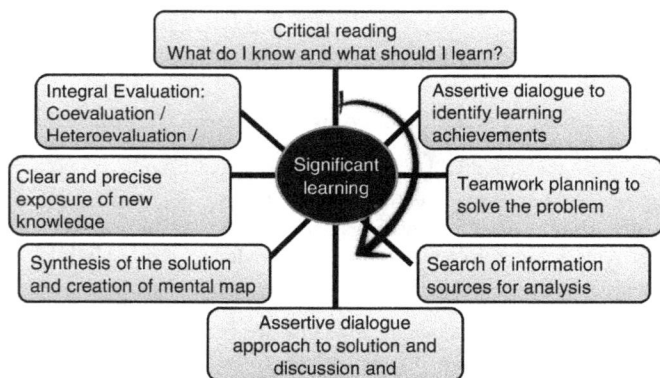

Figure 2: Bases of the plan to achieve meaningful learning.

INTRODUCTION OF SIMULATION SOFTWARE TO IMPROVE LEARNING.

The first introduction was made of the use of virtual simulations in experimental pharmacology to improve learning and respect the ethical norms in the handling of experimental animals motivating the student to be an active participant in their teaching at their own pace.

Design and general description:

The use of virtual simulators in the education of third-year medical students (n = 134) of the UNMSM was examined. Steps:
   a) Raise awareness among teachers about the rational use of experimental animals.
   b) Develop and apply didactic materials for the practices that included a web portal for the use of the software. (Figure 3)

Results and conclusions:

Six trainings were given to professors on the use of virtual simulators. Six practice guides were created for the use of the "Micro Labs" and "Cardiovascular Rat" software.

All the students of the year 2012, who used simulation software, had an average grade higher than the previous year with a significant difference (p = 0.01)

Figure 3: Web portal created to train in the use of simulation software - *http://sanfer1.wix.com/microlabs*

CREATION OF A VIRTUAL LABORATORY IN PHARMACOLOGY. YEAR 2013

The proposal of the physical space was designed, with computer equipment where students and teachers could interact and achieve interactive, creative and clear learning using simulators and accessing information.

Design and general description:

In addition to determining the technical requirements and the architecture of the virtual classroom to be used, a pedagogical and administrative structure (guides and didactic tutorials) was created for training in 4 short sessions with the use of software.

Results:
An area of 58 m2 was implemented with an electrical system necessary for the operation of 27 computers. During the inauguration, a workshop was held with students of the Toxicology course, which showed a high level of satisfaction with the organization, infrastructure, and learning achieved.

INSERTING NEW "PHARMACOGENETIC" EDUCATIONAL TOPICS. 2014

With the implementation of the virtual laboratory, an intervention was planned to include important topics in the medical career that are not included in the curriculum.

Design and general description:
The implementation of PBL and TICs in Pharmacogenetics teaching to third-year Medicine students were evaluated, during the years 2012 (n = 134), 2013 (n = 8) and 2014 (n = 150). It was implemented in the theoretical session of the course using the ABP to solve the cases in blended form: "Dosage of Warfarin in genotypes CYP2C9 / VKORC1" and "Dosage of Abacavir in genotypes HLA-B5701 in patients with HIV" The development of the intervention is summarized in Figure 4.

Results:
The materials were shared online five days before the face-to-face class. In it, they exposed problems, their resolution and the revisions of the subject. Great capacity for synthesis and creativity in the design of what was learned was observed. The level of learning estimated on an score of 10, was 8.24 ± 0.8.

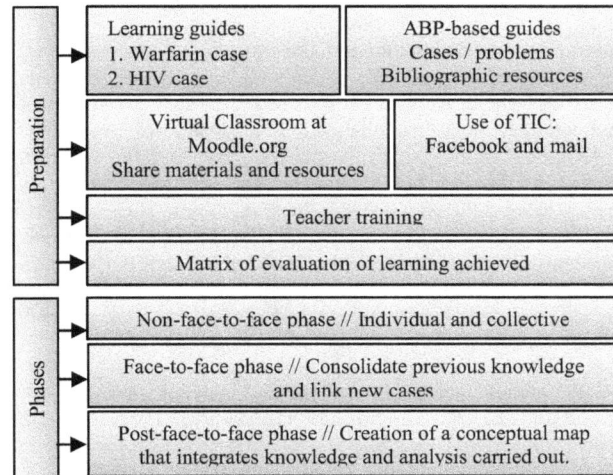

Figura 4. Planificación de ALM para Farmacogenética.

INTERMEDIATE SITUATIONAL DIAGNOSIS – 2014

At the end of 2014, the learning situation was explored again. It was found:
➤ More than 75% of the students declared to achieve high levels of learning.
➤ 90% attended classes for learning motivation
➤ Only 11% did not use electronic resources for self-learning

We also find different proposals for change in the methodology of the course and the expressions of the students.
Opinion about the improvement of the classes: *"I would ask for more interest in the development of the theoretical classes, they are monotonous and many of them with little information".*
Opinions about the methodology: *"Greater horizontality" "Modules must have a good PBL, if they are not used correctly, it causes confusion, train all teachers equally"*

TRANSDISCIPLINARY TRAINING IN THE USE OF ICT. YEARS 2015, 2016

After the interventions in the course of Pharmacology, we began with interventions throughout the Faculty of Medicine

Training was initiated to develop ICT competencies according to the UNESCO model. In the end, although 78% achieved high levels of competence, only 25% of teachers created and implemented virtual classrooms. There were important limitations concerning the technological conditions and university policies to integrate it into their teaching activity [7].

Figure 5: Transdisciplinary training in the use of ICT

INTRODUCTION OF ACTIVE METHODOLOGIES IN HOSPITAL ENVIRONMENTS - 2017, 2018

In the year 2017, the intervention in hospital environments began. Because the form of evaluation could vary from the subjective (based on experiences) to the quantitative (based on a test); an evaluation instrument was developed to standardize the evaluation based on achievement of competences.

Resistance to change was shown; however, the critical point was the constant teacher training and a follow-up plan.

"We are just being aware that we must work as a team and change the traditional methodology"
"We are using the new active methodologies and we feel the difference, I am changing the strategy, with satisfaction"

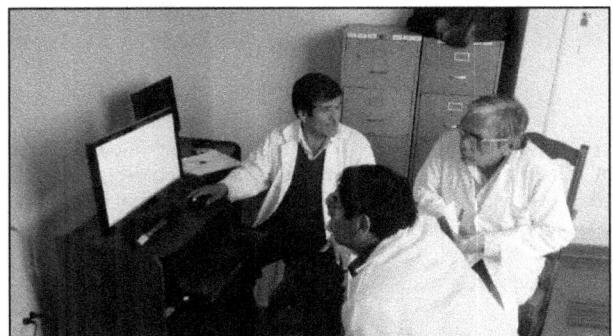

Figure 4. Teaching of ALM in Hospitals

APPLICATION OF B-LEARNING TO IMPROVE SURGICAL SKILLS - 2017, 2018

Finally, in 2017, a project for conducting the course "Surgical Techniques and Anesthesiology" was presented; using the Blended Learning methodology. The design was quasi-experimental research applied to 210 fifth-grade medical students. Among the results of relevance is the continuous use of virtual classrooms, the production of videos by teachers, a restriction of the theoretical content, the evaluation by competencies and the evidence of the improvement of the surgical skills achieved through the use of virtual simulations and face-to-face simulations (laparoscopy or endoscopy).

DISCUSSION

The creation of the Faculty of Medicine of the UNMSM was in 1856. And because it was the first faculty in Peru, it led to the establishment of all the foundations of national medical training in its classrooms since the end of the viceregal period [14]. During the first years, the learning methodology was focused on the teacher considered as the wise and inspiring, and with an educational plan with international bases of anatomy, galenic botany and art [15]. Then, the academic structure was oriented to solve national problems and the use of natural resources [16] but with the same pedagogical form.

Already during the twentieth century, the curricular system was changing due to international and world wars so teaching began to have non-vertical teaching models. But it was not until the 21st century when dizzying changes occurred thanks to the introduction of the Flexner educational process [17] with its methodology of meaningful learning and learning by doing. The construction of meaningful learning then became a transcendental matter in our university system [18].

In this context, the need to give more dynamism to the role of teachers is considered, who should focus much more on the student [19]. However, to empower the great change of this new era, it is necessary to implement more technology and interactivity in educational media, encourage teachers to optimize the teaching process and awaken in students an active participation in their self-learning. Thus, the university would assume its role of training professionals with the capacity to develop their potential based on their career [20].

The success of the application of the MLA seen in the interventions presented here, is due to the motivation and usefulness of the problematization for self-learning in the students, who became stimulators of their own process. They determine the objectives of the solution, develop the strategic plan and discuss what was learned. Although the teachers are guides and received training in the PBL methodology [16], in these 10 years it was striking that the students were the true drivers of this methodology [21].

It can be affirmed now that in the UNMSM, the teaching-learning in some courses of the health sciences, have adopted the model of learning centered on the student and the achievement of this goal contribute the ALM. Especially competency-based education that allows designing curricula based on the health needs of the population, and integrate the achievement of skills and attitudes required.

These educational advances have already been implemented and reported in the local environment by private universities and in countries such as Colombia and Mexico [22, 23, 24]. It is necessary that the teaching staff of a public university also know the bases of education by competence and have an active participation in the design of the tools and in their correct implementation [25]. Support the above, the new educational taxonomy of Dee Fink [4], made explicit in 6 categories, essential to learn something: Initially **"Know"** what it is to remember specific information. For this you need to have basic knowledge

of the subject. The **"Application"** that consists of learning new social, physical and intellectual actions of daily life through critical and creative thinking. The **"special value"** that is to create awareness that learning will provide intellectual and practical power. **"Integration"** is when the student understands the connection between different things. The **"human dimension"** is to understand that what is learned will interact effectively with social and personal implications. And the **"Application of learning"** which is the effective use to solve problems.

Likewise, to design the interventions presented in this report, the Rickenmann didactic was incorporated [26], where it is important to plan the cognitive activity and the tasks that the students must perform. First, the model of teaching materials related to the teaching-learning contents is created and then the stimuli for the critical analysis of the problem and the search for the solution are intensified. Finally, the problem is solved, with teamwork, with argumentative debates based on scientific evidence [27].

In most of the educational blocks developed initially, there was a deficit in the use of ICTs and some potential causes were found: 1. Faculty directors do not add to the academic load of teachers who develop ICTs (the hours spent on tasks of virtual teaching-learning). 2. Lack of confidence of teachers to teach in virtual spaces. 3. Resistance to change, cultural and organizational barriers, which do not differ from other countries. According to Kirkup and Kirkwood, advances in the use of ICTs in higher education have been gradual rather than revolutionary [28]. In the present case, ICTs played an important role as technological tools from acquisition to presentation of information [7].

An important event that favored the educational intervention was the curricular reform of the Human Medicine career that began in 2014, where a curriculum based on the achievement of competences was established. The group of researchers developed training for teachers in Active Learning Methodologies, thanks to their greater benefit for the achievement of basic skills in metacognition and ability for argumentative communication [11]. It is important to emphasize that the ABP is considered as ALM that uses the scientific method for its execution [16] and that after routinizing it as a didactic method, it was used as a key didactic strategy in the learning process.

For the achievement of competencies, academic strengths were important, such as the interdisciplinary nature of the teachers, the transdisciplinarity (members of different careers in the educational research team, teacher educators); a computerized infrastructure and the acquisition of basic laboratory equipment that has allowed the practical development of cognitive, procedural and attitudinal capacities; for the sustainability of these elements in the curriculum. As well as the commitment of the students to develop them, exercising their own responsibility [5, 11]. In the same way, more updated methodologies such as Blended learning (B-Learning), in face-to-face surgical learning (surgical skills), supported by electronic means, in medical education have been started [29, 30].

CONCLUSION

In this decade (2008-2018), important educational changes have been achieved, highlighting the commitment of teachers in the development of ALM methodologies, the use of ICTs, the political support of the authorities of the Faculty of Medicine, which facilitated the training teachers to develop their pedagogical skills, educational management and student satisfaction in the development of their skills with assertive communication and the achievement of meaningful learning for life.

BIBLIOGRAPHY

[1] F. Diaz, G. Fernández, Estrategias docentes para un aprendizaje significativo. Una interpretación constructivista. 3ᵃedición. México: Editorial McGraw-Hill-México, 2010, p. 405.

[2] J. Rivera, El aprendizaje significativo y la evaluación de los aprendizajes. Tecnología educativa. Revista de investigación educativa, 8(14), 2004, pp: 47-52.

[3] P. Paucar, Estrategias de aprendizaje, motivación para el estudio y comprensión lectora en estudiantes de la facultad de educación de la UNMSM. Tesis Magíster en Psicología con mención en Psicología Educativa. 2015,49 pp.

[4] L. Dee Fink. Creating significant learning experiences. An integrated approach to designing College Courses. 2ⁿᵈ edition. San Francisco. USA: Published by Jossey-Bass. 2013. p:334.

[5] W. Lorin, D. Krathwohl (Eds.), A Taxonomy for Learning, Teaching, and Assessing: A Revision of Bloom's Taxonomy of Educational Objectives, Complete Edition. Longman. (2000)

[6] Universidad Nacional Mayor de San Marcos UNMSM. Modelo Educativo, Vice Rectorado Académico 2015. http://viceacademico.unmsm.edu.pe/wcontent/uploads/2015/07/Modelo_Educativo_completo.pdf

[7] M. Placencia, R. Pando, V. Mechan, M. Quintana, J. Carreño, H. Mendoza, J. Silva, Y. Teaching competences using ICT, Faculty of Medicine: San Fernando UNMSM, Lima-Perú: Proceeding of The 22nd World Multi Conference on Systemic Cybernetics and Informatics (WMSCI2018)pp: 54-58.

[8] A, Pinto, O. Cortes, C. Alfaro. Hacia la transformación de la práctica docente: modelo espiral de Competencias. Depósito de Investigación Universidad de Sevilla. 2017; pp: 37-51.

[9] C. Ferro, A. I. Martínez, C. Otero. Ventajas del uso de las TICs en el proceso de enseñanza- aprendizaje desde la óptica de los docentes universitarios españoles. Revista electrónica de tecnología educativa (Edutece): 2009, 29. pp:1-12.

[10] Aneas. Transdisciplinary Design Education Framework. Transdisciplinary technology education: a characterization and some ideas for implementation in the University. Studies in Higher Education. 2015; vol 40 (9), pp: 1715-1728.

[11] G.Sanjay, N. Utsav , U. Parekh, J. Ganjiwale. Student's perception about innovative teaching learning practices in Forensic Medicine. Journal of Forensic and Legal Medicine.2017; 52(1), pp: 137-142.

[12] M. Placencia, C. García, H. Mendoza, L. Tenorio, J. Valencia, J. Escobedo. Nivel de satisfacción de estudiantes en el diseño e implementación del laboratorio de simulación virtual en la sección de Farmacología de la Facultad de Medicina de la UNMSM. Horiz Med. 2015; 15 (3), pp: 51-56.

[13] H.van Wilgenburg, P.Zillesen,I. Krulichova .Experimental design : computer simulation for improving the Precision of an experiment. Altern lab 2004 Jun;32 Suppl 1B, pp: 607-611.

[14] O. Salaverry. El inicio de la educación médica moderna en el Perú. La creación de la Facultad de Medicina de San Fernando. Acta Medica Peruana. 2006; 23 (2), pp: 122-131.

[15] H. Unanue. Oración inaugural que, para la estrena y apertura del Anfiteatro Anatómico, dijo en la real Universidad de San Marcos. Decadencia y Restauración del Perú. Mercurio Peruano; 3 febrero 1793, 7 (218), pp: 82-127.

[16] CE. Paz-Soldán. Heredia y sus discípulos. Biblioteca de Cultura Sanitaria. Lima: Instituto de Medicina Social; 1956, p. 63.

[17] A. Flexner. Medical Education in the United States and Canada. A report to the Carnegie Foundation for the advancement of teaching. Washington, DC: Science and Health Publications, Inc.; 1910.

[18] S. Tobón. Formación integral y competencias. Pensamiento complejo, currículo, didáctica y evaluación. Centro de Investigación en Formación y Evaluación CIFE, 3ᵃ ed. Bogotá-Colombia. Ecoe-Ediciones, 2010.

[19] IHN. Sheriff, F. Ahmed, N. Jivraj, JCM. Wan JCM, J. Sampford, N. Ahmed . Student-led leadership training for undergraduate healthcare students. Leadersh Heal Serv. 2017. doi:10.1108/LHS-03-2017-0018

[20] L. Rodríguez. El aprendizaje basado en problemas, para la educación médica: sus raíces epistemológicas y pedagógicas. Rev Med. 2014;22(2):32-36

[21] I. Valdez. El enfoque de competencias en la virtualidad educativa. Apertura. 2006;6(4):20-30.

[22] D. Champin. Evaluación por competencias en la educación médica. Revista Peruana De Medicina Experimental Y Salud Pública [serial on the Internet]. (2014, July), [cited June 15, 2018]; 31(3): 566-571. Available from: MedicLatina.

[23] G. Risco. Educar por competencias a los profesionales de la salud para transformar la salud. Revista Peruana De Medicina Experimental Y Salud Pública [serial on the Internet]. (2014, July), [cited June 15, 2018]; 31(3) pp. 413-416. Available from: MedicLatina.

[24] A. González-Burboa, C. Acevedo. Percepción de estudiantes de la Salud acerca de la implementación de las macrocompetencias genéricas. Revista Cubana De Educación Médica Superior [serial on the Internet]. (2016, Oct), [cited June 15, 2018]; 30(4),pp: 349-360. Available from: MedicLatina.

[25] M. Durante, A. González, S. López, J. Lozano, M. Mendiola. Educación por competencias: de estudiante a médico. Revista De La Facultad De Medicina De La UNAM [serial on the Internet]. (2011, Nov), [cited June 15, 2018]; 54(6), pp: 42-50. Available from: MedicLatina.

[26] R. Rickenmann. Metodologías clínicas de investigación en didácticas y formación del profesorado: un estudio de los dispositivos de formación en alternancia. Actas del Congreso Internacional de investigación, educación y formación docente. 2006 pp: 1-16.

[27] A. Estrada. El aprendizaje por proyectos y el trabajo colaborativo, como herramientas de aprendizaje, en la construcción del proceso educativo, de la Unidad de aprendizaje TICs. Revista Iberoamericana para la investigación y el desarrollo educativo. 2012; 3 (5), pp: 123-138

[28] G. Kirkup, A. Kirkwood. Information and communications technologies (ICT) in higher education teaching a tale of gradualism rather than revolution. Learn Media Technol. 2005;30(2), pp:185-199. doi:10.1080/17439880500093810

[29] MJ. Cheesman, S.Chenb, M.L Machadia, T. Jacobb, RF.Minchina, PA. Tregloanb. Implementation of a Virtual Laboratory Practical Class (VLPC) module in pharmacology education Pharmacognosy Communications 2014, 4(1), pp: 2-10

[30] A.Estrada .El aprendizaje por proyectos y el trabajo colaborativo como herramienta de aprendizaje, en la construcción del proceso educativo, de la Unidad de aprendizaje TICs. Revista Iberoamericana para la investigación y el desarrollo educativo.2012;3 (5),pp:123-138.

The framework of teacher competencies – an evidence-based generic model for teachers' training in Europe

Paweł Poszytek, PhD

Foundation for the Development of the Education System

National Agency of the Erasmus+ Program

Warsaw 02-305, Poland

ABSTRACT

The article is devoted to the topic of teacher competencies in an international perspective. It presents the recommendations and the generic framework of the Polish Expert Group for Describing Teachers' Competencies[1] in the context of the latest research and data on the national teacher competencies frameworks collected in 28 European countries.

Key words: Teachers' competencies, Teachers' competence profile, Teachers' work pillars

INTRODUCTION

The need to provide high quality school education has become one of reference points of the European Union cooperation in education and training (ET 2020) [1]. It sets out four strategic objectives, responding to challenges the systems of education in Europe are presented with. These objectives include:

- implementation of the concept of lifelong learning and mobility;
- improving the quality and efficiency of education and training;
- promoting equity, social cohesion, and active citizenship;
- enhancing creativity and innovation, and also entrepreneurship, at all levels of education and training.

Consequently, the ET 2020 places a strong emphasis on education and continuing professional development of teachers and on making the profession of a teacher an attractive and conscious career choice. This was also reflected in other documents, i.e. in the Council Conclusions of 26 November 2012 stating that that Member States of the European Union should concentrate their efforts on improving the recruitment to the teaching profession, professional development of teachers, and raising the overall status of teachers, school leaders and teacher trainers [2]. In recent years, a number of introduced reforms directly affected not only teacher education, but also this of head teachers [3].

The literature on the subject proves that the quality of schools and students' educational outcomes to a large extent depend on

the quality of teachers [4,5,6,7] (Hanushek, 2004; Rivkin, Hanushek, Kain, 2005; Rockoff, 2004; Hattie, 2012), and the quality of teachers is correlated with the quality of their education (Barber, Moursed, 2007; Darling-Hammond, 2017) [8,9].

The individual approach to each student, attracting the best candidates for teachers and high quality of teacher education are features, which make top systems of education stand out. This means that teachers are treated as a primary resource for schools and are in fact the factor affecting the quality of education, as it is on teachers, and especially on their competencies, that students' learning outcomes largely rely on [10].

TEACHERS' COMPETENCIES

Speaking of teachers' competencies it is worth describing them as a sophisticated combination of knowledge, skills, understanding, values, attitudes and aspirations, which are at the heart of teachers' profession at and outside the school. These competencies differ from skills, which are defined as the ability to perform complex operations with ease, precision and using adaptability skills [11] .

When investigating teachers'competencies as a pedagogical concept, one should consider their:

- Subjective character - competencies are owned by individuals or collective entities (e.g. society, group of people, organization);
- Complex structure - competencies have different structure, depending on their type. Knowledge, skills, personality traits, value systems, experience, and motivation for work are the factors affecting the competence structure;
- Graduality - an entity achieves competencies at differing levels, which affects their efficiency and ability to perform a given task, whereas a specified competence level of a given entity is defined by the degree of development of individual components that make up the competence (e.g. the level of knowledge or abilities in a given scope);
- Dynamics - it is expressed by the change in the condition of individual correlates of competence, and as a result may lead to a change in the entire competence, which in turn testifies to the possibility of its development;
- Possibility of development - competencies are treated as a result of the process of individual's learning in the course of the acquisition and production of educational

---

[1] The working team is composed of: dr Paweł Poszytek (FRSE), team head; dr Beata Jancarz-Łanczkowska (ORE); dr Piotr Minkiewicz (IBE), and contributing experts: Liliana Budkowska (FRSE), Marta Choroszczyńska (MSCDN), prof. dr hab. Joanna Madalińska-Michalak (UW), Alicja Pietrzak (FRSE), Anna Ryś (ŁCDNiKP), Ewa Sprawka (ŁCDNiKP), dr Dominika Walczak (IBE, APS).

experiences in the course of one's life, which are significant for the individual;

- Expression of competencies in a certain context situation - competencies are expressed when an individual undertakes to execute tasks in certain conditions;
- Interactivity of competencies with the conditions, in which an individual operates - lifelong updating of competencies according to the context (new experiences affect the development of knowledge, skills improvement and attitudes of an individual, which are expressed in action);
- Transferability of competencies to other situations and other frames of reference - this leads to the expansion of freedom and ownership, and the ability to carry out new tasks as a result [12].

Not only teachers' education, but also all pre-professional experiences and those acquired in the course of work affect their competencies. Competencies depend on tacit/hidden and explicit knowledge of teachers', their cognitive and practical skills and also on their predispositions (motivation, beliefs, orientation). Well-developed competencies of a teacher:

- Allow them to meet complex requirements, which are imposed by the school and its stakeholders;
- Allow them to act in a professional manner, which is appropriate in a given situation;
- Allow them to ensure efficient and effective performance of tasks (to achieve the desired result with optimised resources and efforts [13].

In the above context, it is worth emphasising that there is much more to teachers' work than just efficient and effective implementation of tasks. Discussion on the competencies teachers need and on how they are developed over time and recorded is related to a broader discussion on the assumptions concerning the learning process; teaching objectives; social expectations and requirements of teachers; available teaching resources and domestic and international education policy priorities; the status of the teaching profession; existing traditions and culture related to teaching, learning, teachers' work; and a wider social context and environment, in which teaching and learning take place.

One of the most important contributions to this topic has been made by a team of experts working in the ET-2010 programme who established a *Common European Principles for Teacher Competencies and Qualifications* [14].

The common European principles describe the vision of the teaching profession in Europe as follows:
(a) a well-qualified profession;
(b) a profession placed within the context of lifelong learning;
(c) a mobile profession - the professional development should be related to the mobility of teachers;
(d) a profession based on partnership - cooperation between teachers and institutions plays an important role in the development of teachers.

In addition to the common European principles, the text proposes three contexts, in which teachers from the European Union Member States should be able to operate:

(a) work with others;
(b) work with knowledge, technology and information;
(c) work with society and in society.

Apart from the above mentioned text, other documents show the assumptions concerning the development of teachers' profile and good practices in the scope of the development of teachers' skills. These include: *Rethinking education: Investing in skills for better socio-economic outcomes* [15], *Teaching Professions for Better Learning Outcomes* [16], *Policy approaches to defining and describing teacher competencies* [17] and *Supporting teacher competence development for better learning outcomes* [18].

New requirements imposed on schools necessitated a change of thinking about teacher education, which has resulted in the development of legal basis for teacher education and training, and determining the standards for such education in many European countries. In Poland, the regulation of the Minister of Science and Higher Education of 17 January 2012 on the education and training standards for the practice of the profession of a teacher (OJ 2012, item 131)[2], reflects such an approach.

At the European Union level, the Communication from the Commission to the European Parliament *Rethinking Education: Investing in skills for better socio-economic outcomes* [19] stipulates that each Member State needs to establish a competence framework or professional profile for teachers, which will form the basis for the introduction of an efficient system of recruitment to the teaching profession and will make it attractive for the best candidates.

Trends in the policy of the European Union clearly show that teacher education needs to be geared to the development of competencies. Therefore, the proposed below competence framework or professional profile for teachers is a necessary tool in the organisation of teacher education. Such framework is considered indispensable from the point of view of designing teacher education programmes.

TEACHER COMPETENCE FRAMEWORKS ISSUED BY TOP-LEVEL AUTHORITIES IN EUROPE

The report of 2018 *Teaching careers in Europe. Access, Progression and Support* developed by the Eurydice network brings, among others, data on existence and use of teacher competence frameworks in different countries [20].

Teacher competence framework is defined by Eurydice as a collection of statements about what a teacher as a professional should know, understand and be able to do which may be used to support the identification of development needs and improve the skills of the teaching workforce. The level of detail in the

---

[2] The Regulation of the Minister of National Education and Sport of 7 September 2004 on teacher education standards (OJ no. 2017, item 2110) was repealed effective on 1 October 2011, because of the entry into force of the act of 18 March 2011 amending the Law on Higher Education, Law on Academic Degrees and Title and Degrees and Title in the Arts (OJ no. 84, item 455 and no. 112, item 654).

description of the knowledge, skills and competences may vary from one document to another.

The 2017 report of the European Commission's Thematic Working Group Schools underlines the different purposes the teacher competence frameworks or professional standards can serve, namely apart from the use in teacher initial training (ITE), continuing professional development (CPD), career progression or teacher appraisal they provide the opportunity for dialogue, can help promote quality in the teaching profession by increasing transparency, by helping teachers deploy and develop their professional competences and by promoting teacher agency, empowerment and responsibility [21].

Eurydice has undertaken analysis of competence frameworks issued by top level authorities of particular countries, as those with the top leverage. Such frameworks are published in a form of official documents such as decrees or laws, regulations (on ITE or CPD) or national plans. Finally, they are published as individual texts such as e.g. teacher standards, teachers competences, rulebooks or codes of practice.

Teacher competence frameworks issued by top-level authorities, primary and general secondary education (ISCED 1-3), 2016/17

- ■ Competence framework in place
- □ Competence framework under development
- ▨ No competence framework

Source: Eurydice

In nine education systems – the German-speaking Community of Belgium, Bulgaria, Greece, Croatia, Cyprus, Malta, Finland, Iceland and Liechtenstein - there are no competence frameworks in place nor there are plans to elaborate them. As for those countries that have such frameworks in place there are three types of competence areas common to almost all of them: psycho-pedagogical competences, subject knowledge and teaching approaches, organization of learning and evaluation, innovative teaching methods, communication with pupils, cooperation with other teachers and relations with pupils' parents and other stake holders.

The documents vary a lot when one takes into consideration the level of detail of knowledge, competences and skills of teachers. In seven education systems the teacher competence framework list the competence areas but do not provide further details. Competence frameworks in such countries as the French Community of Belgium, Spain, Italy, Hungary, Austria, Slovakia and Switzerland list general competences such as "effective partnership relationships with colleagues and parents" or "working as a team" but no further clarification is given (French Community of Belgium). In remaining systems with such frameworks in place the level of detail in teacher

competences frameworks is much greater and gives more detail e.g. in the Netherlands teacher competences are divided into seven areas, with general objectives defined for each areas together with required skills and knowledge. In the Flemish Community of Belgium, Estonia, Latvia and the United Kingdom competences are described for different stages.

For example in Estonia the framework defines required competences for a Teacher. Additional competences are then listed for the upper levels of the teaching career. A Senior Teacher should support development of other teachers and contribute towards development of teaching methodology in a given school and a Master Teacher should participate in development of creative activities inside and outside school and cooperate closely with a university [22].

In the United Kingdom, the Standards for Registration, the General Teaching Council for Scotland defines for each competence two different levels of attainment: the Standard for Provisional Registration sets out the level needed to provisionally register as a teacher and the Standard for Full Registration sets out the level required to be fully registered at the end of the probationary period [23] .

Teacher competence frameworks can be used for different purposes. First of all they can be used as a reference tool for the various stages of teacher's development, but also as a reference tool for different purposes and stakeholders – for education decision-makers in designing educational reforms, for initial teacher training intuitions, CPD providers, evaluators, and of course for candidate and serving teachers.

According to the Eurydice report (2018) the teacher competence frameworks can be used for the following purposes:

1. In Initial Teacher Education (ITE): for defining the learning outcomes to be acquired by the end of ITE;

2. During entry to the profession for:

   - teacher accreditation/licensing criteria,

   - selection/recruitment criteria,

   - assessing teacher competences at the end of induction;

3. In Continuing Professional Development for:

   - developing CPD programmes,

   - preparing individual teachers' CPD plans;

4. For other puroposes in:

   - teacher appraisal/evaluation criteria,

   - teacher promotion,

   - disciplinary procedures/cases of serious misconduct.

Use of teacher competence frameworks issued by top-level authorities, primary and general secondary education (ISCED 1-3), 2016/17

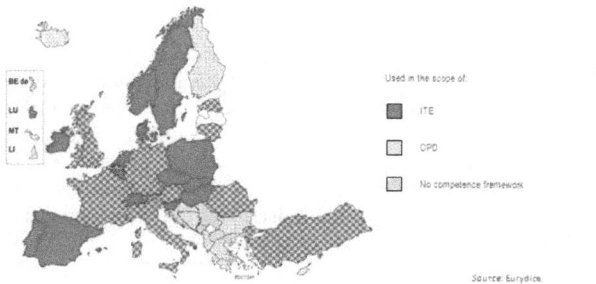

Source: Eurydice.

Approximately one third of the education systems use teacher competence frameworks throughout teachers' careers, i.e. both for ITE and CPD. This is the case of Belgium (Flemish Community), Germany, Estonia, France, Italy, Lithuania, Austria, Romania, the United Kingdom and Turkey [24].

Almost half of the education systems with teacher competence frameworks use them for the initial phase, but not for CPD. This is the case in Belgium (French Community), the Czech Republic, Denmark, Ireland, Spain, Luxembourg, Hungary, the Netherlands, Poland, Portugal, Slovenia, Slovakia, Sweden, Switzerland and Norway. In three countries, the teacher competence framework is used in relation to CPD but not for ITE (the former Yugoslav Republic of Macedonia, Montenegro and Serbia) [25].

It is interesting that some countries use teacher competence frameworks in many different contexts and others only for one or two of the above mentioned purposes. For example Estonia uses teacher competence frameworks in nearly all aspects listed above with two exceptions of teacher accreditation and disciplinary procedures. The UK (England and Wales) also uses teacher competence frameworks for many purposes with an exception of selection and recruitment and disciplinary procedures. Romania is another country which uses such frameworks for all listed by Eurydice purposes with an exception of accreditation. Several countries use frameworks for one purpose and most often this purpose is ITE (French Community of Belgium, Czech Republic, Denmark, The Netherlands, Portugal, Slovakia, Switzerland, Norway and Poland).

It seems worth promoting a consistent and wider use of such frameworks for many different purposes in each country. Poland has just prepared a new proposal of teacher competence framework which could be not only universal and easily adapted to local circumstances but also serve many different purposes.

COMPETENCIES AND PILLARS OF TEACHERS' WORK – THE MODEL FOR THE POLISH TEACHER COMPETENCE FRAMEWORK

The team of experts who worked on the preparation of the model has commenced with the assumption that the teaching

profession and competencies required of teachers (teaching outcomes) are based on three pillars, which are:
(1) professional knowledge;
(2) professional practice;
(3) professional identity and commitment on the part of teachers.

These pillars can be described as follows [26]:
Professional knowledge, generally speaking, means that a teacher:

1. knows their students and knows how they learn, and
2. is familiar with the subject they teach and knows how to teach it.

Teachers who know their students well are sensible of the diversification of pupils in terms of language, culture, and religion. They are aware of the fact that living conditions and life experiences of students affect their learning. They know how to organise their lessons in order to individualise teaching and learning, to promote physical, social, intellectual, emotional, and spiritual development of pupils, and the development of their personal traits. Teachers are familiar with the core curriculum and can assess it critically. They also display knowledge of the subject they teach and of the methodology of teaching it. Not only do they have factual knowledge of the subject taught, but also can teach classes, arouse cognitive curiosity and support intellectual development of students by skilfully selecting activation and teaching methods. Last, but not least, they know how to examine and assess the performance of pupils and their own teaching. Teachers also display knowledge in the area of information and communication technologies and can use it accordingly to expand learning opportunities for pupils.

Professional practice - in the case of this pillar, it can be assumed that teachers have competencies necessary for carrying out tasks related to teaching, education and care over pupils, including the ability to design a curriculum and adapt it to the needs and capabilities of pupils. Teachers are well prepared to carry out professional tasks related to teaching, education and care, which are typical of a role of a teacher. They can:

- Provide a safe environment, which promotes learning by students
- Assess, provide feedback and produce reports on students' learning
- Plan the teaching and learning process and effectively teach and learn with pupils.

Teachers have knowledge of effective teaching and learning strategies, which they use to implement well-designed curricula and to teach classes. On a regular basis, they assess various aspects of their professional practice (performance of tasks with regard to teaching, education, and care) to ensure that they satisfy educational needs of their pupils. They use and interpret pupil assessment data to identify obstacles to learning and challenges faced by pupils, in order to improve their performance. They work effectively at all stages of the teaching and learning cycle, including the planning of learning and assessment, development of curricula, designing the teaching process, providing feedback on learning by the pupils and reporting performance results to their parents/guardians.

Professional commitment/identity of teachers - it is teachers who shape effective learning and development: they show how you can learn and develop and take action to disseminate examples of good practice in teaching. They can manage their personal and professional development thanks to recognising and analysing their educational needs, assessing and broadening their learning, and facing challenges in a group and individually throughout their careers. Teachers are committed to learning and professional development. They cooperate with colleagues, parents, guardians, and external stakeholders in order to forge indispensable partnerships. Teachers demonstrate professionalism in their interactions with pupils, colleagues, parents/guardians and a wider community. They show the ability to cooperate with others and are sensitive to the needs of pupils and their parents/guardians. They effectively communicate with them about the progress and educational attainment of their children. Teachers are characterised by ethical sensitivity, empathy, openness, reflectiveness and socially minded attitudes. They are concerned about students' well-being and build relationships based on trust, mutual respect, acceptance and responsibility. Teachers value opportunities related to their involvement in communities of practice operating in and outside schools. They are willing to enhance their experiences and to develop in order to provide students with increasingly better conditions for education. They understand the relationship between school, home and local community and its importance for social and intellectual development of their pupils. Working on behalf of their profession, they display autonomy, agency, openness, optimism, critical thinking, perseverance, and resistance. They adopt positive attitude to others and are self-conscious.

The pillars of teachers' work allow to identify competencies associated with each of them:

1) professional knowledge, which includes the following competencies:
subject-related (factual) knowledge, knowledge of legal and organisational matters, familiarity with health and safety regulations, psychological and pedagogical knowledge, diagnostic and research-related knowledge, familiarity with supporting institutions acting on behalf of the education system, and familiarity with sources of (factual/subject-related) knowledge.
(2) professional practice, which includes the following competencies:
teaching skills, educational/care-giving/prevention-related skills, research skills, digital skills, communication (language) skills, cognitive skills, leadership skills, adaptation skills.
(3) professional identity and commitment on the part of teachers, which includes the following competencies:
professional ethics, personal improvement and development, emotional and social competencies, cultural and multicultural competencies.

Another aspect of describing teacher competencies is to recognise that these competencies are constantly being developed in the process of professional development of teachers.

For this purpose three levels of professional proficiency and competencies have been identified [27]:
level 1 - beginner teacher
level 2 - specialist teacher
level 3 - expert teacher.

Such a classification allows for the development of individual portfolios, which after a self-analysis can serve as a starting point for designing a professional development path, which can be combined with a promotion system based on state examinations, and which can sometimes be prepared with the help of methodology consultants.

The model presented here takes into consideration both aspects – the three pillars of teacher's work and the above mentioned 3-level structure of professional proficiency. Therefore the model is presented in a form of a table where each pillar of teacher's work is divided into three stages of advancement based on the teachers professional development – from "basic" teaching skills (beginner teacher) to the most advanced competencies of highly experienced teachers (expert teacher).

The pillars themselves are broken into detailed competencies – e.g. professional knowledge includes subject- related competencies, legal competence, familiarity with health and safety regulations as well as psychological and pedagogical knowledge. It also takes into consideration such aspects as diagnostic and research related knowledge, capacity to seek and find factual knowledge and familiarity with the various aspects of education system's functioning including its most important institutions. The aspect of professional practice is also divided into detailed skills and arranged according to the 3-level development model.

As for professional commitment a slightly different approach has been adopted.

The concept of professional ethics refers to the rules of conduct of a given professional group, e.g. teachers. In this sense, professional ethics is normative ethics, which attempts to describe a model teacher, ethical objectives of the profession, rules of conduct in the teaching practice and typical ethical conflicts, which may occur in the course of professional practice.

It can therefore be assumed that values should be a source of objectives and tasks performed by teachers in their teaching and educational activities. Adopting the line of thought of A.M Tchorzewski, who claims that the truth improves intellect, goodness improves will, and beauty improves feelings; the tasks that teachers need to perform include:

- Searching, together with students, for truth in the area of knowledge about the world, to which they belong and to which they contribute;
- Opening to their realities and social life, participation in it, and anticipating future events;
- Continuing efforts to contribute to moral laws, which include objective ethical values, of which all actors of the process of education are aware.

Education perceived as personal development in all its dimensions; physical, mental and spiritual one, is a lifelong process aimed at shaping universal values in its participants.
Teachers who perceive their profession as a mission should be aware that they act as role models for their pupils and should observe professional ethics in their practice.
Competencies in the area of professional ethics included in the proposed Polish model encompass, among others, emotional, social and cultural/multicultural competences, description of

teacher's attitudes towards pupils and their parents, colleagues, as well as tasks and responsibilities. This part of the model also refers to the professional improvement and development of the teacher – his/her attitudes towards continuing professional development, a motivation to learn and acquire new skills, involvement in constant improvement of all competencies and cooperation with other teachers in this respect.

CONCLUSION

If we refer to the Eurydice findings on the teacher competence frameworks issued by top-level authorities presented in the 2018 report it is clear that not only all countries adopted such frameworks, but also many of them have only very general recommendations which don't give the teachers a clear picture of what is expected from them.

Moreover, the existing frameworks, even if formulated in greater detail are not often used in practice. In many countries they are used for one out of four different purposes identified by Eurydice (e.g. only in initial teacher training). It is highly recommended that such frameworks once in place should serve many purposes with a view to a full and multifaceted professional development of teachers.

The recommendations presented above, which contain a description of teachers' competencies and tasks should serve as a starting point for the development of more specific provisions in the area of competencies and become a valuable contribution to their promotion in education circles. The Polish model should be discussed and disseminated so it has a chance to inspire decision makers in all, not only European, countries and can serve as a model for either adjustment of the existing or elaboration of new teacher competence frameworks in the future.

REFERENCES

[1] European Union cooperation in education and training (ET, 2020). Council conclusions of 12 May 2009 on a strategic framework for European cooperation in education and training (ET 2020) (OJ C 119 of 28.5.2009, pp. 2-10)

[2] Council Conclusions of 26 November 2012 on literacy (2012/C 393/01)

[3] Key Data on Teachers and School Leaders in Europe (Eurydice, 2013)

[4] Hanushek, E. Some simple analytics of school quality. Working Paper No. 10229. Cambridge, M.A.: National Bureau of Economic Research (2004)

[5] S.G Rivkin, E.A. Hanushek, J.F. Kain "Teachers, schools and academic achievement": in Econometrica – Journal of the Econometric Society, vol. 73, issue 2 (2005)

[6] J.E. Rockoff "The impact of individual teachers on student achievement: evidence from panel data" in The American Economic Review, vol. 94 no. 2 (2004)

[7] J. Hattie, Visible learning for teachers, Routledge, New York, London (2012)

[8, 10] M. Barber., M. Mourshed, How the world's best performing schools systems come out on top. London: McKinsey & Company (2007)

[9] L. Darling-Hammond, Teacher education around the world: What can we learn from international practice? European Journal of Teacher Education, 40 (3) (2017)

[11, 26] J. Madalińska-Michalak, Filary pracy a kompetencje nauczyciela, Uniwersytet Warszawski (2015)

[12, 13] J. Madalińska-Michalak, „Kompetencje przywódcze dyrektora szkoły – wyzwania wobec teorii i praktyki edukacyjnej" in Kwartalnik Pedagogiczny, Vol. 4 (242) (2016).

[14] Common European Principles for Teacher Competences and Qualifications, European Commission. Directorate–General for Education and Culture (2005)

[15] Communication from the Commission to the European Parliament, the Council, the European Economic and Social Committee and the Committee of the Regions. Rethinking Education: Investing in Skills for Better Socio-Economic Outcomes. Strasbourg, 20.11.2012 COM (2012)

[16] Supporting the Teaching Professions for Better Learning Outcomes. Accompanying the document: Communication from the Commission to the European Parliament, the Council, the European Economic and Social Committee and the Committee of the Regions. Rethinking Education: Investing in Skills for Better Socio-Economic Outcomes. Strasbourg (2012)

[17] Policy approaches to defining and describing teacher competences, Naas, Ireland (2011)

[18] Supporting Teacher Competence Development for Better Learning Outcomes, European Commission (2013)

[19] Supporting the Teaching Professions for Better Learning Outcomes. Accompanying the document: Communication from the Commission to the European Parliament, the Council, the European Economic and Social Committee and the Committee of the Regions. Rethinking Education: Investing in Skills for Better Socio-Economic Outcomes. Strasbourg (2012)

[20, 21,22,23,24,25] Teaching careers in Europe. Access, Progression and Support, Eurydice (2018)

[27] L. Budkowska, P. Poszytek, "Teachers' continuing professional development: trends in European countries. Towards teachers' professionalism". Conference paper WMSCI (2018)

CommunicationS and Political Communication Today:
New World, New Concepts, and Schemes

Svetlana I. ROSENKO
Professor and Chairperson of the Department of Mass Communications
and Technologies in Sports, Lesgaft National State University of Physical Education
Email: s.rosenko@lesgaft.spb.ru

Andrey A. REZAEV
St Petersburg College, Florida, USA
Email: arezae1@live.spcollege.edu

ABSTRACT

The objective of the paper is to discuss theoretical and methodological frames of studying political communication as a part of the phenomena of communication/s as well as to present preliminary research findings of the research developed at the Lesgaft University of Physical Culture in 2015-2018.

On the basis of current sociological and political sciences theories, socio-political analysis the paper will identify the patterns and underlying causes of success and failure in political communication development in the early years of the 21 century.

The argument of the paper is this: contemporary communication thought is more problematic than familiar to academia terms suggest. The new outlook should emerge in the 21st century in response to the changed character and dynamics of the societies. It must attempt to make sense out of a world of communication where identity and order is administered by large organizations rather than achieved by individual consent. It has to consider communication as an agency of culture and politics. The paper argues about the necessity to have a strong interdisciplinary vision for doing research in the field of communication.

Keywords: Communication, Communications, Political Communication, Interdisciplinarity

1. INTRODUCTION

Both the twentieth and the twenty first centuries have begun with a revolution in means of communication. Back one hundred years ago communicationS revolution exploded when radio has been invented. Now, in the early years of the twenty first century, society is confronted with the invasion of Internet, satellites and on-line communications.

Scholarship on communication/S is a modern field of analysis. However, nothing could be done in a productive way in current sciences without proper theoretical understanding of what is the phenomenon of 'communication' and how to cope with the constant flux and revolutions in 'communicationS', i.e. 'means of communication'.

In the 21st century communicationS have emerged as the dominant institution in society. Other institutions - political (state, parties), religious (Church), educational (Universities) - have a decreasing ability to offer effective leadership in comparison with communications today. Their legitimacy increasingly questioned, and in some cases and in some countries even their existence is vulnerable and unstable.

Politicians, academics, priests have neither the resources nor the flexibility to mount an effective response to the challenges people are facing in the age of Internet and On-line communications. Moreover, the political and religious institutions, as well as universities and even businesses are based on the development of the means of communication. Communications begin to assume responsibility for the whole "public sphere" (in the most general sense of the word), but not only for pure exchange of information. CommunicationS (normally being just the means and tools of communication processes) are becoming to play another role in societal development.

Communications have started to produce moral effects. What is really important, communications have started to produce the moral effects and values that are quite opposite to those which were cultivated some twenty five years, even ten years ago.

A list of new research questions for those who are studying communications came to fore. Instead of the traditional (old) questions such as 'Do communications make and transmit information?' becomes 'Do communications creating and insert values?' and "What are human needs for nowadays communication?"

In this regard it becomes clear that new organizational structures are needed for communication institutions to flourish in the future and to serve society according to the new goals and objectives. The basic ideas and environment for a new organizational model is 'telling the truth' and cultural integrity.

2. COMMUNICATIONS AND POLITICAL COMMUNICATION

The "politics" is a notion with which you always end up in trouble. Yet, it is one of the basic notions in current theories of journalism, communication, and media. Politics and communication are very close to each other today. In fact political action is a reaction to communication of one kind or another. Both systems - the political system and the communication system - are parallel one another. Political communication, its practice and technology have always been central to the maintenance of social, economic, and cultural relations among social groups who differentiate themselves from one another according to language, custom, geography, religion.

It has become a truism to say that Political Communication agenda in the 21 century cannot be the same as it was during the Cold War and post-Cold War period. The present stage of world transformation could with equal justice be called the "age of communication" or that of "non-communication". No one image of communication will remain unaffected by the changes through which the world is moving in the 21 century. Like much of the other social processes the process of social communication is again at the cross-roads.

Theory in political communication tries to define a set of elementary concepts that together have complex, but testable, implications. Research on democracy and democratization processes provide a good example of the analytic process, carried out over several decades by many theorists and researchers.

The Western theorists who discussed problems of political communication in the late 1990s have all supposedly begun from the same reflective starting point, namely, what can media do in reinforcing democratization processes in the world assuming that media is an instrument of establishing and reinforcing democracy. The differences and disagreements among them show that although they were supposedly in the same theoretical camp, in fact they were united not by a common philosophical ground and theoretical principles but by a common "image" coming from fairly naive understanding of political processes right after the demise of the USSR and the Soviet bloc countries. Theorists (the people of a pure theoretical work) hate to admit it, but sometimes their work is based on the pictures rather than hard theories and ideas. In attempt to get a handle on both the nature of society and legitimate political communication after the collapse of communism the post- communist studies of communication have struck many as enormously promising. But how that image can be translated into argument has varied considerably.

This paper will attempt to depict some paths for going behind the image, and clarify the different forms of argument in which that image has been used.

The argument of the paper is this: contemporary communication thought is more problematic than familiar to academia terms suggest. When the major themes of this thought are examined (and of the major theme for today is to understand what media and communications are per se in the Internet age) closely, when its assumptions are identified and traced to their theoretical conclusions, they actually limit a political theory, one that derives from classical theories. The new outlook should emerge in the 21st century in response to the changed character and dynamics of the societies. It must attempt to make sense out of a world of communication where identity and order is administered by large organizations rather than achieved by individual consent.

3. CHALLENGES FOR STUDYING COMMUNICATION AS THE AGENCY OF POLITICS AND CULTURE

"Most papers produced by social scientists that deal with computers and society look at the role of information in human history, discuss the social context and consequences of information technology, introduce readers to the ways computers work, debate the effects of computers on individual health and psychology, detect issues of privacy and security. This way or another to the social scientists computer on the one hand is a society's technological product, and on the other hand it is a source of technological progress and hence a source of social change. That was the case in the XX century when debates about post-industrial society flourished all over the world, this continue to be the case in the XXI century when ideas of 'digital society' and post-human evolution spread across scholarly disciplines" [1].

Communication broadly understood is the fundamental agency of culture and politics today and it deals primarily with shaping of consciousness and its conversion. When fully articulated any concept of communication expresses a conception of a world view, a conception of the person, of the relation between persons, and of the general structure and ends of social life. A well-ordered society can be effectively regulated with the help of an advanced conception of communication and media.

Flexibility is a virtue only in pursuit of specific goals, but the goals of the 21st century communication are rarely defines if at all. And pragmatic adjustment to empirically dominant communication (it is quite obvious today) introduces neither flexibility nor pluralism into our social life. [2]

Despite notable instances of fruitful work and the growing number of studies on the mass-media, political communication research faces several challenges. First, is the necessity to focus on "interdisciplinarian" status of communication/s. Research on political communication needs to go further into an integrated field. An important and vantage of a multidisciplinary approach is that it invites methodological pluralism. Literature on political communication published in English generally concentrates on three major topics: developments in mass-media, public opinion, and dynamics of policy makers. Yet, the scholarship lately has concentrated also on the necessity to have interdisciplinary perspective in viewing the relations between media, communication, and general public.

Scholars today are committed to interdisciplinarity. This commitment depends upon listening to—and learning from—those researchers who are studying the ''same'' things in methodologically different ways, raising different research questions. Contemporary interdisciplinarity requires intellectual and methodological breadth and expertise that extends across the disciplinary boundary.

Second, it could be argued that the press in recent years is finally telling the true story of politics, that public officials are an ineffective and untrustworthy. Candidates for political positions routinely make promises they have no intention of keeping, and which are' made, not only to deceive the voters, but to trick them into supporting actions that are contrary to their interests.

Third, it seems that communications research has already demolished believes that news is "value free". The professional reporting is absolutely consistent with the selection of facts, the framing of interpretations, the attribution of importance through front page headlines, for example. Moreover, "objectivity" as a principle of democratic press seems to have eroded. Of course, this topic is quite debatable, and there are opposite voices and suggestions. Nonetheless, there is enough evidence to argue that professional media, communication, and understanding of what has be covered tend to invest in political values expressed in new stories. We would argue that this is exactly the area where more research is needed.

4. DEMOCRACY AND DEMOCRATIZATION IN THE AGE OF INTERNET

That communication should be a "democratic" no one in a democracy would seriously dispute. But what such an announcement would commit anyone to is far from clear. This is partly because of different interpretations which it is possible to give to the notion 'democratic'. It is also because of the vagueness which all such general terms of commendation must have if they are to fulfil their function of reminding a people of their ultimate valuations.

It can be argued that, in a society that acknowledges allegiance to democratic processed, the very idea of communication cannot be understood without attention to the meaning of democracy. First of all 'democracy' in 'communication' could mean that communication system of a community should be democratically distributed and organized.

Internet and on-line communication bring to fore very interesting and really important facts for discussion and organization of research in the field of 'democratic communications' [2].

The research that has been organized and conducted by the research group at the Lesgaft State University of Sports and Health in 2015 – 2018 was oriented towards answering the question "What kind of communication shall we advocate and support in the course of communications transformation?" On the one hand, if we hope to make of communication a constructive force on behalf of a better world rather than a worse one, we must be fundamentally concerned with the directions in which we desire the world to move. On the other hand, we must be equally concerned with determining and avoiding the directions in which we do not desire to move.

The materials and preliminary results of our study show that there are some similarities but also differences between development of communications and political communication in western and eastern societies, specifically in the societies that are on their way to organize market based socio-economic development. Materials of the research show that that the productive answer to these problems can be found on the way of reciprocal investigation of Eastern and Western perspectives of political communication. It does not mean that western patterns must be copied for application in the East. Everything has its peculiarities and overtones. There is no, of course, one single model for the development of the new communication systems in different societies despite of the reality of globalization processes.

One widely circulated story is that communications in current times are becoming increasingly shaped by and sacrificed to global forces [3]. These forces might` include transnational corporations, global flows of ideas, global financial institutions, and influential international regulatory authorities, such as IMF, or the European Commission. In fact, today few doubt the reality of globalization or rather glocalization, yet not many people agree how to measure 'globalization' and even less would find common ground in measuring effects of communications for a better world.

Our research is an on-going Project and we believe to have an opportunity to present specifics and detailed outcomes of the Project in the future.

5. REFERENCES

1. A. V. Rezaev, A.A. Ivanova "Studying Artificial Intelligence and Artificial Sociality in Natural Sciences, Engineering, and Social Sciences: Possibility and Reality" **Proceedings of the 22nd World Multi-Conference on Systemics, Cybernetics and Informatics (WMSCI'18)**, Orlando, 2018

2. A. V Rezaev, Tregubova N. D. (2018) "Are sociologists ready for 'artificial sociality'? Current issues and future prospects for studying artificial intelligence in the social sciences". **Monitoring of Public Opinion: Economic and Social Changes.** No.5.,pp.91-108. https://doi.org/10.14515/monitoring.2018.5.10.

3. R. Newman **The Structure of Communication. Continuity and Change in a Digital Age**, Chicago: University of Chicago Press, 2013

Modeling Workplace Conflict With "Systems Theatre"

Tom SCHOLTE

Department of Theatre and Film, University of British Columbia
Vancouver, BC, V6T 1Z4, Canada

ABSTRACT

Applying systemic analysis to examples of the author's practice, this paper presents evidence for the efficacy of a theatre-based mode of systems modeling.

Keywords: Augusto Boal, Theatre of the Oppressed, Systems Thinking, Workplace Conflict, Causal Loop Diagrams

1. INTRODUCTION

Conflict Theatre @ UBC (CT@UBC) is an initiative of the Human Resources Department of the University of British Columbia (UBC) in Vancouver, Canada. In collaboration with UBC's Department of Theatre and Film, and in line with the goals of the university's Conflict Engagement Framework, the program seeks to cultivate "conflict literacy" across faculty and staff defined as the basic awareness, knowledge, skill and practical wisdom for productively engaging in conflicts in which we find ourselves.. The principal modality of CT@UBC's work is Forum Theatre featuring plays created and performed by diverse casts of UBC employees for audiences of their peers at various professional development events.

Forum Theatre was originally developed in the 1960's and 70's by Brazilian artist and activist, Augusto Boal, as part of his "arsenal of the Theatre of the Oppressed" (TO). Given Boal's explicit wish that his methods be strictly employed within a "social justice" context and certainly not in any kind of "corporate" environment, some in the TO community might object to its use in the university context. However, the CT@UBC initiative is adamantly not focused upon simply making employees more "efficient" in the manner that Boal feared [1]. In the spirit of the aforementioned UBC Conflict Engagement Framework it seeks, rather, to explicitly "enable all members of the university community to pursue our commitment to inclusion, collaboration, and innovation as three priorities to be advanced by all the work of our institution." Conflict engagement aims to concretize these commitments through realistic and practical efforts, noting that the pursuit of inclusion, collaboration and innovation *requires* engaging with conflict.. The Framework also aims to make concrete the aims of UBC's Respectful Environment Statement in "establishing employment and educational practices that respect the dignity of individuals and make it possible for everyone to live, work, and study in a positive and supportive environment, free from harmful behaviours such as bullying and harassment." [2] Finally, the work of CT@UBC is anchored in an ongoing commitment to the vision of a university as a public good. In pursuing the ideals outlined above, CT@UBC is designed to serve as much as a mechanism for openly and safely critiquing the structures and policies of the institution itself as it is for the development of the personal capacities of individuals within the institution.

Forum Theatre has been further developed by many international practitioners including Vancouver's David Diamond whose Theatre for Living (TfL) has "moved away from the binary language and model of "oppressor/oppressed"

and now "approaches community-based cultural work from a systems-based perspective; understanding that a community is a complexly integrated, living organism." (theatreforliving.com).

The Theatre for Living website describes Forum Theatre as follows:

In Forum Theatre, we show the audience the play all the way through once – the play builds to a crisis, and stops, offering no solutions. The play is then performed a second time, where audience members can then stop the action and enter the stage themselves, by replacing characters with whom they identify and try to solve problems or issues inside the story. The rest of the cast stays in character and improvises. [...] The theatre becomes a creative laboratory where we can try ways to transform ourselves, our communities, and the world. (theatreforliving.com)

While Diamond is not the only contemporary practitioner to be influenced by developments in Systems Theory (see [1]) and the potential benefit of a more direct and overt engagement with the tools and techniques of Systems Thinking has been recognized and brought to the attention of the TO community [3] major adaptations to Forum Theatre practice in order to maximize the mutual support these bodies of work might lend each other have not been forthcoming in any pronounced manner. The need for such innovations appears more acute in light of Luong and Arnold's reflection upon the "frustration at the lack of change and impact in their communities" expressed by many TO practitioners and their suggestion that " perhaps the missing link between the frustrations the facilitators experienced and creating the change that Boal once envisioned for TO techniques may lie in the conscious ability to use systems thinking skills." They go on to reflect that:

Currently, forum theatre seems to be the TO form of choice to use in tackling problems. It provides a great structure that facilitators may adapt and utilize to explore different perspectives, allowing a community of viewers to make changes. However, the forum theatre pieces that we have participated in often tackle issues on a surface level, lacking a big picture view. Whether this issue is caused by inadequate facilitation or a need to present a more holistic and systemic scenario seems to depend on the performance. If further development can improve these workshops, we believe the TO facilitators can help create bigger changes in their communities.

Like Luong and Arnold, who "envision formal, long term research" to assess and address these gaps in TO practice, I have embarked on a program of research to try and remedy this state of affairs through the development of Systems Theatre [4]. To that end, Conflict Theatre @ UBC has served as the test-bed for the gradually increased application of systems tools within the creation and performance of Forum Theatre events. Conversely, it is vital to note that this effort is equally inspired by a desire to be of value to the Systems Theory/Thinking/Science communities; in particular, by going some ways to fulfill the wish, expressed most directly by Werner Ulrich, to "pragmatize the kernel of the systems idea" for the wider public. [5] In my view, an adapted form of Forum Theatre is the ideal vehicle for this task and my hope is that efforts like those of Luong and Arnold and myself to make explicit the natural affinities between TO/TfL and Systems Theory can lend credence to Ross Ashby's assertion that ' "the discovery that two branches are related leads to each branch helping in the development of the other. " [6] The general features of the proposed Systems Theatre can be found in [4] and empirical evidence of the increased levels of reflective awareness it can facilitate for those involved in its practice are detailed in [7] The current paper will offer examples of the kinds of generalizable insights that can be teased out of the dynamic flux of a Forum Theatre event when Systems Thinking "lenses" are applied to the analysis of individual audience interventions. It is hoped that these examples will add credence to Luong and Arnold's claim that "the conscious ability to use systems thinking skills" is, indeed, the "missing link" to greater long-term "change and impact" in our communities of concern.

2. SYSTEMS THEORETICAL FRAMEWORK

The proposed Systems Theatre seeks to unveil leverage points at both the organizational and personal level. In order to do so, it engages two distinct methods of analysis: Systems Thinking at the organizational level and Perceptual Control Theory (PCT) at the personal.

Systems Thinking

The phrase "Systems *Thinking"* is grounded in Donella Meadows popular book, THINKING IN SYSTEMS: A PRIMER [8] and is used advisedly to indicate that, while Causal Loop and Stock and Flow Diagrams will be employed as analytical tools, the rigorous mathematics of fully-fledged System Dynamics will not be applied. Instead, these tools will be used to more generally illustrate interactive relationships and systemic structures and to help identify the "archetypes" of systemic dysfunction identified by Meadows. To visually communicate these insights to audiences, it is proposed that the online modeling platform LOOPY be employed. (https://ncase.me/loopy/)

Perceptual Control Theory

Perceptual Control Theory (PCT) is a cybernetic theory of behaviour originally developed by William T. Powers [9] applying selected ideas from control engineering to a conception of the human nervous system as a hierarchical organization of control systems. These systems seek to match present perceptual experiences with preferred, internally set goal states via homeostatic negative feedback loops that generate goal-seeking behaviour. This hierarchy begins with the most fundamental sensory perceptions, and subsequent basic motor activities (e.g. maintaining balance), at the bottom, and extends to more abstract principles of self-perception (e.g. ethical behaviour, aspirations for personal character etc,), and subsequent complex social behaviour, at the top. Each level has its intrinsic reference value set by the level above it. This theory offers profound utility to the Systems Theatre project given that it is entirely consistent with research on the cybernetic nature of the Stanislavski System of Acting and the Naturalist theatre [10, 11], provides a method of cyber-systemic analysis at the level of the individual that is compatible with those employed at the organizational level (e.g. System Dynamics inspired Systems Thinking) and is supported by a robust body of empirical validation [12]. It also contains a parsimonious theory of conflict as the struggle between two or more control systems seeking to bring the same variable to different states; either

interpersonally (e.g. a negotiation between employee and employer over compensation) or intra-personally (e.g. during an emotionally charged department meeting, an individual's desire to both question authority and to be liked by everyone.)

Object of Study

In the next section, the kind of systemic analysis outlined above will be applied to the examination of two interventions into a play made by members of an audience from a unit within UBC's Sauder School of Business. Due to restrictions of length, they will focus only upon organizational levels insights drawn from Systems Thinking while those drawn from PCT will be featured in a separate paper. While the interventions and discussions described below reflect the events that took place during the actual performance, the systemic analyses outlined here were formulated upon subsequent reflection and, as such, were not presented to the audience as part of a standard CT@UBC performance. The represent a model of the fully integrated Systems Theatre toward which the author is working and are being used to inspire new modes of play creation and analysis in further exploratory work.

3. THE PLAY

The following excerpt is the final section of a short Forum play developed by an ensemble of UBC employees[1] during CT@UBC's 2011 intensive. It portrays a meeting in the fictitious "Department of Excellence" between department head, Chantal (a recent external hire), long-time administrator, Jen, long-time faculty member, Fran, and recently hired communications specialist, Maura. After a bumpy beginning due to chronic lateness, and an awkward interaction around overlapping requests for vacation time, the group finally gets to the main item on their agenda.

Chantal: Next item: orientation. We are going to brainstorm around what our unit wants to do for faculty and staff orientation. *(Jen raises her hand)* Yes Jen.
Jen: We did this at the last meeting Chantal. You weren`t there, but we did it. We spent at least 2 hours brainstorming and we had a whole flipchart full of ideas.
Fran: We did.
Chantal: Ok, perhaps you could update me on that.
Jen: Maura?
Maura: So at the brainstorming we came up with a ton of ideas for orientation which I have handy here. Although at some point we did spin our wheels. Most of the ideas are related to the resource booths that we're going to have for the whole orientation.
Fran: Not with faculty session, no.
Maura: This will be my first orientation, so I guess I am confused about how I'm working with you Fran for the faculty orientation.
Fran: You aren't working with me for the faculty session!
Chantal: Actually it is my expectation that you should be, Fran. We have talked as a team, about the faculty and staff becoming a joint session and perhaps you could take a couple of minutes to inform your new colleague here in terms of what happens in faculty orientations.

---

[1] The ensemble members included Maura Cruz, Julie Stockton, Judy Chan, Joseph Topornycky, Zack Lee and Nihan Sevinc.

Fran: Yes, of course, Chantal. Maura, at orientations Staff and Faculty do a joint session in the morning and then we break into two groups for the afternoon sessions. We have always done it this way. You and Jen look after staff; I look after faculty – they break into two groups, one focused on research, the other on teaching and learning.

Maura: How am I involved with the faculty then?

Fran: You`re not involved in the faculty sessions! You do staff orientation.

Jen: Can I say something, Chantal?

Chantal: If it's relevant Jen.

Jen: It is. Can I be honest? I really resent the fact that we`re spending so much time on this when, really, it's Maura's responsibility. Sorry, Maura.

Fran: I have to agree. (*Meanwhile, she has already started checking her e-mails on her phone*)

Chantal: Well PEOPLE, let's step back for a moment and think about how we can better incorporate Maura to our team. I think that… || Fran, do I have your attention right now? You seem a little preoccupied.

Fran: I`m actually trying to get urgent stuff done cause this doesn`t really apply to me.

Chantal: Actually it does apply to you. As a team, what we`re trying to do is to come up with strategies on what to do around staff and faculty orientations.

Fran: So, you`ve been talking a lot lately, Chantal, about us as a team. Quite frankly my understanding of "team" is we participate in all operational aspects of the team.

For example: the selection of a new team member. Jen and I weren't included in Maura's recruitment, nor were we consulted before you hired her. You made the decision entirely on your own, and now I`m suddenly expected to train her. No disrespect to Maura - I'm sure she's a nice person – but I don't have the time to train somebody new right before the orientation, especially when they're not getting it.

Chantal: Fran! I think that this conversation has crossed a boundary.

Fran: Boundaries were crossed long before this conversation, Chantal. I'm sorry, I have to excuse myself.

Leaves the room.

End of Scene

4. INTERVENTIONS

Intervention One – *Action*

Audience member *A* chose to replace the character of Chantal and, as an introduction to the topic of the orientation session, praised the many years of excellent work that Fran had put into developing a very successful template for the faculty sessions and commended the very solid foundation upon which any innovations generated with their new team member, Maura, would rest. As the conversation moved fully into the discussion of potential adjustments to the format, Fran still seemed somewhat uneasy but did not attempt to completely block Maura's involvement. Subsequently, the tone of the meeting did not escalate and the meeting proceeded in a calm and collegial manner until the Joker (facilitator) called an end to the scene and began to facilitate discussion of the intervention.

Intervention One – *Discussion*

Speaking as the character, the actor playing Fran confirmed that the acknowledgement of her long-standing contributions to the

workplace did, indeed, make it easier for her to begin to engage in a discussion with Maura about possible innovations to the procedures she had developed. Of particular importance was the sense that the extant faculty orientation sessions that she had designed had legitimate value and that the desire for innovation was not an indication that the work that she had done previously was fundamentally flawed or inadequate. Drilling down a little further in our discussion, "Fran" revealed that, having been in her job for so long, much of her very sense of self-worth was enmeshed with her professional identity. Thus, urgent and repeated demands for change left her feeling deeply threatened and triggered what Systems Dynamics practitioner, John Sterman, might call "defensive routines." [13]. These feelings, and subsequent behaviours, were significantly mitigated by the alternative approach enacted by audience member *A*.

Intervention One – *Systemic Analysis*

Given that many audience members raised their hands when asked if they identified with Fran's close association between professional identity and self-worth, it seems prudent to attempt to generalize the insight gained from this particular intervention in an attempt to extract a principle that might be applied in similar "change management" situations beyond the scope of this particular play and the particular individuals that it portrays. One way in which this can be approached is through a pair of Causal Loop Diagrams illustrating the feedback loops at work in both the initial scenario portrayed and the subsequent intervention. As with all descriptions of "non-physical" systems (and possibly other types as well), the names given to the interacting "elements" do not reflect an objective definition of reality but are, rather, dependent on the conceptual schemas employed by the observer (in this case, the Conflict Theatre Joker.) As such, these diagrams are not offered as "the" way to see and describe the dynamics at work but, simply, as "a" way to see and describe them that will only prove its worth if it results in insights and applications that lead to "successful" interactions in the future. Even then, the diagrams will not function as descriptions of the "truth."

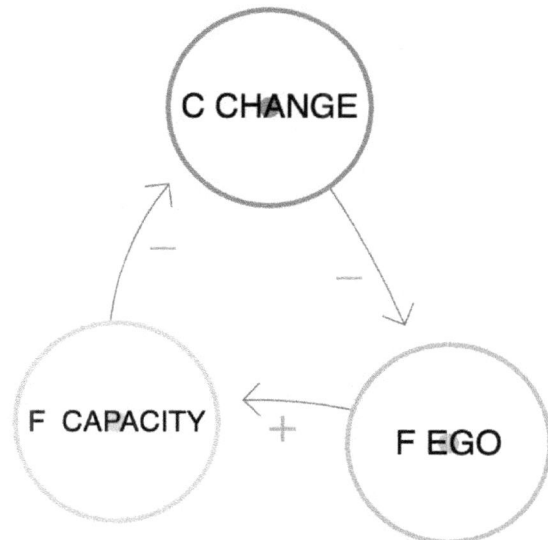

FIG. 1
Fig. 1 utilizes the modeling platform, LOOPY, to portray the initial scenario as a feedback loop which is structured so that

Chantal's increasing demands for change will drive down Fran's ego strength which will drive down her capacity for change which will drive up Chantal's demands for change. The presence of an even number of negative links guarantees, of course, that this will be a reinforcing loop.

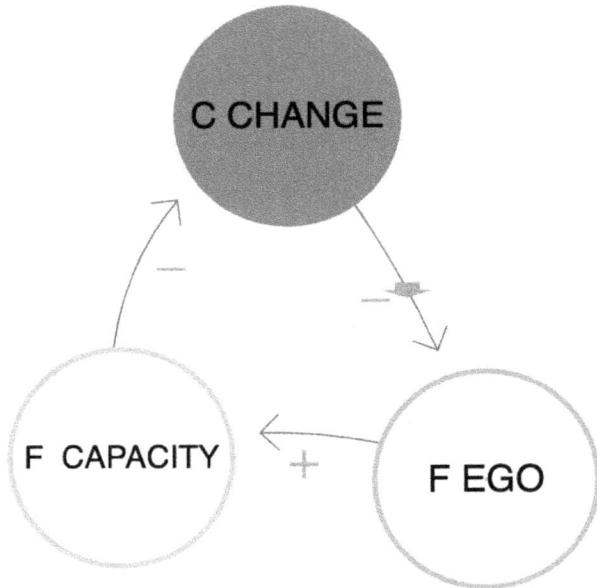

FIG. 2

Fig. 2 shows the states of these variables after LOOPY has run the model for 8 time steps beginning with the introduction of one unit of "Chantal's demand for change" into the system. Fran's ego strength and capacity for change have bottomed out at the lowest possible level and Chantal's demand for change has reached its upper limit.

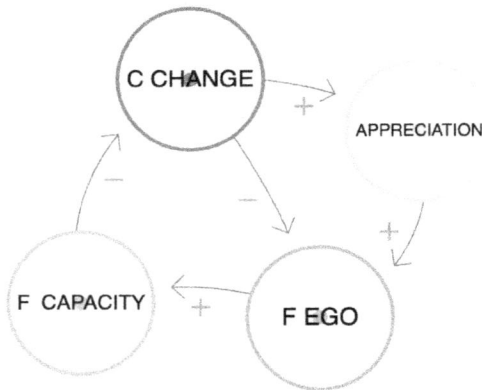

FIG. 3

Fig. 3 shows a new structure reflecting audience member *A*'s intervention in which an additional balancing loop (with only one negative link) has been created through which expressions of "honest appreciation" are triggered upwards by increasing demands for change. Both will reach Fran's ego strength at the same time.

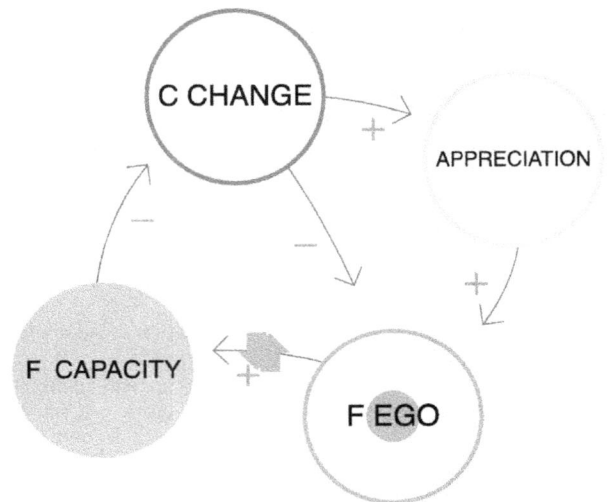

FIG. 4

Fig. 4 shows the states of these variables after LOOPY has run the model for 9 time steps; again beginning with the introduction of one unit of "Chantal's demand for change". Chantal's demands for change and expressions of appreciation are now both at zero while Fran's ego strength is at a median position and her capacity for change is at its maximum.

The overall effect of the model is to demonstrate that, if the leader of an organization in need of change learns to link an equal amount of honest expressions of appreciation for work done up to the present with demands for innovation, there may not be a complete and automatic conversion (as evinced by the lingering sense of unease exhibited by Fran during the intervention) but new conversations will at least become possible through the correction of runaway positive feedback and, with persistence, there may eventually be a tipping point at which team members with less robust ego-strength may experience a lasting shift in their ongoing capacity for change. While such a general principle may already be recognized within the Organizational Development, Change Management, and other social science literatures [14] creating and projecting the Systems Thinking diagrams above for a Forum Theatre audience to view during post-intervention discussion may provide a novel and engaging way to communicate this idea in its systemic fullness and can, as in this case, provide a powerful short-hand method for generalizing insight from what may have begun simply as a kind of "gut instinct" for positive action from a community member. It is also an efficient manner in which to quickly and clearly "pragmatize the kernel of the systems idea" (namely, circularly causal and non-linear interactions of elements) for a general audience.

Interaction Two – *Action*

Audience member *B* chose to replace the character of Maura and de-escalated the entire situation by taking any immediate innovations off the table. Instead, she offered to simply shadow Fran for this year with an eye to developing any possible innovations to the faculty orientation sessions for implementation the following year. As a result, Fran, Jen and Maura then quickly agreed in a friendly and enthusiastic manner that the meeting was basically ready to wrap-up while

Chantal was left looking on with a rather disconcerted expression on her face. It was at this point that I, as the session Joker, froze the scene and began facilitating discussion of the intervention.

Intervention Two- *Discussion*

In our discussion, audience member *B*, who, not coincidentally, was the head of the unit hosting this performance, said she was motivated to make this intervention by having personally learned the lesson of "too much, too fast" when she had first assumed leadership of the unit and attempted to implement a fairly sweeping program of change. Her colleagues smiled and nodded knowingly and there was even some laughter as the group seemed to acknowledge a shared experience that had been difficult but that they had come through together in a positive manner. The candidness with which *B* owned the self-created difficulties she had experienced early in her tenure demonstrated a remarkably mature leadership style. However, from my point of view as the Joker, it was vital that the group confront the fact that this intervention was carried out by the highest-ranking member of a real-life unit replacing the most junior member of the fictitious unit portrayed. Employing a Joking technique learned from my mentor, David Diamond, I asked the original "Maura" how easy or difficult it would be for her character to implement the kind of approach we had just witnessed by the intervening "Maura". Unsurprisingly, she replied that it would, basically, be impossible given her position as the newest member of the team who had been specifically brought in to help implement Fran's program of change. For her to feel sufficiently empowered to unilaterally change course in this manner was a stretch to say the least. This led to some further rich and frank discussion about differing levels of equity in hierarchical organizations and their impact on the ways in which conflicts unfold. The need to build mechanisms to support newer employees in this area was identified.

I then turned the conversation to the actress playing Chantal and asked how the meeting had gone for her. She revealed that the look of displeasure I had noticed indicated her uncertainty around explaining to the Dean, to whom she must report, that the program of renewal for which she was specifically hired would be proceeding at a pace slower than requested.

Intervention Two – *Systemic Analysis*

An intervention such as this provides a perfect opportunity to discuss the System Archetype identified by Donella Meadows as "Escalation" in which two sides of a conflict are locked in a mutually amplifying feedback loop of resistance to each other. It does so via *B's* demonstration of the only real antidote Meadows offers beyond not getting locked into such a loop in the first place; namely, "unilateral disarmament." (Meadows and Wright, 2015, p. 124-126)) By completely letting go of her immediate need in favour of a longer-term solution down the road *B* was able to stabilize the situation in the meeting room.

From a systems perspective, the aforementioned discussion around "equity" could also be framed in terms of the concept of "leverage", and the similar hierarchical factors that impact individuals' perceived possession of this potent systemic element when faced with challenging and confrontational situations, could also be explored.

The dilemma that Chantal found herself in at the conclusion of this intervention also opens the door to a discussion of system boundaries. While the "interaction system" comprised of the four individuals onstage in our play may have been stabilized in terms of escalating conflict, it is nested inside a larger system that will be subsequently perturbed by the actions taken in the intervention. This perturbation may lead to very difficult emergent outcomes for Chantal. Even the very decision as to what to put onstage and what to leave offstage in a particular Forum Theatre play represents a boundary judgment to which various methods of critique can be applied and demonstrated.

5. CONCLUSION

The LOOPY diagramming platform has some obvious limitations compared with other more advanced platforms such as Insight Maker. The most obvious of these is the fact that feedback is always emanating throughout the system in a single unalterable unit per time step and the user is unable to employ various mathematical functions to adjust differing amounts of feedback at different points in the system. Similarly, one cannot build in other mathematical functions that could regulate flows based on their comparison with desired levels of stocks. However, remembering that they do not represent the totality of the system but simply the relationships illuminated by the intervention at hand (whose impacts are, obviously, rippling throughout various other elements and relationships not visibly captured at this point) as well as the types of leverage revealed, LOOPY diagrams are certainly adequate for the kinds of introductory systemic insights generated "on the fly" in the heat of a Forum Theatre performance. Perhaps it is possible to build more detailed models of extant Forum Plays complete with mathematically specified feedback and flow functions that would make other types of insights available to Forum Theatre audiences. Efforts to do so remain part of the ongoing Systems Theatre research program.

In the meantime, it is hoped that the example interventions offered in this paper, as well as their basic analysis in systemic terms, have provided sufficient evidence that the relationship between Forum Theatre and system modeling proposed by the Systems Theatre project is a rich one that is well worth pursuing through future, expanded research collaborations.

6. REFERENCES

[1] B. Fitz. **InExArt: The Autopoietic Theatre of Augusto Boal**. Ibidim Press, Stuttgart. 2012

[2] A. Erfran, **UBC Conflict Engagement Framework – Draft** January, 2019.

[3] J. Luong and R. Arnold Enhancing Theatre of the Oppressed through Systems Thinking: Reflections on an Applied Workshop. **Pedagogy and Theatre of the Oppressed Journal,** Volume 1, Article 8, 2016

[4] Scholte T. "Toward a Systems Theatre: Proposal for a Program of Non-Trivial Modeling." **Futures,** vol. 103, pp. 94–105., doi:10.1016/j.futures.2018.03.008. (2018).

[5] W. Ulrich, "Reflective practice in the civil society: the contribution of critically systemic thinking", **Reflective Practice**, Vol. 1 No. 2, pp. 247-268, doi: 10.1080/713693151. (2000)

[6] R. Ashby (1956), **An Introduction to Cybernetics**, Chapman & Hall, London.

[7] M. Ryland and T. Scholte "Rehearsing Resilience (and beyond)." **Kybernetes,** 2018. doi:10.1108/k-11-2017-0459.

[8] D. H. Meadows and D. Wright (2015). **Thinking in Systems: a Primer**. Chelsea Green Publishing

[9] W. T. Powers (2005) **Behavior: the Control of Perception.** Benchmark Publications.

[10] T. Scholte, "Proto-Cybernetics in the Stanislavski System of Acting." **Kybernetes**, vol. 44, no. 8/9, 2015. pp. 1371–1379., doi:10.1108/k-11-2014-0234.

[11] T. Scholte "'Black Box' Theatre: Second-Order Cybernetics and Naturalism in Rehearsal and Performance." **New Horizons for Second-Order Cybernetics,** pp. 271–292., doi:10.1142/9789813226265_0044. 2017.

[12] R. S. Marken, **Doing Research on Purpose: a Control Theory Approach to Experimental Psychology.** Newview. 2014.

[13] J. D. Sterman, **Business Dynamics: Systems Thinking and Modeling for a Complex World**. Irwin, Boston. 2014

[14] D. L. Cooperrider and L. N. Godwin. "Positive Organization Development." **Oxford Handbooks Online,** 2011, doi:10.1093/oxfordhb/9780199734610.013.0056.

Evaluation model about behavior, quality perception and satisfaction of the drinking water service in Trujillo- Peru

Bertha ULLOA RUBIO
Programa Académico de Investigación – Universidad César Vallejo
Trujillo, 13001/La Libertad, Perú

Irma Luz YUPARI AZABACHE
Programa Académico de Investigación – Universidad César Vallejo
Trujillo, 13001/La Libertad, Perú

Rosa Patricia GÁLVEZ CARRILLO
Programa Académico de Investigación – Universidad César Vallejo
Trujillo, 13001/La Libertad, Perú

Julio Antonio RODRIGUEZ AZABACHE
Programa Académico de Investigación – Universidad César Vallejo
Trujillo, 13001/La Libertad, Perú

Higinio Guillermo WONG AITKEN
Programa Académico de Investigación – Universidad César Vallejo
Trujillo, 13001/La Libertad, Perú

ABSTRACT

The present research had as an objective to develop an evaluation model about behavior, quality perception and user´s satisfaction of the drinking water service regarding the drinking water service in Trujillo - Peru in the year 2018. The population was made up of the inhabitants with drinking water connections in the district of Trujillo that make a total of 62,166. The sample was made up of 651 people who reside in the district. The applied technique was the survey and the instrument was the questionnaire, which includes the user´s characterization, the user´s environmental behavior, either connected or not connected to public network. The results obtained were the habits and/or customs in the use of water by the users of the drinking water service and 14% believe that it is convenient; as far as the repairs on the public network in the users of the drinking water service, 92% do it externally and in relation to the sanitary guarantee in the drinking water by the users of the drinking water service, 61% consider it moderate. It is concluded that there is an optimal evaluation model about behavior, quality perception and user´s satisfaction regarding the drinking water service in Trujillo-Peru-2018.

Keywords: Model, evaluation, behavior, quality perception, user´s satisfaction, water.

1. INTRODUCTION

Users' perception is of vital importance for a company; before that they must focus their efforts to identify how to achieve their user's satisfaction.

Defining the quality of the service and how to evaluate it depends on the observer's point of view. For this reason, there are controversies among authors; however, in the proposal we used the systemic approach of company, university and society represented by water users. [1].

Many users of the liquid element (water) do not have priority to comply with the payment of their water bill. [2].

In La Libertad region, the company that provides drinking water serves thirteen localities: El Porvenir, Trujillo, Víctor Larco, La Esperanza, Florencia de Mora, Huanchaco, Moche, Salaverry, Puerto Malabrigo, Chocope, Paiján, Chepén and Pacanguilla, whose coverage reaches 86.08% of the population. That means that the remaining 13.22 % lacks the attention of the liquid element for the human being.

Regarding the factors associated with the quality of drinking water service, 76.1% are in the medium level, 19.38% are satisfied and 4% are dissatisfied, while 74.8% have a regular perception regarding the quality of service; concluding that there is an average satisfaction and regular perception (62.2%) and that the factors analyzed have a significant relationship with the perception of quality. [3].

Public services are currently one of the fastest-growing sectors worldwide, and over time this has become an important aspect of development for all countries. Also, the ease of the digital age and the internet allows customers easy access to be informed by giving them the choices they need and how to meet their respective needs. [4].

In Trujillo, the fundamental problem is the shortage of drinking water supply due to the rupture of the mother canal of the Chavimochic Special Project which has affected 426,000 users in this province of La Libertad. Districts such as La Esperanza, Florencia de Mora, El Porvenir and part of Huanchaco (El Milagro) and Trujillo are affected by water shortages and the rupture of the pipes. For this reason, the main goal of this research was to determine an evaluation model about behavior, quality perception and user´s satisfaction regarding the drinking water service in Trujillo. This allowed us to know the aspects to evaluate among the main actors that provide and receive this service and, at the same time, with the results to be obtained to offer the possible alternatives of solution so that the water resource is to the availability of the inhabitants and they can carry out their basic necessities inside their homes and that the company can offer a better service of quality and attention to their clients as well as the opportunity of improvement in relation to the personnel that has communication with the users, and also to offer the suitable information in relation to the complementary services, consultancy and insurance. information in relation to the complementary services, consultancy and insurance.

The research was applied to a population of 738 people residing in the district. The applied technique was the survey and the instrument was the questionnaire to develop the Model of evaluation on behavior, quality perception and user´s satisfaction of the drinking water service regarding the drinking water service in Trujillo - Peru in the year 2018. This questionnaire was validated by experts. The results obtained were the habits and/or customs in the use of water and the drinking water service where 14% believe that it is convenient; as far as the repairs on the public network in the users of the drinking water service, 92% do it externally, and in relation to the sanitary guarantee in the drinking water in the users of the drinking water service, 61% consider it moderate. It is concluded that there is an optimal evaluation model about behavior, quality perception and user´s satisfaction regarding the drinking water service in Trujillo-Peru-2018.

2. OBJECTIVES

General

To determine the evaluation model about behavior, quality perception and user´s satisfaction of the drinking water service in Trujillo.

Specific

To evaluate users' behavior regarding water quality.
To analyze users' perception of water quality with respect to drinking water service.
To analyze user's satisfaction in relation to the sanitary sewerage service in Trujillo

3. MATERIAL AND METHODS

According to the design, the research is explanatory. In the case study the population was 62166 and a sample of 738 people calculated with the formula for finite population with a 95% confidence level, a success rate of 19% obtained from a similar research previous to ours, and an adjusted error of 4.9%.

Sampling: The sampling was carried out by strata, considering the following sectors

Sectors	No.	Records	Sample size
901	440	0.00707782	5
902	3202	0.05150725	38
903	5403	0.08691246	64
904	2766	0.04449377	33
905	2508	0.0403436	30
906	2368	0.03809156	28
907	3323	0.05345366	39
908	2710	0.04359296	32
909	4044	0.06505164	48
911	2923	0.04701927	35
912	2130	0.0342631	25
913	1744	0.02805392	21
914	3258	0.05240807	39
915	4248	0.06833317	50
916	4959	0.07977029	59
917	2418	0.03889586	29
918	1371	0.02205386	16
919	2239	0.03601647	27
920	2051	0.03299231	24
921	579	0.00931377	7
922	2152	0.03461699	26
924	4150	0.06675675	49
923-925	1180	0.01898144	14
	62166	100%	738

Data collection techniques and instruments
The technique used was the survey and the instrument was the questionnaire about user behavior and drinking water quality of service in Trujillo-Peru-2018 (See Annex N°01). It is made up of three parts:
Part I: Characterization of the user.
Part II: Behavior of the connected, not connected user to the public network and for all.
Part III: Perception of quality and user's satisfaction that includes problems with the water and sewer service that are present, the perception of quality with respect to water service, sewer service and the care provided by the service company, user's satisfaction with respect to water service and sanitary sewerage.

Methods of data analysis
Descriptive statistics, statistical tables and graphs, SPSS version 25 Amos were used to model structural equations that allow us to support our research by extending standard multivariate analysis methods to create models of behavior and attitudes that more accurately reflect complex relationships than standard multivariate statistical techniques through an intuitive programmatic or graphical user´s interface.

4. RESULTS

Behavior

Table 1
Frequency of drinking water Behavior by potable water service Users in Trujillo-Peru-2018

Frequency	N°	%
Adequate	103	14%
Inadequate	635	86%
Total	738	100%

Table 2
Frequency of drinking water use by potable water service users in Trujillo- Peru-2018

Frequency	N°	%
A lot	150	20%
Moderate	372	50%
Normal	216	29%
Total	738	71%

Table 3
Repairs in public network by users of drinking water in Trujillo- Peru-2018

Repairs	N°	%
External	678	92%
Service company	60	8%
Total	738	100%

Perception of quality

Table 4
Sanitary guarantee of drinking water in users of drinking water service in Trujillo- Peru-2018

Guarantee	N°	%
Good	248	34%
Moderate	453	61%
Normal	37	5%
Total	738	100%

Table 5
Cost of drinking water service in users of drinking water service in Trujillo- Peru-2018

	N°	%
High	341	46%
Normal	397	54%
Total	738	100%

Table 6
Evacuation of water used by users of drinking water services in Trujillo - Peru-2018

Evacuation	N°	%
Bad	461	62%
Very bad	64	9%
Total	738	100%

Table 7
Individualized attention of drinking water by the users of drinking water service in Trujillo- Peru-2018

Attention	N°	%
Efficient	511	69%
Inefficient	227	31%
Total	738	100%

Satisfaction of quality

Table 8
User's satisfaction regarding the drinking water service in Trujillo- Peru-2018

Satisfaction	N°	%
Very satisfied	131	18%
Satisfied	414	56%
Dissatisfied	132	18%
Very dissatisfied	61	8%
Total	738	100%

Table 9

User's satisfaction regarding the sanitary sewerage service in Trujillo- Peru-2018

Satisfaction	N°	%
Very satisfied	158	21%
Satisfied	316	43%
Dissatisfied	160	22%
Very dissatisfied	104	14%
Total	738	100%

Table 10

User's satisfaction regarding the attention of the drinking water service in Trujillo- Peru-2018

Satisfaction	N°	%
Very satisfied	40	5%
Satisfied	262	36%
Regularly Satisfied	336	46%
Dissatisfied	83	11%
Very dissatisfied	17	2%
Total	738	100%

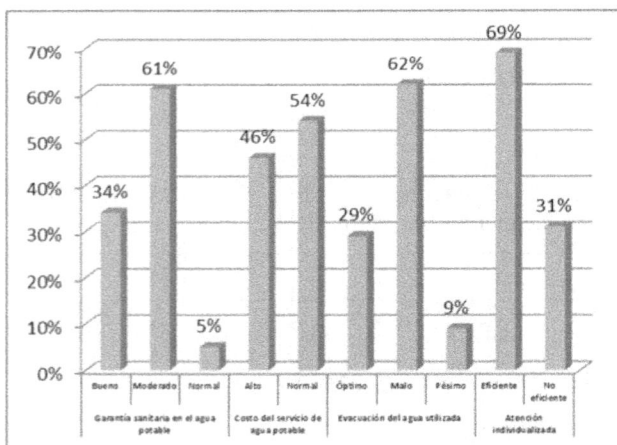

Figure 1: Quality Levels the drinking water service in Trujillo – Peru - 2018

Amos Model

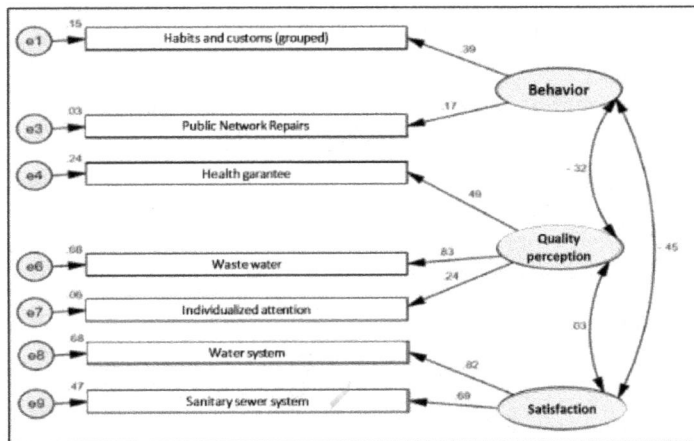

Figure 2. Three-factor model related to ten indicators

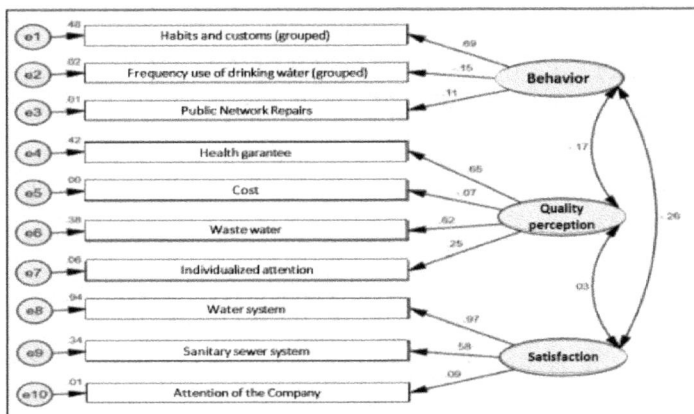

Figure 3. The Model proposal is presented, which would have three factors related to seven indicators.

5. DISCUSSION

The main objective of this research was to determine an evaluation model about the user's behavior, perception of quality and satisfaction regarding the drinking water service in Trujillo and we found that with regard to the behavioral dimension in Table 1 the habits and/or customs in the use of the drinking water service, 14% have adequate habits while 86% have inadequate habits. In Table 2, regarding the frequency of the use of the drinking water service, in 50% it is moderate and in 20% it is a lot. In Table 3, with respect to repairs in the public network in users of the drinking water service, 92% do so externally and 8% use the company's service. In Table 4, regarding the sanitary guarantee in the drinking water service, 61% consider it moderate and 5% consider it normal. An investigation was carried out in order to know the perception of the Federal District inhabitants about the quality of the drinking water service, as well as their willingness to pay a higher rate, and their consumption habits. Among the main results of the survey, it was reported that 96% of households have piped water and 82% receive it every day, but there is a high perception that water is scarce. Although the interviewees consider water to be the second most important public service and the one for which they pay the least, they do not perceive it as the cheapest and they are reluctant to increase the tariff. There is inequality in the perception of service quality among socio-economic strata and among delegations. Finally, the perception of such quality encompasses all aspects of the service, from the supply conditions to the service in the operator's offices, as shown in Tables 1 and 2. [6].

.

Based on the dimension perception of quality regarding the drinking water sanitary guarantee in the users of the drinking water service, 61% consider it moderate and 5% consider it normal; with respect to the cost of the drinking water service in Table 5, 54% of the users consider it high and 46% consider it normal. Likewise, González, Aguirre and Lartigue (2016) conducted a quantitative research and concluded that there is a reluctance on the part of the population to increase the water resource tariff and there is inequality among the population of the different social strata.It could be assumed that the moderate type perception is due to the treatment of water for human consumption by the company, because being a vital and important resource for the population it ensures that this type of water quality be suitable for human consumption. Regarding the evacuation of water used in users of drinking water services in Trujillo, in Table 6, 62% consider it bad and 9% very bad, and in Table 7 regarding individualized attention to drinking water in users of drinking water services, 69% believe that it is efficient and 31% that it is not efficient.

In Table 8, regarding user's satisfaction with drinking water service, 56% are satisfied and 8% dissatisfied. These results are similar to those reported by Márquez and Ortega who conducted a quantitative investigation in the state of Veracruz in which the population was all the inhabitants of the city of Xalapa.The technique used was the survey and the instrument the questionnaire; the sampling used was of a probabilistic type, concluding that the population is dissatisfied with the high water rates as well as the lack of water resource supply. This would be because users would be willing to pay a higher value for the water service in order to receive a better quality product. In this same category, respondents believe that by improving the quality of water used for human consumption, the risk of contracting diseases is reduced, as shown in Tables 6, 7 and 8. [7].

In Table 9, 43% of users are satisfied with the sewerage service whereas 14% are dissatisfied. These results are similar to those reported by Alvarado, Rodríguez and Iturralde who analyzed the distribution of the infrastructure of the drinking water and health systems in the state of Nuevo León, in which the municipalities with the greatest social marginalization (without drinking water or access to health services) tend to present the worst health outcomes. Therefore, it is assumed that there could be an unequal distribution of material and human resources in the drinking water and health systems, since there is a high concentration of these resources in the metropolitan area and the consequent neglect of the peripheral municipalities. [8].

In table 10, in terms of user satisfaction with the provision of drinking water service, 46% are regularly satisfied, 11% are dissatisfied and 2% are very dissatisfied. Thus, Lascuráin (2012) conducted a qualitative descriptive research, concluding that problem solving is one of the most important factors which directly affects long-term satisfaction. [9]. Data are also provided regarding the economic and social assessment of the drinking water service which can be used to improve the city's service. The most outstanding results show that for the inhabitants of the

city the amount to pay for a better water service expresses the social and economic value of this vital resource. On the other hand, the probability that someone accepts a payment for improving the service is greater when the respondent is a woman. In addition, as with environmental goods, the water service for the homes of the city has a normal characteristic. However, the proportion of families that responded with a "yes" in their willingness to pay being higher in the low income range. [10] When evaluating the proposed model using the AMOS software, the indicators include habits and customs, repairs in the public network for the dimension Behavior, health guarantee, wastewater and individualized attention for the perception of quality and water and sanitary sewer service for Satisfaction, deciding to eliminate from the model the indicators Frequency of use of drinking water, Cost and Service of the company that provides service due to having less standardized factorial load and positions to be evaluated through the Satorra-Bentler test. Each model focuses the evaluation on the different aspects of the organization of education and in function to its processes, being the purpose of the model to measure the level of location of an institution or company that seeks quality. [10]. Finally, a simple and practical methodology was reported that allows the selection of the internal services that will evaluate and improve, identify clients, develop, apply instruments and mechanisms for the assessment of the level of service and finally, carry out improvement actions. [11]..

6. CONCLUSIONS

The water is a principal service to life of human being. With this work, the research team do their contribution analizing the indications and suggesting a model to evaluate the dimensions of behaviour, quality and user satisfaction in relation to potable water service.

7. REFERENCES

[1] Contreras, A. & Ulloa, R. (2017). Systemic Dynamic Methodology for Complex Systems "SDMCS", (Memories Sixteenth Ibero-American Conference on Systems, Cybernetics and Informatics, 2017).

[2] Rubio, G., & Rodríguez, M. (2012). Analysis of customers' perception of the quality of the service received by the personnel working in the large supermarkets in the city of Ibagué. Business Dimension. 10 (2), pp21-31.

[3] Ulloa, B., Yupari, I., Gálvez, R., & Anticona, M. (2017). Factors associated with the perception of the quality of service of water users in the district of Víctor Larco. UCV-SCIENTIA Magazine, 9 (1). ISSN 2077-172X, ISSN 2410-891X.

[4] Rubio, G., & Rodríguez, M. (2012). Analysis of customers' perception of the quality of the service received from the personnel working in the large supermarkets in the city of Ibagué. Business Dimension. 10 (2), pp21-31.

[5] Pastor C. (2014). Evaluation of the satisfaction of urban water and sanitation services in Peru: From the imposition of the offer to listen to the demand.

Recovered
http://tesis.pucp.edu.pe/repositorio/bitstream/handle/12345
6789/5470/PASTOR_PAREDES_OSCAR_EVALUACIO
N_SERVICIO.pdf?sequence=1&isAllowed=y

[6] González, F., Aguirre, R. and Lartigue, C. (2016). Perceptions, attitudes and behaviors regarding drinking water service in Mexico City. Tecnología y Ciencias del Agua, vol.7 (6). Redalyc. pp. 41-56. Mexican Institute of Water Technology. Morelos, Mexico.

[7] Márquez, O and Ortega M. (2017). Social perception of the drinking water service in the Municipality of Xalapa, Veracruz. Mexican Journal of Public Opinion, year 12 number 23. Elsevier pp. 41-59. ISSN 1870-7300

[8] Rodríguez e Iturralde (2016), Accessibility to drinking water and health systems: A spatial analysis for Tabasco, Mexico. Universidad Autónoma de Nuevo León. Health issues and international affairs. 3CIN.tps Foundation: //github.com/ttezel/nn. [Last access: 17 07 2018].

[9] Lascuráin, I. (2012). Diagnosis and Proposal of the improvement of quality in the service of a company of uninterrupted electric power units. Thesis to obtain a Master's degree in Quality Engineering. . Mexico D.F: Universidad Iberoamericana.].

[10] Giorgetti, C., & Romero, L. (2014.). Study of existing quality assessment models for the conceptualization of a suitable model for Higher Education Institutions that implement Distance Education in Argentina. Ibero-American Congress on Science, Technology, Innovation and Education, ISBN: 978-84-7666-210-6-Article 1466.

[[11] Balmori, G. (2014). MECSI. Model to evaluate the quality of the internal service (MECSI: Evaluation model for internal service quality). . Business Innovations, 11 (22): 191-213.

Data Distribution Assessment and Optimal Splitting of Data Sets

Tim Heinz and Oliver Nelles

Department of Mechanical Engineering, University of Siegen

Paul-Bonatz-Str. 9-11, 57076 Siegen, Germany

ABSTRACT

A new method for assessing the quality of a data distribution based on the calculation of the Kullback-Leibler (KL) divergence is proposed. The pdf of the data is estimated by a kernel density estimator. In the case without any prior knowledge the target distribution is assumed to be uniform. Then Monte Carlo sampling of the estimated pdf allows to approximate the KL divergence as criterion for the space-filling properties of the data distribution. Applications of this KL-based criterion are manifold. Sobol sequences and maximin latin hypercubes, most frequently applied for space-filling design of experiments, are compared. Finally, strategies for optimally splitting data sets are discussed and illustrated.

Keywords: Data distribution, kernel density estimation, Kullback-Leibler divergence, training and test set, domain adaptation.

1. INTRODUCTION

The data point distribution influences the quality of a data-based model decisively. Therefore it is important to assess the quality of a design of experiments before the (expensive) measurement takes place. Without any prior knowledge, the data points should be evenly spread across the input space (space-filling design) [1]. For optimization purposes, several loss functions are popular like maximin [2] and Φ_p [3] which evaluate the data distribution on the locally worst point pairs, but these loss functions are not able to reflect the overall distribution quality.

In this contribution, the probability density function (pdf) of a given data set is estimated with a kernel density estimator and compared to a uniform distribution using the Kullback-Leibler divergence (see Sec. 2). This approach is more global compared to the above mentioned loss functions (see Sec. 2 for further discussion) and can be used to compare different designs (see Sec. 3 and 4). Optimal splitting of a data set in training and test data in Sec. 5 is an important application for the proposed approach. Both subsets should be close to the uniform distribution for space-filling properties. The strategy proposed in Sec. 5 is similar to the distribution stratified cross-validation as in [4] and requires no repetitions as in [5] with random splitting.

2. DISTRIBUTION QUALITY

The data distribution quality in the n-dimensional input space spanned by $\underline{u} = [u_1, u_2, \ldots, u_n]^T$ should be assessed by comparing the data distribution with pdf $q(\underline{u})$ to a desirable target distribution with pdf $p(\underline{u})$. For a comprehensive survey on how measuring distances between pdf's refer to [6]. The most widely and successfully used measure is the Kullback-Leibler (KL) divergence also called relative entropy. It measures how one probability distribution $q(\underline{u})$ (here: the data) diverges from a second, expected probability distribution $p(\underline{u})$ (here: the desired target distribution).

In order to evaluate the Kullback-Leibler divergence in practice, a (quasi) Monte Carlo sampling of the pdfs is carried out, see e.g. [7]. For M sampling points the Kullback-Leibler divergence in its discrete version is given by

$$J_{\mathrm{KL}} = \sum_{i=1}^{M} P(i) \log \frac{P(i)}{Q(i)} \,. \tag{1}$$

For space-filling designs, the target distribution is uniform, i.e., $P(i) = 1/M$.

The data distribution shall be estimated by a density estimator $q(\underline{u})$ and therefore at the M sampling points the probabilities become $Q(i) = q(\underline{u}(i))/M$. Thus, in this case, (1) simplifies to

$$J_{\mathrm{KL}}^{(\mathrm{uniform})} = -\frac{1}{M} \sum_{i=1}^{M} \log q(\underline{u}(i)) \,. \tag{2}$$

Kernel Density Estimation

Given the input data distribution of any data set $\{\underline{u}(1), \underline{u}(2), \ldots, \underline{u}(N)\}$ with N data points, the estimation of the n-dimensional pdf $q(\underline{u})$ can be carried out by any density estimator. For standard books on that topic refer to [8] or [9]. Here a kernel estimator with a Gaussian kernel function shall be used, i.e., a Gaussian is placed on each data point:

$$\hat{q}(\underline{u}) = \frac{1}{N} \sum_{i=1}^{N} \frac{\exp\left(-\frac{1}{2}[\underline{u} - \underline{u}(i)]^T \underline{\Sigma}^{-1} [\underline{u} - \underline{u}(i)]\right)}{\sqrt{(2\pi)^n |\underline{\Sigma}|}} \,. \tag{3}$$

Throughout this paper the covariance matrix is chosen diagonal with individual standard deviations for each dimension: $\underline{\Sigma} = \mathrm{diag}(\sigma_1^2, \sigma_2^2, \ldots, \sigma_n^2)$. The standard deviations of the estimator in dimension $i = 1, 2, \ldots, n$ are fixed according to Silverman's rule-of-thumb given in [8]

$$\sigma_i = \sigma_{ui} \left(\frac{4}{n+2}\right)^{\frac{1}{n+4}} N^{-\frac{1}{n+4}} \tag{4}$$

where σ_{ui} is the standard deviation of the data in dimension i.

a)   b)

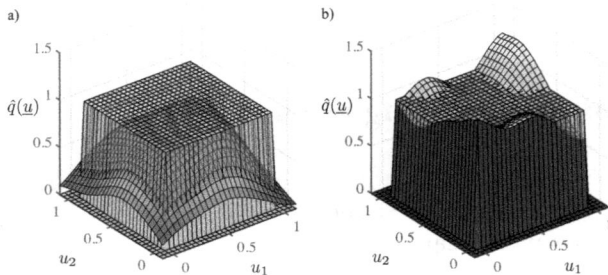

Figure 1: Data distribution of a maximin latin hypercube with 20 points in 2D shown in $[-0.1, 1.1]^2$ compared to a uniform pdf: a) ordinary density estimator, b) density estimator with boundary correction.

For sufficiently accurate (quasi) Monte Carlo sampling of the estimated pdf in (3) the number of sampling points M should be at least one or two orders of magnitude larger than the number of data points N of the data distribution to be assessed: $M \gg N$. The computational demand grows with $\mathcal{O}(N^2)$ making the proposed approach practical infeasible for huge data sets. However, if this is the case usually enough data is available for choosing separate training, validation, and test sets. Also for reducing the computational load, the proposed strategies can be applied on a cluster level after some clustering algorithm has reduced the data to $N^{(clust)}$ clusters with $N^{(clust)} = 1\,000$ or so.

Boundary Effects

In many applications the input space represents a unit hyper-square $[0, 1]^n$ – at least after normalization. If the inputs can be controlled by the experimenter and no or little prior knowledge about sensitivities is available then it is common practice to choose a space-filling design, i.e., asking for a uniform distribution of the data in the input space. If the actual data distribution is evaluated directly with a kernel density estimator as in (3) a lot of probability mass falls out of $[0, 1]^n$ as shown in Fig. 1a. It is remarkable that $\hat{q}(\underline{u}) < 1$ for all $\underline{u}$ in this toy example.

In consequence the (hyper)volume below $\hat{q}(\underline{u})$ in $[0, 1]^n$ is much smaller than 1 and thus leads to a large negative bias. Therefore it is common to correct/compensate for this lost (hyper)volume. For example the MATLAB function `mvksdensity` offers a logarithmic transformation or, more sensible in the discussed context, the method `'reflection'` which adds the lost pdf mass to the kernel being responsible. This results in a pdf estimate with a (hyper)volume equal to 1 in $[0, 1]^n$ as illustrated in Fig. 1b. The (hyper)volume under $\hat{q}(\underline{u}) < 1$ where data is too sparse balances with the (hyper)volume under $\hat{q}(\underline{u}) > 1$ where data is too dense, compared to a uniform distribution. The Kullback-Leibler divergence is then calculated with these two pdfs in Fig. 1b.

In future, different boundary correction methods shall be analyzed and compared with respect to the specific requirements of this application. The `'reflection'` method pretends data outside the boundaries; thus the estimated pdf is unrealistically large there.

Unsuitability of d^2 and Φ_p for Quality Assessment

Low-discrepancy sequences based on Halton [10], Hammersley [11], or Sobol [12] sets can be utilized for generating space-filling point distributions. This can be carried out in a computationally cheap way for an arbitrary amount of data points for an arbitrary dimensional input space. Also anytime new, additional points can be included without altering the already existing ones. Due to all these advantages, they are commonly applied for space-filling designs. Alternatively, latin hypercubes (LHs) also offer some attractive features. In particular they are non-collapsing designs which means that all data projected to one axis ends up in a unique position and furthermore is uniformly distributed. However, LHs are not necessarily space-filling; they need to be optimized for this purpose. Maximin optimization which maximizes the minimal (squared) nearest neighbor distance d^2 between the closest point pair is a very popular strategy. This approach is strictly local as it only considers the worst point pair(s); a more global alternative is minimizing Φ_p which effectively considers a wider environment by replacing the ∞-norm with the (inverse) p-norm and consequently requiring a delicate fine-tuning of p. Refer to [3] for a survey on LH optimization heuristics.

Although d^2 or Φ_p are good criteria for *optimizing* LHs as they drive the points farther away from each other, they are unsuitable for *assessing* a data distribution's quality. To immediately see this: Imagine the perfect distribution of LH data points with optimal value d^2_{opt}. One new or existing point coinciding with an already existing one would change the criterion immediately to $d^2 = 0$ although the quality of the data distribution hardly has changed. In consequence, the data distribution quality of LHs (or any other design) cannot be assessed with these optimization criteria. This paper proposes an alternative. It is computationally much more demanding and therefore not advisable for optimization except for very small problems but it can be utilized for comparing different LH optimization schemes and additionally comparing those with other designs.

3. COMMON DISTRIBUTIONS

In this section some typical input data shall be compared to convey an idea how well the proposed approach works for assessing the space-filling properties of a distribution. In the demonstration examples throughout this paper the number of Monte Carlo sampling points was chosen as $M = 10\,000$. All the examples in this section are 2-dimensional and with $N = 20$ data points.

Figure 2 (top) contrasts a normal distribution with standard deviation 1/6 and center at [0.5, 0.5] with a diagonally equally spaced point distribution. Both are incapable to cover the whole input space which is also illustrated by the large KL value according to (2).

The uniform distribution is also incapable to cover the input space very well with just 20 data points. The KL value varies significantly with the realization. A histogram of 1000 realizations in Fig. 3a reveals that the realization shown in Fig. 2 represents a very inferior one. Figure 3b shows the histogram of the KL values of 1000 realizations

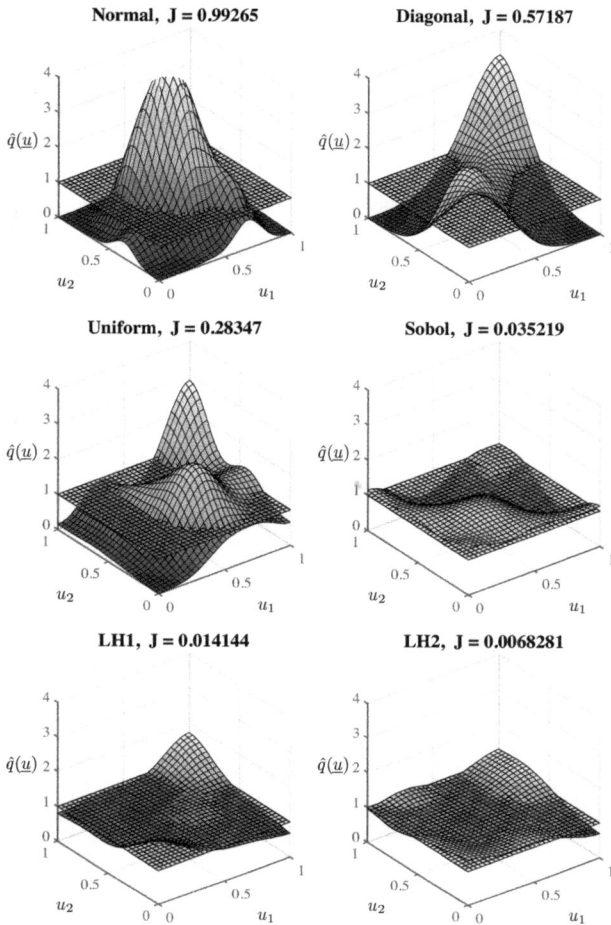

Figure 2: Density estimation for different data distributions with 20 points in $[0,1]^2$ with associated KL value according to (2).

of uniform distributions for $N = 200$ points. It scales roughly with $\sqrt{N}$ as statistically expected. These KL values are in the range of Sobol sequence or latin hypercubes for 10 times fewer data points. This underlines the benefits of *quasi*-random sampling, compare also [7].

The final three point distributions in Fig. 2 are extremely close to the ideal uniform distribution. The Sobol sequence seems to be inferior to maximin latin hypercube for few data points. This topic is discussed in more detail in the next section. LH2 represents a superior but computationally more demanding maximin latin hypercube optimization than LH1.

4. MAXIMIN LATIN HYPERCUBES VS. SOBOL SEQUENCES

The previous section has demonstrated the extreme variation in different random uniform designs, see Fig. 3. Note that Sobol sequences and LHs also are not unique. Different initializations are possible in both cases. However, the variance in the KL values is tiny compared to the random uniform distribution. Figure 4a illustrates the histogram for 20-point Sobol sets with different skippings. Figure 4b demonstrates that 20-point maximin LHs optimized with

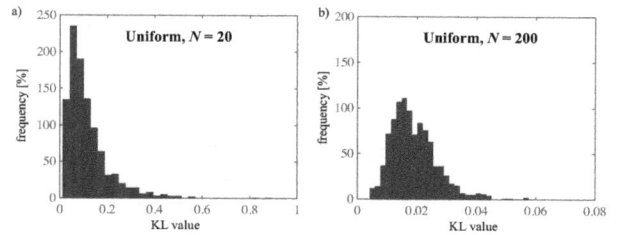

Figure 3: Histograms of the KL values for 1000 realizations of a uniform distribution in 2D for a) $N = 20$ (mean = 0.1), b) $N = 200$ (mean = 0.02).

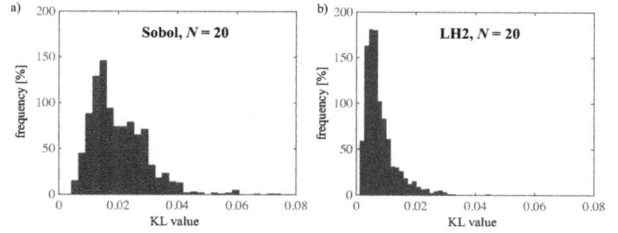

Figure 4: Histograms of the KL values for 1000 realizations of a) different Sobol sequences in 2D for $N = 20$ (mean = 0.02), b) different maximin latin hypercubes LH2 in 2D for $N = 20$ (mean = 0.008); LH1 is slightly worse (mean = 0.009).

the Extended Deterministic Local Search (EDLS) algorithm (phase 2) proposed in [13] perform even better than Sobol and with lower variance. This is true even for the simpler and faster optimization strategy (phase 1) discussed in [13]. This EDLS algorithm exchanges LH points with minimal d^2 value to their nearest neighbor until swapping point pairs does not make any progress (phase 1, LH1) or any swap is unsuccessful (phase 2, LH2).

In our investigations the maximin LH designs were superior to Sobol sequences regarding their space-filling properties if the number of data points was relatively small. Since optimizing the LHs is prohibitively slow as the number of points becomes large, studies with $N > 100$ have to be postponed to the future investigating more advanced, still to be developed, suboptimal maximin LH schemes.

Figure 5 compares the relative KL values for a) Sobol vs. LH1 and b) Sobol vs. LH2 for 4-10 dimensions and 10-100 data points given by

$$\text{rel. KL value} = \frac{J_{\text{KL}}^{(\text{Sobol})} - J_{\text{KL}}^{(\text{LH})}}{J_{\text{KL}}^{(\text{Sobol})}}. \qquad (5)$$

The superiority of the LH designs is obvious. The winning margin of the LHs decreases with growing data size. For the 2- and 3-dimensional cases the plots (not shown) are less concise. Also Sobol sequences win for $N > 30$ and $N > 90$, respectively. Presumably, for higher dimensions a similar behavior occurs for $N \gg 100$. A practical recommendation therefore could be: For small data sets: Utilize maximin LHs; for large data sets: Utilize Sobol sequences. Since maximin LHs can be optimized reliably only for small data sets anyway this approach also matches the computational constraints.

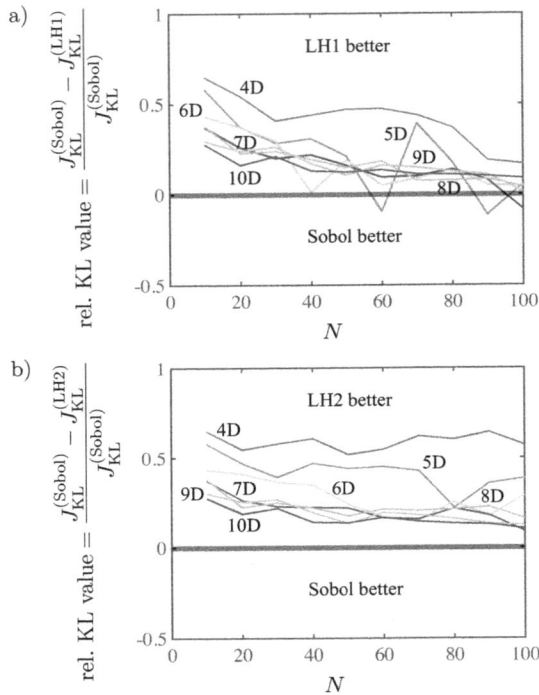

Figure 5: Relative space-filling KL value of maximin LHs vs. Sobol sequences in 4- to 10-dimensional space for 10-100 data points. 0 corresponds to identical KL values; 0.5 corresponds to 50% superior LH performance: a) LH1 vs. Sobol, b) LH2 vs. Sobol.

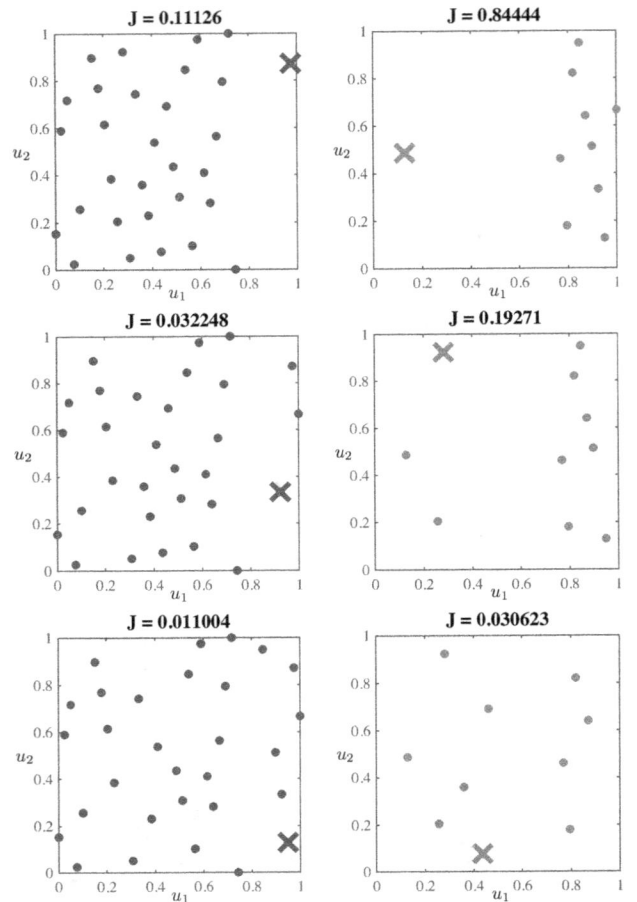

Figure 6: Point distribution for training (left) and test (right) data for iteration 1, 3, 6. The cross marks the currently swapped point.

5. SPLITTING DATA SETS

In all machine learning or system identification problems the available data has to be split in training and test set. Usually the training set again is split in a training and a validation part, either once or multiple times for cross validation. High discrepancies in performance on training set and validation/test set normally indicate overfitting. However, it can also be the result of very different data distributions for training and validation/test. In machine learning the field dealing with these issues is called *domain adaptation*.

Thus, it is advisable to take extreme care in making sure that the training and validation/test data distributions are as similar as possible. In the space-filling design scenario discussed in the previous sections, they all should be close to uniform. In consequence, the validation/test error cannot be attributed to different data distributions guaranteeing a reliable assessment of the model quality. This section discusses ways to optimally split a data set into parts which is a universally useful tool for all data-driven modeling.

The literature on this topic is scarce. A famous first approach was taken with the DUPLEX algorithm in [14] which lists the data based on pairwise distances and then subsequently sorts them in training and test sets. [15] compare three different splitting methods for real-world data in the field of water resources and discuss the benefits of the different algorithms with regard to the type of data

distribution.

One simple, greedy algorithm which exploits the KL value estimation proposed in this paper, starts with a (i) random split in training and test data, (ii) swaps data points between both sets; thereby improving the KL values of training and test distribution, (iii) stops if no improvement can be achieved anymore. Point exchange algorithms are very popular in the field of DoE; refer e.g. to [16] for a review in the area of D-optimal designs.

Various implementations of step (ii) are possible. The algorithm employed in this paper selects the point with highest estimated density in the test set

$$\underline{u}_{\text{test}}^* = \operatorname*{argmax}_i q(\underline{u}(i)), \quad i = 1, \ldots, N_{\text{test}} \qquad (6)$$

and swaps it with the point in the training set that minimizes a combination of the KL values on training and test data. Here we choose the geometric mean $\sqrt{J^{(\text{train})} J^{(\text{test})}}$ as overall criterion but other measures are possible as well. The proposed algorithm is illustrated with two toy examples in 2D. The first example artificially partitions a space-filling maximin LH design of 40 data points in 30 training and 10 test points in a worst-case scenario. The training set covers the left-hand side of the input space, the test set covers the right-hand side. This artificial initial point

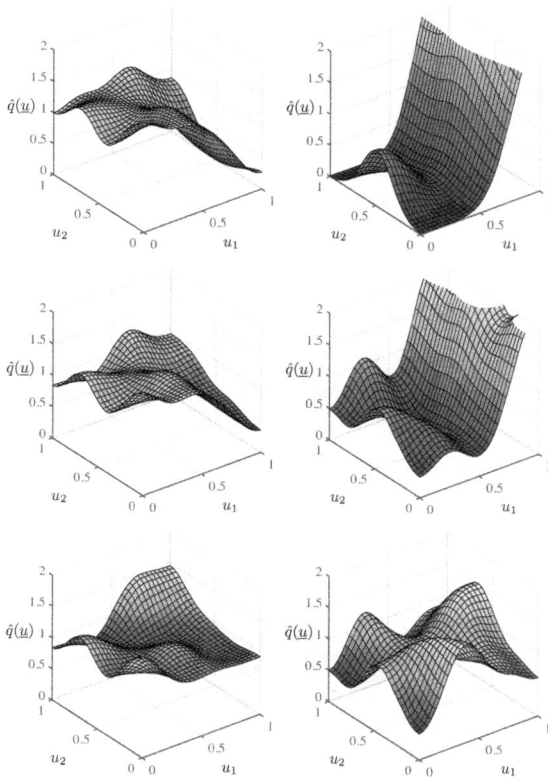

Figure 7: Estimated pdfs for training (left) and test (right) data for iteration 1, 3, 6.

distribution (iteration 0) is so bad that the KL measure on the test data equals infinity. Iterations 1, 3, and 6 of the point-swapping algorithm are visualized in Fig. 6 together with the values of $J^{(\text{train})}$ and $J^{(\text{test})}$, and the corresponding density estimates are shown in Fig. 7. Clearly, the final data distributions of training and test sets are space-filling. The convergence curve is shown in Fig. 8a. Note that for such a simple greedy approach this curve necessarily is monotonously decreasing and generally achieves only a local optimum.

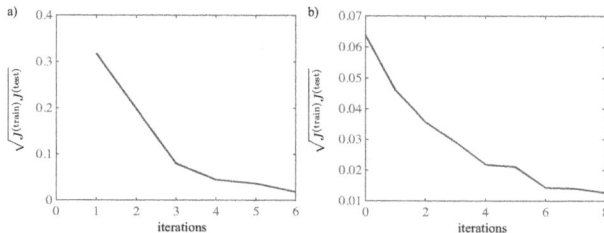

Figure 8: Convergence of the data exchange algorithm for the a) 30:10 LH data split (compare Fig. 6, 7), b) 80:20 random data split (compare Fig. 9, 10).

The second example demonstrates a more realistic scenario where 100 uniform random data points are split randomly in a ratio 80:20 in a training and test set. Nevertheless, the initial point distribution looks very poor. After 8 iterations of the swapping algorithm significant improvement could

be achieved. Iterations 1, 5, 8 are shown in Fig. 9 and Fig. 10 and the convergence curve is given in Fig. 8b.

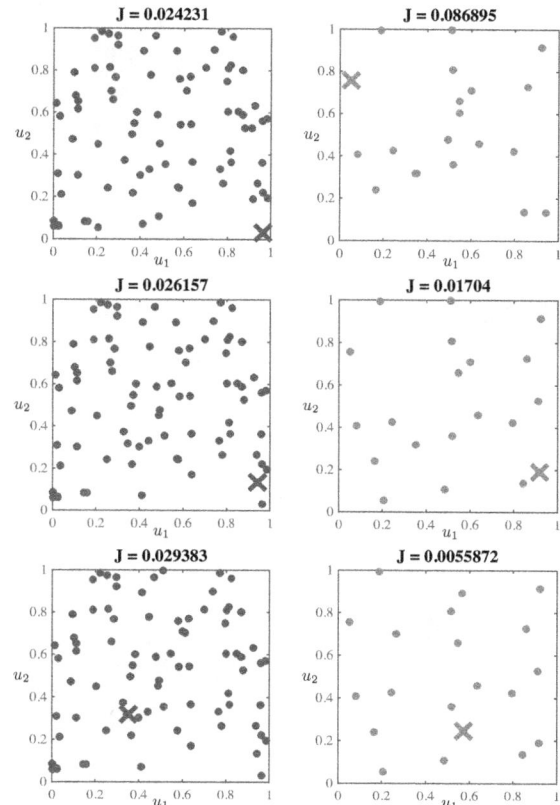

Figure 9: Point distribution for training (left) and test (right) data for iteration 1, 5, 8. The cross marks the currently swapped point.

Although the proposed swapping algorithm utilizes *both* KL values for training and test set it is asymmetrical in that it first picks the worst point in the test set for swapping. This results in an emphasis on the quality of the test data. In many cases this effect may be desirable as the test set typically is chosen significantly smaller. However, clearly, alternative algorithms need to be investigated in the future.

6. SUMMARY AND OUTLOOK

A new approach for assessing the quality of a data distributions has been proposed. It is based on the evaluation of the Kullback-Leibler divergence with a Monte Carlo sampling of the estimated probability density functions. This paper focused on situations where a space-filling point distribution is desirable. Different typical point distributions have been compared. In particular, Sobol sequences have been contrasted with maximin latin hypercubes for up to 10 dimensions and 100 data points where latin hypercubes proved superior w.r.t. their space-filling properties. Finally, a point-swapping algorithm for optimizing the split into training and test data sets was proposed and its performance was proven and illustrated with two examples. With just a couple of point swaps significant improvements

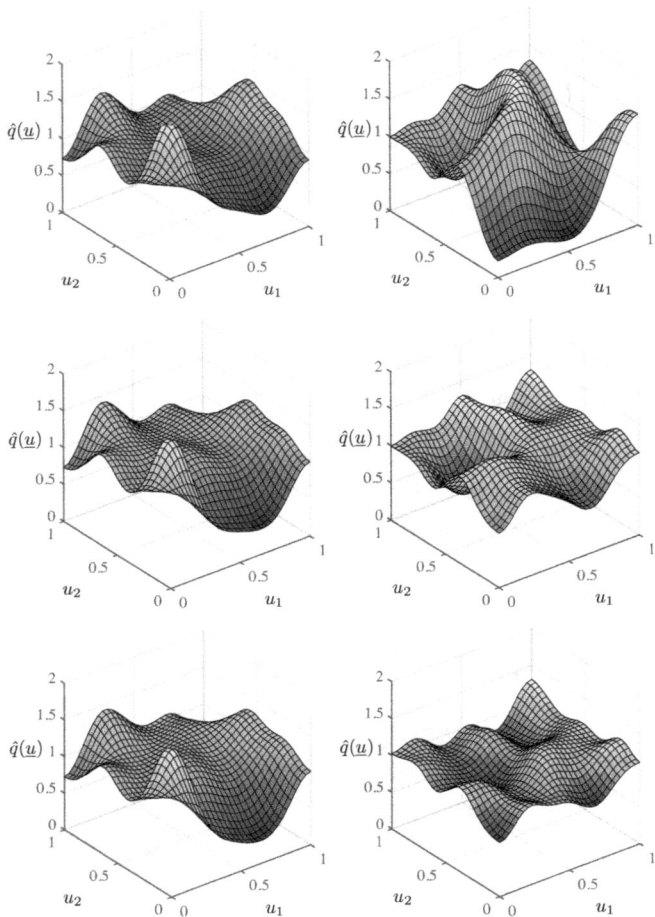

Figure 10: Estimated pdfs for training (left) and test (right) data for iteration 1, 5, 8.

can be obtained.

A couple of further investigations are obviously due for the future. Achieving good space-filling properties in DoE is not always feasible or even desirable. Often the focus is on approximating some target distribution $p(\underline{u})$ which is not uniform. Then the proposed approach can be extended by describing or estimating $p(\underline{u})$. For splitting data into training and test set then the objective could be $\hat{p}(\underline{u}) \approx \hat{q}(\underline{u})$. Another interesting extension is to formulate an algorithm that splits data in k folds for k-fold cross validation.

References

[1] L. Pronzato and W. G. Müller, "Design of computer experiments: space filling and beyond," *Statistics and Computing*, vol. 22, no. 3, pp. 681–701, 2012.

[2] M. E. Johnson, L. M. Moore, and D. Ylvisaker, "Minimax and maximin distance designs," *Journal of statistical planning and inference*, vol. 26, no. 2, pp. 131–148, 1990.

[3] A. Rimmel and F. Teytaud, "A survey of metaheuristics used for computing maximin latin hypercube," in *European Conference on Evolutionary Computation in Combinatorial Optimization*. Springer, 2014, pp. 25–36.

[4] X. Zeng and T. R. Martinez, "Distribution-balanced stratified cross-validation for accuracy estimation," *Journal of Experimental & Theoretical Artificial Intelligence*, vol. 12, no. 1, pp. 1–12, 2000.

[5] D. Krstajic, L. J. Buturovic, D. E. Leahy, and S. Thomas, "Cross-validation pitfalls when selecting and assessing regression and classification models," *Journal of cheminformatics*, vol. 6, no. 1, p. 10, 2014.

[6] S.-H. Cha, "Comprehensive survey on distance/similarity measures between probability density functions," *City*, vol. 1, no. 2, p. 1, 2007.

[7] A. B. Owen, "Quasi-monte carlo sampling," *Monte Carlo Ray Tracing: Siggraph*, vol. 1, pp. 69–88, 2003.

[8] B. W. Silverman, *Density estimation for statistics and data analysis*. CRC press, 1986, vol. 26.

[9] D. W. Scott, *Multivariate density estimation: theory, practice, and visualization*. John Wiley & Sons, 2015.

[10] H. Chi, M. Mascagni, and T. Warnock, "On the optimal halton sequence," *Mathematics and computers in simulation*, vol. 70, no. 1, pp. 9–21, 2005.

[11] T.-T. Wong, W.-S. Luk, and P.-A. Heng, "Sampling with hammersley and halton points," *Journal of graphics tools*, vol. 2, no. 2, pp. 9–24, 1997.

[12] I. M. Sobol, "On quasi-monte carlo integrations," *Mathematics and Computers in Simulation*, vol. 47, no. 2, pp. 103–112, 1998.

[13] T. Ebert, T. Fischer, J. Belz, T. O. Heinz, G. Kampmann, and O. Nelles, "Extended deterministic local search algorithm for maximin latin hypercube designs," in *Computational Intelligence, 2015 IEEE Symposium Series on*. IEEE, 2015, pp. 375–382.

[14] R. W. Kennard and L. A. Stone, "Computer aided design of experiments," *Technometrics*, vol. 11, no. 1, pp. 137–148, 1969.

[15] W. Wu, H. R. Maier, G. C. Dandy, and R. May, "Exploring the impact of data splitting methods on artificial neural network models," *Procceedings of the 10th International Conference on Hydroinformatics, Hamburg, Germany*, 2012.

[16] N.-K. Nguyen and A. J. Miller, "A review of some exchange algorithms for constructing discrete d-optimal designs," *Computational Statistics & Data Analysis*, vol. 14, no. 4, pp. 489–498, 1992.

Generic integration of VR and AR in product lifecycles based on CAD models

Jessica ULMER
Department of Mechanical Engineering and Mechatronics, FH Aachen University of Applied Sciences
Aachen, 52064, Germany

Sebastian BRAUN
Department of Mechanical Engineering and Mechatronics, FH Aachen University of Applied Sciences
Aachen, 52064, Germany

Chow Yin LAI
Department of Manufacturing, Materials and Mechatronics, RMIT University
Melbourne, VIC 3000, Australia

Chi-Tsun CHENG
Department of Manufacturing, Materials and Mechatronics, RMIT University
Melbourne, VIC 3000, Australia

Jörg WOLLERT
Department of Mechanical Engineering and Mechatronics, FH Aachen University of Applied Sciences
Aachen, 52064, Germany

ABSTRACT

Augmented Reality (AR) and Virtual Reality (VR) play an important role for the implementation of Industry 4.0 - especially in the area of virtual prototyping, manufacturing and maintenance. Thus, a holistic integration of these technologies in existing processes structures is essential to ensure future competitiveness of companies. Current research mostly focuses on some aspects of the lifecycle and not on the whole process. Furthermore, mostly specific tools are developed to create AR and VR contents instead of using already existing and widespread programs for example the 3D CAD software Inventor [1] or game engines like Unity [2]. The tools are used to create VR content providing a user-friendly environment with limited options for content creation. On one side the use of these programs decreases the required knowledge to create Mixed Reality applications, however they are associated with high implementation and running costs. This increases the entry barrier for small and medium sized enterprises (SME) to adopt AR and VR into their value chains significantly.

The presented work discusses concepts and proposes information models for adding VR-specific information directly in CAD environments. A generic model of necessary interaction options as well as VR properties is created and applied to a use case in the Industry 4.0 model factory at FH Aachen, Germany. Furthermore, a workflow for combined evaluation of product and equipment developments is developed focusing on VR integration.

Keywords: Industry 4.0, VR, AR, Integrated Engineering, Product Lifecycle Management, Virtual Prototyping.

1. INTRODUCTION

Anyone who speaks about Industry 4.0 can hardly avoid VR and AR. Current studies show that the demand for VR and AR emerging technologies will increase significantly in the next few years, while at the same time more and more extended reality products will reach the consumer market and the industry [3-5]. The mass production of VR and AR equipment makes them affordable and economically viable even for SMEs. The fields of applications for virtual helpers are numerous, ranging from virtual prototyping, AR-supported assembly, to maintenance tasks. [6]

While technical breakthroughs continue to happen thanks to technological advancements, customers' expectation for new products intensifies as product lifecycles are greatly shortened. In order to maintain and expand the competitiveness of companies, it is necessary to accelerate development services through integrated engineering across the entire value chain [7]. Especially virtual prototyping [8, 9] and virtual training [10, 11] are gaining importance. Products and entire plants can be tested, validated, and improved in virtual space before the costly manufacturing process starts. Training on commissioning, plant operation, and maintenance can also be carried out virtually leading to fast and efficient implementations of new processes in production [10-13].

However, the full potential of VR and AR applications is not yet fully exploited in practice. Mixed reality technologies are mostly used to solve specific problems [15] and seldom reach into the general product development processes. This means that generated CAD data generated during the design process of a product can only be reused to a limited extent for new problems, which leads to a high implementation overhead, making the technology not viable for SMEs.

An example on an investigation of cross-process usage of AR and VR technologies is shown in the AVILUS project [16], where different research projects are conducted with the goal of creating a company-wide information source including various software tools. As result, an ontology is created to enable automatic extraction of CAD data (NX) and wiring information (EPLAN). However, the research only shows flagship projects conducted in different companies and facilities, thus no complete integration over a system lifecycle is demonstrated [16].

The presented work emphasizes the necessity to develop generic information models and concepts for effective CAD integration without the need of highly specialized and cost-intensive VR/AR authoring tools.

2. VR IN PRODUCT DEVELOPMENT

To achieve a pervasive deployment of VR technologies especially in SMEs, a deeper look into possible integration stages during the development of a new product and its production process is necessary. This should ensure a consistent use of available CAD data in the sense of integrated engineering throughout the entire product life cycle and over various technologies.

ISO/IEC 15288 [14] defines six lifecycle stages (concept, development, production, utilization, support and retirement stage). Additionally, a technical process consisting of 11 processes starting with the stakeholder requirements definition process and ending with the disposal process is determined. A typical product development process can be derived based on this standard (Fig. 1, black font). A similar process can be assumed for the design of operating equipment like for example a gripper for picking parts or tools.

For VR applications, the product development process is the most important part [15]. During this stage, virtual design reviews can take place in simulations [16], visualization of engineering data [17], and usability tests [18]. To include VR simulations, additional information is required (Fig. 1, red font).

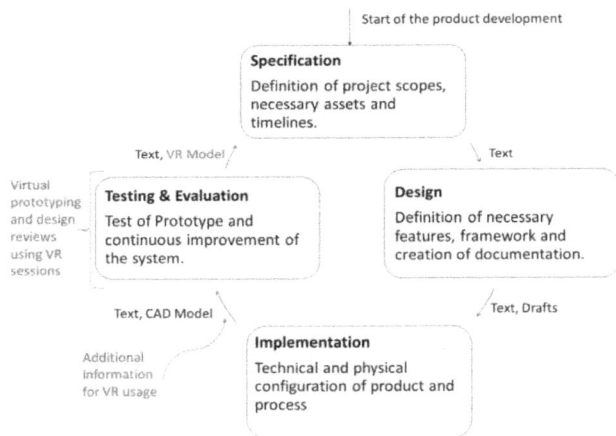

Fig. 1: Typical product development process

For a smooth integration of VR into the product development, different concepts were developed. Wolfartsberger *et al.* [17] show a multimodal VR-supported tool for design review. To integrate CAD models into 3D graphics software, they propose a three steps approach, converting a native CAD model (e.g. .ipt, .stp, etc.) to a 3D editable mesh (using 3DS Max, Blender etc.), and then importing this model into authoring tools (e.g. Unity3D) as interactive 3D models (typically .fbx). To integrate actions in Unity, an automatic creation of Colliders for the imported objects was implemented. Based on that, haptic feedback is provided to the user when a virtual object is touched. Their study showed that context-specific interaction processes, like pushing a button, are essential for an immersive user experience.

Berg *et al.* [19] state that a typical VR integration process consists of seven steps. First, VR sessions must be requested, and the relevant data are acquired. Next, the modelling process of the CAD data takes place, which lasts for hours to days. This step is considered as the most time-consuming part. Then, the virtual environment based on the application is created including object manipulations, physical properties, and animations. After finishing the VR scene, a proof-of-concept is conducted and then the VR session takes place. Finally, the outcomes are summarized.

Another approach for automatic integration of CAD models into VR environments is shown by Lorentz *et al.* [20]. Their work focuses on creating VR models out of CAD including previously defined animations (e.g. explosion views) and kinematic relationships. Their comparison on different 3D data exchange formats shows that VRML fulfills their requirements best. The presented conversion concept includes three main functionalities: 3D model reduction (using a special program like GPure from DeltaCAD [21]), animation transition (using VRML or capturing of motions on a time step basis), and interactive kinematics (use of CAD model for kinematics calculation, exchange information with VR system).

It can be concluded that the generation of VR applications for testing and evaluation is a time-consuming process. Typically, VR specialists are needed to create VR environments and to manage VR meetings due to their high complexities. Wolfartsberger *et al.* [17] show that the assignment of scripts in Unity is done using two ways: Automatic assigning of basic scripts (for example the generation of Colliders to all imported objects) and manual allocation of interactions to specific objects. However, no method is available for selecting the appropriate interactions that exist in the CAD programs. To solve this problem, an information model comprises basic interactions and physical properties, which are necessary to generate VR models automatically out of CAD models, is developed in our work.

Information model for VR interactions

The proposed information model consists of five main topics: physical properties, graphics, kinematic constraints, animations and interactions (Fig. 2). As the import process of kinematic constraints and animations is already covered in [17], the focus in this work lies on the interchange of physical properties and interactions. Additionally, graphical properties are considered. The naming and categories are based on the conventions used in Unity as it is widely adopted by the research community [6, 8, 17, 22]. For the same reason, Unity is adopted as the testing environment for the presented concept.

For every imported CAD object (GameObject), the physical properties must be selected. If a Rigidbody is attached, the physical behavior of the GameObject is enabled and the object will respond to gravity. If Colliders are added to an object, the object reacts to incoming collisions. Additionally, the specification of mass and air friction are essential for creating a realistic virtual environment [23].

The selection of the graphics parameters also has a significant influence on the realistic representation of objects. Thus, the definition of a mesh, a material (specification of the surface being rendered), a shader (script to calculate the color of pixels during rendering) and a texture (bitmap image applied over the mesh surface) must be presented in the CAD model [23].

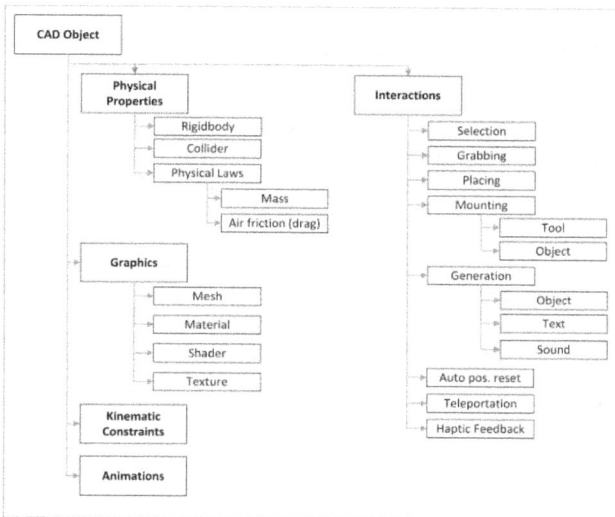

Fig. 2: Information model for VR interactions

Moreover, different kinds of user interactions are specified in the information model covering most typical use cases. To handle objects, four interactions are defined: selection, grabbing, placing, and mounting. Mounting is used if a tool is needed to interact with a virtual object, for example if a screwdriver is needed to tighten a screw. In this case, the interaction can only be finished if the right tool and the right object are selected.

Additionally, the option of generating new objects, text or sounds based on triggers, for instance a collision or pressing a button, is included. Furthermore, the option for an automatic position reset (for example if the object is released or if a specific button is pressed) is taken into account. As the virtual worlds may vary in size and to minimize motion sickness, a teleportation option should be available. Finally, the extensibility for haptic feedback like vibrations of a controller is added.

A manual workstation of the Industry 4.0 model factory at FH Aachen is chosen (Fig. 3) as a physical platform for study in this work.

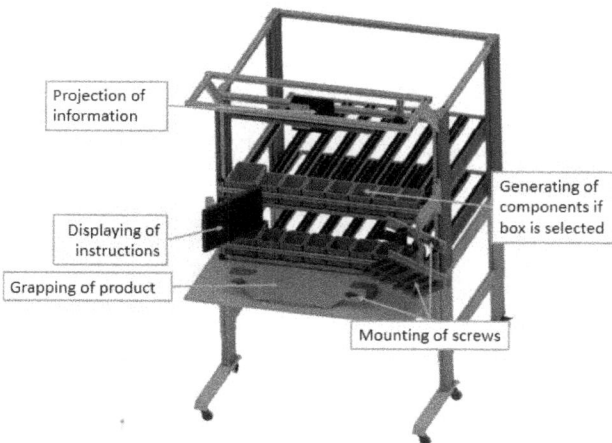

Fig. 3: Example for VR interactions (manual workstation at FH Aachen)

The station offers a variety of interaction possibilities to build virtual longboards. The projector in the upper part can be selected to project assembly information onto the desk. Besides, the status

of the order can be reviewed at the monitor. When the user reaches a box in the storage area, a corresponding virtual component stored in the box is generated. All parts lying on the table can be grabbed and placed in the virtual working environment.

The in the information model (Fig. 2) specified properties and interactions of virtual objects can be allocated to CAD models in Unity manually. However, this is a time-consuming process and difficult to create synergy between the CAD designer and the VR modeler. Thus, an adapted workflow is proposed in Fig. 4.

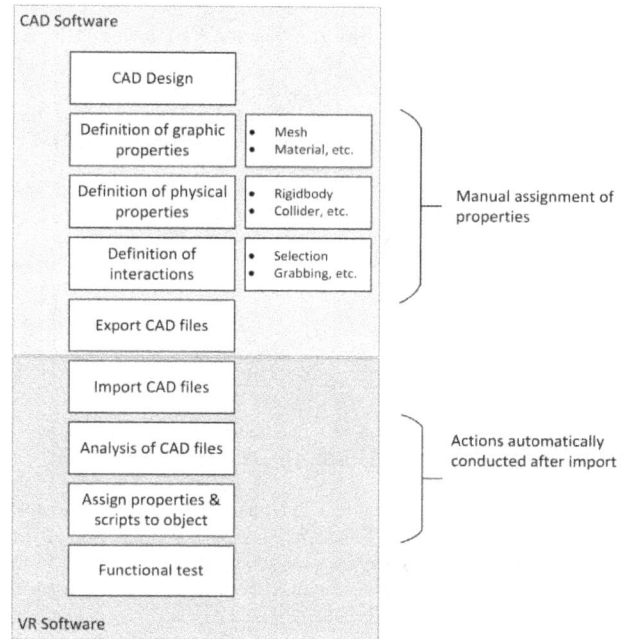

Fig. 4: Workflow for VR content generation

Adding properties & interactions to CAD files

To enable the workflow shown in Fig. 4, a process sequence using different environments (Inventor, 3ds Max, Unity) is suggested. The CAD model is expanded with additional properties in json format (Fig. 2, Fig. 5) to the objects, for instance in Inventor or 3ds Max (Fig. 6). As the export of files in Unity-readably formats is not fully supported in CAD programs (e.g. Inventor does not support the export of fbx-files), an intermediate step between Inventor and Unity using 3ds Max is utilized in the current design. However, solutions that support direct export of the appropriate formats from CAD programs like Inventor or SolidWorks will be explored in future projects.

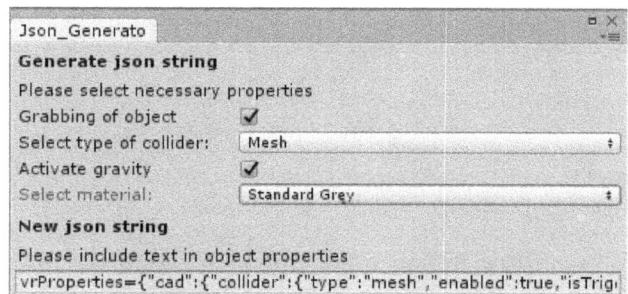

Fig. 5: User interface to generate json string

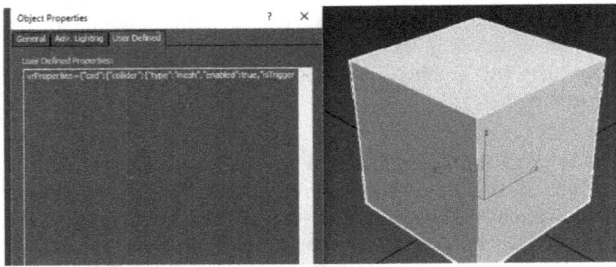

Fig. 6: Adding object properties in 3ds Max

Additionally, the property information must be included in the available file formats (i.e. .fbx, .dae (Collada), .3ds, .dxf, .obj, and .skp for Unity imports). According to our studies, the file format .fbx contains most previously added information and thus is selected as the file format in the tests in this work (Fig. 7).

```
Model: 2348822650400, "Model::Cube_1", "Mesh" {
    Version: 232
    Properties70: {
        P: "PreRotation", "Vector3D", "Vector", "",-90,-0,0
        P: "RotationActive", "bool", "", "",1
        P: "InheritType", "enum", "", "",1
        P: "ScalingMax", "Vector3D", "Vector", "",0,0,0
        P: "DefaultAttributeIndex", "int", "Integer", "",0
        P: "Lcl Rotation", "Lcl Rotation", "", "A",90.0000093346676,-0,0
        P: "UDP3DSMAX", "KString", "", "U", "vrProperties={"cad":{"collider":

        P: "MaxHandle", "int", "Integer", "UH",1
    }
    Shading: T
    Culling: "Cullingoff"
}
```

Fig. 7: Extract of the fbx-file including the property "mesh collider"

To generate the VR environment in Unity, the GameObjects must be added to the scene by drag and drop. Next, a parsing of the .fbx files of the present objects can be started via user interface. This results in an automatic allocation of properties and scripts to the corresponding GameObjects.

3. COMBINING PRODUCT AND EQUIPMENT DEVELOPMENT IN VR

Due to synchronous engineering processes, the development of new products as well as the corresponding equipment must be coordinated, and a well-defined information exchange standard must be available. Hence, the product and equipment development progress require a standardized connection (Fig. 8, upper part). Additionally, a generation of VR or AR training sessions by including extra information after the design process is possible (Fig. 8, lower part). The uniqueness lies in the reuse of CAD models for three different purposes (product/equipment evaluation, combined production analysis, and training sessions) by exploiting existing design information and adding further details.

For a combined VR analysis of the two models, three steps must be conducted: integration, testing and evaluation. The goal is to enable an automatic integration by mapping the CAD models of the product and the equipment with the corresponding process step. Typically, product assemblies are imported in VR for review processes [15]. Thus, the focus of the developed concept for VR analysis lies on compound products, which need different resources (machines, tools, etc.) to be assembled. As a basis for combined product and equipment VR reviews, a work schedule is taken. There are different concepts in the area of Computer Aided Process Planning (CAPP) available to generate automatically assembly sequences. [24, 25] Therefore, an

ordered list of tasks is considered as given in this case. However, the assembly sequence must be enriched with all information necessary for VR integration (Fig. 9).

The expanded work schedule includes three main aspects: definition of the working area, specification of the final product, and determination of the necessary process steps. The working area defines the required space for operation as well as the area in which interactions can take place. In case of the manual work station, (Fig. 3) this would be the size of the room and the surface of the table. Additionally, the properties related to the final version of the product are included. For evaluation purposes, the position as well as the possible interactions (Fig. 2) must be considered. Using this information, a transparent view of the final product similar to the one in [17] can be generated automatically.

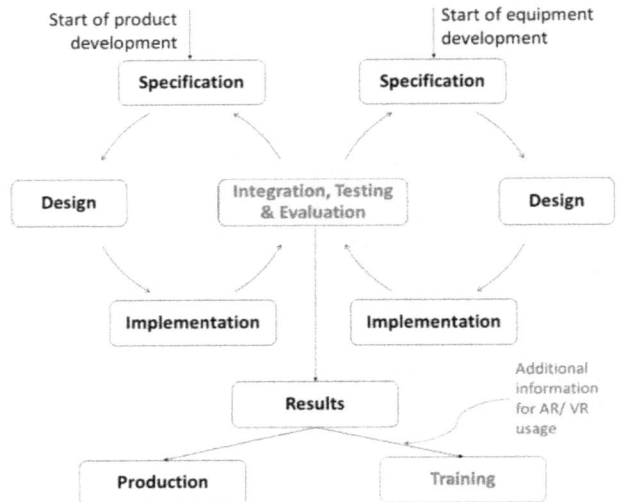

Fig. 8: Combination of product and equipment lifecycles (VR and AR integration highlighted in red)

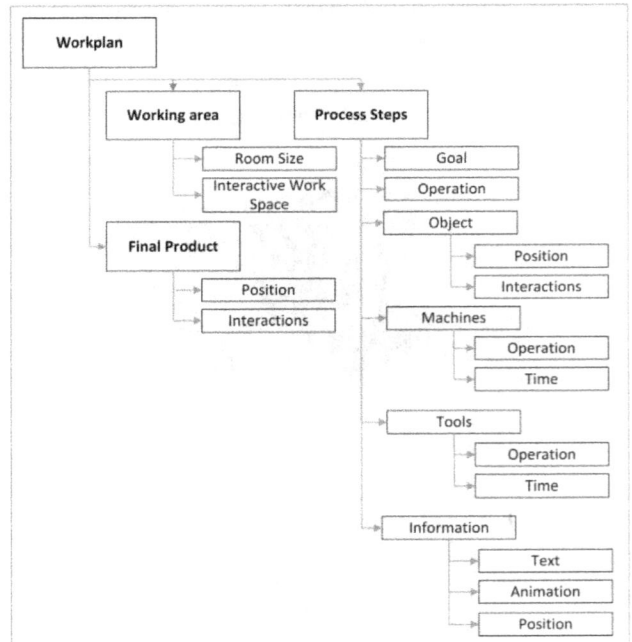

Fig. 9: Required information in the work plan for VR integration

The following process information is needed for the realized of a process step in VR. First, the goal and the corresponding required operations are assigned. In the example of the manual workstation, this would be the mounting of screws (Fig. 10). Additionally, the necessary tools (Fig. 10, green box) and/or the machines (Fig. 10, blue box) are defined.

To enable a process-oriented simulation in VR, operation times of machines and tools can be added. The objects required for the process step (Fig. 10, red boxes) including their positions in the workspace and the possible interactions are defined. Furthermore, the CAD designer should be able to display supplementary information during VR sessions (Fig. 10, yellow box) at designated areas.

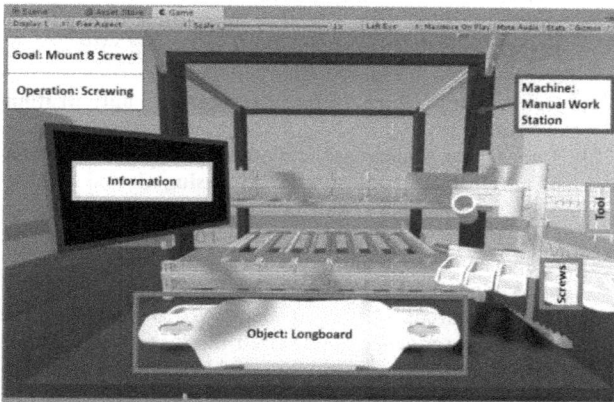

Fig. 10: Example for essential information for the realization of one process step in VR

The required process to generate the VR environment shown in Fig. 10 starts with two CAD models (Fig. 11). Next, all required information is added in the CAD program for the product and the equipment designs. Additionally, a work plan is generated out of the product CAD files. Then, both CAD models are exported into a .fbx file and imported in Unity. In Unity, automated processes are started using the information provided in the .fbx file. First, all CAD models are transformed into GameObjects. Second, the scripts enabling user interactions are added to the GameObjects. After finishing the scene according to the work plan, the VR application can be used for design reviews.

4. DISCUSSION AND LIMITATIONS

The use of the presented information models to generate a VR manual work station showed that the process to include user defined information in .fbx files via user interfaces can be seamlessly integrated in already existing CAD design processes. Following, the designer only has to put the CAD models into the VR environment and maybe adjust them in size, position or orientation. The VR properties are added automatically via scripts.

However, limitations occur for the automatic allocation process. First, a standardized and consistent naming through all programs is the basis for the whole process to match the defined properties in the .fbx file with GameObjects in Unity. Second, only objects which are important for the functionality of the whole system should be enhanced with additional information. Less important parts or for example frames, screws, etc. must often not be part of the physical simulation, which reduces the work effort and the required computing power. It must also be conducted that only

general properties like physical behavior or the property "grabbing" can be added in the CAD system. Specific requirements like for example the grabbing of tools only on the handle must be adjusted manually in Unity.

5. CONCLUSION AND FUTURE WORK

VR based review sessions in development of new products as well as VR trainings are mostly used for highly complex and costly products like those in the automotive and aerospace industries [19]. However, due to the availability of low-cost VR devices, potential applications for SMEs are emerging. To support smaller companies, concepts and applications, which enable the use of VR by lowering its technical entry barrier.

The concepts and information models proposed in this work enable a consistent usage of the already available CAD models in VR by including additional information. This process can minimize the time and personnel expenditure to use VR reviews along value chains [17, 19, 26]. Using the presented approach, the CAD models generated during the design process can be reused three times (product/ equipment review, combined review, training) in the same environment. As all information are already included in the CAD programming environment, the CAD designer can directly import models into VR.

The proposed concept was tested using different scripts for interactions (grabbing, placing and object generation). Additionally, an automatic assignment of physical properties to imported object is included. This results in time and complexity reductions as manual allocation is not needed in Unity. The specification of the room creates the floor, walls, and a roof of the virtual space. The collection of scripts can be further expanded to incorporate other specified interactions.

In our future work, the connection between product and equipment will be implemented using Inventor and Unity. Supplementary user studies are scheduled to identify additional required information and interactions.

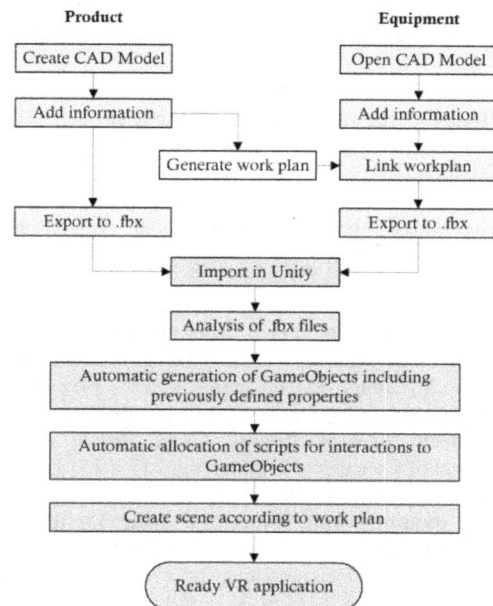

Fig. 11: Complete process to model the VR environment (blue: CAD software; red: VR software; white: assembly plan generator)

6. REFERENCES

[1] Autodesk GmbH: **Inventor. 3D-CAD-Software für Produktentwicklung**. 2018

[2] Unity Technologies: **Unity**. 2018

[3] IDC: **Prognose zum Absatz von Virtual-Reality- und Augmented-Reality-Brillen weltweit von 2016 bis 2022 (in Millionen Stück)**. Statista - Das Statistik-Portal. 2018

[4] SuperData Research: **Prognose zum Umsatz mit Virtual Reality weltweit in den Jahren 2016 bis 2021 (in Milliarden US-Dollar)**. Statista - Das Statistik-Portal. 2018

[5] Brandt, M.: **Rosige Zukunft für erweiterte Realität**. Statista - Das Statistik-Portal.2017

[6] Schreiber, W. u. Zimmermann, P.: **Virtuelle Techniken im industriellen Umfeld. Das AVILUS-Projekt; Technologien und Anwendungen**. Springer-Verlag 2011

[7] Wollert, J.: **Industrie 4.0 – warten bis die Revolution vorbei ist? Ängste und Chance rund um Industrie 4.0**. Kommunikation und Bildverarbeitung in der Automation. Springer Berlin Heidelberg (2018), p. 177–186

[8] Exner, K. u. Stark, R.: **Validation of Product-service Systems in Virtual Reality**. Procedia CIRP 30 (2015), p. 96–101

[9] Butenuth, M., Kallweit, R. u. Prescher, P.: **Vehicle-in-the-Loop Real-world Vehicle Tests Combined with Virtual Scenarios**. ATZ worldwide 119 (2017) 9, p. 52–55

[10] Grajewski, D., Buń, P. u. Górski, F.: **Examination of Effectiveness of a Performed Procedural Task Using Low-Cost Peripheral Devices in VR**. In: Chen J., Fragomeni G. (eds) Virtual, Augmented and Mixed Reality: Interaction, Navigation, Visualization, Embodiment, and Simulation. VAMR 2018. Lecture Notes in Computer Science, vol 10909. Springer, Cham (2018), p. 403–415

[11] Werrlich, S., Lorber, C., Nguyen, P.-A., Yanez, C. E. F. u. Notni, G.: **Assembly Training: Comparing the Effects of Head-Mounted Displays and Face-to-Face Training**. In: Chen J., Fragomeni G. (eds) Virtual, Augmented and Mixed Reality: Interaction, Navigation, Visualization, Embodiment, and Simulation. VAMR 2018. Lecture Notes in Computer Science, vol 10909. Springer, Cham (2018), p. 462–476

[12] Neges, M., Adwernat, S. u. Abramovici, M.: **Augmented Virtuality for maintenance training simulation under various stress conditions**. Procedia Manufacturing 19 (2018), p. 171–178

[13] Fehling, D.: **Enhancing Vocational Training with Augmented Reality**. International Conference on Knowledge Technologies and Data-driven Business (i-KNOW 2016)

[14] DIN Deutsches Institut für Normung e. V.: **DIN ISO 15226. Technische Produktdokumentation – Lebens-zyklusmodell und Zuordnung von Dokumenten** (2017)

[15] Choi, S., Jung, K. u. Noh, S. D.: **Virtual reality applications in manufacturing industries: Past research, present findings, and future directions**. Journal of Concurrent Engineering 23 (2015) 1, p. 40–63

[16] Almusawi, A. R. J., Dulger, L. C. u. Kapucu, S.: **Robotic arm dynamic and simulation with Virtual Reality Model (VRM)**. Proceedings of International Conference on Control, Decision and Information Technologies (CoDIT). IEEE (2016), p. 335–340

[17] Wolfartsberger, J., Zenisek, J., Sievi, C. u. Silmbroth, M.: **A virtual reality supported 3D environment for engineering design review**. Proceedings of the 2017 23rd International Conference on Virtual Systems and Multimedia (VSMM). IEEE (2017), p. 1–8

[18] Grajewski, D., Górski, F., Hamrol, A. u. Zawadzki, P.: **Immersive and Haptic Educational Simulations of Assembly Workplace Conditions**. Procedia Computer Science 75 (2015), p. 359–368

[19] Berg, L. P. u. Vance, J. M.: **Industry use of virtual reality in product design and manufacturing: a survey**. Journal of Virtual Reality 21 (2017) 1, p. 1–17

[20] Lorenz, M., Busch, M., Rentzos, L., Tscheligi, M., Klimant, P. u. Frohlich, P.: **I'm There! The influence of virtual reality and mixed reality environments combined with two different navigation methods on presence**. IEEE Virtual Reality Conference (VR 2015), p. 223–224

[21] DeltaCAD: **GPure. The engineering optimization software**. 2011

[22] Tamas, G. u. Fodorean, D.: **Model in the loop simulation of an electric propulsion system using virtual reality**. 52nd International Universities Power Engineering Conference (UPEC) (2017), p. 1–4

[23] Unity Technologies: **Unity Manual**, 2018. https://docs.unity3d.com/Manual/

[24] Bahubalendruni, M. R.A. u. Biswal, B. B.: **A review on assembly sequence generation and its automation**. Proceedings of the Institution of Mechanical Engineers, Part C: Journal of Mechanical Engineering Science 230 (2016) 5, p. 824–838

[25] Park, H.-S., Park, J.-W., Park, M.-W. u. Kim, J.-K.: **Development of Automatic Assembly Sequence Generating System Based on the New Type of Parts Liaison Graph**. Bernard A., Rivest L., Dutta D. (eds) Product Lifecycle Management for Society. PLM 2013. IFIP Advances in Information and Communication Technology, vol 409. Springer, Berlin, Heidelberg (2013), p. 540–549

[26] Fite-Georgel, P.: **Is there a Reality in Industrial Augmented Reality?** 10th IEEE International Symposium on Mixed and Augmented Reality (2011), p. 201–210

Augmented Reality Systems in Total Hip Arthroplasty

Amal YASSIN

Computer Science Department, Faculty of Computer and Information Sciences, Ain Shams University
Cairo, 11566, Egypt

Mamdouh HEFNY
Orthopaedics Department, Warwick Hospital
Warwick, CV34 5BW, United Kingdom

Taha ELARIF
Computer Science Department, Faculty of Computer and Information Sciences, Ain Shams University
Cairo, 11566, Egypt

ABSTRACT

Augmented Reality (AR) is the technology of viewing a real physical environment with its real objects as well as virtual computer-generated objects. AR technology has been applied in several fields in medicine as an entity of Computer-Assisted Surgery (CAS). Using AR improved the results of conventional surgery and also had a great impact on the development of Minimally Invasive Surgeries (MIS). One of the surgeries that revealed promising outcomes when using AR intraoperatively is Total Hip Arthroplasty (THA).

The aim of this paper is to present the benefits of using AR in the cup placement of THA and to compare the results of the two available systems implementing this technology. PubMed and Cochrane Library were searched, and two systems were identified. Both had superior results when compared to conventional surgery with some advantages for one over the other. Despite the good results of both systems, further research and software development are required to address the challenges of using AR technology intraoperatively. In addition, this study recognized the paucity of the published research in this field.

Keywords: Augmented reality, minimally invasive surgery, orthopaedics, total hip arthroplasty, intra-operative planning, X-ray, surgical navigation.

1. INTRODUCTION

Augmented Reality (AR) is the technology of viewing a real physical environment with its real objects as well as computer-generated virtual objects [1]. AR has already invaded the medical field and has been applied in many operations as a form of Computer-Assisted Surgery (CAS) [2]. CAS was initially proposed to improve the outcomes of conventional surgical techniques, however more recently its implementation assisted the development of Minimally Invasive Surgeries (MIS) and showed very promising progress over the last decade [3][4].

MIS is a particular type of surgeries performed using smaller incisions [5]. It has shown broad interest from both surgeons and patients since it provides many advantages. It minimizes the tissue damage and therefore reduces the morbidity associated with surgery such as wound infection and bleeding. In addition, smaller scars offer better cosmesis [6]. It also allows for faster recovery, shorter hospital stays and therefore reduction of the overall cost. However, small incisions make the visualization of the surgical field challenging [3], and thus surgeons are guided using intraoperative imaging which may have hazards on patients and theatre staff [7].

The use of AR technology in MIS can provide direct visualization without the need for large incisions or the use of extensive hazardous imaging [8]. It enriches the surgeon's view of his surroundings by displaying information gathered from patient medical images on an AR surgical interface [9]. As a result, implementing AR in surgeries, particularly MIS, is developing with good results. One of the surgical applications of AR that is showing promising results is the cup placement in conventional and minimally invasive Total Hip Arthroplasty (THA) [10].

THA has been described as the operation of the century since it is a curative treatment for disabling diseases and its results are satisfactory with excellent patient-reported outcomes [11][12][13]. It has evolved over the last decades achieving excellent results and reducing its complications rate. In THA, the acetabular component mal-alignment is a known cause of the most preventable complications of THA including dislocation, impingement, wear, reduced range of movements, and leg length discrepancy following the surgery [14][15][16]. Joint dislocation, which is reported to be the second most common cause of failure requiring revision surgery, is described as the dissociation of the femoral and acetabular components. It is a very painful condition, usually recurrent, and more common in the hands of the less experienced surgeons [17]. Moreover, recent studies have reported joint dislocation to occur in around 10% of patients receiving a primary total hip replacement and up to 28% in revision surgery [18].

THA complications may be a consequence of the complexity of the pelvic anatomy, its variable orientation, and its deep position concealed by overlying tissues which make it challenging for the surgeon to position the prosthesis correctly. Therefore, recent studies have reported the use of computer-assisted surgery to allow the placement of the component to be more accurate, reliable and reproducible when compared to conventional surgery [11][19][20]. In addition, it standardizes cup placement in the hands of all surgeons and leads to significantly better results in recovering the leg length of the patients after the surgery [21].

2. METHODOLOGY

In this work, PubMed and Cochrane Library were comprehensively searched for key terms (total hip replacement) or (total hip arthroplasty) AND (augmented reality). The last search was performed on the 2nd of March 2019. Only papers discussing cup placement in THA using AR were included. Two relevant articles using different AR systems were identified. Both of them used AR in THA to enhance the accuracy of the cup placement. This paper aims to present the benefits of using AR in THA over conventional surgery and compare the methodologies and results of the two available systems applying AR for acetabular cup placement in THA.

3. "TECHNICAL NOTE: AN AUGMENTED REALITY SYSTEM FOR TOTAL HIP ARTHROPLASTY"

Fotouhi et al. [22] proposed an augmented reality system to be used in THA to guide the surgeons intraoperatively. We will refer to this system throughout the paper as "*System A*". The system uses an intraoperative planning strategy based on two intraoperative C-arm X-ray images. The planning results are then combined with 3D augmented reality visualization to display a live RGBD data overlay. The quick planning and visualization increase the accuracy of placing acetabular components and reduces radiation exposure, surgery time, and the risk of revision surgery.

System Components

The system comprises three components: **(1)** a visual marker, **(2)** a C-arm X-ray imaging system, and **(3)** an RGBD camera mounted on the C-arm and is located near its detector plane to have a direct view onto the surgical site.

Surgical Techniques

Using the three components of the system, surgeons can do the following steps as in Figure 1.

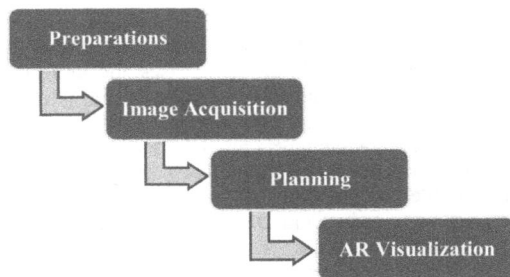

Figure 1: *System A* Surgical Techniques

1. **Preparations:** The femoral head is dislocated, the acetabulum is reamed, and then the size of the acetabular implant is determined according to the size of the reamer.

2. **Image Acquisition:** Two C-arm X-ray images are acquired from two different perspectives. While moving the C-arm to obtain a new image, the relative poses of the C-arm are determined using the RGBD camera and a visual marker on the surgical bed. The C-arm is self-contained which requires only a single offline calibration, and it does not need any external tracker.

3. **Planning:** Based on the two stereo X-ray images, the surgeon plans the position of the cup. The location of the planned cup and impactor (the straight cylindrical stick that is rigidly attached to the cup) are estimated relative to the RGBD camera to be displayed. The surgeon can manually adjust the orientation of the cup in the X-ray images, or it could be automatically preset based on desired angles relative to the anterior-posterior (AP) plane, or any other known position of the pelvis.

4. **AR Visualization:** To place the real acetabular cup in the planned position correctly, the surgeon aligns the real impactor on the monitor (the real-time cloud of points of the

real impactor obtained from the RGBD camera as shown in Figure 2) with the virtual planned impactor (the superimposed 3D representation of the impactor estimated from planning as shown in Figure 3) in all of the virtual perspectives provided as shown in Figure 4 .

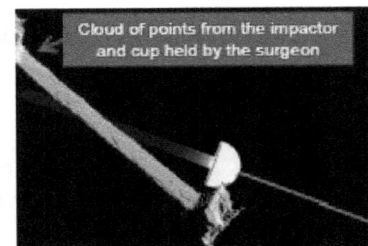

Figure 2: Real-time cloud of points of the real cup and impactor captured by the RGBD camera Abduction, (Source: SPIE 2018 - Copyright © 2018 SPIE) [22]

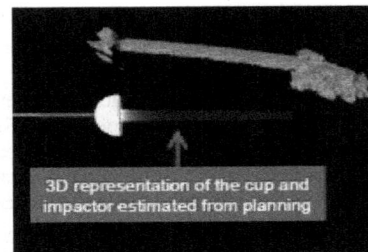

Figure 3: The 3D virtual representation of the planned cup and impactor, (Source: SPIE 2018 - Copyright © 2018 SPIE) [22]

Figure 4: The surgeon aligns the cloud of points of the real impactor with the 3D virtual representation of the planned impactor in all aspects, (Source: SPIE 2018 - Copyright © 2018 SPIE) [22]

System Methodology & Evaluation

The system methodology comprises four main steps as shown in Figure 5.

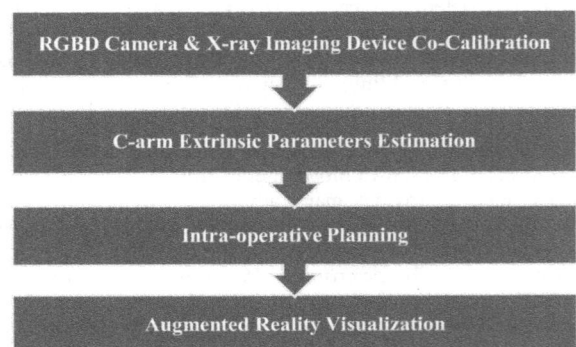

Figure 5: *System A* Methodology

1. RGBD Camera & X-ray Imaging Device Co-Calibration

To achieve AR visualization in the system, the RGBD camera and the X-ray imaging device have to be co-calibrated. A multi-modal checkerboard pattern is used in the calibration process. Each black square in the checkerboard pattern is backed with a thin radiopaque square of metal of the same size. Then the next steps are followed to accomplish the calibration process:

i. The checkerboard is placed at different positions. In each new position, a pair of images (RGB and X-ray images) are captured simultaneously.

ii. The RGB channel and the X-ray imaging device intrinsic parameters are determined.

iii. The intrinsic parameters are used to determine the 3D locations of the checkerboard corners in both the RGB and X-ray coordinate frames.

iv. The least squares minimization algorithm is used to estimate the stereo relation between the X-ray and RGB imaging devices. The RGBD camera manufacturer provides the stereo relation between the RGB and the depth of the RGBD sensor.

Experiments were held to evaluate the offline stereo co-calibration of the X-ray source and the RGBD camera using 22 image pairs. The results of individual mean reprojection errors for X-ray and RGBD cameras were 1.46 and 0.74 pixels, respectively, with a mean reprojection error of 1.10 pixels.

2. C-arm Extrinsic Parameters Estimation

The RGBD camera is used to estimate the relative extrinsic parameters of the C-arm and determine the stereo relation between C-arm X-ray images acquired at different positions. Therefore, the visual marker is first tracked in the RGBD camera coordinate frame, then the outcome is transformed into the X-ray coordinate frame. The visual marker appears in the surgery for a short period between acquiring the two X-ray images. However, it could be removed from the scene as long as an RGBD-based simultaneous localization and mapping algorithm is used instead of tracking the surgical scene.

3. Intra-operative Planning

For intra-operative planning, the system uses the extrinsic parameters, as well as the two X-ray images captured from different perspectives. Through a user interface, the surgeon can rotate and translate the cup in 3D with six degrees of freedom (DOF) rigid parameters. Then the planned cup is forward projected onto the two X-ray images planes. Using these two X-ray perspectives allows the surgeon to correctly adjust the depth of the cup, which is not possible when using only one X-ray image view.

Experiments were carried out to assess the planning of placing acetabular cups on simulated stereo X-ray images (Digitally Reconstructed Radiographs "DRRs"). 21 DRRs of the hip were generated. In each experiment, the acetabular cup is placed and correctly aligned in two DRR views: a randomly selected DRR and the AP plane DRR.

The experiments results showed that the translational error in placing the cup was below 3mm if the lateral opening between the two images was larger than 18°, and it maximized when using only the AP X-ray image for planning.

The orientation errors in abduction and anteversion were compared to conventional AP-based surgery errors. Acetabular abduction and anteversion measurements are shown in Figure 6 and Figure 7, respectively.

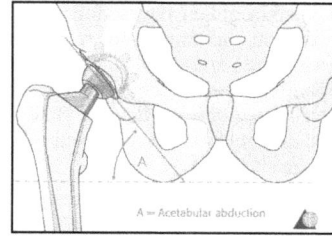

Figure 6: Acetabular Abduction, (Source: AO Surgery Reference, www.aosurgery.org - Copyright © AO Foundation, Switzerland) [23]

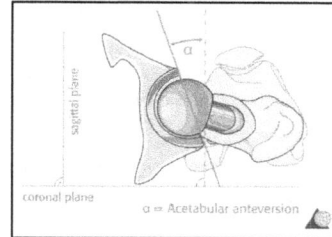

Figure 7: Acetabular Anteversion, (Source: AO Surgery Reference, www.aosurgery.org - Copyright © AO Foundation, Switzerland) [23]

The abduction and anteversion errors of *System A* along with those of the conventional surgery are shown in Table 1.

Planning Error/System	System A	Conventional Surgery
Abduction Error	0°	6.52° ± 5.97°
Anteversion Error	0°	1.82° ± 1.89°

Table 1: The planning error measurements of *System A* and the conventional surgery

The abduction and anteversion errors were computed as zero since the angles were set in advance, which shows apparent minimization of errors in the system compared to the conventional surgery.

4. Augmented Reality Visualization

The AR environment consists of: **(1)** a real-time cloud of points from the real surgical scene captured by the RGBD camera, and **(2)** surface meshes of the virtual cup and the virtual impactor superimposed on the position estimated in the planning phase.

To construct the AR environment; the RGBD sensor position is estimated relative to the planned cup. Then a 3D mesh of the virtual cup and impactor is superimposed with the real-time cloud of points, all in the RGBD coordinate frame. After displaying the real and planned impactors, the surgeon aligns only the cloud of points from the impactor with the 3D virtual representation of the planned impactor. The acetabular cup disappears behind the skin tissues, and only the impactor is visible during the fixing process as shown in Figure 8. Therefore, aligning the real impactor and the planned model in all aspects means that the surgeon correctly placed the cup in the planned position.

Figure 8: Only the impactor is visible during the fixing process, (Source: SPIE 2018 - Copyright © 2018 SPIE) [22]

For evaluating AR environment interaction, the orientation error of the impactor position was measured, relative to the planning position, after placing the impactor. The experiment was repeated for ten various positions, and each time four virtual perspectives of the surgical scene were used. Then a CBCT scan of the cup was acquired after the cup was placed using AR guidance. The evaluation results are shown in Table 2.

Error Type	Measurement
Orientation Error	0.74° ± 0.41°
Translation Error	1.98 mm
Abduction Error	1.10°
Anteversion Error	0.53°

Table 2: The error measurements of *System A*

4. "A PILOT STUDY OF AUGMENTED REALITY TECHNOLOGY APPLIED TO THE ACETABULAR CUP PLACEMENT DURING TOTAL HIP ARTHROPLASTY"

Ogawa et al. [24] proposed a new system that uses the augmented reality to allow the surgeon to visualize the real-time surgical scene with the virtual image of the acetabular cup superimposed using the display of a smartphone. The system is used as a measurement tool. We will refer to this system as "*System B*" throughout the paper. It shows the abduction, anteversion, and placement angles of the acetabular cup, which provides more accurate information than the conventional surgery.

System Components

The system comprises four components:

1. A standard CT-scan.
2. A smartphone (placed in a sterilized waterproof sealable bag).
3. A software application developed by the authors (using software Unity 3D and Vuforia SDK).
4. An intraoperative guide (a stainless steel guide with 50 mm legs with an attached cube-type AR marker. The legs of the guide are placed on the skin of the bilateral anterior superior iliac spine and pubic symphysis).

Surgical Techniques

Using the four components of the system, surgeons can do the following steps as in Figure 9.

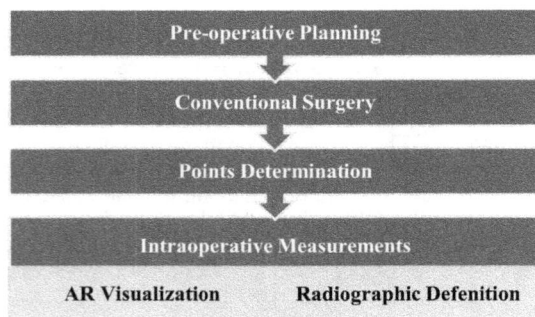

Figure 9: *System B* Surgical Techniques

1. **Pre-operative Planning**: For the preoperative planning, CT images are captured and transferred to multi-planar reconstruction.

2. **Conventional Surgery**: THA is performed using the conventional mechanical guide (goniometer) to estimate the acetabular cup installation angles. After the acetabular cup is impacted, it needs 1 or 2 screws to be fixed which may result in changing the position of the cup. Thus the impactor is combined with the acetabular cup after screw fixation.

3. **Points Determination**: Using the CT images, the user manually set four 3D coordinate points (shown in Figure 10): the bilateral anterior superior iliac spine (ASIS), pubic symphysis, and cup center position.

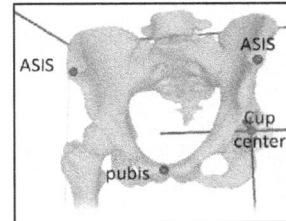

Figure 10: The four 3D coordinate points, (Source: The Journal of Arthroplasty, 2018 - Copyright © 2018 Elsevier Inc.) [24]

4. **Intraoperative Measurements:** The acetabular cup placement angles are measured using both *System B* and the goniometer.

   (i) **AR Visualization**: To measure the abduction and anteversion angles of the cup using *System B*; the image of the virtual cup and impactor is superimposed on the view of the real cup and impactor, then the image can be managed through the abduction and anteversion buttons on a touch panel as shown in Figure 11.

   (ii) **Radiographic Definition:** In the measurement using the goniometer, the radiographic definition is used to measure abduction and anteversion angles.

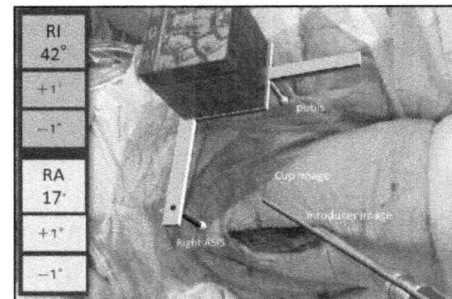

Figure 11: AR Visualization, (Source: The Journal of Arthroplasty, 2018 - Copyright © 2018 Elsevier Inc.) [24]

System Methodology

The system methodology comprises three main steps as shown in Figure 12.

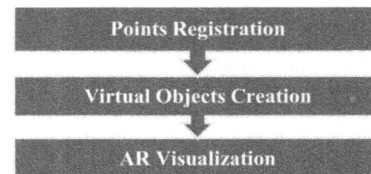

Figure 12: *System B* Methodology

1. **Points Registration**: The system registers the four points (shown in Figure 10) that were set by the surgeon.

2. **Virtual Objects Creation**: The system automatically creates:

(i)   A cube AR marker.

(ii) 3D model data of the acetabular cup.

(iii) Cup impactor.

(iv) An image of the guide.

3. **AR Visualization**: The image of the virtual cup and impactor is displayed in the planned position.

System Evaluation

For evaluating the performance of the system, the acetabular cup placement angle was measured postoperatively using CT-scan according to the radiographic definition. Postoperative measurements for each case were performed twice by a single examiner, and the mean value was determined.

The absolute value of the difference between the intraoperatively and postoperatively placement angle was defined as the absolute difference. The absolute difference results of using *System B* and the goniometer intraoperatively were compared to estimate the placement accuracy of *System B*. The results are shown in Table 3.

The results show that the abduction is not remarkably different in both approaches, but *System B* shows more accurate anteversion results, leading to accurate intraoperative placement angles of the acetabular cup than the goniometer approach.

Comparison / System	System B	Goniometer Approach
Intraoperative mean abduction	39.3° ± 4.1° (mean ± SD; range 31.0° - 46.0°)	39.4° ± 4.2° (mean ± SD; range 31.0° - 48.0°)
Intraoperative mean anteversion	20.9° ± 4.9° (mean ± SD; range 10.0° - 32.0°)	15.9° ± 4.2° (mean ± SD; range 5.0° - 27.0°)
Postoperative mean abduction	40.4° ± 4.7° (mean ± SD; range 32.0° - 51.0°)	
Postoperative mean anteversion	22.3° ± 5.8° (mean ± SD; range 8.0° - 32.0°)	
Abduction absolute difference	2.1° ± 1.5° (range 0° - 5.0°)	2.7° ± 1.7° (range 0° - 8.3°)
Anteversion absolute difference	2.7° ± 1.7° (range 0° - 8.0°).	6.8° ± 3.8° (range 0° - 15°)

Table 3: Comparison of *System B* and goniometer approach results

5. DISCUSSION

The two systems, *System A* and *System B*, both used AR in THA and provided better results than those of the conventional surgery. Although, *System A* showed more advantages and more accurate results than *System B*, as follows:

1. Planning the cup intra-operatively after removing the femoral head and reaming the acetabulum provides more accurate planning results in *System A* than those of the conventional mechanical guide (goniometer) used for pre-operative planning in *System B*.

2. Rotating and translating the cup in 3D with six DOF rigid parameters and setting the angles to the desired values in the planning process in *System A* resulted in zero planning abduction and anteversion errors.

3. Using monitors in *System A* to display the cup and impactor in many perspectives provides more accurate results than using only one perspective on the display of a smartphone in *System B*.

4. Using the smartphone in *System B* instead of cameras and monitors in *System A* to capture and display videos respectively may be less expensive; however, the use of dedicated hardware may be more reliable and professional.

5. The use of CT-scan in *System B* exposes patients to higher radiation dose and is more expensive than the use of X-ray in *System A*.

A brief comparison between the two systems is shown in Table 4.

Comparison	System A	System B
Usage	Navigation Tool	Measurement tool
Methodology	AR is used intraoperatively to plan the cup position and guide the surgeon to place the cup correctly	The surgery is performed using the conventional mechanical guide, then AR is used to measure the abduction and anteversion angles of the cup
Imaging	Intra-operative X-ray	Preoperative CT-scan
Planning	Intra-operative	Preoperative
Pelvic movement during surgery	Affects the measurements	Does not affect the measurements
Capturing Video	RGBD camera	Smartphone
AR Display	Monitors	Smartphone
Accuracy	Accurate in translation, abduction, and anteversion	Accurate in anteversion
Abduction Error	1.10°	1° - 3°
Anteversion Error	0.53°	1° - 3°

Table 4: Systems comparison

The limitation of our study is that only two systems were identified for comparison, however, this reflects the paucity of the literature in this field. Therefore, further research is required to enhance the reliability of using AR technology intraoperatively.

6. CHALLENGES AND FUTURE RESEARCH

Some challenges were identified and need more future research to enhance both systems as follows:

In *System A*:

1. The patient has to be stable during the cup placement process. In the case of patient movement, the surgeon has to repeat the planning or continue the surgery using the conventional fluoroscopy-based approach. To solve this issue, more motion compensation techniques can be explored and applied to the system.

2. RGBD-based simultaneous localization and mapping algorithm can be used instead of tracking the surgical scene using the visual marker.

In *System B*, the accuracy needs further investigations to be used as a navigation tool with accurate results of placing the acetabular cup instead of being used as a measurement tool.

In both systems, using monitors to display the AR visualizations can be distracting for the surgeon. Instead, using an optical see-through head-mounted display makes it easier for the surgeon to view the surrounding world with the virtual objects superimposed.

7. CONCLUSION

The two systems discussed in this paper used AR in THA and provided superior results when compared to conventional surgery. However, *System A* showed more accurate results and more advantages over *System B*.

System A was used as a navigation tool, in which AR was used intraoperatively to plan the cup position and guide the surgeon to place the cup correctly. While *System B* was used as a measurement tool, where the cup planning took place preoperatively, the surgery was performed using the conventional mechanical guide, and then AR was used intraoperatively to measure the abduction and anteversion angles of the cup.

Further research and software development is required to address the challenges of using AR intraoperatively such as the implications of patient movement on the accuracy of the results. In addition, systems should evolve to minimize the use of imaging and reduce the hazards of exposure to radiation.

8. REFERENCES

[1] J. Carmigniani and B. Furht, "Augmented Reality: An Overview," 2011, pp. 3–46.

[2] M. Van Oosterom, H. G. van der Poel, N. Navab, C. J.H. van de Velde, and F. W. B. Leeuwen, *Computer-assisted surgery: Virtual- and augmented-reality displays for navigation during urological interventions*, vol. 28. 2017.

[3] I. D. Learmonth, C. Young, and C. Rorabeck, "The operation of the century: total hip replacement," *Lancet*, vol. 370 (9597), pp. 1508–1519, 2007.

[4] M. Siddaiah-Subramanya, K. W. Tiang, and M. Nyandowe, "A New Era of Minimally Invasive Surgery: Progress and Development of Major Technical Innovations in General Surgery Over the Last Decade.," *Surg. J. (New York, N.Y.)*, vol. 3, no. 4, pp. e163–e166, Oct. 2017.

[5] B. McCrory, C. A. LaGrange, and M. Hallbeck, "Quality and safety of minimally invasive surgery: past, present, and future," *Biomed. Eng. Comput. Biol.*, vol. 6, pp. 1–11, Apr. 2014.

[6] J. Allegrone et al., "Chapter 19 - Physical Rehabilitation after Total Hip Arthroplasty," D. J. Magee, J. E. Zachazewski, W. S. Quillen, and R. C. B. T.-P. and I. in M. R. (Second E. Manske, Eds. W.B. Saunders, 2016, pp. 692–712.

[7] J. M Lloyd, T. Wainwright, and R. G Middleton, *What is the role of minimally invasive surgery in a fast track hip and knee replacement pathway?*, vol. 94. 2012.

[8] R. Van Krevelen and R. Poelman, *A Survey of Augmented Reality Technologies, Applications and Limitations*, vol. 9. 2010.

[9] P. Lamata, *Augmented reality for minimally invasive surgery: Overview and some recent advances*. 2010.

[10] L. Chen, T. Day, W. Tang, and N. John, *Recent Developments and Future Challenges in Medical Mixed Reality*. 2017.

[11] S. O. Mavrogenis A Mimidis G, Papanastasiou J, Koulalis D, Demertzis N, Papagelopoulos P., "Computer-assisted Navigation in Orthopedic Surgery," *Orthopedics*, vol. 36, pp. 631–642, 2013.

[12] I. Reininga et al., *Minimally invasive and computer-navigated total hip arthroplasty: A qualitative and systematic review of the literature*, vol. 11. 2010.

[13] T. P. Sculco, L. C. Jordan, and W. L. Walter, "Minimally invasive total hip arthroplasty: the Hospital for Special Surgery experience.," *Orthop. Clin. North Am.*, vol. 35, no. 2, pp. 137–142, Apr. 2004.

[14] K. Deep, S. Shankar, and A. Mahendra, *Computer assisted navigation in total knee and hip arthroplasty*, vol. 3. 2017.

[15] T. Cheng, J. G. Feng, T. Liu, and X. L. Zhang, "Minimally invasive total hip arthroplasty: a systematic review," *Int. Orthop.*, vol. 33, no. 6, pp. 1473–1481, 2009.

[16] K.-H. Widmer and P. A. Grutzner, "Joint replacement-total hip replacement with CT-based navigation.," *Injury*, vol. 35 Suppl 1, p. S-A84-9, Jun. 2004.

[17] "National Joint Registry for England, Wales, Northern Ireland and the Isle of Man. 15th annual report," 2018.

[18] J. Dargel, J. Oppermann, G.-P. Bruggemann, and P. Eysel, "Dislocation following total hip replacement.," *Dtsch. Arztebl. Int.*, vol. 111, no. 51–52, pp. 884–890, Dec. 2014.

[19] A. M. Digioia, B. Jaramaz, C. Nikou, R. S. Labarca, J. E. Moody, and B. D. Colgan, "Surgical navigation for total hip replacement with the use of hipnav," *Oper. Tech. Orthop.*, vol. 10, no. 1, pp. 3–8, Jan. 2000.

[20] R. G. A. Haaker, K. Tiedjen, A. Ottersbach, F. Rubenthaler, M. Stockheim, and J. B. Stiehl, "Comparison of conventional versus computer-navigated acetabular component insertion.," *J. Arthroplasty*, vol. 22, no. 2, pp. 151–159, Feb. 2007.

[21] A. Manzotti, P. Cerveri, E. De Momi, C. Pullen, and N. Confalonieri, "Does computer-assisted surgery benefit leg length restoration in total hip replacement? Navigation versus conventional freehand," *Int. Orthop.*, vol. 35, no. 1, pp. 19–24, Jan. 2011.

[22] J. Fotouhi et al., *Technical note: an augmented reality system for total hip arthroplasty*, vol. 10576. SPIE, 2018.

[23] "AO Foundation - AO Surgery Reference." [Online]. Available: www.aosurgery.org.

[24] H. Ogawa, S. Hasegawa, S. Tsukada, and M. Matsubara, "A Pilot Study of Augmented Reality Technology Applied to the Acetabular Cup Placement During Total Hip Arthroplasty," *J Arthroplast.*, vol. 33, no. 6, pp. 1833–1837, Elsevier Inc., 2018.

AUTHORS INDEX

VOLUME III

Alzate, Marco A.	37	Minami Koyama, Yukihiro	55
Andersone, Ieva	13	Nelles, Oliver	103
Ascacivar Placencia, Yanelli Karen	76	Ozolins, Modris	31
Babica, Viktorija	7	Pīlēna, Arta	25
Bapat, Arun	43	Pando Álvarez, Rosa	76
Braun, Sebastian	109	Placencia Medina, Maritza	76
Carreño Escobedo, Jorge Raúl	76	Poszytek, Pawel	82
Čevers, Aldis	1	Quintana Salinas, Margot Rosario	76
Cheng, Chi-Tsun	109	Rezaev, Andrey A.	88
Elarif, Taha	115	Rodriguez Azabache, Julio Antonio	97
Estrada-Domínguez, Jesús Eduardo	49	Rosenko, Svetlana I.	88
Gaile-Sarkane, Elīna	1	Rustenova, Elvira	7
Gaile-Sarkane, Elina	31	Salazar Guerrero, Evelyn	55
Gálvez Carrillo, Rosa Patricia	97	Sceulovs, Deniss	7; 13
Gregori, Giovanni	43	Scholte, Tom	91
Grikke, Laura	13	Silva Valencia, Javier	76
Gutiérrez Arenas, Rodrigo Alejandro	55	Straser, Valentino	43
Hefny, Mamdouh	115	Straujuma, Anita	31
Heinz, Tim	103	Torres-Castro, Alejandro	49
Hinojosa-Rivera, Moisés	49	Ulloa Rubio, Bertha	97
Hissink, Louis	43	Ulmer, Jessica	109
Karulis, Miervaldis	59	Valdez, Edgar	71
Kasperovica, Ludmila	19	Venkatanathan, Natarajan	43
Kavosa, Maija	25	Wollert, Jörg	109
Lace, Natalja	19	Wong Aitken, Higinio Guillermo	97
Lai, Chow Yin	109	Wu, Hong-Chun	43
Lara Gracia, Marco A.	65	Yassin, Amal	115
Laracy, Fr. Joseph R.	71	Yupari Azabache, Irma Luz	97
Leybourne, Bruce	43		
Liddy, Msgr. Richard	71		
López-Lira Arjona, Alfonso	49		
Marlowe, Thomas	71		
Martínez Alavez, Jacquelyn	55		
Mechan Mendez, Víctor	76		
Mejia, Marcela	37		

www.ingramcontent.com/pod-product-compliance
Lightning Source LLC
Chambersburg PA
CBHW081537220326
41598CB00036B/6461